SEVENTH EDITION
GRAMMAR IN CONTEXT 2

SANDRA N. ELBAUM

Australia • Brazil • Canada • Mexico • Singapore • United Kingdom • United States

National Geographic Learning,
a Cengage Company

Grammar in Context 2, Seventh Edition
Sandra N. Elbaum

Publisher: Sherrise Roehr

Executive Editor: Laura Le Dréan

Managing Editor: Jennifer Monaghan

Director of Global Marketing: Ian Martin

Heads of Regional Marketing:

   Joy MacFarland (United States and Canada)

   Charlotte Ellis (Europe, Middle East, and Africa)

   Kiel Hamm (Asia)

   Irina Pereyra (Latin America)

Product Marketing Manager: Tracy Bailie

Content Project Manager: Beth F. Houston

Media Researcher: Leila Hishmeh

Art Director: Brenda Carmichael

Senior Designer: Lisa Trager

Operations Support: Rebecca G. Barbush, Hayley Chwazik-Gee

Manufacturing Planner: Mary Beth Hennebury

Composition: MPS North America LLC

© 2021 Sandra N. Elbaum

ALL RIGHTS RESERVED. No part of this work covered by the copyright herein may be reproduced or distributed in any form or by any means, except as permitted by U.S. copyright law, without the prior written permission of the copyright owner.

"National Geographic," "National Geographic Society" and the Yellow Border Design are registered trademarks of the National Geographic Society ® Marcas Registradas

For permission to use material from this text or product, submit all requests online at **cengage.com/permissions**
Further permissions questions can be emailed to
permissionrequest@cengage.com

ISBN-13: 979-8-214-33349-6

National Geographic Learning
5191 Natorp Boulevard
Mason, OH 45040
USA

Locate your local office at **international.cengage.com/region**

Visit National Geographic Learning online at **ELTNGL.com**
Visit our corporate website at www.cengage.com

Printed in China
Print Number: 01   Print Year: 2023

CONTENTS

1 ANIMALS

GRAMMAR The Simple Present
Frequency Words

READING 1	**Special Friends**	4
1.1	*Be* Simple Present—Form	5
1.2	Contractions with *Be*	5
1.3	*Be*—Use	7
1.4	Negative Statements with *Be*	8
1.5	*Yes/No* Questions and Short Answers with *Be*	10
1.6	*Wh-* Questions with *Be*	12
READING 2	**Beneficial Bugs**	15
1.7	The Simple Present Affirmative Statements—Form	16
1.8	The Simple Present—Use	17
1.9	The Simple Present—Negative Statements	18
READING 3	**Lucy Cooke, Zoologist**	20
1.10	The Simple Present—Questions	21
1.11	*Wh-* Questions with a Preposition	25
1.12	Questions about Meaning, Spelling, Cost, and Time	26
READING 4	**Bottlenose Dolphins**	28
1.13	Frequency Words with the Simple Present	29
1.14	Position of Frequency Words	30
1.15	Questions about Frequency	32
1.16	Questions with *How Often*	33

UNIT SUMMARY 36
REVIEW 37
FROM GRAMMAR TO WRITING 38

2 ACROSS GENERATIONS

GRAMMAR The Present Continuous
The Future

READING 1	**Iris Apfel: Still Going Strong**	42
2.1	The Present Continuous—Form	43
2.2	The Present Continuous—Use	45
2.3	Questions with the Present Continuous	46
READING 2	**Digital Natives and Digital Immigrants**	50
2.4	Contrasting the Simple Present and the Present Continuous	51
2.5	Action and Nonaction Verbs	53
READING 3	**The Future Population of the United States**	57
2.6	The Future with *Will*	58
2.7	The Future with *Be Going To*	60
2.8	Choosing *Will*, *Be Going To*, or Present Continuous for Future	62
2.9	The Future + Time or *If* Clause	64

UNIT SUMMARY 66
REVIEW 67
FROM GRAMMAR TO WRITING 68

Contents iii

3 WHAT IS SUCCESS?

4 WEDDINGS

| GRAMMAR | The Simple Past |
| | The Habitual Past with *Used To* |

READING 1	Failure and Success	72
3.1	The Simple Past—Form	73
3.2	The Simple Past—Use	74

READING 2	Never Too Late to Learn	75
3.3	The Past of *Be*	76
3.4	The Simple Past of Regular Verbs	77
3.5	The Simple Past of Irregular Verbs	78

| READING 3 | If at First You Don't Succeed | 81 |
| 3.6 | Negatives and Questions with the Simple Past | 82 |

| READING 4 | Success in Changing Laws | 85 |
| 3.7 | The Habitual Past with *Used To* | 86 |

UNIT SUMMARY	88
REVIEW	89
FROM GRAMMAR TO WRITING	90

| GRAMMAR | Possessives |
| | Pronouns |

READING 1	A Traditional American Wedding	94
4.1	Overview of Possessive Forms and Pronouns	95
4.2	Possessive Forms of Nouns	96
4.3	Possessive Adjectives	98
4.4	Possessive Pronouns	99
4.5	Questions with *Whose*	101

READING 2	A Destination Wedding	102
4.6	Object Pronouns	103
4.7	Reflexive Pronouns	106

READING 3	New Wedding Trends	108
4.8	Direct and Indirect Objects	109
4.9	*Say* and *Tell*	110

READING 4	Questions and Answers about American Weddings	112
4.10	Subject Questions	113
4.11	*Wh-* Questions	114

UNIT SUMMARY	118
REVIEW	119
FROM GRAMMAR TO WRITING	120

AMERICAN HERITAGE

A HEALTHY PLANET, A HEALTHY BODY

GRAMMAR Nouns
There + Be
Quantity Words

READING 1	**Thanksgiving**	124
5.1	Noun Plurals—Form	125
5.2	Using the Plural for Generalizations	128
5.3	Special Cases of Singular and Plural	129
READING 2	**Cranberry Sauce**	130
5.4	Count and Noncount Nouns	131
5.5	Nouns That Can Be Both Count and Noncount	132
5.6	Units of Measure with Noncount Nouns	133
5.7	*A Lot Of, Much, Many*	135
READING 3	**The First Americans**	137
5.8	*There* + a Form of *Be*	138
5.9	*Some, Any, A, No*	141
READING 4	**Navajo Code Talkers**	142
5.10	*A Few, Several, A Little*	143
5.11	*A Few* vs. *Few*; *A Little* vs. *Little*	143
5.12	*Too Much/Too Many* vs. *A Lot Of*	145
UNIT SUMMARY		146
REVIEW		147
FROM GRAMMAR TO WRITING		148

GRAMMAR Modifiers
Adverbs

READING 1	**Feeding the Planet**	152
6.1	Modifying a Noun	153
6.2	Adjectives	154
6.3	Noun Modifiers	157
READING 2	**The Happiest City in the U.S.**	159
6.4	Adverbs	160
6.5	Adjectives vs. Adverbs	162
READING 3	**A Good Night's Sleep**	164
6.6	*Too, Too Much, Too Many,* and *Enough*	165
6.7	*Too* and *Very*	166
UNIT SUMMARY		168
REVIEW		169
FROM GRAMMAR TO WRITING		170

Contents **v**

7 A NEW START

8 WHERE WE LIVE

GRAMMAR Time Words
The Past Continuous

READING 1	Ellis Island	174
7.1	Time Words	175
7.2	*When* and *Whenever*	178

READING 2 Immigrants: Building Businesses and Communities 179

7.3	The Past Continuous—Form	180
7.4	The Past Continuous with a Specific Time	182
7.5	The Past Continuous with a *When* Clause	184

READING 3 Albert Einstein: Refugee from Germany 185

7.6	The Past Continuous with a *While* Clause	186
7.7	The Simple Past vs. The Past Continuous with *When*	188
7.8	Using the *-ing* Form after Time Words	189

UNIT SUMMARY	190
REVIEW	191
FROM GRAMMAR TO WRITING	192

GRAMMAR Modals

READING 1	An Apartment Lease	196
8.1	Overview of Modals	197
8.2	Phrasal Modals	197
8.3	Obligation/Necessity—*Must* and Phrasal Modals	199
8.4	Permission/Prohibition—*May* and Phrasal Modals	200
8.5	Expectation—*Be Supposed To*	201
8.6	Ability/Permission—*Can, Could*, and Phrasal Modals	202

READING 2 Frequently Asked Questions: Recycling Plastic in Your Home 204

8.7	Advice—*Should, Ought To, Had Better*	205
8.8	Negatives of Modals	207

READING 3 Starting Life in a New Country 211

8.9	Conclusions or Deductions—*Must*	212
8.10	Possibility—*May/Might*	214

READING 4 How to Furnish Your New Apartment Cheaply 216

| 8.11 | Using Modals for Politeness | 217 |

UNIT SUMMARY	220
REVIEW	221
FROM GRAMMAR TO WRITING	222

9 VIRTUAL COMMUNITIES

GRAMMAR The Present Perfect
The Present Perfect Continuous

READING 1 Google — 226
9.1 The Present Perfect—Forms — 227
9.2 The Past Participle — 229
9.3 The Present Perfect with an Adverb — 233

READING 2 Crowdfunding — 234
9.4 The Present Perfect—Overview of Uses — 235
9.5 The Present Perfect with Continuation from Past to Present — 236
9.6 The Simple Past, the Present Perfect, the Simple Present — 238

READING 3 Khan Academy — 240
9.7 The Present Perfect with Repetition from Past to Present — 241
9.8 The Present Perfect with an Indefinite Time in the Past — 243
9.9 The Present Perfect vs. the Simple Past — 246

READING 4 Genealogy and the Genographic Project — 248
9.10 The Present Perfect Continuous—Forms — 249
9.11 The Present Perfect Continuous—Use — 251

UNIT SUMMARY — 254
REVIEW — 255
FROM GRAMMAR TO WRITING — 256

10 JOBS

GRAMMAR Gerunds
Infinitives

READING 1 Finding a Job — 260
10.1 Gerunds—An Overview — 261
10.2 Gerunds as Subjects — 263
10.3 Gerunds as Objects — 265
10.4 Preposition + Gerund — 267

READING 2 Employee Engagement — 270
10.5 Infinitives—An Overview — 271
10.6 Infinitives after Expressions with *It* — 272
10.7 Infinitives after Adjectives — 273
10.8 Infinitives after Verbs — 274
10.9 Objects before Infinitives — 276
10.10 Infinitives to Show Purpose — 277
10.11 Infinitives or Gerunds after Verbs — 278

UNIT SUMMARY — 280
REVIEW — 281
FROM GRAMMAR TO WRITING — 282

MAKING CONNECTIONS

GRAMMAR Adjective Clauses

READING 1 **Reconnecting with Old Friends** 286
11.1 Adjective Clauses—Overview 287
11.2 Relative Pronouns as Subjects 288
11.3 Relative Pronouns as Objects 291

READING 2 **Making Connections Using Meetup** 295
11.4 Relative Pronouns as Objects of Prepositions 296
11.5 *Whose* + Noun 298

READING 3 **The Science of Friendship** 300
11.6 Adjective Clauses with *Where* and *When* 301

UNIT SUMMARY 304
REVIEW 305
FROM GRAMMAR TO WRITING 306

SPORTS AND ATHLETES

GRAMMAR Superlatives
Comparatives

READING 1 **Gregg Treinish: Extreme Athlete and Conservationist** 310
12.1 The Superlative Forms of Adjectives and Adverbs 311
12.2 Superlatives—Use 313

READING 2 **Americans' Attitude toward Soccer** 316
12.3 The Comparative Forms of Adjectives and Adverbs 317
12.4 Comparatives—Use 319

READING 3 **An Amazing Athlete** 323
12.5 *As . . . As* 324
12.6 *As Many/Much . . . As* 326
12.7 *The Same . . . As* 327

READING 4 **Football and Soccer** 330
12.8 Showing Similarity with *Like* and *Alike* 331

UNIT SUMMARY 334
REVIEW 335
FROM GRAMMAR TO WRITING 336

13 THE LAW

GRAMMAR Active and Passive Voice

READING 1 The Supreme Court — 340
13.1 Active and Passive Voice—Overview — 341
13.2 The Passive Voice—Form — 342

READING 2 Jury Duty — 344
13.3 The Passive Voice—Use — 345
13.4 Negatives and Questions with the Passive Voice — 347

READING 3 Who Owns the Photo? — 349
13.5 Transitive and Intransitive Verbs — 350

UNIT SUMMARY — 354
REVIEW — 355
FROM GRAMMAR TO WRITING — 356

14 MONEY

GRAMMAR Articles
Other/Another
Indefinite Pronouns

READING 1 Millennials and Money — 360
14.1 Articles—An Overview — 361
14.2 Making Generalizations — 362
14.3 Classifying or Defining the Subject — 363

READING 2 Kids and Money — 365
14.4 Non-Specific Nouns — 366
14.5 Specific Nouns — 367
14.6 Specific or Non-Specific Nouns with Quantity Words — 370

READING 3 Billionaires — 372
14.7 *Other* and *Another* — 373
14.8 More about *Other* and *Another* — 374
14.9 Definite and Indefinite Pronouns — 376

UNIT SUMMARY — 378
REVIEW — 379
FROM GRAMMAR TO WRITING — 380

APPENDICES

A	Summary of Verb Tenses	382
B	Nonaction Verbs	383
C	Irregular Verb Forms	384
D	Gerunds and Infinitives	386
E	Verbs and Adjectives Followed by a Preposition	387
F	Noncount Nouns	388
G	Uses of Articles	390
H	Connectors	394
I	Capitalization and Punctuation	396

GLOSSARY 398

INDEX 402

ACKNOWLEDGMENTS

The Author and Publisher would like to acknowledge and thank the teachers who participated in the development of the seventh edition of *Grammar in Context*.

A special thanks to our Advisory Board for their valuable input during the development of this series.

ADVISORY BOARD

Andrea Gonzalez, BYU English Language Center, Provo, UT, USA
Ellen Rosen, Fullerton College, Fullerton, CA, USA
Erin Pak, Schoolcraft College, Livonia, MI, USA
Holly Gray, Prince George's Community College, Largo, MD, USA
John Halliwell, Moraine Valley Community College, Palos Hills, IL, USA
Katherine Sieradzki, FLS Boston, Boston, MA, USA
Maria Schirta, Hudson County Community College, Jersey City, NJ, USA
Oranit Limmaneeprasert, American River College, Sacramento, CA, USA
Susan Niemeyer, Los Angeles City College, Los Angeles, CA, USA

REVIEWERS

Adriana García, Institut Nord-America, Barcelona, Spain
Alena Widows, Institut Nord-America, Barcelona, Spain
Augustine Triantafyllides, So Easy, Athens, Greece
Bilal Aslam, GTCC, High Point, NC, USA
Carmen Díez, CFA Les Corts, Barcelona, Spain
David Finfrock, QU, Doha, Qatar
Deanna Henderson, LCI, Denver, CO, USA
Ellen Barrett, Wayne State University, Detroit, MI, USA
Francis Bandin, UAB, Barcelona, Spain
Jonathan Lathers, Macomb Community College, Warren, MI, USA
Karen Vallejo, University of California, Irvine, CA, USA
Kathy Najafi, Houston Community College, Houston, TX, USA
Katie Windahl, Cuyahoga Community College, Cleveland, OH, USA
Laura Jacob, Mt. San Antonio College, Walnut, CA, USA
Leah Carmona, Bergen Community College, Paramus, NJ, USA
Luba Nesterova, Bilingual Education Institute, Houston, TX, USA
Marcos Valle, Edmonds Community College, Lynnwood, WA, USA
Marla Goldfine, San Diego Community College, San Diego, CA, USA
Milena Eneva, Chattahoochee Technical College, Marietta, GA, USA
Monica Farling, University of Delaware, Newark, DE, USA
Naima Sarfraz, Qatar University, Doha, Qatar
Natalia Schroeder, Long Beach City College, Long Beach, CA, USA
Paul Schmitt, Institut d'Estudis Nord-Americans, Barcelona, Spain
Paula Sanchez, Miami Dade College, Miami, FL, USA
Paulette Koubek-Yao, Pasadena City College, Pasadena, CA, USA
Robert Yáñez, Hillsborough Community College, Tampa, FL, USA
Samuel Lumbsden, Essex County College, Newark, NJ, USA
Sarah Mikulski, Harper College, Palatine, IL, USA
Steven Lund, Arizona Western College, Yuma, AZ, USA
Teresa Cheung, North Shore Community College, Lynn, MA, USA
Tim McDaniel, Green River College, Auburn, WA, USA
Tristinn Williams, Cascadia College, Seattle, WA, USA
Victoria Mullens, LCI, Denver, CO, USA

WELCOME TO *GRAMMAR IN CONTEXT*, SEVENTH EDITION

Grammar in Context, the original contextualized grammar series, brings grammar to life through engaging topics that provide a framework for meaningful practice. Students learn more, remember more, and use language more effectively when they study grammar in context.

ENHANCED IN THE SEVENTH EDITION

National Geographic photographs introduce unit themes and pull students into the context.

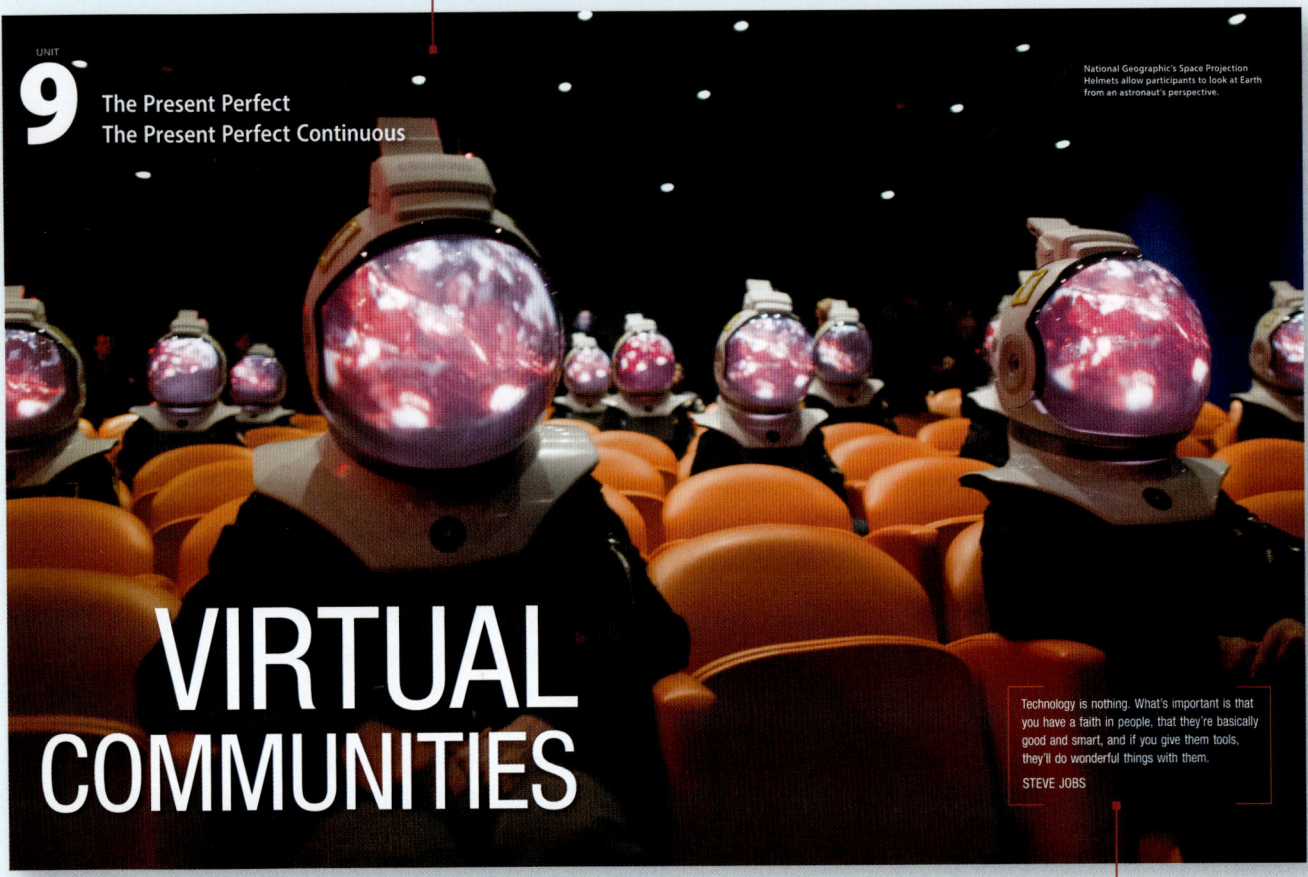

Unit openers include an inspirational quote to help students connect to the theme.

New and updated readings introduce the target grammar in context and provide the springboard for explanations and practice.

New Think About It questions give students the opportunity to personalize and think critically about what they are reading.

CROWDFUNDING

Read the following article. Pay special attention to the words in bold.

■ **Have** you ever **had** an idea for a business but no way to fund it? **Have** you **asked** relatives and friends for money to help you? If you **have done** these things, you know it isn't easy to get people interested in investing in your dream. After getting money from relatives and friends, it's hard to find more people willing to invest. Lately, people **have found** a different way to raise cash: through crowdfunding. Crowdfunding is a method of "collecting small amounts of money from a lot of different people, usually by using the Internet." While the idea **has been** around for possibly hundreds of years, the word *crowdfunding* **has** only **existed** since 2006.

Crowdfunding websites, which started to appear on the Internet in 2010, **have helped** individuals raise billions of dollars worldwide. So how does it work? A person demonstrates his idea in a short video and states his financial goal and the time frame for raising money. Usually the first investors are family and friends. Little by little, strangers become interested and donate money.

Not all crowdfunding plans are for profit. Some people **have used** crowdfunding websites that are specifically for philanthropic[1] projects. These sites **have attracted** people who want to make the world a better place. The 97 Supermarket in Changchun, China, is one example of this. Jiang Naijun used crowdfunding to get the money to open a supermarket. She named her market 97 because that was her age when she did this. Since she became profitable, she **has given** at least half the money she earns to charity[2], to help children in need. "I wanted to do more for society," she said.

If you want more information, just google "crowdfunding" and you will find a number of different sites specializing in different types of projects.

[1] philanthropic: intended to help others
[2] charity: an organization that helps people in need

Crowdfunding has become one of the most popular ways for people to raise money for a cause, project, or event. In 2017, $34 billion was raised globally. This number is expected to grow to more than $300 billion by 2025.

98-year-old Jiang Naijun used crowdfunding to start her supermarket and donates the profits to charity.

COMPREHENSION Based on the reading, write T for *true* or F for *false*.
1. _____ Sometimes strangers help fund a crowdfunding project.
2. _____ The idea of crowdfunding is old, but it has become easier to do with the Internet.
3. _____ The "97 Supermarket" project didn't reach its financial goal.

THINK ABOUT IT Discuss the questions with a partner or in a small group.
1. What would you like to crowdfund for? Why?
2. What might be some challenges with crowdfunding? Explain.

9.4 The Present Perfect—Overview of Uses

EXAMPLES	EXPLANATION
People **have used** crowdfunding since 2010. Google **has been** in existence for over 20 years.	We use the present perfect to show that an action or state started in the past and continues to the present.
I **have used** my laptop in coffee shops many times. How many articles about crowdfunding **have** you **read**?	We use the present perfect to show that an action repeated during a period of time that started in the past and includes the present.
Have you ever **asked** relatives for money?	We use the present perfect to show that an action occurred at an indefinite time in the past.

EXERCISE 7 Tell if the sentences show continuation from past to present (C), repetition from past to present (R), or an indefinite time in the past (I).

1. Larry Page has been interested in computers since he was a child. __C__
2. How many emails have you received today? _____
3. I've had my laptop for one year. _____
4. The word *crowdfunding* has been in existence since 2006. _____
5. Internet security has become a big problem. _____
6. Has your computer ever had a virus? _____
7. My cousin has used crowdfunding two times. _____
8. Have you ever used your laptop in a coffee shop? _____

GRAMMAR IN USE
When an event happened in the recent past, and the effect is still felt, we often use the present perfect. This is especially common for speakers of British English. In American English, we use either the present perfect or the simple past.

Someone **has just donated** $10,000!   Someone just donated $10,000.
I **have forgotten** my password again.   I forgot my password again.
Have you **heard** the news?   Did you hear the news?

New Grammar in Use notes highlight practical usage points to help students communicate more effectively.

New listening comprehension activities encourage students to listen for meaning through natural spoken English.

EXERCISE 17 Listen to the information about the U.S. Census. Write T for *true*, F for *false*, or NS for *not stated*.

1. _____ At first, children were not counted in the census.
2. _____ All census information is available to everyone.
3. _____ Most Americans complete the census questionnaire.

New Fun with Grammar allows the class to practice grammar in a lively game-like way.

FUN WITH GRAMMAR

Race to write. Form three teams. One person from each team goes to the board. Your teacher will say an irregular verb, and you will write the past participle of that verb on the board. Every student has a turn. The first to finish writing the word correctly wins a point.

For an extra challenge, the first to write a sentence using the verb in the present perfect wins another point.

Summary and Review sections help students revisit key points and assess their progress.

From Grammar to Writing gives editing advice and practice to set students up to successfully apply the grammar to writing.

New Writing Tips further connect the grammar to the unit writing task.

ADDITIONAL RESOURCES

FOR STUDENTS The **Online Practice** provides a variety of interactive grammar activities for homework or flexible independent study.

GO TO ELTNGL.COM/MYELT

FOR TEACHERS The **Classroom Presentation Tool** allows the teacher to project the student book pages, open interactive activities with answers, and play the audio program.

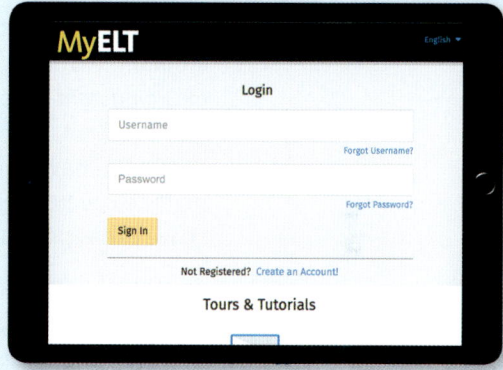

The Teacher's Website hosts the teacher's guide, audio, and ExamView® Test Center, so teachers have all the materials they need in one place.

ELTNGL.COM/GRAMMARINCONTEXTSERIES

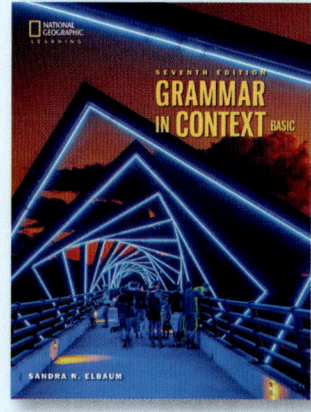 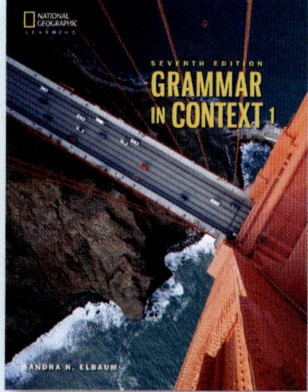 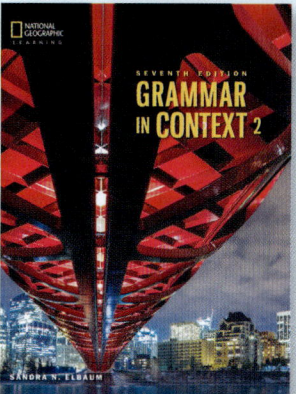 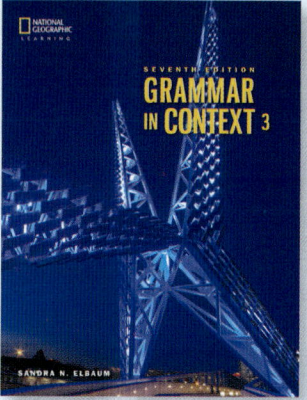

A WORD FROM THE AUTHOR

My parents immigrated to the United States from Poland and learned English as a second language as adults. My sisters and I were born in the United States. My parents spoke Yiddish to us; we answered in English. In that process, my parents' English improved immeasurably. Such is the case with many immigrant parents whose children are fluent in English. They usually learn English much faster than others; they hear the language in natural ways, in the context of daily life.

Learning a language in context, whether it be from the home, from work, or from a textbook, cannot be overestimated. The challenge for me has been to find a variety of high-interest topics to engage the adult language learner. I was thrilled to work on this new edition of *Grammar in Context* for National Geographic Learning. In so doing, I have been able to combine exciting new readings with captivating photos to exemplify the grammar.

I have given more than 100 workshops at ESL programs and professional conferences around the United States, where I have gotten feedback from users of previous editions of *Grammar in Context*. Some teachers have expressed concern about trying to cover long grammar units within a limited time. While ESL is not taught in a uniform number of hours per week, I have heeded my audiences and streamlined the series so that the grammar and practice covered is more manageable. And in response to the needs of most ESL programs, I have expanded and enriched the writing component.

Whether you are a new user of *Grammar in Context* or have used this series before, I welcome you to this new edition.

Sandra N. Elbaum

For my loves
Gentille, Chimene, Joseph, and Joy

CREDITS

ILLUSTRATIONS

15 (b) ©VectorShow/Shutterstock.com; **137** (tc) ©Source: National Park Service: all others © Cengage Learning

PHOTOS

2–3 (c) ©Frans Lanting/National Geographic Image Collection; **4** (bc) ©Manny Ceneta/Getty Images News/Getty Images; **9** (bc) ©Hero Images Inc./Alamy Stock Photo; **15** (tc) ©Berggren, Hans/Johner Images Royalty-Free/Getty Images; **17** (bc) ©frank60/Shutterstock.com; **18** (tr) ©Nigel Milner/EyeEm/Getty Images; **19** (bc) ©Davemhuntphotography/Shutterstock.com; **20** (t) ©Cengage; **28** (c) ©Flip Nicklin/Minden Pictures/National Geographic Image Collection; **34–35** (bc) ©viridis/E+/Getty Images; **40–41** (c) ©Chang Lee/The New York Times/Redux; **42** (r) ©Dia Dipasupil/Getty Images Entertainment/Getty Images; **50** (bc) ©Samo Trebizan/Shutterstock.com; **55** (bc) ©KidStock/Blend Images/Getty Images; **57** (bc) ©Rob Marmion/Shutterstock.com; **70–71** (c) ©Alfred Eisenstaedt/Time Life Pictures/Getty Images; **72** (bc) ©Science History Images/Alamy Stock Photo; **75** (tc) ©Carolyn Bauman/Tribune News Service/DALLAS/TX/USA/Newscom; **81** (t) ©AMIL LAGE/AFP/Getty Images; **81** (c) ©Image Source/Getty Images; **85** (t) ©Francis Miller/The LIFE Picture Collection/Getty Images; **92–93** (c) ©VCG/Visual China Group/Getty Images; **94** (bc) ©Roberto Westbrook/Tetra images/Getty Images; **102** (bc) ©Ben Horton/National Geographic Image Collection; **108** (r) ©Marmaduke St. John/Alamy Stock Photo; **111** (bc) ©IVASHstudio/Shutterstock.com; **112** (t) ©Hero Images/Getty Images; **122–123** (c) ©Eric Kruszewski/National Geographic Image Collection; **124** (t) ©TIMOTHY A. CLARY/AFP/Getty Images; **130** (c) ©YinYang/E+/Getty Images; **137** (bl) ©Larry Lahren, Ph.D.; **142** (bc) ©Hemis/Alamy Stock Photo; **150–151** (c) ©Andy Isaacson/The New York Times/Redux; **152** (t) ©Noelia Ramon - TellingLife/Moment/Getty Images; **155** (bc) ©Citizen of the Planet/Citizen of the Planet/Superstock; **156** (bc) ©David Sacks/David Sacks/Getty Images; **159** (bc) ©Matthieu Paley/National Geographic Image Collection; **164** (t) ©Magnus Wennman; **172–173** (c) ©Eric Rojas/The New York Times/Redux; **174** (t) ©Fotosearch/Archive Photos/Getty Images; **179** (bc) ©Johannes Arlt/The New York Times; **185** (t) © John Treslian/New York Daily News Archive/Getty Images; **194–195** (c) ©martin-dm/E+/Getty Images; **196** (bc) ©Maskot/Getty Images; **204** (t) ©Syed Mahabubul Kader/EyeEm/Getty Images; **208** (bc) ©Hinterhaus Productions/DigitalVision/Getty Images; **211** (t) ©Hero Images/Getty Images; **216** (t) ©Alex Potemkin/E+/Getty Images; **219** (b) ©Alexander Spatari/Moment/Getty Images; **224–225** (c) ©Eduardo Munoz/National Geographic Image Collection; **226** (t) ©Jb Reed/Bloomberg/Getty Images; **231** (b) ©Ashley Gilbertson/VII /Redux; **234** (b) ©TPG/Getty Images Entertainment/Getty Images; **240** (t) ©Robyn Twomey/Redux; **248** (b) ©Rick Friedman/Corbis Historical/Getty Images; **258–259** (c) © Zay Yar Lin; **260** (t) ©Frances Roberts/Alamy Stock Photo; **270** (t) ©Gary Friedman/Los Angeles Times/Getty Images; **279** (b) ©SolStock/E+/Getty Images; **284–285** (c) ©Photograph by Tyler Metcalfe; **286** (t) ©ZUMA Press Inc/Alamy Stock Photo; **295** (t) ©Hero Images/Getty Images; **300** (b) ©kate_sept2004/E+/Getty Images; **308–309** (c) ©Handout/Getty Images Sport/Getty Images; **310** (b) ©GREGG TREINISH/National Geographic Image Collection; **315** (b) ©Alexander Hassenstein/Getty Images Sport/Getty Images; **316** (t) ©Meg Oliphant/Getty Images Sport/Getty Images; **321** (c) ©Al Bello/Getty Images Sport/Getty Images; **323** (bl) ©Abramorama/Courtesy Everett Collection; **329** (b) ©Adam Pretty/Getty Images Sport/Getty Images; **330** (t) ©Tom Szczerbowski/Getty Images Sport/Getty Images; **338–339** (c) ©CSP_teshimine/AGE Fotostock; **340** (t) ©Photo by Mike Kline (notkalvin)/Moment/Getty Images; **344** (t) ©Hero Images/Getty Images; **349** left ©DAVID SLATER; **353** (b) ©Bill Perry/Shutterstock.com; **358–359** (c) ©KAZUHIRO NOGI/AFP/Getty Images; **365** (t) ©kate_sept2004/E+/Getty Images; **372** (t) ©Photo Courtesy of Kleiner Perkins

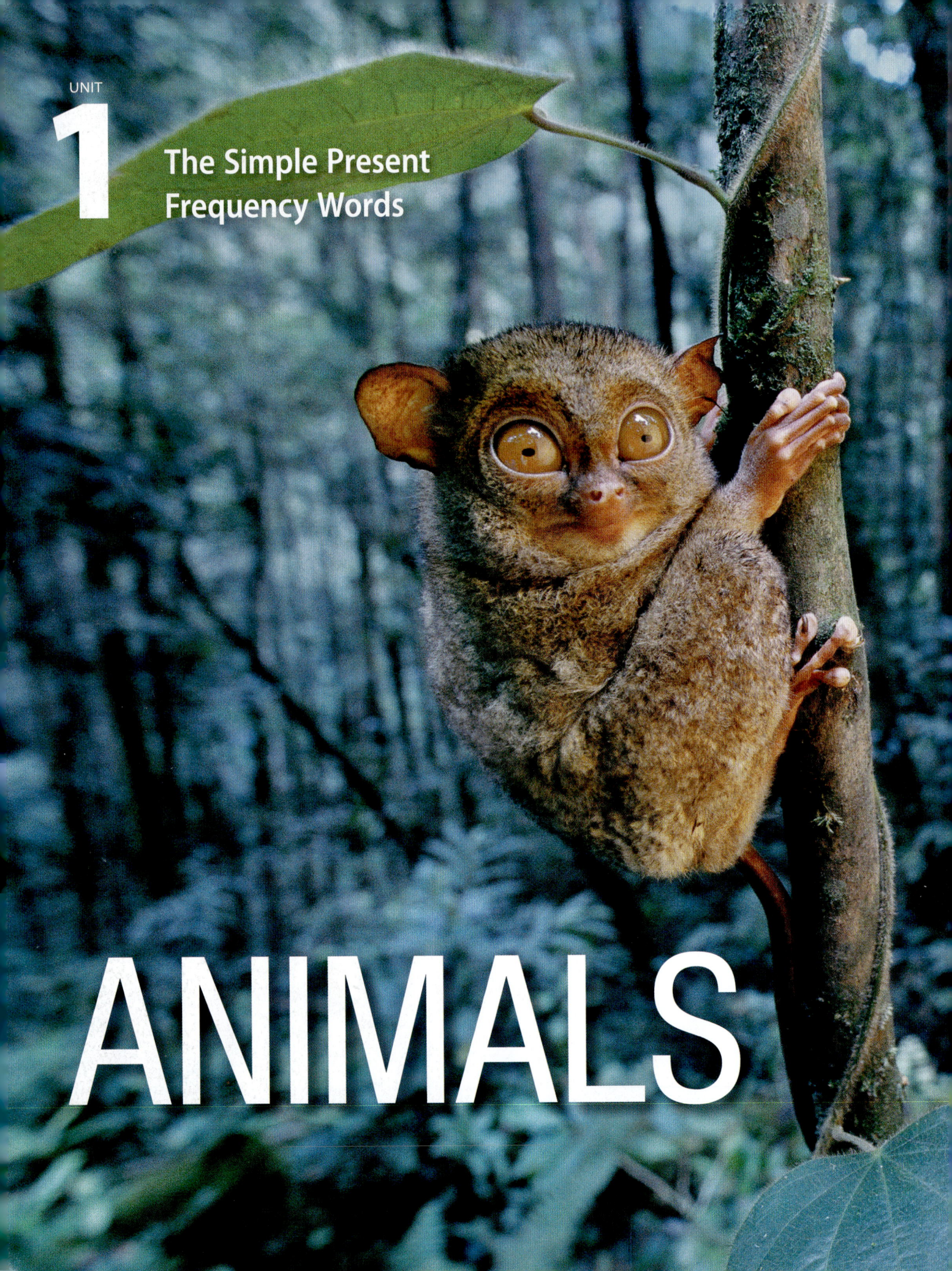

UNIT
1 The Simple Present
Frequency Words

ANIMALS

The Western tarsier is nocturnal. Its big eyes and ears help it see and hear in the dark.

Some people talk to animals. Not many listen though. That's the problem.

A.A. MILNE

Special Friends

Read the following article. Pay special attention to the words in bold. 1.1

They **are** our friends. We play with them. We talk to them. We spend a lot of money on them. We love them. Who **are** they? Our pets, of course. About 68 percent of Americans live with one or more animals. There **are** about 94 million pet cats and 90 million pet dogs in the United States. There **are** more pets than children in the United States! The most popular pets **are** cats and dogs. Other popular pets **are** fish, birds, and rabbits.

Pet ownership **isn't** cheap. Americans spend more than $69 billion a year on their pets. There **are** schools, toys, hotels, clothes, and cemeteries for pets. The average dog owner spends over $257 a year on vet[1] bills.

For many Americans, pets **are** part of the family. Many owners sleep with their dogs or cats. Some people travel with their pets. (The average cost to fly with a pet **is** $125 each way.) Some hotels allow guests to bring their pets.

Pets **are** great for your health. Contact with an affectionate[2] dog or cat can lower a person's blood pressure. Also, pets **are** a comfort to lonely people.

Pets **are** fun, but **they're** also work. Animals need a lot of attention. Before you buy a pet, it **is** important to answer these questions:
- **Are** you patient?
- **Are** you home a lot?
- If you have children, **are** they responsible?
- **Is** this a good animal for children?
- **Are** pets allowed where you live?
- **Are** you or your family members allergic[3] to pets?

It's important to understand that a pet **is** a long-term responsibility—and a long-term friend.

---
[1] vet: short for *veterinarian*; an animal doctor
[2] affectionate: loving
[3] allergic: very sensitive to a particular animal or plant

A man and his dog check in for their flight.

COMPREHENSION Based on the reading, write T for *true* or F for *false*.

1. _____ The most popular pets in the U.S. are dogs and cats.
2. _____ About 94 percent of Americans have a pet.
3. _____ Pets are not allowed on airplanes.

THINK ABOUT IT Discuss the questions with a partner or in a small group.

1. Do you have a pet? If so, what kind? If not, what kind do you think you would like?
2. In addition to lowering a person's blood pressure, what other ways can a pet make a person's life better?

1.1 *Be* Simple Present—Form

EXAMPLES			EXPLANATION
SUBJECT	**BE**		
I	am	happy with my dog.	We use *am* with *I*.
The child He She The cat It That There	is	responsible. intelligent. lonely. happy. cute. a friendly cat. a dog in the yard.	We use *is* with *he, she, it, this, that,* and singular subjects (*the child, the cat,* etc.). We use *there is* with a singular noun.
We You Pets They Those There	are	hard working. home a lot. fun. good friends. cute kittens. schools for dogs.	We use *are* with *we, you, they, these, those,* and plural subjects (*pets, cats,* etc.). We use *there are* with a plural noun.

1.2 Contractions with *Be*

EXAMPLES		EXPLANATION
I am You are She is He is It is We are They are	**I'm** responsible. **You're** patient. **She's** happy. **He's** kind. **It's** necessary. **We're** busy. **They're** cute.	A contraction combines two words. We can make a contraction with the subject pronoun and *am, is,* or *are*. We put an apostrophe (') in place of the missing letter.
There is Here is That is	**There's** a pet store near my house. **Here's** an idea. Let's get a dog. **That's** a friendly cat.	We can make a contraction with *there is, here is,* and *that is*.
cat is dog is	The **cat's** hungry. Your **dog's** cute.	We can make a contraction with most singular nouns and *is*.
A fo**x is** a relative of a dog. A mou**se is** a small animal. Thi**s is** a cute cat.		We don't make a contraction with *is* if the word before ends in *s, se, ce, ge, ze, sh, ch,* or *x*.

EXERCISE 1 Listen to the conversation. Fill in the blanks with the words you hear.

A: I want a dog. My friend has a dog with new puppies. There ___are___ nine puppies, and they
1.
need a home. The puppies _____ two months old. They _____ so cute. I want
2.   3.
one. Look—this _____ a picture of my favorite puppy.
4.

B: Dogs _____ a big responsibility.
5.

A: Mom, I _____ nine years old now, and I _____ responsible. I love dogs.
6.   7.
They _____ so affectionate. They _____ great friends. And dogs
8.   9.
_____ fun.
10.

B: They _____ expensive, too. For example, there _____ the cost of food.
11.   12.

EXERCISE 2 Fill in the blanks with the correct form of *be* to finish the conversation from Exercise 1. Use contractions wherever possible.

B: There ___are___ also vet bills.
1.

A: Vet bills?

B: Yes. A vet ___is___ an animal doctor. Dogs need doctors just like we do. It ___is___
2.   3.
important to think about that, too.

A: But the puppies ___are___ healthy.
4.

B: You ___are___ healthy, too. But sometimes you ___are___ sick and you need a
5.   6.
doctor. Also, your little brother ___is___ only three years old. He ___is___
7.   8.
afraid of dogs. Here ___is___ another problem: It ___is___ summer now, so it
9.   10.
___is___ easy to take the dog out. But in winter, it ___is___ so cold.
11.   12.

A: Please, Mom.

B: Let me think about it. I have to talk to Dad. We ___are___ your parents, and we want to make
13.
the right decision.

A: Thanks, Mom.

6 Unit 1

1.3 Be—Use

EXAMPLES	USES
I **am** patient.	With a description (an adjective)
A vet **is** an animal doctor.	With a classification or definition of the subject
My dog **is** in the yard.	With a location
This dog **is** from Alaska.	With a place of origin
The dog **is** cold. It **is** cold outside.	With a reaction to the temperature (*hot, cold, warm*) and with weather. The subject for sentences about weather is *it*.
My dog **is** three (years old).	With age
The cat **is** hungry. I **am** afraid of dogs.	With a physical or emotional state: *hungry, thirsty, afraid*
There **are** toys for dogs. There **is** an animal hospital near my house.	With *there*, to show that something exists
It **is** ten o'clock now.	With time. The subject for sentences about time is *it*.
It **is** important to be responsible with a pet.	With certain expressions beginning with *it*

Note:
Some words that end in *-ed* are adjectives: *tired, married, worried, interested, bored, excited, crowded, located.*
   The pet shop is **located** on the corner.
   The children are **excited** about the new puppy.

EXERCISE 3 Fill in the blanks with the correct form of *be*. Then write **D** for description, **C** for classification, **L** for location, **O** for origin, **W** for weather, **A** for age, **P** for a physical or emotional state, **TH** for *there*, **T** for time, or **I** for expressions beginning with *it*. Use contractions wherever possible.

1. My dog **'s** small. **D**
2. You _____ home a lot. _____
3. This dog _____ friendly. _____
4. There _____ a lot of pets in the U.S. _____
5. It _____ fun to own a pet. _____
6. It _____ hot today. _____
7. The dog _____ thirsty. _____
8. The puppies _____ three months old. _____
9. It _____ 7 a.m. _____
10. I _____ from Vietnam. _____
11. Vietnam _____ a country in Asia. _____

1.4 Negative Statements with *Be*

EXAMPLES	EXPLANATION
The dog owner **is not** home now. She **isn't** home during the day. You **are not** ready for a pet. You **aren't** patient.	To make a negative statement with *be*, we put *not* after a form of *be*. The negative contractions are *isn't* and *aren't*.

We can make contractions in negative statements with most subject pronouns + a form of *be* or with a form of *be* + *not*. (Exception: *I am not*)

I am not	I'm not		—
you are not	you're not	OR	you aren't
he is not	he's not	OR	he isn't
she is not	she's not	OR	she isn't
it is not	it's not	OR	it isn't
we are not	we're not	OR	we aren't
they are not	they're not	OR	they aren't

Notes:

1. We can make contractions with most nouns:
   The dog is not friendly. = The **dog's not** friendly. = The **dog isn't** friendly.
2. Remember: We cannot make a contraction with certain words + *is*. (See 1.2.)
   This is not a good pet. = This isn't a good pet. (NOT: This's not)

EXERCISE 4 Fill in the first blank with the correct form of *be*. Then fill in the second blank with a negative form. Use contractions wherever possible. In some cases, more than one answer is possible. Write all possible answers.

1. Today **'s** my daughter's birthday. It **isn't** a holiday.
2. My daughter and I **are** at the pet shop. We **aren't** at home.
3. My husband **is** at work now. He **isn't** with me.
4. I **'m** patient with dogs. I **'m not** patient with cats.
5. This puppy **is** for my daughter. It **is not** for my son.
6. My daughter **is** responsible. My son **isn't** responsible.
7. Dogs **are** good for protection. Cats **aren't** good for protection.
8. This **is** a small dog. It **is not** a big dog.
9. There **are** a lot of puppies here. There **aren't** a lot of kittens here.

8 Unit 1

EXERCISE 5 Circle the correct words to complete the sentences. In some cases, both answers are possible, so circle both options.

1. My dog (*is*/*are*) sick.
2. (*She's not*/*She isn't*) young.
3. She (*is*/*'s*) 15 years old.
4. She (*isn't*/*not*) hungry.
5. This (*is*/*'s*) a serious problem.
6. My dog and I (*am*/*are*) at the vet.
7. (*I'm not*/*I amn't*) happy.
8. We (*is*/*are*) worried about the dog.
9. (*The vet's*/*The vet*) a good doctor.
10. There (*'s*/*are*) many dogs in the waiting room.
11. (*They aren't*/*They're not*) all sick.
12. There (*are*/*is*) one cat in the waiting room.
13. (*It's*/*It*) in a box.
14. The box (*is*/*'s*) small.
15. There (*are*/*'re*) pet magazines in the waiting room.
16. (*Is*/*It's*) important to have a healthy pet.
17. (*It's*/*It*) my turn with the vet now.
18. (*I'm*/*I*) next.

A father and his sons wait to see their dog's veterinarian.

The Simple Present, Frequency Words

1.5 Yes/No Questions and Short Answers with *Be*

Compare statement word order with *yes/no* question word order.

STATEMENT WORD ORDER	YES/NO QUESTION	SHORT ANSWER
I am patient.	**Am I** patient with pets?	Yes, you are.
You are happy.	**Are you** happy with the new dog?	Yes, I am.
The vet is kind.	**Is the vet** patient?	Yes, she is.
It is important to take the dog to the vet.	**Is it** important to give the dog exercise?	Yes, it is.
We are at the vet.	**Are we** in her office?	No, we're not.
Pets are fun.	**Are pets** interesting?	Yes, they are.
They are interested in a pet.	**Are they** interested in a bird?	No, they aren't.
Those are cute puppies.	**Are those** your puppies?	Yes, they are.
That is a friendly dog.	**Is that** your dog?	No, it's not.
There are dogs at the vet.	**Are there** birds at the vet?	No, there aren't.

Notes:
1. In a question, we put *am, is,* or *are* before the subject.
2. We use a contraction for a short *no* answer. We don't use a contraction for a short *yes* answer.
   Is your son responsible? No, he isn't. OR *No, he's not.*
   Is your daughter responsible? Yes, she is. (NOT: *Yes, she's.*)
3. We use a pronoun (*he, we, you,* etc.) in a short answer.
4. When the question contains *this* or *that,* the answer uses *it,* even for people.
   Is that the vet? Yes, it is.

Pronunciation Note: We usually end a *yes/no* question with rising intonation.

Is that your dog?

EXERCISE 6 Fill in the blanks to complete each item. Use contractions wherever possible.

1. **A:** _____Is a bird_____ a good pet?

   B: Yes, it is. A bird is a very good pet.

2. **A:** _____Are you_____ happy with your new kitten?

   B: Yes, I am. My new kitten is fun.

3. **A:** _____Is your son_____ interested in birds?

   B: No, he _____is not_____. My son's interested in fish.

4. **A:** _____Is there_____ a vet near here?

   B: Yes, _____there's_____. There's a vet on the next block.

5. **A:** _Is she_ in the yard?

   B: No, she _is not_. The dog is in the house.

6. **A:** _Are you_ ready for a dog?

   B: No, I'm not. _I'm_ not home enough.

7. **A:** _Am I_ good with pets?

   B: No, you _'ve not_. You're not patient enough.

EXERCISE 7 Fill in the blanks to complete this conversation. Use contractions wherever possible. In some cases, more than one answer is possible.

A: _Is_ (1) this your dog?

B: Yes, it _is_ (2).

A: He _is_ (3) beautiful.

B: Thanks. But it's a "she."

A: _Is she_ (4) friendly?

B: Yes, she _is friendly_ (5).

A: She's so small. _Is she_ (6) a puppy?

B: No, she _isn't_ (7). _She's_ (8) four years old.

A: _Is it_ (9) hard to take care of a dog?

B: No, it _isn't_ (10).

A: _Are you in_ (11) home a lot?

B: No, _I'm not_ (12). _I'm_ (13) a student. But my parents _are at_ (14) home a lot.

A: I love dogs, but I _'m not in_ (15) home very much, and I live alone. So that _it's_ (16) a problem.

B: Cats _are_ (17) good pets, too. With a cat, it _is not_ (18) necessary to be home a lot. I think a cat _is_ (19) the perfect pet for you. _Am I_ (20) right?

A: No, you _aren't_ (21). I'm allergic to cats.

The Simple Present, Frequency Words 11

1.6 Wh- Questions with Be

Compare statement word order with wh- question word order.

AFFIRMATIVE STATEMENTS	AFFIRMATIVE WH- QUESTIONS
I am lost.	Where **am I**?
You are lonely.	Why **are you** lonely?
That is a nice dog.	What kind of dog **is that**?
The cat is old.	How old **is the cat**?
It is important to choose the right pet.	Why **is it** important to choose the right pet?
She is at work.	When **is she** at home?
There are a lot of dogs in my neighborhood.	How many dogs **are there** in your neighborhood?

NEGATIVE STATEMENTS	NEGATIVE WH- QUESTIONS
The dogs aren't friendly.	Why **aren't the dogs** friendly?
You aren't happy with the dog.	Why **aren't you** happy with the dog?

Notes:

1. Most question words can contract with *is*. The exceptions are *which is* and *how much is*.

    What's a vet?

    Where's your cat?

    Which is bigger, my dog or your dog?

2. After *what*, we can use a noun:

    what kind, what color, what country, what time

3. After *how*, we can use an adjective or adverb:

    how long, how hard, how old, how big, how much, how many

4. After *which*, we can use a noun:

    which dog, which vet, which animal

GRAMMAR IN USE

We ask different wh- questions to get information about specific topics.

Where	for a place	**A:** *Where* is your school?	**B:** *It's on Maple Street.*
Why	for a reason	**A:** *Why* are you here?	**B:** *Because I am a student.*
What kind	for a description	**A:** *What kind* of book is that?	**B:** *It's an English book.*
How old	for age	**A:** *How old* is Miguel?	**B:** *He's 18.*
When	for time	**A:** *When* is the concert?	**B:** *At 7 p.m./Tomorrow.*
How many	for number	**A:** *How many* students are here?	**B:** *15.*
How much	for amount	**A:** *How much* time is there?	**B:** *About ten minutes.*
How long	for length of time	**A:** *How long* is the flight?	**B:** *Two hours.*

EXERCISE 8 Fill in the blanks with the words you hear.

A: __Is that__ your dog?

B: No. It's my neighbor's dog.

A: __What kind of dog is it__? It's so cute.

B: I think it's a mutt.

A: __What is__ a mutt?

B: It's a mixed breed dog.

A: My daughter wants a dog. But dogs are so expensive.

B: A mutt isn't so expensive.

A: __Why isn't__ expensive?

B: Because you can get a mutt at an animal shelter. Dogs aren't expensive there.

A: __What's__ an animal shelter?

B: It's a place for unwanted pets. Those animals need a loving family.

A: __Are the animals__ healthy?

B: Yes, they __are__. The vets check the animals' health.

A: Why __are there__ so many unwanted pets?

B: There are a lot of unwanted pets because some people aren't responsible. They get a pet and then realize it's too much trouble to take care of it. What about your daughter? __Is she responsible__ responsible?

A: Yes, __she is__.

B: __How old is she__?

A: She's almost 10 years old.

B: I love dogs, but it's not a good idea for our family.

A: __Why isn't__ a good idea?

B: We're all too busy.

The Simple Present, Frequency Words   13

EXERCISE 9 Fill in the blanks to complete the phone conversation.

A: Hello?

B: Hi, Betty. This is Lara. How ___are you___?
   1.

A: I'm fine. I'm not home now.

B: Where ___are you___?
   2.

A: I'm at the animal hospital with the cat.

B: You have two cats. Which cat ___is___ sick?
   3.

A: Fluffy.

B: ___What's___ wrong with Fluffy?
   4.

A: He isn't hungry or thirsty.

B: ___How old is he___?
   5.

A: He's only four years old.

B: ___Are you___ alone?
   6.

A: No, I'm not.

B: ___Who's___ with you?
   7.

A: My daughter's with me.

B: Why ___isn't she___ at school?
   8.

A: She's on spring break now. She's very worried.

B: Why ___is she___ worried?
   9.

A: Fluffy is tired all the time. Oh, I have to go. The vet is ready to see us now.

B: OK. Call me later.

ABOUT YOU Find a partner. Ask each other these questions and share your answers.

1. Are pets popular in your native country? What kind?
2. What's a popular name for dogs in your native culture?
3. What's a better pet in your opinion—a dog or a cat?

FUN WITH GRAMMAR

Race your classmates. Form two or three teams. Your teacher will write a statement on the board. Each team writes a *yes/no* question and a *wh-* question for the statement. The team to write two correct questions first wins a point.

Statement: *Sam is in Prague.*   Yes/No question: *Is Sam in Prague?*
Wh- questions: *Where is Sam?/Who is in Prague?*

Dung beetles keep the land healthy for grazing cattle.

BENEFICIAL BUGS[1]

Read the following article. Pay special attention to the words in bold. 1.4

Are you afraid of spiders? How about insects such as roaches, ants, or bees? If your answer is "yes," you are not alone. Most people **don't like** them—and for good reason. Insects and spiders **look** scary. They **have** lots of legs, and they **fly** or **move** fast. Also, some of them **bite**, and sometimes this **causes** pain or even illness. (Usually, a spider's bite **doesn't hurt**, though.)

Insects and spiders can be scary, but they aren't all bad. In fact, many **help** us. Here's how.

 They **feed** us.

Bees **do** a lot for us, for example. Everyone **knows** that bees **make** honey, which we **use** in food, drinks, and medicine. But bees also **pollinate**[2] plants. When they **do** this, it **gives** us many fruits and vegetables. In fact, the U.S. **uses** bees to grow about 30 percent of its crops[3].

 They **protect** our food.

Farmers **grow** crops for food, but many insects **eat** these plants. Luckily, we **have** ladybugs and spiders. They **kill** bad bugs and **protect** our food. A ladybug, for example, **eats** about 5,000 insects a year, and a spider **eats** about 2,000. Thanks to spiders and ladybugs, a farmer **doesn't need** to use as many pesticides.

 They **clean** the environment.

Many insects and spiders **eat** waste on the ground—for example, old food or dead animals and plants. On one street in New York City, spiders, ants, and roaches **consume** about 2,100 pounds (950 kilos) of food on the ground each year. That's the same as 60,000 hot dogs! Eating this food waste **cleans** the environment and **keeps** it healthy.

DID YOU KNOW?
Spiders and insects are members of the largest group of animals on Earth (called *arthropods*). For every one person, there are 1.4 billion insects and millions of spiders. Luckily, many are small, and they **don't live** very long.

[1] bug: an informal word for *insect*
[2] to pollinate: to give material from one plant to another so that the plant reproduces and makes seeds and fruit
[3] crops: plants that we grow for food

The Simple Present, Frequency Words 15

COMPREHENSION Based on the reading, write T for *true* or F for *false*.

1. _____ Spiders and insects are a type of animal. There are more of them on Earth than people.
2. _____ Farmers dislike bees because they kill plants.
3. _____ Spiders and insects don't like human food.

THINK ABOUT IT Discuss the questions with a partner or in a small group.

1. How do the following help people? Explain with an example from the reading.

    bees   spiders   ladybugs   ants and roaches

2. Are you afraid of spiders and insects? Did the reading change your feelings about them?

1.7 The Simple Present Affirmative Statements—Form

A simple present tense verb has two forms: the base form and the *-s* form.

EXAMPLES			EXPLANATION
SUBJECT	**BASE FORM**	**COMPLEMENT**	
I You We They Many people	**dislike**	insects.	We use the base form of the verb when the subject is *I, you, we, they,* or a plural noun. NOTE: *People* is a plural noun.
SUBJECT	**-S FORM**	**COMPLEMENT**	
He She It The child Everyone	**dislikes**	insects.	We use the *-s* form of the verb when the subject is *he, she, it,* or a singular noun. NOTE: *Everyone* is a singular noun.

Notes:
1. *Have* is an irregular verb. The *-s* form is *has*.

    Insects **have** six legs. A spider **has** eight legs.

2. We use the *-s* form in the following expression: It **takes** (time) to do something.

    It **takes** time for bees to make honey.

3. We use the *-s* form after an *-ing* subject (gerund).

    Eating food waste on the ground **cleans** the environment.

16 Unit 1

EXERCISE 10 Complete the sentences with the base form or the -s form of the verb given. Then listen and check your answers. 1.5

Amazing Ants

Ants __live__ (1. live) in a large group called a *colony*. Usually, the colony __has__ (2. have) one queen. She __lays__ (3. lay) eggs. Female "worker" ants __find__ (4. find) food and __protect__ (5. protect) the group. Male ants __have__ (6. have) one main function in the colony: to mate with the queen.

Many people __think__ (7. think) that the queen is the group's leader, but she isn't. No single ant __controls__ (8. control) the colony. Instead, each ant __does__ (9. do) its part to help the colony, and the group __fixes__ (10. fix) any problems together. For example, when a worker ant __goes__ (11. go) out to find food, she usually __brings__ (12. bring) it back by herself. But sometimes an object is large, and the worker ant can't carry it alone. So she __sends__ (13. send) a chemical message to other ants, and they __come__ (14. come) to help her. Then everyone __carries__ (15. carry) the large object together. Working as a group __makes__ (16. make) the difficult task easier. People can learn a lot from these little animals.

1.8 The Simple Present—Use

EXAMPLES	USES
Some insects **bite**. Everyone **knows** that bees **make** honey. The U.S. **uses** bees to grow 30 percent of its crops.	To talk about general truths, habits, or customs
A spider **eats** about 2,000 insects a year. I **see** ants in the kitchen all the time.	To show regular activity or repeated action

Ants work together to solve problems.

EXERCISE 11 Fill in the blanks with the base form or the -s form of a verb in the box. You will use the verbs *catch* and *make* twice.

| catch | have | hope | know | make | see ✓ | take |

1. You probably __see__ spiders' webs all the time.
2. A spider's web __catches__ insects for the spider to eat. Everyone __knows__ this.
3. Making a new web __takes__ about an hour.
4. A spider __makes__ its web from silk.
5. This silk is very strong. Some people __make__ fishing nets from it, and they __catch__ fish.
6. In the future, scientists __hope__ to make clothes from spider silk.
7. Spider silk also __has__ the ability to stop bleeding in humans.

1.9 The Simple Present—Negative Statements

EXAMPLES	EXPLANATION
The girl **likes** ladybugs. She **doesn't like** spiders.	We use *doesn't* + the base form with *he, she, it,* or a singular subject. Compare: likes doesn't like / hurts doesn't hurt
A bee sting **hurts**. A spider bite **doesn't hurt** as much.	*Doesn't* is the contraction for *does not*.
Many insects **live** for only a few hours. They **don't live** very long.	We use *don't* + the base form with *I, you, we, they,* or a plural subject. Compare: like don't like / live don't live. *Don't* is the contraction for *do not*.

EXERCISE 12 Fill in the blanks with the negative form of the underlined verb.

1. A spider <u>makes</u> a web. An insect __doesn't make__ a web.
2. A spider <u>has</u> eight legs. An insect __doesn't have__ eight legs. It has six.
3. Most spiders <u>have</u> eight eyes. Insects __don't have__ eight. They have two.
4. An ant <u>lives</u> in a colony. It __doesn't live__ alone.
5. Pesticides <u>kill</u> many bugs, but they __don't kill__ many spiders.
6. My brother <u>likes</u> spiders. I __doesn't like__ them at all!
7. Elena and Carlos are entomologists. She <u>studies</u> bees. He __doesn't study__ bees. He specializes in ants.

18 Unit 1

8. We know many bees are dying today. We _don't know_ why.

9. Some people raise bees for honey. It takes time, but raising bees _doesn't take_ a lot of work.

10. Some insects bite people. But bees _don't bite_. They sting.

EXERCISE 13 Fill in the blanks with the correct negative form of a verb in the box. Use each verb only once.

| break ✓ | die ✓ | have | kill ✓ | know |
| like ✓ | live ✓ | make ✓ | see | want ✓ |

1. Most spiders _don't live_ very long—only about a year.
2. Many people _don't like_ spiders because they look scary.
3. My sister is afraid of spiders, but I _don't know_ why.
4. A typical spider has eight eyes, but it _doesn't see_ very well.
5. Take my advice: If you _don't want_ spiders in your house, keep your home clean.
6. Using pesticides _don't kill_ most spiders. Instead, try vinegar. It kills most bugs.
7. Unlike many spiders, a tarantula _doesn't make_ a web. It makes a hole in the ground.
8. In a famous story, a dangerous spider bites a man, but he _doesn't die_. He lives and becomes the superhero Spider-Man.
9. A spider's web _doesn't break_ easily because it is very strong.
10. We _don't have_ any more time today to talk about these eight-legged animals.

A tarantula is a large spider with a hairy body and legs.

The Simple Present. Frequency Words 19

Lucy Cooke wants to help animals that aren't so cute, such as this frog.

LUCY COOKE, ZOOLOGIST

Read the following article. Pay special attention to the words in bold. 1.6

Which animal **do** you **prefer** to see? A baby panda, a toad, or a snake? Most people choose the baby panda. Why **do** people **choose** this animal? Most people like cute, furry animals with big eyes, like the panda. These animals get a lot of attention. Why **don't** people **like** snakes and toads? They're just not cute like pandas.

Lucy Cooke wants people to respect all animals. Who is Lucy Cooke? Why **does** she **want** to show people the importance of other animals? Cooke is a zoologist, a scientist who studies animals. She worries about the future of all animals. Scientists need money to study and protect these animals, but they get less money for toads and snakes than for pandas.

"There are so many television shows about koala bears and kittens," Cooke says. To get people interested in less popular animals, Cooke writes stories about them in a blog. She also makes videos about them and puts them online. People love her videos. They are fun to watch.

Cooke is especially interested in frogs and other amphibians[1]. Some of these are in danger of disappearing. She wants to save these animals. Why **does** she **want** to save these animals? Other animals depend on them for food. If we save frogs, we save other animals, too.

Do you **know** about the flying frog in Borneo? It has wings. It lives in the treetops and goes from tree to tree without going down to the ground. **Do** you **know** about the poison[2] dart frog? It is only one centimeter long. But it has enough poison to kill ten people.

Scientists need research money to protect all animals. Cooke's videos and blog make people aware of all kinds of animals.

---

[1] amphibian: an animal that can live on land or in water
[2] poison: a substance that harms or kills people or animals

COMPREHENSION Based on the reading, write T for *true* or F for *false*.

1. _____ Cooke makes videos about animals.
2. _____ The Borneo frog goes to the ground to get food.
3. _____ Cooke writes a blog about animals.

THINK ABOUT IT Discuss the questions with a partner or in a small group.

1. Do you think it is important to protect all animals? Why or why not?
2. What are some unpopular animals? Why are they unpopular?

1.10 The Simple Present—Questions

Compare statements, *yes/no* questions, and short answers.

STATEMENT	YES/NO QUESTION & SHORT ANSWER	EXPLANATION
Cooke **studies** animals. She **writes** a blog.	**Does** she **study** frogs? Yes, she **does**. **Does** she **write** about pets? No, she **doesn't**.	For *yes/no* questions with *he, she, it*, or a singular subject, we use *Does* + subject + base form.
People **like** cute animals. Koala bears **get** attention.	**Do** people **like** insects? No, they **don't**. **Do** pandas **get** attention? Yes, they **do**.	For *yes/no* questions with *I, we, you, they*, or a plural subject, we use *Do* + subject + base form.

Note:

Compare *yes/no* questions and short answers with *be* and other simple present verbs:

Is Cooke a zoologist? Yes, she **is**.   **Does** Cooke research amphibians? Yes, she **does**.

Compare statements and *wh-* questions.

STATEMENT	WH- QUESTION	EXPLANATION
Cooke **studies** frogs. She **makes** videos.	How **does** Cooke **study** frogs? Why **does** she **make** videos?	For *wh-* questions with *he, she, it*, or a singular subject, we use *wh-* word + *does* + subject + base form.
Some frogs **live** in trees. Some frogs **have** wings.	Where **do** other frogs **live**? Why **do** these frogs **have** wings?	For *wh-* questions with *I, we, you, they*, or a plural subject, we use *wh-* word + *do* + subject + base form.
Cooke **doesn't study** plants. Borneo frogs **don't live** on the ground.	Why **doesn't** Cooke **study** plants? Why **don't** Borneo frogs **live** on the ground?	For negative *wh-* questions, we use *wh-* word + *don't* or *doesn't* + subject + base form.

Note:

Compare *wh-* questions with *be* and other simple present verbs:

What kind of animals **are** *you interested in?*   *Why* **aren't** *people interested in some animals?*

What kind of animals **do** *you* **like**?   *Why* **don't** *people* **like** *some animals?*

EXERCISE 14 Listen to the conversation. Then write T for *true* or F for *false*. 🎧 1.7

1. _____ Search and rescue dogs help find people after a disaster.
2. _____ They rely on their excellent eyesight.
3. _____ Small dogs make the best rescue dogs.

EXERCISE 15 Listen to the conversation again. Fill in the blanks with the words you hear. 🎧 1.7

A: There's a program on TV tonight about search and rescue dogs. __Do you want__ to watch it with me?
1.

B: I __know__ about guide dogs. But I __don't know__ anything about search and
2. 3.
rescue dogs. What __does__ search __mean__?
4. 5.

A: Search __means__ "look for."
6.

B: __How do you spell__ search?
7.

A: S-E-A-R-C-H.

B: What __do__ these dogs __do__?
8. 9.

A: When there is a disaster, like an earthquake, they __help__ the workers find missing people.
10.
They __save__ people's lives.
11.

B: How __do__ they __do__ that?
12. 13.

A: They __have__ a great sense of smell. They can find things that people can't.
14.

B: __Do they need__ a lot of training?
15.

A: Yes, they __do__.
16.

B: What kind of dogs __do they use__?
17.

A: They usually __use__ large, strong dogs. Labrador retrievers or golden retrievers are often
18.
search and rescue dogs. Let's watch the program together tonight.

B: What time __does it begin__?
19.

A: At 9 p.m.

B: __Does__ your dog __want__ to watch the program with us?
20. 21.

A: Ha! I __don't__ think so. My dog is lazy. She just __likes__ to eat, play, and sleep.
22. 23.

22   Unit 1

EXERCISE 16 Fill in the blanks to complete the conversation. Use context clues to help you.

A: Do you ____*like*____ animals?
               1.

B: Yes, I ____do____. In fact, I like animals very much, especially dogs.
            2.

A: ____Do you have____ a dog?
         3.

B: No, I don't have a dog, but my sister has two Labradors. I love to play with them when I visit her.

A: If you love dogs, why ____don't you have____ a dog?
                             4.

B: Because my landlord ____doesn't like____ dogs.
                            5.

A: That's too bad. ____Does____ he allow cats?
                        6.

B: Yes, he ____does____.
               7.

A: Why ____does he allow____ cats but not dogs?
           8.

B: He says dogs make a lot of noise. I have a cat, but I have to find a new home for her. ____Do____
                                                                                                9.
you know anyone who wants a cat?

A: No, I ____don't____. Sorry. Why ____don't you want____ your cat?
             10.   11.

B: I want my cat, but my girlfriend doesn't.

A: Why ____doesn't she want____ your cat?
           12.

B: She's allergic to cats.

A: That's a problem.

ABOUT YOU Choose Part 1 to interview a student who has a dog, or Part 2 to interview a student who has a cat. Then report what you learned to another student.

PART 1

1. your dog/big
   A: *Is your dog big?*
   B: *Yes, she is.*

2. your dog/sleep a lot (how many hours)
   A: *Does your dog sleep a lot?*
   B: *Yes, she does.*
   A: *How many hours does she sleep?*
   B: *She sleeps about fifteen hours a day.*

continued

3. how old/your dog
4. it/a male or a female
5. what/your dog's name
6. what/your dog/eat
7. how often/you/take your dog out
8. your dog/do tricks (what kind)
9. your dog/have toys (what kind)
10. your dog/friendly
11. your dog/bark a lot (when)
12. why/you/like dogs

PART 2

1. how old/your cat
2. it/a male or a female
3. what/your cat's name
4. your cat/eat special food (what kind)
5. your cat/friendly
6. your cat/sit on your lap a lot
7. your cat/have toys (what kind)
8. your cat/sleep with you (where)
9. why/you/like cats

EXERCISE 17 Circle the correct words to complete the conversation.

A: We're late. Hurry. The train is ready to leave.

B: Let's go . . . (on the train) . . . Why (*that dog is*/*is that dog*) on the train? (*Are*/*Do*) they allow dogs on trains?
                                                    1.   2.

A: Not usually. But that's not an ordinary dog. That's a guide dog. It's a dog that helps people with disabilities.

B: How (*do they help*/*they help*) people?
                       3.

A: They (*help*/*helps*) blind people move from place to place, on foot and by public transportation.
             4.

B: (*Are*/*Do*) they need a lot of training?
       5.

A: Yes, they (*are*/*do*).
               6.

B: Where (*do*/*are*) they get their training?
             7.

A: They get their training at special schools. There are guide dogs for the blind, the deaf, and people in wheelchairs.

B: Why (*are you*/*you are*) such an expert on guide dogs?
　　　　　　　　8.

A: My cousin is blind. He has a guide dog.

B: Then you know a lot about guide dogs.

A: Yes, I (*am*/*do*). A guide dog (*need*/*needs*) to concentrate.
　　　　　9.　　　　　　　　　10.

B: When (*are*/*do*) they play?
　　　　　　11.

A: They (*play*/*plays*) when the owner (*take*/*takes*) off the dog's harness. Then the dog (*know*/*knows*) its
　　　　　12.　　　　　　　　　　　　13.　　　　　　　　　　　　　　　　　　　　　　　14.
work is finished.

B: It's amazing what a dog can do.

1.11 Wh- Questions with a Preposition

EXAMPLES	EXPLANATION
A: What does Lucy Cooke write **about**? **B:** She writes about animals in danger. **A:** What are these animals in danger **of**? **B:** They're in danger of disappearing.	In conversation, most people put the preposition at the end of the *wh-* question.
A: Where does Lucy Cooke **come from**? **B:** She comes from England. **A:** Where **is** she **from**? **B:** She's from England.	For place of origin, we use *be from* or *come from*.
A: What time does the program begin? **B:** It begins **at** 9 p.m.	We omit *at* in a question about time.

> **GRAMMAR IN USE**
>
> Putting the preposition before a question word is grammatically correct, but very formal. When the preposition comes at the beginning, we use *whom*, not *who*. This formal style is rarely used in everyday speech.
>
> 　　Formal: **With whom does the dog play?**
> 　　Informal: **Who does the dog play with?**

The Simple Present, Frequency Words 25

EXERCISE 18 Complete each question using the underlined words as clues.

1. Lucy Cooke <u>comes from</u> England. What city _____does_____ she _____come from_____?
2. <u>I'm interested in</u> pandas. What animals _____are_____ you _____interested in_____?
3. What _____does_____ Lucy Cooke _____write about_____? She <u>writes</u> a blog <u>about</u> animals in danger.
4. Who _____does she study with_____? She <u>studies</u> animals <u>with</u> other zoologists.
5. She <u>travels to</u> other countries. Which countries _____does she travel to_____?
6. Cooke <u>worries about</u> certain animals. Which animals _____does Cooke worry about_____?
7. I <u>want to learn</u> more <u>about</u> tree frogs. What animals _____do_____ you _____want to learn about_____?

1.12 Questions about Meaning, Spelling, Cost, and Time

WH- WORD	DO/DOES	SUBJECT	VERB (BASE FORM)	COMPLEMENT
What	does	*puppy*	mean?	
How	do	you	spell	*puppy*?
How	do	you	say	*puppy* in Spanish?
How much	does	a puppy	cost?	
How long	does	it	take	to train a puppy?

EXERCISE 19 Fill in the blanks to complete the conversation.

A: _____Do you have_____₁ a pet?

B: Yes. I have a new kitten.

A: I don't know the word *kitten*. What _____does kitten mean_____₂?

B: *Kitten* means "baby cat."

A: Oh. What's his name?

B: Romeo.

A: How _____do you spell puppy_____₃?

B: R-O-M-E-O. _____Do you have_____₄ any pets?

26 Unit 1

A: Yes, I do. I have a bird.

B: What kind of bird _do you have_ ?
           5.

A: I have a bird that talks. I don't know the word in English.

How _do you say_ loro in English?
       6.

B: Parrot. So you have a parrot.

A: Yes. His name is Chico.

B: How old _is he_ ?
              7.

A: He's almost 20 years old.

B: How long _do parrot live_ ?
               8.

A: They live a long time. Some live up to 80 years.

B: How much _do it cost_ ?
               9.

A: It depends on what kind you get. But they usually cost between $175 and $1,000.

B: Wow! _Are_ parrots affectionate?
           10.

A: Oh, yes. They're very affectionate. Chico sits on my shoulder all the time.

B: What _does he eat_ ?
           11.

A: He eats fruit, vegetables, rice, nuts, and seeds.

B: _Does he talk_ a lot?
       12.

A: Yes. He talks a lot.

B: What _does he say to_ ?
           13.

A: He says, "Good-bye," "Hello," "I love you," and many more things. He speaks Spanish and English.

B: How long _does it take_ to teach a parrot a word?
               14.

A: My parrot is very smart. It takes a few weeks to teach him one word.

FUN WITH GRAMMAR

Role-play a conversation. You have five minutes to write and practice a conversation with a partner about his or her job. It can be a real job, or you can choose from the ideas below. Use information questions and *wh-*questions to ask what your partner does, where he/she works, if he/she likes the job, and why/why not. The pair with the most original conversation wins.

   dolphin trainer   fashion blogger   race car driver   video game tester
   A: Why do you like to train dolphins?
   B: Dolphins are more fun to work with than people.

Bottlenose DOLPHINS

Read the following article. Pay special attention to the words in bold. 1.8

Bottlenose dolphins are very popular animals. We **often** see them in aquariums, sea parks, TV shows, and movies. Because of the shape of their nose, they look like they **always** have a smile on their faces.

Bottlenose dolphins live in warm climates. They live underwater, but they **rarely** stay there for more than seven minutes. Humans are involuntary[1] breathers. We don't **usually** think about breathing. But dolphins have to remember to breathe. One side of their brain is **always** active. This means they **never** fully sleep.

Dolphins have an excellent sense of hearing. They use clicking sounds to find food. The sound echoes[2] back and tells them where the food is.

Bottlenose dolphins are social animals. They **usually** swim in groups of 10 to 15. Together they hunt[3] for food. They **sometimes** hunt with fishermen near their fishing boats. **Once in a while** a dolphin hunts alone. **Sometimes** a dolphin gets lost. Each dolphin has a unique[4] whistle, so it uses its whistle to call out to the group.

Bottlenose dolphins **usually** live about 40 to 50 years.

---

[1] involuntary: done without thinking
[2] to echo: to be repeated by bouncing off a surface
[3] to hunt: to search for
[4] unique: one of a kind; not like anything else

COMPREHENSION Based on the reading, write T for *true* or F for *false*.

1. __F__ Bottlenose dolphins are involuntary breathers.
2. __F__ Bottlenose dolphins usually hunt alone.
3. __T__ The whistle of the bottlenose dolphin helps it find other dolphins.

THINK ABOUT IT Discuss the questions with a partner or in a small group.

1. What is a "social animal"? In addition to dolphins, what other animals are social?
2. Why do you think dolphins are popular?

1.13 Frequency Words with the Simple Present

EXAMPLES	EXPLANATION
Dolphins **never** fully sleep. They **always** come up for air. They **sometimes** hunt with fishermen.	We use the simple present with frequency words to show a regular activity.
Whenever a dolphin gets lost, it uses sound to find its group.	*Whenever* shows a regular activity. It means "any time."

FREQUENCY WORDS	FREQUENCY
always	100%
usually/generally	↑
often/frequently	
sometimes/occasionally	
rarely/seldom/hardly ever	↓
never/not ever	0%

GRAMMAR IN USE

Hardly ever is more informal than *rarely* or *seldom*. We use it a lot in speaking.

FORMAL: I **rarely** go to the movies.
INFORMAL: I **hardly ever** go to the movies.

EXERCISE 20 Fill in the blanks with a phrase from the box.

always come	is always	are never ✓	usually live	sometimes get	usually think

1. Dolphins ___are never___ completely asleep.
2. Dolphins ___always come___ up for air.
3. They ___sometimes get___ lost.
4. People don't ___usually think___ about breathing.
5. The dolphin's brain ___is always___ active.
6. Dolphins don't ___usually live___ more than 50 years.

ABOUT YOU Fill in the blanks with an appropriate frequency word to talk about your native country or culture. Find a partner and compare your answers.

1. People in my native culture ____rarely____ have cats in the house.
2. Dogs in my native culture _____ sleep with their owners.
3. Dogs are _____ part of the family.
4. Cats are _____ part of the family.
5. People _____ feed pet food to cats and dogs.
6. People _____ travel with their pets.
7. People _____ take dogs into restaurants.
8. Blind people _____ use dogs to help them.
9. People are _____ kind to animals.

EXERCISE 21 Look again at the sentences in the exercise above. Does the frequency word come before or after the verb? Write *B* for *before* or *A* for *after*.

1. __B__   4. _____   7. _____
2. _____   5. _____   8. _____
3. _____   6. _____   9. _____

1.14 Position of Frequency Words

EXAMPLES	EXPLANATION
A dolphin's brain **is always** active.	A frequency word can come after the verb *be*.
A dolphin **rarely stays** under water for more than seven minutes.	A frequency word can come before other verbs.
Sometimes a dolphin gets lost. A dolphin **sometimes** gets lost. Dolphins **usually** swim in groups. **Usually** dolphins swim in groups.	*Sometimes* and *usually* can come close to the verb or at the beginning of the sentence.

Note:
Always and *never* are rarely at the beginning of the sentence.
    I'm **always** interested in animal TV programs. (NOT: Always I'm interested . . .)
    Fish **never** live on land. (NOT: Never fish live . . .)

30 Unit 1

EXERCISE 22 Rewrite the sentence, adding the word given.

1. A guide dog stops at an intersection. (*always*)
   A guide dog always stops at an intersection.

2. Dogs like to play. (*often*)
   Dogs often like to play.

3. Lucy Cooke is excited about animals. (*always*)
   Lucy Cooke is always excited about animals.

4. Dolphins hunt with fishermen. (*sometimes*)
   Dolphins sometimes hunt with fishermen.

5. Dolphins come up for air. (*always*)
   Dolphins always come up for air.

6. People go to sea parks to see dolphins. (*sometimes*)
   People sometimes go to sea parks to see dolphins.

7. Sea parks are crowded in the summer. (*always*)
   Sea parks are always crowded in the summer.

8. A dolphin hunts alone. (*rarely*)
   A dolphin rarely hunts alone.

9. A dolphin is awake. (*always*)
   A dolphin is always awake.

10. A dolphin leaves its group. (*hardly ever*)
    A dolphin hardly ever leaves its group.

11. Dogs are happy to see their owners. (*always*)
    Dogs are always happy to see their owners.

12. Cats are friendly to strangers. (*rarely*)
    Cats are rarely friendly to strangers.

1.15 Questions about Frequency

Yes/No Questions with *Ever*

DO/DOES	SUBJECT	EVER	VERB		SHORT ANSWER
Do	you	ever	sleep	with your cat?	No, I **never** do./No, **never**.
Does	the teacher		talk	about her dog?	Yes, she **often** does./Yes, **often**.

BE	SUBJECT	EVER		SHORT ANSWER
Are	dogs	ever	lonely?	Yes, they **sometimes** are./Yes, **sometimes**.
Is	your cat		home alone?	Yes, she **often** is./Yes, **often**.

Notes:
1. In a short answer, the frequency word comes between the subject and the verb.
2. The verb after *never* is affirmative.
    Does your cat ever drink milk?
    *No, she **never drinks** milk.*

EXERCISE 23 Answer the questions with a short answer and the frequency word given.

1. Do dogs ever bark? (*sometimes*)
    Yes, they sometimes do.

2. Do people ever travel with their dogs? (*sometimes*)
    Yes, they sometimes do.

3. Do fish ever make noise? (*never*)
    No, they never do.

4. Do birds ever make noise? (*always*)
    Yes, they always do.

5. Do parrots ever live for more than 20 years? (*usually*)
    Yes, they usually do.

6. Do dogs ever live for more than 20 years? (*hardly ever*)
    No, they hardly ever do.

7. Does a dolphin ever swim alone? (*sometimes*)
    Yes, it sometimes does.

8. Are parrots ever affectionate? (*sometimes*)
    Yes, they sometimes are.

9. Do dolphins ever hunt in groups? (*usually*)

   Yes, they usually do

10. Are pets ever lonely? (*sometimes*)

    Yes, they sometimes are

1.16 Questions with *How Often*

EXAMPLES	EXPLANATION
How often do you take your dog out? I take her out **three times a day**. **How often** do you take your cat to the vet? I take my cat to the vet **twice a year**.	We use *how often* when we want to know about the frequency of an activity. We answer with a frequency expression.
Once in a while, a dolphin gets lost. A dolphin gets lost **once in a while**. **Every seven minutes**, a dolphin needs air. A dolphin needs air **every seven minutes**.	A frequency expression can come at the beginning or at the end of a sentence. When it comes at the beginning of the sentence, we sometimes separate it from the rest of the sentence with a comma.

Note:
Some frequency expressions are:
- every (other) day/week/month/year
- several/many/a few/five times—a day/week/month/year
- once/twice—a day/week/month/year
- from time to time
- once in a while

EXERCISE 24 Fill in the blanks to complete each item.

1. **A:** How ___*often*___ do you take your dog to the vet?

   B: I take her to the vet ___once___ a year, in April.

2. **A:** Do guide dogs ___ever___ play?

   B: Yes. They usually play when they finish their work.

3. **A:** Do dolphins ___ever___ swim in groups?

   B: Yes. They usually swim in groups.

4. **A:** ___How___ often do dolphins come up for air?

   B: They come up for air ___every___ seven minutes.

5. **A:** ___How often___ do you put your dog in a pet hotel?

   B: I never ___do___.

continued

6. **A:** _How often_ does your dog want to go out?

   B: She wants to go out three times _a day_.

7. **A:** Does your dog _ever_ sleep with you?

   B: Yes. My dog sleeps with me _every_ night.

8. **A:** _Once_ in a while, I take my dog to a dog park. What about you?

   B: I hardly _ever_ go there. It's too crowded.

EXERCISE 25 Fill in the blanks to complete the conversation. Use contractions wherever possible.

A: I know you love dogs. _Do you have_ a dog now?
                                1.

B: No, I _don't_. But I have two cats. I don't have time for a dog.
           2.

A: Why _don't you have_ time for a dog?
          3.

B: Because I'm not at home very much. I work in the day and go to school in the evening.

A: How _often do you have class_?
          4.

B: I have class three nights a week. I love dogs, but dogs need a lot of attention.

A: Cats need attention, too.

B: When I'm not home, sometimes my sister comes to play with them.

A: _How_ often does she come?
       5.

B: Two or three times _a_ week. What about you? _Do you have_ any pets?
                         6.   7.

A: I have several tropical fish.

B: How _much does it cost_?
          8.

34 Unit 1

A: Some tropical fish cost more than $100.

B: Wow! How many fish ___do you have___ ?
 9.

A: I have about 14 or 15. My favorite is my Oranda.

B: How ___do you spell___ Oranda?
 10.

A: O-R-A-N-D-A. It's a kind of goldfish.

B: You spend a lot of money for a boring pet.

A: Fish ___aren't___ boring. It ___is___ interesting to look at them. And
 11. 12.
they ___are___ easy to take care of. When I go to work, they _____
 13. 14.
get lonely, like dogs and cats.

B: Yes, but they _____ affectionate like dogs and cats.
 15.

A: They _____ make noise like dogs do, so neighbors never complain about fish. One thing
 16.
isn't easy: cleaning the fish tank.

B: _____ clean the tank?
 17.

A: About once _____ . I usually clean the tank every Saturday.
 18.

B: Do you _____ forget to clean it?
 19.

A: No, I _____ do. I can see when it needs to be cleaned.
 20.

B: _____ get a new fish?
 21.

A: Not very _____ . They can live for many years.
 22.

The Simple Present, Frequency Words **35**

SUMMARY OF UNIT 1

The Simple Present with *Be*

	WITH *IS*	WITH *ARE*
Affirmative Statement	Your dog **is** smart.	Dolphins **are** smart animals.
Negative Statement	It **isn't** big.	They **aren't** afraid of fishermen.
Yes/No Question	**Is** it friendly?	**Are** dolphins fish?
Short Answer	No, it **isn't**.	No, they **aren't**.
Wh- Question	What kind of dog **is** it?	How smart **are** they?
Negative *Wh-* Question	Why **isn't** it friendly?	Why **aren't** they afraid of fishermen?

The Simple Present with Other Verbs

	BASE FORM	-*S* FORM
Affirmative Statement	My friends **have** a dog.	She **likes** birds.
Negative Statement	They **don't have** a cat.	She **doesn't like** cats.
Yes/No Question	**Do** they **have** a bird?	**Does** she **like** small birds?
Short Answer	No, they **don't**.	Yes, she **does**.
Wh- Question	What kind of dog **do** they **have**?	Why **does** she **like** birds?
Negative *Wh-* Question	Why **don't** they **have** a cat?	Why **doesn't** she **like** cats?

Frequency Words and Expressions

FREQUENCY WORDS	FREQUENCY	FREQUENCY EXPRESSIONS
always	100%	once in a while
usually/generally	↑	from time to time
often/frequently		every day
sometimes/occasionally		once a year
rarely/seldom/hardly ever	↓	several times a day
never/not ever	0%	every other month

Questions and Answers with Frequency Words

QUESTION	ANSWER
Does he **ever** take his dog to the park?	Yes, he often does.
How often does he feed his dog?	Twice a day.

REVIEW

Circle the correct words to complete the conversation.

A: Your dog (**is**/are) very friendly.
　　　　　　1.

B: Yes, he (love/**loves**) people. His name is Buddy.
　　　　　　　2.

A: How (**do you spell**/you spell) Buddy?
　　　　　3.

B: B-U-D-D-Y. He's a therapy dog.

A: What (a therapy dog does/**does a therapy dog do**)?
　　　　　　　　　　4.

B: He (make/**makes**) sick people feel better.
　　　　5.

A: How (**does a therapy dog make**/is a therapy dog make) sick people feel better?
　　　　　　　6.

B: People (**feel**/feels) happy when they're with a nice dog. Buddy and I (**often visit**/visit often) patients in the
　　　　　7.　　　　　　　　　　　　　　　　　　　　　　　　　　　　　　8.
hospital. Everyone at the hospital (love/**loves**) him.
　　　　　　　　　　　　　　9.

A: How (**does a dog become**/a dog becomes) a therapy dog?
　　　　　10.

B: First, the owner (need/**needs**) to answer a few questions such as these: "(Is your dog likes/**Does your dog like**)
　　　　　　　　11.　　　　　　　　　　　　　　　　　　　　　　　　　　12.
people?" or "Does he (**have**/has) a calm personality?" But that's not enough.
　　　　　　　13.
(Always the dog/**The dog always**) needs training.
　　　　　14.

A: How much (costs the training/**does the training cost**)?
　　　　　　　15.

B: (It's cost/**It costs**) about $500.
　　　16.

A: (How long it takes/**How long does it take**) to train the dog?
　　　　　17.

B: That (depend/**depends**) on the dog.
　　　　18.

A: (Are/**Do**) the dog owners make money?
　　　19.

B: No. We (**work**/are work) as volunteers.
　　　　　20.

A: How (**often**/ever) (**do you visit**/you visit) the hospital with Buddy?
　　　　21.　　　　　22.

B: (We once a week go/**Once a week we go**) to the hospital. For more information, check the TDI website.
　　　23.

A: What (means TDI/**does TDI mean**)?
　　　　　24.

B: (It's mean/**It means**) "Therapy Dogs International."
　　　25.

A: (**Do you ever**/Do ever you) get tired of working with sick people?
　　　26.

B: No, I (don't never/**never do**). I have to go now. Buddy (**needs**/is needs) water.
　　　　27.　　　　　　　　　　　　　　　　　　　28.

A: How (does you know/**do you know**) that?
　　　　29.

B: His tongue is out. That's dog talk for "(I/**I'm**) thirsty."
　　　　　　　　　　　　　　30.

The Simple Present, Frequency Words　37

FROM GRAMMAR TO WRITING

PART 1 Editing Advice

1. Don't use *have* with age. Don't use *years* without *old*.

   The dog ~~has~~ **is** 10 years **old**.

2. Don't use *have* with *hungry, thirsty, hot, cold,* or *afraid*.

   The dog ~~has~~ **is** thirsty. She wants water.

3. Don't forget the verb *be*. Remember that some words that end in *-ed* are adjectives, not verbs.

   We **are** excited about our new puppy.

4. Use the correct question formation.

   Why ~~your sister doesn't~~ **doesn't your sister** like dogs?

   Why ~~Lucy Cooke studies~~ **does Lucy Cooke study** animals?

5. Don't use *be* with another present verb.

   ~~We're~~ have a new cat.

6. Use the *-s* form when the subject is *he, she, it,* a singular noun, *everyone,* or *family*.

   The cat sleep**s** all day.

   Everyone love**s** the new puppy.

   My family want**s** a cat.

7. Use *doesn't* when the subject is *he, she, it,* a singular noun, or *family*.

   He ~~don't~~ **doesn't** have a pet.

   My family ~~don't~~ **doesn't** like cats.

8. Use the base form after *does*.

   My brother doesn't ~~has~~ **have** a pet.

   How does a dolphin get~~s~~ air?

9. Use regular question formation for *spell, mean, cost,* and *take*.

   What ~~means "obey"~~ **does "obey" mean**?

   How **do you** spell "dolphin"?

   How much ~~costs~~ **does** a parrot **cost**?

   How long ~~it takes~~ **does** it **take** to train a guide dog?

10. Use the correct word order with frequency words.

    ~~Never my dog~~ **My dog never** sleeps with me.

11. Don't put longer frequency expressions between the subject and the verb.

    She ~~all the time~~ plays with her cat **all the time**.

PART 2 Editing Practice

Some of the shaded words and phrases have mistakes. Find the mistakes and correct them. If the shaded words are correct, write C.

    The relationship between people and pets in the U.S. **is sometimes** strange to me. [C] (1.) **I surprised** (2.) that Americans **thinks** (3.) of their pets as part of the family. **I'm have** (4.) a new American friend, Marianne. She **live** (5.) alone, but **she's has** (6.) a dog, Sparky. Marianne **treats** (7.) him like a child. **I not** (8.) very interested in him, but **always she wants** (9.) to show me pictures of him on her phone. She thinks everyone **want** (10.) to see them, but I think **she wrong** (11.). She often **buy** (12.) toys for him, especially on his birthday. He **has** (13.) 12 years old, so she **spends** (14.) a lot of money on vet bills, too. **How much cost a visit to the vet?** (15.) At least $100!

    She **have** (16.) several coats for him for the winter weather, but he **don't like** (17.) to wear them. So when they **go** (18.) outside in winter, he **has** (19.) cold. She **buys sometimes** (20.) expensive food for him. (He **likes** (21.) steak.) She sometimes **calls** (22.) him on the telephone when **she not** (23.) home and **talks** (24.) into the answering machine which she keeps just for this purpose. **Sparky always sleeps** (25.) in bed with her.

    Once a month, she (26.) takes him to a dog groomer. **What means "dog groomer"?** (27.) This is a professional who gives Sparky a bath and cuts and paints his nails. Nothing **cost** (28.) too much money when it comes to Sparky.

    Sometimes **I'm think** (29.) American dogs live better than most people in the world.

WRITING TIP

When you write about an animal, introduce it by making a statement with *be* + an adjective to describe it:

    The zebra **is a social** animal.

When you write about the animal's behavior, use the simple present. Choose the correct form:

    A zebra **runs** very quickly./Zebras **live** in grasslands.

To describe animal behavior, use frequency words and expressions:

    Zebras **often** move around to find fresh grass.

PART 3 Write

Read the prompts. Choose one and write a paragraph about it.

1. Look for a Lucy Cooke video online. Watch the video and describe the behavior of the animal. What does this video teach you about the animal? (Provide your teacher with a link to the video.)
2. Describe the behavior of an animal you know about. This can be a pet or a wild animal.

PART 4 Edit

Reread the Summary of Unit 1 and the editing advice. Edit your writing from Part 3.

UNIT
2

The Present Continuous
The Future

ACROSS
GENERATIONS

Grandmothers attend a school trip in South Korea with their classmates, who are also their grandchildren.

In youth we learn; in age we understand.
MARIE VON EBNER-ESCHENBACH

IRIS APFEL:
STILL GOING STRONG

Read the following article. Pay special attention to the words in bold. 🎧 2.1

Many people in the United States retire in their sixties, but not fashion icon[1] Iris Apfel. Born in 1921 in New York City, Apfel is now in her late nineties. But unlike many people her age, she **isn't relaxing** at home. Instead, she **is creating** a new line of clothing and jewelry. She**'s planning** a fashion show, too. And she**'s traveling** all over the world. "I**'m working** harder than ever," she says, "but I**'m having** so much fun."

For many years, Apfel was an interior designer[2]. Now she**'s working** in fashion. Her style is unique. She**'s** always **wearing** colorful clothing, jewelry, and large black glasses. On the street, people **are** constantly **approaching**[3] her and **taking** her photo.

On Instagram, Apfel has over a million followers, but she is worried about social media. She thinks it**'s ruining** fashion. People **are copying** each other, Apfel says. Everything **is becoming** the same everywhere—in New York, Hong Kong, Paris. It's boring, Apfel believes. When things are different, then they are interesting.

Don't follow others, Apfel tells people. "Be your own person"—in fashion and in life. Ask yourself: "**Am** I **doing** the right thing for *me*?" This can be about your clothing choices, or even the subject you**'re studying** in school. Apfel lives her life this way. And at almost one hundred years old, she **is** still **going strong**.

Iris Apfel's style is unique. Here, she is wearing black and white with red accessories, and, as always, her famous large black glasses.

---

[1] icon: a person who is well known and important
[2] interior designer: a person who decorates the inside of a home or other building
[3] to approach: to come close to someone

COMPREHENSION Based on the reading, write T for *true* or F for *false*.

1. _____ Iris Apfel is in her sixties, and she is planning to retire soon.
2. _____ A lot of people like Iris Apfel's style.
3. _____ Iris Apfel likes social media. In her opinion, it is improving fashion.

THINK ABOUT IT Discuss the questions with a partner or in a small group.

1. The last sentence of the reading says that Iris Apfel "is still going strong." What does the expression "still going strong" mean? Why does this expression describe Ms. Apfel?
2. Do you think it's a good idea for people to work into their sixties and beyond? Why or why not?

2.1 The Present Continuous—Form

For the present continuous, we use a form of *be* (*am, is, are*) + verb + *–ing*.

SUBJECT	BE (AM, IS, ARE)	VERB + -ING	
I	am	working	hard.
Iris/She	is	traveling	all over the world.
Social media/It	is	ruining	fashion.
Some people/They	are	taking	Ms. Apfel's photo.
You	are	learning	about Iris Apfel.

Notes:

1. We can make a contraction with the subject pronoun and a form of *be*. Most nouns can also contract with *is*.

    I'm having so much fun.
    She's traveling all over the world.
    Iris Apfel's creating a new clothing line. Her **team's** helping her.

2. To form the negative, we put *not* after *am/is/are*. In many cases, we can make a negative contraction in two ways:

    She is not relaxing. = **She isn't** relaxing. = **She's not** relaxing.
    You are not working. = **You aren't** working. = **You're not** working.

3. For *I am not,* there is only one contraction:

    I am not traveling. = **I'm not** traveling.

4. We do not repeat the *be* verb after *and* or *or*.

    She **is traveling** and **planning** a fashion show.

5. We can put an adverb between *be* and the verb + *–ing*.

    She's <u>still</u> **going** strong.

6. The present continuous is also called the present progressive.

EXERCISE 1 Fill in the blanks with the present continuous form of the words given. Use correct spelling and capitalization. Make contractions when possible.

A: What are you doing?

B: ___I'm looking___ at something on Instagram.
          1. I/look

A: Yeah, what?

B: _____ about Iris Apfel in class, right? Well, there is this married couple, Alisa
         2. we/learn

and Min Soo. They're 70, and _____ around the U.S. on their bikes.
                                    3. they/travel

A: _____ me!
        4. you/kid

B: No, I'm serious. _____ to visit every state park in the U.S.
                         5. they/try

A: Wow, that's cool. So where are they now?

B: _____ Yosemite National Park, in California. Look at this photo.
        6. they/hike

A: _____. It's so beautiful!
        7. it/snow

B: I know. _____ classes in the park, too. _____ to paint,
              8. they/take   9. Min Soo/learn

and _____ photography.
        10. Alisa/study

A: So how can they do this? Do they have a lot of money?

B: No, _____ only 80 dollars a day. _____ in hotels.
           11. they/spend   12. they/not stay

_____ home-sharing sites.
    13. they/use

A: That's great. I love that _____ them from doing new things, just like Iris Apfel!
                                  14. age/not stop

EXERCISE 2 Read the items. Then listen and fill in the blanks with the words you hear. 2.2

1. Today, many older people ___are starting___ new careers later in life. They _____

   and _____ nothing.

2. For example, for years, 70-year-old Judy Pearlman was an engineer. These days, _____ high

   school students in math.

3. "_____ really _____ my new job," Pearlman says. "_____

   a lot of money, but _____ people. I like that."

4. The work is hard sometimes, but Judy _____. "_____ a lot," she says,

   "and that's a good thing."

44 Unit 2

2.2 The Present Continuous—Use

EXAMPLES	EXPLANATION
Iris Apfel **is talking** with two people. They **are taking** her photo.	We use the present continuous to describe an action in progress at this moment.
These days, Ms. Apfel **is working** in fashion. "I'm working harder than ever," she says.	We use the present continuous to show a long-term action that is in progress. It may not be happening at this exact moment.
A lot of people on social media **are copying** each other. More retired people **are starting** a second career.	We use the present continuous to describe a trend. A trend is a behavior that many people are doing at this time. It describes a change in behavior from an earlier time.

> **GRAMMAR IN USE**
>
> We use the present continuous to describe the actions in an image.
>
> > In this photo, my friends and I **are hanging out** at the beach. This is Jeff. He **is learning** to surf. Martina **is making** a sandcastle.
>
> The present continuous is also used to describe action in a piece of art such as a painting or a drawing.

EXERCISE 3 Fill in the blanks with the present continuous form of one of the verbs from the box. Use each verb only once. You will not use all the verbs.

happen	exercise	lift ✓	not swim ✓
not take ✓	ride ✓	take ✓	visit ✓

1. Jack _'s visiting_ a new gym. He _is taking_ a tour.
2. Some people _re exercising_ in the main room.
3. A woman _'s riding_ an exercise bike.
4. A man _is lifting_ weights.
5. In a yoga class, Jack sees his friend Naomi. But she _isn't taking_ the class. She's the instructor.
6. There's a pool, but people _aren't swimming_ in it today.

EXERCISE 4 Are these things happening at this point in time in the United States, in the world, or in another country you know about? Explain your ideas to a partner.

1. Fewer senior citizens are retiring.
2. The world is becoming a safer place.
3. Everyone is spending more time on social media.
4. More people in their twenties are traveling.

continued

5. A lot of people are losing their jobs.
6. Fewer people in their twenties are buying cars.
7. More women are starting businesses.
8. Kids are growing up faster than before.
9. More young adults are living with their parents longer.
10. People are living longer.
11. Fewer people are smoking.
12. Fewer people are voting in elections.

ABOUT YOU Find a partner and discuss your answers to these questions.

1. What kinds of things are you doing in your free time these days?
2. What classes are you taking this semester?
3. What are you doing at work this month?

2.3 Questions with the Present Continuous

Compare statements, *yes/no* questions, short answers, and *wh-* questions.

STATEMENT	YES/NO QUESTION AND SHORT ANSWER	WH- QUESTION AND ANSWER
You **are studying** at Cornell.	**Are** you **studying** full time? Yes, I **am**.	What **are** you **studying**? I'**m studying** interior design.
They **are living** in New York.	**Are** they **going** to school? No, they'**re not**.	What **are** they **doing** in New York? They'**re working** at the U.N.
Iris **isn't relaxing** at home.	**Is** she **traveling**? Yes, she **is**.	Why **isn't** she **relaxing**? She **isn't relaxing** because she's **working**.

Notes:

1. We sometimes leave a preposition at the end of a question.

    What **are** you **listening** to?   I'**m listening** to a podcast on second careers.

2. In spoken English, we often give a short answer to a *wh-* question. The short answer to a *why* question often starts with *because*.

    What are you studying?   Computer science.
    Why are you studying that?   Because it pays well.

3. When the question is "What … doing?" we usually answer with a different verb. The short answer starts with the *-ing* word.

    What **are** they **doing** in New York?   **Working** at the U.N.

46   Unit 2

EXERCISE 5 Use the words given to make a *yes/no* question. Fill in the second blank to complete the short answer.

1. those students/interview

    A: _Are those students interviewing_ Iris Apfel?

    B: Yes, _they are_. Ms. Apfel is visiting their school today.

2. you/plan

    A: _Are you planning_ your next vacation?

    B: Yes, _I'm_. I'm thinking about visiting Costa Rica.

3. Alisa/take

    A: _Is Alisa taking_ a painting class?

    B: No, _she isn't_. She's studying photography.

4. social media/ruin

    A: _Is social media ruining_ fashion?

    B: No, _it isn't_. It's making fashion more interesting.

5. Iris Apfel/still live

    A: _Is Iris Apfel still living_ in New York City?

    B: Yes, _she is_. She loves it there.

6. Alisa and Min Soo/stay

    A: _Are Alisa and Min Soo staying_ in Yosemite long?

    B: No, _they aren't_. They're only there for three days.

7. I/ask

    A: _Am I asking_ too many questions?

    B: No, _you aren't_. You can ask as many questions as you want.

8. you/write

    A: _Are you writing_ down this information?

    B: No, _I'm not_. I can check the website later.

EXERCISE 6 Read each statement and write a question about it using the word in parentheses. Then think of a short answer to the question.

1. Some older people are starting new careers. (*when*)

   When are some older people starting new careers?   Later in life.

2. Iris Apfel is wearing a colorful outfit in this photo. (*what*)

   What is Iris Apfel wearing in this photo?   A colorful outfit

3. Jack is learning to paint. (*where*)

   Where is Jack learning to pain?   At Art academy

4. I'm taking an interesting class. (*what*)

   What interesting class are you taking?   An astronomy class

5. My grandparents are visiting Mexico. (*who*)

   Who else visiting Mexico?   My grandparents

6. People are living longer nowadays. (*why*)

   Why are people living longer nowadays?   Because the good medicines

7. My sister is applying to college. (*where*)

   Where is your sister applying to college?

8. In this photo, we're not smiling. (*why*)

   Why aren't we smiling in this photo?   Because I'm sad

9. My parents aren't planning to retire. (*why*)

   Why aren't your parents planning to retire?   Because they're young

10. I'm doing an internship. (*where*)

    Where are you doing an internship?   At a computer company

11. My brother isn't working now. (*why*)

    Why isn't your brother working now?   Because he's sick

12. I'm eating a sandwich for lunch. (*what*)

    What are you having for lunch?   A sandwich

EXERCISE 7 Fill in the blanks with the present continuous to complete the conversation between a career coach (speaker A) and a retired firefighter (speaker B). Use contractions wherever possible.

A: So, I understand that ___you're looking___ for part-time work.
    1. you/look

B: Yes, I am.

A: Great. I work with a local community center. It has many part-time job openings right now. ___Are you working___ at the moment?
    2. you/work

B: No. I retired from the fire department six months ago.

A: Oh? Two retired firefighters ___are working___ for us now.
    3. work

B: Really? What kind of things ___are they doing___?
    4. they/do

A: ___One's teaching___ a CPR¹ class. ___Another's helping___ people with their taxes.
    5. one/teach   6. another/help

B: I can do those things. How many hours ___are they working___?
    7. they/work

A: Twenty hours a week. The community center needs another CPR teacher.

B: Great, but ___is the CC hiring___ right away?
    8. the community center/hire

A: Yes. Why?

B: ___I'm planning___ to take a short trip.
    9. I/plan

A: That's not a problem. Where are you going?

B: Florida. My good friend Marcos ___is living___ there now.
    10. live

A: ___What's he doing___ in Florida? Is he retired, too?
    11. what/he/do

B: Yes, but he enjoys cooking, so ___he's making___ online cooking tutorials. Two thousand
    12. he/make
___people are watching___ his channel now!
    13. people/watch

---

¹ CPR: a method used to help a person who isn't breathing

Digital Natives and Digital Immigrants

Read the following article. Pay special attention to the words in bold.

They're everywhere: in coffee shops, on the train, in restaurants, at work. They**'re texting**; they**'re tweeting**; they**'re googling**; they**'re checking** social media; they**'re taking** selfies; they**'re listening** to music. And yes, they**'re** even **working**. They're always connected. These are the "digital natives."

Born at the end of the twentieth century and the beginning of the twenty-first century, digital natives **don't know** life without technology. The first generation of digital natives **is** now **entering** the workforce and **changing** the way we work. More and more younger people **are working** from home, in coffee shops, or anyplace. They**'re bringing** their personal equipment into the workplace, too. They **switch** back and forth between their social and professional lives. They **don't see** the need to separate the two.

Some older people **are adapting** well to technology. Some people call them "digital immigrants." Others **are having** trouble. Some **are refusing** to use any new technology. Older people often **think** that technology **is growing** too fast. Look at the older people around you. **Do** they **have** smart phones? **Do** they **have** earbuds in their ears? **Are** they **texting**? Many older people **prefer** to share information with a small group of friends. Digital natives **share** information globally[1].

The younger generations **want** high-tech devices that do everything: take pictures, send texts and photos, provide music and videos, and connect them with friends around the world. What **does** the older generation **want** from technology? In many cases, Grandma and Grandpa just **want** a device that **connects** them to family and friends. They **like** to see pictures of grandchildren. Some even **love** to have a video chat with family.

As more and more technology **is entering** every aspect of our lives, the digital divide between generations **is widening**.

---

[1] globally: throughout the world

A digital immigrant is improving his computer skills with help from a digital native.

COMPREHENSION Based on the reading, write T for *true* or F for *false*.

1. _____ Many digital natives are always connected.
2. _____ Digital natives separate their personal and professional lives.
3. _____ Digital immigrants usually want a device that does many things.

THINK ABOUT IT Discuss the questions with a partner or in a small group.

1. Do you think being connected all the time is positive or negative? Explain.
2. Do you agree that the digital divide between generations is widening? Or are digital immigrants starting to catch up with digital natives? Explain with examples.

2.4 Contrasting the Simple Present and the Present Continuous

Form

THE SIMPLE PRESENT	THE PRESENT CONTINUOUS
Grandma **uses** email.	Marc **is sending** a message.
She **doesn't use** a smart phone.	He **isn't making** a phone call.
Does she **use** the Internet? Yes, she **does**.	**Is** he **sending** a message to his friend? Yes, he **is**.
When **does** she **use** the Internet?	How **is** he **sending** a message?
Why **doesn't** she **use** a smart phone?	Why **isn't** he **sending** a message to his friend?

Use

EXAMPLES	EXPLANATION
People **use** their phones to text. I sometimes **send** photos to my grandmother. Older people **prefer** to talk on the phone.	We use the **simple present** for: • a general truth. • a habitual activity. • a custom.
I'm getting a text message right now. My grandfather **is learning** about technology. Technology **is growing** quickly.	We use the **present continuous** for: • an action that is in progress now. • a longer action in progress at this general time. • a recent trend.
My grandparents **live** in a retirement home. My sister **is living** in a dorm this semester.	We use *live* in the simple present to talk about a person's home. We use *live* in the present continuous to talk about a temporary, short-term residence.
A: What does she do (for a living)? **B:** She's an English teacher. **A:** What is she doing now? **B:** She's texting her grandson.	"What does she do?" asks about a job or profession. "What is she doing?" asks about an activity now.

The Present Continuous, The Future   51

EXERCISE 8 Fill in the blanks with the simple present or the present continuous form of the verb given.

1. Conversation between a grandmother and grandson:

    A: You 're eating and working on your essay at the same time.
                  a. eat and work

    B: That's not a problem, Grandma.

    A: What _are you eating_ ? Is that a hamburger?
               b. you/eat

    B: No, it isn't. It's a veggie burger. I never _eat_ meat.
                                             c. eat

    A: You don't eat enough. Look at you. You're so thin.

    B: I _'m trying_ to lose weight.
         d. try

    A: You always _eat_ in front of your computer. Take a break.
                     e. eat

    I _'m making_ soup now. When it's ready, please come to the table.
       f. make

    B: But I _'m working_ on something important now.
              g. work

    A: How is that possible? You _'re eating and listening_ to music, too.
                                 h. eat and listen

    B: I always _listen_ to music when I _work or study_ .
                 i. listen   j. work or study

    A: Whenever I _work_ , I _concentrate_ on my work.
                    k. work   l. concentrate

    I _don't do_ other things at the same time.
      m. not/do

    B: You _don't understand_ the world of young people. We often multitask.
             n. not/understand

    A: You're right. I don't.

2. Conversation between two brothers:

    A: _Are you sleeping_ ? Wake up. It's almost time for class.
        a. you/sleep

    B: I'm so tired. I never _get_ enough sleep.
                        b. get

    A: That's because you're always on your computer or phone. How many hours _do you sleep_
                                                                  c. you/sleep

    a night?

    B: About four or five.

    A: That's not enough. You _need_ more sleep. Turn off your computer
                                  d. need

    and phone at night, and get some sleep.

    B: I never _turn off_ my devices. I always _want_
             e. turn off   f. want

    to know when I get a message.

A: That's ridiculous! Let's go get breakfast. Mom __is making__ pancakes.
           g. make

B: I __don't want__ breakfast. I just __drink__ coffee.
         h. not/want   i. drink

A: That's not good. You __need__ to live a healthier life.
                              j. need

3. Conversation between two friends:

    A: What __does your mother__ for a living?
                  a. your mother/do

    B: She's retired now.

    A: __Is she__ old?
             b. she/be

    B: No. She's only 58.

    A: What __does she do__ with her free time?
                   c. she/do

    B: A lot of things. In fact, she __doesn't have__ any free time at all.
                                           d. not/have
    She __is taking__ a course at the art center this semester. Right now
          e. take
    she __is painting__ a picture of me.
          f. paint

2.5 Action and Nonaction Verbs

EXAMPLES	EXPLANATION
He **is texting** his friend. I **am listening** to music.	Some verbs are action verbs. These verbs express physical or mental activity.
Young people **know** a lot about technology. Many people **have** a smart phone now. **Do** you **remember** a time without cell phones?	Some verbs are nonaction verbs. These verbs express a state, condition, perception, or feeling, not an action. We do not usually use the present continuous with nonaction verbs. We use the simple present even if we are talking about now.
She'**s looking at** the text message. I want to learn about technology, but it **looks hard**. Your photo **looks like** a selfie.	Some verbs can express an action or a perception. When they express an action (for example, *look at*), they are action verbs. When they express a perception (for example, *look* + adjective or *look like*), they are nonaction verbs.
I'**m looking** at my cell phone. I **see** a text from my father. She **is listening** to music. She **hears** her favorite song.	*Look* and *listen* are action verbs. *See* and *hear* are nonaction verbs.
Grandma **is thinking about** getting an e-reader. She **thinks that** technology is a good thing.	When we think *about* or *of* something, *think* is an action verb. When *think* shows an opinion about something, it is a nonaction verb.
My grandfather **is having** a hard time with technology. He'**s having** lunch with his friends now. Grandma **has** free time now. She **has** five grandchildren. I can't visit her now. I **have** a cold.	When *have* means to experience something or to eat or drink something, it is an action verb. When *have* shows possession, relationship, or illness, it is a nonaction verb.

continued

Note:

Some common nonaction verbs are verbs that show:
- Perception: *smell, taste, look, sound,* followed by an adjective or *like*
- Feelings and desires: *like, dislike, love, hate, hope, want, need, prefer, agree, disagree, care about, expect, matter*
- Mental states: *believe, know, hear, see, notice, understand, remember, think that, suppose, recognize*
- Other nonaction: *mean, cost, spell, weigh*

EXERCISE 9 Circle the correct words to complete the conversation.

A: Listen, Marco, (**I'm thinking**/*I think*) about getting a new computer. Can you help me choose?
  1.

B: Sure, Grandma. How about on Saturday?

A: Saturday's good. What's that noise? It (*sounds*/*is sounding*) like rock music (*comes*/*is coming*) from
  2. 3.
your pocket.

B: It's my cell phone. It's my new ringtone. (*I receive*/*I'm receiving*) a text message now. It's a message from
  4.
Dad. See?

A: It (*looks*/*is looking*) like Greek to me. What does it say?
  5.

B: (*He tells*/*He's telling*) me to come home early. (*He wants*/*He's wanting*) to give me another driving lesson.
  6. 7.
(*I learn*/*I'm learning*) to drive, you know.
  8.

A: When (*I have*/*I'm having*) something to say, (*I use*/*I'm using*) the phone.
  9. 10.

B: (*I prefer*/*I'm preferring*) to text. (*It saves*/*It's saving*) time. You can text me, too, Grandma.
  11. 12.

A: (*It looks*/*It's looking*) hard. Let me try to send a note to Grandpa. "Jim. Where are you? See you later."
  13.

B: (*You're writing*/*You write*) so slowly. And (*you use*/*you're using*) whole words. Use abbreviations, like this:
  14. 15.
"where r u c u later." Don't use punctuation. (*You need*/*You're needing*) to write fast.
  16.

A: You know I'm an English teacher, and (*I don't like*/*I'm not liking*) to write without punctuation.
  17.

B: Text messages don't need punctuation.

A: (*I don't think*/*I'm not thinking*) I can do it.
  18.

B: But (*you send*/*you're sending*) email every day.
  19.

A: That's different. (*I write*/*I'm writing*) slowly, and (*I check*/*I'm checking*) my spelling.
  20. 21.

B: You're so old-fashioned!

A: No, I'm not. This month (*I study*/*I'm studying*) photo editing at the senior center.
  22.
(*I make*/*I'm making*) a digital family album.
  23.

B: That's great, Grandma! I'm proud of you.

54   Unit 2

EXERCISE 10 Fill in the blanks with the simple present or the present continuous form of the verb given.

1. **A:** My grandfather is a volunteer. Twice a week he ____helps____ in the local school.
   a. help

   B: That's great! My grandmother ____works____ part-time in a bookstore. She ____loves____
   b. work   c. love

   books. She usually ____rides____ her bike to work. She ____likes____ the exercise.
   d. ride   e. like

   A: Where is she now? ____Is she working____?
   f. she/work

   B: Right now she's on vacation. She ____'s visiting____ her sister in Florida.
   g. visit

2. **A:** Can I borrow your dictionary?

   B: I'm sorry. I ____'m using____ it now. Where's your dictionary?
   a. use

   A: I never ____bring____ it to class. It's too heavy.
   b. bring

   B: ____Do you expect____ to use my dictionary all the time? You ____need____
   c. you/expect   d. need

   a dictionary app for your phone.

   A: I ____don't have____ a smart phone.
   e. not/have

3. **A:** What ____'s the teacher saying____? She ____'s talking____ too fast, so
   a. the teacher/say   b. talk

   I ____don't understand____ her.
   c. not/understand

   B: I don't know. I ____'m not listening____. I ____'m texting____ a friend.
   d. not/listen   e. text

   A: I ____think____ you should pay attention in class.
   f. think

   continued

4. **A:** What _are you writing_ (a. you/write) ?

   B: I _'m writing_ (b. write) an essay about my grandparents. I _love_ (c. love) them very much.

   A: _Do they live_ (d. they/live) with you?

   B: No, they don't. They live in Pakistan. They _visit_ (e. visit) us once a year.

   A: How _do you communicate_ (f. you/communicate) ? By email?

   B: We usually _do_ (g. do) a video chat once a week. But right now their computer _isn't working_ (h. not/work), so we _use_ (i. use) the phone.

5. **A:** _Do you see_ (a. you/see) that guy over there? Who is he?

   B: That's my technology teacher.

   A: He _'s wearing_ (b. wear) jeans and running shoes. And he _has_ (c. have) an earring in his ear. He _looks_ (d. look) like a student.

   B: I _know_ (e. know). Everyone _thinks_ (f. think) he's a student. But he's a very professional teacher.

6. **A:** My parents _are planning_ (a. plan) to put Grandma in a nursing home. Mom _thinks_ (b. think) she'll receive better care there.

   B: It _sounds_ (c. sound) like a difficult decision.

   A: It is. Mom _doesn't know_ (d. not/know) what else to do. Grandma _sometimes falls_ (e. sometimes/fall).

   B: Maybe she _needs_ (f. need) a cane or a walker.

   A: Her memory is bad, too. She _never remembers_ (g. never/remember) where she puts things.

   B: Can I call you back later? I _hear_ (h. hear) my other phone. My son _is calling_ (i. call) me.

FUN WITH GRAMMAR

Categorize. Work with a partner. Sort the words below into three columns: *action verbs, nonaction verbs*, and *both*. Then write a sentence for each verb that can be used in the present continuous. Be careful: some words can be both action and nonaction verbs but have a different meaning in the present continuous. The team with the most correct sentences wins.

listen	be	believe	have	hear	help	recognize	taste
know	learn	look	mean	ask	need	see	think

56   Unit 2

THE FUTURE POPULATION OF THE UNITED STATES

Read the following article. Pay special attention to the words in bold. 2.4

The population of the United States is growing slowly. Today it's about 328 million. By 2050, it**'s going to be** about 400 million. This is not a big increase, but one group is growing very fast—the elderly. The 65-and-over population **will** more than **double** by 2050. The 85-and-over population **will** more than **triple**.

There are two reasons for this increase of older Americans. First, the "baby boomers" are getting old. Baby boomers are people born between 1946 and 1964. During that time, a very large number of babies were born. The oldest are now entering their senior years. Many more **will** soon **be** elderly. As these people retire, young people **are going to have** many more job opportunities. In fact, there**'s going to be** a shortage[1] of workers to take their place. The number of jobs in health care **will increase**. There **will be** many jobs for pharmacists, physical therapists, and home health aides.

There is another reason for the increase in older Americans: life expectancy is increasing. Some scientists predict that half the babies born in 2007 **will live** to be 104 years old. But according to Dr. Harrison Bloom of the Longevity Center of New York, many young people **won't reach** this age because they don't have a healthy lifestyle. Or, if they do live a long time, they**'re going to need** a lot of medical help.

When today's young people retire at age 65 or 70, they**'ll have** a lot of years ahead of them. They need to think about how they**'ll spend** their later years. If they want to have good health later, they need to think about it now.

---
[1] shortage: a state of not having enough

COMPREHENSION Based on the reading, write T for *true* or F for *false*.

1. __F__ There will be a shortage of jobs in health care in the future.
2. __T__ The biggest growth in population will be in people over 85.
3. __F__ The baby boomers will live longer than younger generations.

THINK ABOUT IT Discuss the questions with a partner or in a small group.

1. What are some reasons that the current generation might not have a healthy lifestyle? How could young people improve their lifestyles?
2. Do you think it is a good idea to prepare to live a long time? Why or why not?

2.6 The Future with *Will*

EXAMPLES	EXPLANATION
The number of older people **will increase** in the future. My grandfather **will be** 85 next week.	We use *will* + the base form for the future.
I'**ll be** 72 years old in 2050. We'**ll retire** at age 65.	We can contract *will* with the subject pronouns. The contractions are *I'll, you'll, he'll, she'll, it'll, we'll,* and *they'll*.
The population **will not decrease**. I **won't retire** soon.	To form the negative, we put *not* after *will*. The contraction for *will not* is *won't*.
You'**ll probably have** a long retirement.	We can put an adverb between *will* and the main verb.

Compare statements, *yes/no* questions, short answers, and *wh-* questions.

STATEMENT	YES/NO QUESTION AND SHORT ANSWER	WH- QUESTION
She **will help** her parents.	**Will** she **help** her parents? Yes, she **will**.	How **will** she **help** her parents?
You **will retire** soon.	**Will** you **retire** next year? No, I **won't**.	When **will** you **retire**?
There **won't be** enough health workers.	**Will** there **be** a lot of jobs? Yes, there **will**.	Why **won't** there **be** enough health workers?

EXERCISE 11 Listen to the conversation between a 60-year-old mother and her 29-year-old daughter. Then write T for *true* or F for *false*. 🎧 2.5

1. _____ The woman's retired friends say she won't have any free time.
2. _____ The daughter won't be in New York in August.
3. _____ The grandfather will appreciate an email on his birthday.

EXERCISE 12 Listen to the conversation again. Fill in the blanks with the words you hear.

A: Tomorrow ____will be____ my last day of work.
   　　　　　　　　1.

B: What ____will you do____ with all your free time?
   　　　　　2.

A: Our retired friends all say I ____won't have____ any free time. They say
   　　　　　　　　　　　　　　　　3.
   ____I'll say____ plenty of things to do.
   　　　4.

B: So, ____what will you do____ first?
   　　　　　　5.

A: Dad and I are planning to travel.

B: ____Where will you go____ first?
   　　　6.

A: To the Grand Canyon.

B: That's great! How long ____will you be____ there?
   　　　　　　　　　　　　　　　7.

A: For about two weeks. Then ____we'll visit____ Grandpa in Nevada.
   　　　　　　　　　　　　　　　8.

B: I'm sure ____he'll be happy____ happy to see you.
   　　　　　　9.

A: ____He'll be____ 85 at the end of August. ____We'll be____ there for his
   　10.　　　　　　　　　　　　　　　　　　　　11.
   birthday.

B: What ____will you do____ with the dog?
   　　　　12.

A: Can you take care of her for us while we're gone?

B: Sorry. I ____won't be____ here the first week in August.
   　　　　　13.

A: Why ____won't you be____ here?
   　　　14.

B: I'm going to New York. ____You'll need____ to find someone else to take
   　　　　　　　　　　　　　15.
   care of the dog.

A: ____I'll ask____ my neighbor. Maybe ____she'll do____ it. Don't forget to send
   　16.　　　　　　　　　　　　　　　　　17.
   Grandpa a birthday card.

B: ____I'll send____ him an email on his birthday.
   　18.

A: You know Grandpa. He doesn't use his computer much.

B: All right. ____I'll send____ him a card then.
   　　　　　19.

A: I'm sure ____he'll appreciate____ it.
   　　　　　20.

The Present Continuous, The Future 59

EXERCISE 13 Fill in the blanks with *will* and one of the verbs from the box. You may use the same verb more than once.

spend	have	increase	triple	live ✓	need	move	find	be

1. Today's generation _____will live_____ longer.
2. The population of old people ___will increase___.
3. The over-85 population ___will triple___ by 2050.
4. ___will___ young people ___have___ more job opportunities?
5. Many young people ___will find___ jobs in health care.
6. Some older people ___will move___ into retirement housing.
7. How ___will___ you ___spend___ your retirement years?
8. Why ___will___ we ___need___ more health care workers?
9. How old ___will___ you ___be___ in the year 2050?

2.7 The Future with *Be Going To*

EXAMPLES	EXPLANATION
People **are going to live** longer. We **are going to need** more pharmacists in the future.	We can use a form of *be* + *going to* + the base form to express future time.
I'**m not going to work** after retirement. He **isn't going to retire** soon.	To form the negative, we put *not* after *am, is,* or *are*.
We're **going to go** to the Grand Canyon. We're **going** to the Grand Canyon.	We often shorten *going to go* to *going*.

Compare statements, *yes/no* questions, short answers, and *wh-* questions.

STATEMENT	YES/NO QUESTION AND SHORT ANSWER	WH- QUESTION
We **are going to travel**.	Are we **going to travel** by car? Yes, we **are**.	When **are** we **going to travel**?
She **is going to work** as a nurse.	Is she **going to work** at a hospital? No, she **isn't**.	Where **is** she **going to work**?
You **aren't going to send** Grandpa a present.	Are you **going to send** an e-card? Yes, I **am**.	Why **aren't** you **going to send** Grandpa a present?

Pronunciation Note:
In informal speech, *going to* before another verb often sounds like "gonna." In academic and formal English, we don't write "gonna."

  I'm not "gonna" work after retirement.

60 Unit 2

EXERCISE 14 Fill in the blanks with *be going to* and one of the verbs from the box. You may use the same verb more than once.

| need | spend | study | be | live | find | become | double | have |

1. Many people _are going to live_ to the age of 100.
2. Young people _are going to have_ a lot of job possibilities.
3. I _'m going to become_ a nurse because it _is going to be_ easy to find a job.
4. Some people _are going to have_ a long retirement.
5. Some old people _are going to need_ a lot of medical help.
6. _Are_ you _going to study_ to be a physician's assistant?
7. Younger people _are going to have_ jobs in health care.
8. By 2050, the population of people over 65 _is going to double_.
9. _Are_ your grandparents _going to live_ with your family?
10. You need to think about how you _are going to spend_ your retirement years.
11. In the future, there _is going to be_ a shortage of workers.
12. _Am_ I _going to live_ to be 100?

EXERCISE 15 Fill in the blanks with *be going to* and the words given to complete the conversation between two co-workers.

A: I'm so excited. I _'m going to retire_ at the end of this year!
                              1. retire

B: That's wonderful news. What _are you going to do_ next?
                                    2. you/do

A: I don't really know yet. I _'m going to explore_ new things.
                                3. explore

B: What _are you going to explore_?
                4. you/explore

A: I think I have a talent for art. I _'m going to take_ art classes.
                                   5. take

B: _Are you going to work_ part-time?
    6. you/work

A: No way! I want to have fun.

B: Is your husband happy about your retirement?

A: Yes. He _'s going to retire_, too.
            7. retire

B: But you're not that old.

continued

A: I'm 58 and he's 56. Our children <u>aren't going to need</u> us much anymore.
8. not/need

B: Why <u>aren't they going to need</u> you?
9. not/need

A: Our youngest son <u>is going to graduate</u> from college in June. And the other two are
10. graduate

already on their own. The oldest <u>is going to get</u> married next year, and the
11. get

middle one has her own apartment and a job.

B: I <u>'m going to miss</u> you at work. It <u>'s not going to be</u> the same
12. miss .... 13. not/be

without you.

A: I <u>'m not going to miss</u> the boss and the long hours.
14. not/miss

2.8 Choosing *Will, Be Going To,* or Present Continuous for Future

EXAMPLES	EXPLANATION
The U.S. population **will be** 400 million by 2050. The U.S. population **is going to be** 400 million by 2050.	For a prediction about the future, we use either *will* or *be going to*. *Will* is more formal than *be going to*.
Grandpa **will be** 85 years old in August. Grandpa **is going to be** 85 in August.	For a fact about the future, we use either *will* or *be going to*.
A: I'm interested in health care. I **am going to become** a nurse. **B:** My sister's a nurse. I'**ll tell** her about your plan. Maybe she can give you some advice.	When we have a definite plan for the future, we use *be going to*. When we are thinking about the future at the moment of speaking, we use *will*.
A: I want to buy a cell phone. What kind should I buy? **B:** I'**ll help** you. I'**ll take** you shopping. **A:** You always say that. But you never have time. **B:** I'**ll make** time. I promise.	To make a promise or offer to help with no previous plan, we use *will*. The decision comes at the moment of speaking.
My grandmother **is moving** into a retirement home on Friday. I'**m helping** her move. The weather report says it'**s going to rain** on Friday, so the move won't be easy.	We can use the present continuous with definite plans for the near future. We don't use the present continuous if there is no plan. (NOT: It is raining on Friday.)

Note:
For a scheduled event, such as a flight, movie, or class, we often use the simple present.

*The semester **begins** in August.*

*My nursing course **ends** next month.*

62 Unit 2

EXERCISE 16 Listen to the conversation. Fill in the blanks with the words you hear. 2.6

A: I hear _you're retiring_ next month.
    1.
B: Yes. Isn't it wonderful? _I'll be_ 65 in September.
    2.
A: What _are you going to do_ after you retire?
    3.
B: _I'm moving_ to Florida.
    4.
A: What _are you going to do_ in Florida?
    5.
B: _I'm going to buy_ a sailboat. Maybe _I'll learn_
    6.   7.
to play golf. What about you?
A: I don't know. _I'm not going to retire_ any time soon. I'm only 45.
    8.
B: I hope _you'll visit_ me in Florida.
    9.
A: Of course _I will_! Do you need help packing?
    10.
B: Yes. _I'm starting_ to pack this weekend.
    11.
A: _I'll help_ you.
    12.
B: Thanks. _That'll make_ my life a lot easier!
    13.

EXERCISE 17 Circle the correct words to complete the conversation. In some cases, both choices are possible. If so, circle both.

1. **A:** Do you want to go for a cup of coffee?

    B: Sorry. I don't have time. (*I'm going to visit*/*I'll visit*) my grandfather this afternoon.
    a.
    (*I'm going to help*/*I'll help*) him with his computer. And I need to return some books to the library.
    b.

    A: Give them to me. I'm going that way on my way home. (*I'll return*/*I'm going to return*) them for you. Do you
    c.
    want to get together for coffee tomorrow?

    B: I'm not sure. (*I'll text*/*I'm going to text*) you tomorrow to let you know.
    d.

2. **A:** I have to go to the airport. My grandparents' plane (*is arriving*/*is going to arrive*) at four o'clock this
    a.
    afternoon.

    B: (*I'll go*/*I'm going*) with you. (*I'll*/*I'm going to*) stay in the car while you go into the airport.
    b.   c.

    A: Thanks.

    B: How long (*are they going to stay*/*are they staying*)?
    d.

continued

A: (*They'll come*/*They're coming*) because (*my sister's graduating*/*my sister will graduate*) on Sunday.
   e.   f.

After the graduation, (*they'll*/*they're going to*) visit my cousins in Denver.
                        g.

3. **A:** My mother's so happy. (*She's going to retire*/*She'll*) retire next month.
                                            a.

   B: Are you (*going to have*/*having*) a party for her?
                        b.

   A: Yes. Do you want to come to the party?

   B: What's the date?

   A: June 16.

   B: I have to check my calendar. (*I'm going to*/*I'll*) let you know later.
                                              c.

2.9 The Future + Time or *If* Clause

TIME OR *IF* CLAUSE (SIMPLE PRESENT)	MAIN CLAUSE (FUTURE)	EXPLANATION
When I **retire**,	I'**m going to start** a new hobby.	Some sentences have a time or *if* clause and a main clause. We use the future in the main clause; we use the simple present in the time or *if* clause.
If I **am** healthy,	I'**ll continue** to work.	
MAIN CLAUSE (FUTURE)	**TIME OR *IF* CLAUSE (SIMPLE PRESENT)**	
He'**ll move** to a warm climate	as soon as he **retires**.	
My parents **are going to travel**	if they **have** enough money.	

Note:
If the time or *if* clause comes before the main clause, we use a comma to separate the two parts of the sentence. If the main clause comes first, we don't use a comma.

   If they have enough money, they're going to travel.
   They're going to travel if they have enough money.

EXERCISE 18 Choose the correct words to complete the conversation. In some cases, both choices are possible. If so, circle both choices.

A: What (*are you doing*/*will you do*) later today?
              1.

B: After class (*will be*/*is*) over, I'm going to drive my grandfather to the airport.
                    2.

A: Where (*is he going*/*will he go*)?
                3.

B: To Hawaii to play golf.

A: That's great! How old is he?

B: (*He's going to*/*He'll*) be 78 next month.
          4.

64 Unit 2

A: He's pretty old.

B: He's in perfect health. (*He's getting/He'll get*) married in two months.
                                        5.

A: That's great! What are you and your family (*doing/going to do*) when (*he's/he'll be*) no longer able to take
                                                              6.   7.
care of himself?

B: We never think about it. He's in great health. I think he's (*outliving/going to outlive*) us all.
                                                                            8.

A: But (*he's probably going to need/he'll probably need*) help when (*he'll get/he gets*) older.
                           9.   10.

B: If (*he'll need/he needs*) help, (*he has/he'll have*) his wife to take care of him.
              11.   12.

A: My grandparents are in their sixties now. But when (*they're/they'll be*) older, they're going to live with my
                                                                     13.
parents. In our country, it's an honor to take care of our parents and grandparents.

B: That sounds like a great custom. But I think older people should be independent. I'm glad that Grandpa
doesn't depend on us. And when (*I'm/I'll be*) old, (*I'm going to take/I'm taking*) care of myself. I don't
                                         14.   15.
want to depend on anyone.

A: (*You'll change/You're changing*) your mind when (*you're/you'll be*) old.
                 16.   17.

ABOUT YOU Think about a specific time in your future (when you graduate, when you get married, when you have children, when you find a job, when you return to your native country, when you retire, etc.). Write three sentences to tell what will happen at that time. Find a partner who is close to your age. Compare your answers to your partner's answers.

1. When I have children, I won't have as much free time as I do now.
2. When I retire, I'm going to start a new hobby.
3. When I graduate, I'm going to look for a good job.
4. When I buy my first car, it will be pretty and fast.
5. If I travel to Colombia, I'm going to eat a lot.

> **FUN WITH GRAMMAR**
>
> Role-play a conversation. You have five minutes to write and practice a conversation with a partner about next weekend. Include the weather forecast, definite plans, and scheduled events. When you role-play the conversation, your teacher and classmates will listen for the various uses of the future and count them. The pair with the most correctly used statements in the future wins.
>
>   A: Hey, Gina. What are you doing this weekend?
>   B: Oh hi, Steve. Actually, I have big plans. First, I'm going to . . .

The Present Continuous, The Future

SUMMARY OF UNIT 2

SIMPLE PRESENT	
For general truths	Many people **retire** in their sixties. Most young people **have** smart phones.
For regular activities, habits, customs	Jack **plays** golf twice a week. I **always** visit my grandparents on the weekend.
With a place of origin	My grandfather **comes** from Mexico. My grandmother **comes** from Peru.
In a time clause or in an *if* clause of a future statement	When she **retires**, she'll start a new hobby. If Grandma **needs** help, she'll live with us.
With nonaction verbs	I **care** about my grandparents. Your grandfather **needs** help now. My grandfather **prefers** to live alone now.
For scheduled events	The plane **leaves** at 8 p.m. tonight.

PRESENT CONTINUOUS (WITH ACTION VERBS ONLY)	
For an action happening now, at this moment	My friend **is texting** me now. She'**s sending** me her photo.
For a long-term action in progress at this general time	Judy **is earning** money by tutoring students. Jack is retired now. He **is starting** a new career.
For a trend in society	The population of the U.S. **is getting** older. Americans **are living** longer.
For a definite plan in the near future	She **is retiring** next month. She **is going** on a long trip soon.
With a descriptive state	Mary **is standing** over there. She **is wearing** jeans and a T-shirt.

FUTURE	WILL	BE GOING TO
For a plan		He **is going to retire** in two years.
For a fact	The number of old people **will increase**.	The number of old people **is going to increase**.
For a prediction	There **will be** more jobs in health care.	There **are going to be** more jobs in health care.
For a decision made at the time of speaking, usually with a promise or an offer	I promise I'**ll take care of** you when you're old.	

REVIEW

Circle the correct words to complete the conversation. If both answers are correct, circle both choices.

A: Hi, Maya.

B: Hi, Liz. How are you?

A: Fine. What (**are you doing**/you are doing)? (**Do**/Are) you want to go out for a cup of coffee?

B: (**I'm not having**/I don't have) time now. (I pack/**I'm packing**). (We're moving/**We're going to move**) next Saturday.

A: Oh, really? Why (**are you**/you are) moving? You (**have**/are having) such a lovely apartment now.

B: Yes, I know we do. But my father (comes/**is coming**) soon, so we're (**going to need**/needing) a bigger apartment.

A: When (**is he**/he is) going to come?

B: He (**leaves**/**'ll leave**) as soon as he (**gets**/'ll get) his visa. That (is probably/**will probably be**) in about four months.

A: But your present apartment (**has**/have) an extra bedroom.

B: Yes. But my husband (**likes**/is liking) to have an extra room for an office. He usually (**brings**/is bringing) a lot of work home. He doesn't (likes/**like**) noise when he works.

A: (**Is your father**/Your father is) going to get his own apartment after he (will find/**finds**) a job?

B: He's retired now. He's going to (**live**/living) with us. He (isn't liking/**doesn't like**) to live alone.

A: (**Do you need**/Are you needing) help with your packing?

B: No, thanks. Bill and I are (stay/**staying**) home this week to finish the packing. And my sister (**is helping**/helps) me now, too.

A: I'd like to help. (**I come**/**I'll come**) over next Saturday to help you move.

B: (**We're going to use**/We use) professional movers on Saturday. We (aren't/**don't**) want to bother our friends.

A: It's no bother. I (**want**/'m wanting) to help.

B: Thanks. I have to go now. (**I hear**/I'm hearing) Bill. (He calls/**He's calling**) me. He (need/**needs**) help in the basement. (I call/**I'll call**) you back later.

A: That's not necessary. (I see/**I'll see**) you on Saturday. Bye.

The Present Continuous, The Future **67**

FROM GRAMMAR TO WRITING

PART 1 Editing Advice

1. Always include a form of *be* in a present continuous verb.

   She ^is working now.

2. Don't use the present continuous with a nonaction verb.

   I am ~~liking~~ like my new hobby.

3. Include *be* in a future sentence that has no other verb.

   You will ^be busy when you retire.

4. Don't combine *will* and *be going to*.

   He will ~~going to~~ leave. OR He's going to leave.

5. Don't use the future after a time word or *if*.

   When I ~~will~~ retire, I'll have more free time.

   If I ~~will~~ have enough money, I'll travel.

6. Use a form of *be* with *going to*.

   He ^is going to help his grandfather.

7. Use the correct word order in questions.

   When ~~you will~~ will you retire?

   Why ~~she isn't~~ isn't she going to work part-time?

PART 2 Editing Practice

Some of the shaded words and phrases have mistakes. Find the mistakes and correct them. If the shaded words are correct, write C.

My grandfather is retired now, and he's not happy. He wakes up every day and says, "What ~~I will~~ **will I** do today?" On the other hand, my grandmother is very busy. My grandparents **live** (C)
1.   2.
in a retirement village, and Grandma **is learning** how to draw. She's also **take** singing lessons,
                                       3.   4.
and she **studying** photography. Next month, she **going to** take a trip to India with a group of older
         5.   6.
people. When Grandma **will get** back from India, she's **going to make** a photo slideshow of her
                     7.   8.
trip.

68   Unit 2

Grandpa doesn't want to travel. He says, "What I'm going to do in India?" I'm thinking that
                                                                        9.   10.
Grandpa is needing to find a hobby. Grandma always tells him, "You will happy if you find
            11.   12.
something to do." Will I going to have a hard time like Grandpa when I will retire? I'll think
                  13.   14.   15.
about it when the time comes.
                       16.

> **WRITING TIP**
>
> When you write, it's important to think about the verb forms you need to express your ideas.
>
> If you choose prompt 1 below, you might start with a general statement such as "My generation uses more technology than my parents' generation." If your supporting examples are of past events, use the simple past. If your examples are of habitual or general actions, use the simple present.
>
> For prompt 2, decide which verb forms are necessary to ask someone questions about current activities and about plans for the future.
>
> > habitual actions: "How do you spend your time?"
> >
> > future plans: "What are you looking forward to?"
>
> Remember that there are various future forms, depending on the context.

PART 3 Write

Read the prompts. Choose one and write a paragraph about it.

1. Write about the differences in generations and their use of technology. Use examples from your own life or the lives of people you know.
2. Interview a retired person. What is this person doing with his or her life now? What are this person's plans for the future?

PART 4 Edit

Reread the Summary of Unit 2 and the editing advice. Edit your writing from Part 3.

UNIT

3

The Simple Past
The Habitual Past with *Used To*

What is
SUCCESS?

Walt Disney, seen here working on figures for a Disneyland exhibit, was once fired from a newspaper job for not having any good ideas or imagination. The Walt Disney Company is worth an estimated $130 billion today.

Success consists of going from failure to failure without loss of enthusiasm.

WINSTON CHURCHILL

FAILURE and SUCCESS

Read the following article. Pay special attention to the words in bold. 3.1

What is success? What do we learn from failure[1]? When we try something new, failure is always a possibility. In the nineteenth century, many explorers **attempted** to reach the North Pole by land, but they **died** trying. Salomon Andrée **was** a Swedish engineer. He **wanted** to be the first person to arrive at the North Pole. He **knew** that travel over land **was** very dangerous. He **had** an idea. He **thought** he **had** the perfect way to reach the North Pole: by balloon. On a windy day in July 1897, Andrée and two other men **climbed** into the basket of a balloon. They **took** with them enough food for several months. When they **left**, people **cheered** and **waved**.

As soon as they **lifted** off, strong winds **hit** the balloon. Fog[2] **froze** on it, making it too heavy. The men **traveled** by balloon for 65 hours. **Were** they successful? **Did** they **arrive** safely? Unfortunately, no. They **landed** almost three hundred miles from the North Pole. No one **heard** from them again. Thirty-three years later, hunters **found** their frozen bodies, their cameras, and their diaries.

Failure is part of all exploration. Robert Ballard, a famous ocean explorer, says that success and failure go together. Failure helps us do things differently the next time. Mountain climber Peter Athans said, "I **learned** how *not* to climb the first four times I **tried** to summit[3] Everest."

In 1914, a polar explorer, Ernest Shackleton, **led** an expedition across Antarctica. His ship became trapped in the ice. However, he **brought** the 27 men on his team home safely. The expedition **was** a failure, but the rescue of his men **was** a success.

Failure helps us on our next try. Failure is a good teacher. Without failure, success would be impossible.

---

[1] failure: an activity or project that does not succeed
[2] fog: a heavy gray vapor near the ground that makes it difficult to see
[3] to summit: to reach the top of a mountain

Salomon Andrée and Knut Fraenkel look at their balloon after it crashed on ice. The photograph was taken by the third team member, Nils Strindberg.

COMPREHENSION Based on the reading, write T for *true* or F for *false*.

1. _F_ Salomon Andrée was the first person to reach the North Pole.
2. _T_ The weather caused problems with the balloon.
3. _F_ Robert Ballard successfully climbed Mt. Everest.

THINK ABOUT IT Discuss the questions with a partner or in a small group.

1. What did Peter Athans mean when he said, "I learned how *not* to climb the first four times I tried to summit Everest."? Do you think he eventually climbed Everest?

2. Do you agree that without failure, success would be impossible? Do you have any examples from *your* life of failing at something before eventually succeeding?

3.1 The Simple Past—Form

EXAMPLES	EXPLANATION
Andrée's balloon **landed** far from the North Pole. Peter Athans **learned** from his mistakes.	Some simple past verbs are regular. Regular verbs end in *–ed*. land—landed learn—learned
They **had** bad weather. Hunters **found** the bodies.	Some simple past verbs are irregular. Irregular verbs do not end in *–ed*. have—had find—found
Shackleton's expedition **was** a failure. The men **were** safe.	The verb *be* is irregular. It has two forms in the past: *was* and *were*.

Notes:
1. Except for *be*, the simple past form is the same for all subjects.
    *I **had** an idea.* ***He had** an idea.*
2. The verb after *to* does not use the past form.
    *He wanted to **reach** the North Pole.*

EXERCISE 1 Listen to the article. Then write T for *true* or F for *false*. 3.2

1. _____ Robert Ballard became interested in the ocean when he was young.
2. _____ There were many unsuccessful attempts to find the *Titanic*.
3. _____ Robert Ballard was not successful in finding the *Titanic*.

EXERCISE 2 Listen again. Fill in the blanks with the words you hear. 3.2

The famous ship *Titanic* __sank__ in 1912. It __rested__ on the ocean floor for over 70 years. There __were__ many attempts to find it—all of them unsuccessful. Oceanographer Robert Ballard __decided__ to look for it.

continued

Ballard __grew__ up in California near the ocean. When he __was__
       5.   6.
young, he __became__ interested in ocean exploration. He __wanted__ to find
           7.   8.
the *Titanic*. He __needed__ money for his exploration. He __asked__ the
                 9.   10.
U.S. Navy for money, and they __gave__ it to him. Ballard __created__ a
                              11.   12.
submersible called the *Argo*. He __invited__ a French research team to join his
                                 13.
exploration. His team __was__ on a ship called the *Knorr* while the *Argo*
                      14.
__stayed__ underwater for many weeks. The *Argo* __sent__ pictures to
  15.   16.
Ballard and his team. On September 1, 1985, the *Argo* __found__ the *Titanic*.
                                                       17.
It __was__ the first view of the *Titanic* in 73 years.
   18.

3.2 The Simple Past—Use

EXAMPLES	EXPLANATION
In 1897, Andrée **left** for the North Pole in a balloon.	We use the simple past with a single, short past action.
The balloon **traveled** for 65 hours.	We use the simple past with a longer past action.
Peter Athans **climbed** Mt. Everest seven times.	We use the simple past with a repeated past action.

EXERCISE 3 In Exercise 2, underline the regular verbs once and the irregular verbs twice. Circle the forms of the verb *be*.

EXERCISE 4 Write the base form of the verbs. Write *R* for a regular verb. Write *I* for an irregular verb. Write *B* for the verb *be*.

1. __cheer__   cheered   __R__
2. __be__   were   __B__
3. __Attempt__ attempted __R__
4. __think__   thought   __I__
5. __die__   died   __R__
6. __wave__   waved   __R__
7. __freeze__   froze   __I__
8. __lift__   lifted   __R__
9. __hear__   heard   __I__
10. __learn__   learned   __R__
11. __take__   took   __I__
12. __leave__   left   __I__
13. __climb__   climbed   __R__
14. __bring__   brought   __I__

74   Unit 3

George Dawson learned to read and write when he was 98 years old.

NEVER TOO LATE TO LEARN

Read the following article. Pay special attention to the words in bold.

George Dawson **was** a successful man. **Was** he famous? No, he **wasn't**. He **was** just an ordinary man who **did** something extraordinary.

George Dawson **lived** in three centuries—from 1898 to 2001. He **was** born in Texas, the grandson of slaves. At that time, there **were** fewer opportunities for African Americans[1]. Dawson **was** the oldest of five children. His family **was** very poor, so George **had** to work to help his family. He **started** working for his father when he **was** only four years old. As a result, he **didn't have** a chance to get an education. He **didn't learn** to read and write. He **signed** his name with an *X*.

When Dawson **was** 98 years old, he **decided** to go to school. He **wanted** to learn to read and write. He **went** to adult literacy[2] classes. The teacher **asked** him, "Do you know the alphabet?" When he **answered** "No," his teacher **was** surprised. Over the next few years, his teacher **taught** Dawson to read and write. Dawson **said**, "Every morning I get up and I wonder what I might learn that day."

Richard Glaubman **read** an article about Dawson in the newspaper and **wanted** to meet him. Glaubman **helped** Dawson write a book about Dawson's life, called *Life Is So Good*. Dawson **was** 102 when the book was published. Dawson **wrote** about what makes a person happy. He **learned** from his father to see the good things in life. They **had** a close family, and George never **felt** lonely. Dawson says in the book, "People worry too much. Life is good, just the way it is."

Was George Dawson a success? He definitely **was**. He **enjoyed** life and **accomplished** his goal: learning to read and write.

---

[1] African American: an American whose ancestors came from Africa
[2] literacy: the ability to read and write

The Simple Past, The Habitual Past with *Used To*

COMPREHENSION Based on the reading, write T for *true* or F for *false*.

1. _____ George Dawson was born a slave.
2. _____ Richard Glaubman helped Dawson write his book.
3. _____ Dawson learned to enjoy life from his father.

THINK ABOUT IT Discuss the questions with a partner or in a small group.

1. What kind of student do you think Dawson was?
2. Dawson's philosophy is that "People worry too much. Life is good, just the way it is." Do you live by this philosophy? Explain.

3.3 The Past of *Be*

EXAMPLES	EXPLANATION

Dawson **was** from a poor family.
His grandparents **were** slaves.
	The past of the verb *be* has two forms: *was* and *were*.
	  I, he, she, it → **was**
	  we, you, they → **were**

There **was** an article about Dawson in the newspaper. There **were** many changes in his lifetime.	After *there*, we use *was* or *were* depending on the noun that follows. We use *was* with a singular noun. We use *were* with a plural noun.
Dawson's life **wasn't** easy. Education and books **weren't** available to him as a child.	To make a negative statement, we put *not* after *was* or *were*. The contraction for *was not* is *wasn't*. The contraction for *were not* is *weren't*.
Dawson **was born** in 1898.	We use a form of *be* with *born*.
Dawson **was able to** live a happy life.	We use a form of *be* with *able to*.

Compare statements, *yes/no* questions, short answers, and *wh-* questions.

STATEMENT	YES/NO QUESTION AND SHORT ANSWER	WH- QUESTION
Dawson **was** poor.	**Was** he successful? Yes, he **was**.	How **was** he successful?
His grandparents **were** slaves.	**Were** they from the North? No, they **weren't**.	Where **were** they from?
Dawson **wasn't** unhappy.	**Was** he in school as a child? No, he **wasn't**.	Why **wasn't** he in school?

EXERCISE 5 Fill in the blanks to complete these affirmative and negative statements and questions.

1. George Dawson _____was_____ poor.
2. Dawson _____was_____ born in 1898.
3. At that time, there _____weren't_____ many opportunities for him.
4. His parents _____were_____ poor.
5. He _____wasn't_____ unhappy.
6. George Dawson wasn't able to write his name. Why _____wasn't_____ he able to write his name?
7. _____Was_____ he happy to go to school? Yes, he _____was_____.
8. How old _____was_____ he when he learned to read? He _____was_____ 98 years old.
9. _____Was_____ there slavery in the U.S. when Dawson was born? No, there wasn't.
10. _____Were_____ there a lot of opportunities for African Americans at that time? No, there weren't.

ABOUT YOU Find a partner and discuss your answers to these questions.

1. What do you think makes a person successful?
2. What personal goals do you have? What steps do you need to take to reach those goals?
3. Were your goals different when you were younger? Do you think your goals will change over time?

3.4 The Simple Past of Regular Verbs

EXAMPLES	EXPLANATION
Dawson **signed** his name with an *X*. He **learned** a lot from his father. Dawson **accomplished** his goal.	sign—sign**ed** learn—learn**ed** accomplish—accomplish**ed**

Note:
If the verb ends in an *e*, we add only *–d*.
   Dawson decide**d** to get an education. He die**d** in 2001.

GRAMMAR IN USE

A common error in speaking is to add a syllable to simple past verbs that end in a consonant. Remember—only the consonant sounds /d/ and /t/ add a syllable in the *-ed* form.

   waited = /weʸ-tɪd/   *started* = /stɑr-tɪd/
   lived = /lɪvd/   NOT: /lɪ-vɪd/
   laughed = /læft/   NOT: /læ-fɪd/

The Simple Past, The Habitual Past with *Used To* 77

EXERCISE 6 Fill in the blanks with the simple past form of one of the verbs from the box. In some cases, more than one answer is possible.

fail	ask	live	decide	discover	try
land	attend	want	attempt	learn	
die	occur	rescue	help	start	

1. Dawson ____lived____ from 1898 to 2001.
2. He __started__ to work when he was four years old.
3. Many changes __occured__ during his long life.
4. His teacher __asked__ him, "Do you know the alphabet?"
5. He __attempted__ school when he was 98.
6. Richard Glaubman __helped__ Dawson write a book.
7. Salomon Andrée __decided__ to explore the North Pole.
8. Many people __tried__ to reach the North Pole by land, but they weren't successful.
9. Andrée __decided__ to use a balloon.
10. The balloon __landed__ far from the North Pole.
11. Andrée and his men __died__.
12. In 1914, Ernest Shackleton __failed__ when he tried to cross Antarctica.
13. He __learned__ from his failure.
14. He __rescued__ his men.
15. Robert Ballard __discovered__ the *Titanic* on the ocean floor.

3.5 The Simple Past of Irregular Verbs

Many verbs are irregular in the past. An irregular verb does not use the *–ed* ending.

EXAMPLES	EXPLANATION
A teacher **taught** Dawson to read.	teach—taught
Dawson **had** a close family.	have—had
Andrée and his men **went** up in a balloon.	go—went

Notice the different kinds of changes to form the simple past of irregular verbs.

VERBS WITH NO CHANGE				FINAL *D* CHANGES TO *T*	
beat	fit	put	spit	bend—bent	send—sent
bet	hit	quit	split	build—built	spend—spent
cost	hurt	set	spread	lend—lent	
cut	let	shut			

VERBS WITH VOWEL CHANGES		VERBS WITH VOWEL CHANGES	
feel—felt	mean—meant	dig—dug	sting—stung
keep—kept	sleep—slept	hang—hung	strike—struck
leave—left	sweep—swept	spin—spun	swing—swung
lose—lost	weep—wept	stick—stuck	win—won
awake—awoke	speak—spoke	begin—began	sing—sang
break—broke	steal—stole	drink—drank	sink—sank
choose—chose	wake—woke	ring—rang	spring—sprang
freeze—froze		shrink—shrank	swim—swam
bring—brought	fight—fought	blow—blew	grow—grew
buy—bought	teach—taught	draw—drew	know—knew
catch—caught	think—thought	fly—flew	throw—threw
arise—arose	rise—rose	bleed—bled	meet—met
drive—drove	shine—shone	feed—fed	read—read
ride—rode	write—wrote	flee—fled	speed—sped
		lead—led	
sell—sold	tell—told	find—found	wind—wound
mistake—mistook	take—took	lay—laid	say—said
shake—shook		pay—paid	
swear—swore	wear—wore	bite—bit	light—lit
tear—tore		hide—hid	slide—slid
become—became	forgive—forgave	fall—fell	run—ran
come—came	give—gave	hold—held	sit—sat
eat—ate	lie—lay		
forget—forgot	shoot—shot	stand—stood	
get—got		understand—understood	

MISCELLANEOUS CHANGES			
be—was/were	go—went	hear—heard	see—saw
do—did	have—had	make—made	

Pronunciation Notes:

1. *Meant* rhymes with *sent*.
2. The past form of *read* is pronounced like the color *red*.
3. *Said* rhymes with *bed*.

*For an alphabetical list of irregular past verbs, see Appendix C.

EXERCISE 7 Fill in the blank with the simple past form of the verb given.

1. Andrée ___flew___ to the Arctic in a balloon.
   fly
2. Andrée ___thought___ he could reach the North Pole in a balloon.
   think
3. He and his men ___left___ in July 1897.
   leave
4. Fog ___made___ the balloon heavy.
   make
5. Strong winds ___hit___ Andrée's balloon.
   hit
6. They ___had___ problems with the weather.
   have
7. The *Titanic* ___sank___ in 1912.
   sink
8. Robert Ballard ___grew___ up near the ocean.
   grow
9. He ___became___ an oceanographer.
   become
10. He ___found___ the *Titanic* on the ocean floor.
    find
11. Earnest Shackleton ___led___ an expedition to Antarctica.
    lead
12. He ___brought___ all of his men home safely.
    bring

EXERCISE 8 Fill in the blanks with the simple past form of one of the verbs from the box. You may use the same verb more than once.

teach	write	begin	see	say	have	go	become

1. Dawson ___had___ a hard life.
2. He ___began/went___ to work for his father when he was four years old.
3. He ___saw___ many changes in his lifetime.
4. He ___became___ interested in reading when he was 98.
5. He ___went___ to school when he was 98.
6. His teacher ___taught___ him the alphabet.
7. Dawson ___said___, "I wonder what I might learn today."
8. Dawson ___wrote___ a book about his life.

FUN WITH GRAMMAR

Play a matching game. Work in groups of three. Choose 10 verbs from chart 3.5. Cut 20 evenly sized pieces of paper. Write the base form of the verbs on 10 of the papers and the matching irregular simple past forms on the other 10 papers. Place all of the papers face-down on a desk and mix the papers up. Take turns turning two cards over at a time to find a matching base form–past form pair. If you find a pair, you get to go again. The person with the most pairs wins.

Diana Nyad on her fifth attempt to swim between Cuba and Florida

IF AT FIRST YOU DON'T SUCCEED

Read the following article. Pay special attention to the words in bold. 3.4

Diana Nyad was a professional swimmer. She was in her twenties when she decided to swim around Manhattan. The first time she tried, she **didn't succeed**. But she **didn't give** up. She tried again and swam the 28 miles in less than eight hours. Then she had another goal: to swim from Cuba to Florida, a distance of 110 miles. She swam 79 miles in 42 hours. She **didn't stop** to sleep. But she **didn't finish**. Jellyfish attacked her, and the weather threw her off course[1]. **Did** she **try** again? Yes, but not until 33 years later.

Nyad retired from competitive swimming in her twenties. For the next 30 years, she **didn't swim** at all. She became a sportscaster[2] and a journalist. But she **didn't stop** all physical activity. She always kept in shape. Every Friday she took a 100-mile bike ride.

In 2007, when Nyad was 60 years old, her mother died. She started to think about her own life. In the 30 years that she **didn't swim**, she always thought about the possibility of trying again. She **didn't want** to die without achieving her goal. She started to train again. By the summer of 2011, she tried again—and failed again—after 29 hours in the water. She tried two more times—and failed to reach Florida each time. What kinds of problems **did** she **face**? There were attacks by jellyfish, bad weather, and breathing problems from asthma[3]. How **did** she **solve** the problem of jellyfish? For her fifth attempt, she wore a bodysuit and mask to protect against jellyfish stings. On August 31, 2013, after 53 hours of swimming, she reached the Florida shore, 35 years after her first attempt. Nyad achieved[4] what younger and stronger swimmers could not.

Nyad always tells people, "Never give up."

Jellyfish

[1] to throw off course: to send in an unintended direction
[2] sportscaster: someone who gives news about sports on the TV or radio
[3] asthma: a medical condition that causes difficulty in breathing
[4] to achieve: to succeed in doing something

COMPREHENSION Based on the reading, write T for *true* or F for *false*.

1. _____ Nyad made four attempts to swim from Cuba to Florida before she was finally successful.
2. _____ She didn't do any hard physical activity for 30 years.
3. _____ The death of her mother made her think about her own life.

THINK ABOUT IT Discuss the questions with a partner or in a small group.

1. Think about the details of Diana Nyad's life and the successes and failures described in the article. Then write six adjectives to describe her.
2. Diana Nyad had three obstacles to completing her goal: jellyfish, bad weather, and asthma. Think of a big goal you have in your life. What obstacles do you have? How can you overcome them?

3.6 Negatives and Questions with the Simple Past

EXAMPLES	EXPLANATION
Diana **succeeded** on her fifth attempt. She **didn't succeed** on her first attempt. She **swam** around Manhattan in her twenties. She **didn't swim** from Cuba to Florida in her twenties.	For the negative of the simple past, we use *didn't* (*did not*) + base form for regular and irregular verbs (except *be*). succeeded—didn't succeed swam—didn't swim

Did Nyad **face** difficulties? Yes, she **did**.
Did she **succeed** the first time? No, she **didn't**.
	For *yes/no* questions about the past, we use *did* + base form for regular and irregular verbs (except *be*).
	For a short answer, we use:
	   Yes, + subject pronoun + *did*.
	   No, + subject pronoun + *didn't*.

What kind of difficulties **did** Nyad **face**? When **did** she **succeed**?	For *wh-* questions about the past, we use: Wh- word + *did* + subject + base form.

Compare statements, *yes/no* questions, short answers, and *wh-* questions.

STATEMENT	YES/NO QUESTION AND SHORT ANSWER	WH- QUESTION
Diana **swam** to Florida.	**Did** she **swim** around Manhattan? Yes, she **did**.	When **did** she **swim** around Manhattan?
She **didn't succeed** the first time.	**Did** she **succeed** the second time? No, she **didn't**.	When **did** she **succeed**? Why **didn't** she **succeed** the first time?

Note:
We don't use *did* with the verb *be*.
Compare: Nyad **wasn't** successful her first time.   What **was** her goal?
           She **didn't reach** Florida on her first try.   What **did** she **want** to accomplish?

EXERCISE 9 Fill in the blanks with the negative form of the underlined verbs.

1. Andrée and his men <u>landed</u> on ice. They ___didn't land___ on the North Pole.

2. George Dawson <u>knew</u> how to do many things. He _____ how to read and write.

3. His father <u>taught</u> him many things. His father _____ him to read or write.

4. He <u>had</u> the chance for an education when he was old. He _____ the chance when he was young.

5. He <u>wrote</u> a book about his life. He _____ it alone.

6. Diana Nyad <u>wanted</u> to swim from Cuba to Florida. She _____ to die without achieving her goal.

7. She <u>swam</u> a lot when she was young. She _____ for many years.

8. Nyad <u>went</u> to Cuba. She _____ alone.

EXERCISE 10 Fill in the blanks to complete the conversation. Use context clues to help you.

A: ___Did you read___ the Harry Potter books?
1.

B: Yes, I ___did___. I read all of them. I recently wrote a paper about
2.
the author, J.K. Rowling. She's the first author to become a billionaire from her writing. When she first started writing, she considered herself a failure. ___Did you know___ that?
3.

A: No, I ___didn't___. But I'd like to know more. When
4.
___did she write___ the first Harry Potter book?
5.

B: She wrote the first one in 1995. She always wanted to be a writer. But her parents
___didn't like___ the idea. They thought she needed a "real" job.
6.

A: Why ___didn't they think___ that writing novels was a real job?
7.

B: They were worried that it wouldn't pay the rent for her. She was very poor. She went on welfare. At that time in her life, she was very depressed.

A: Why ___did she go___ on welfare?
8.

B: She was divorced and a single parent. She ___didn't have___ enough money to
9.
support her daughter. She was also very depressed because her mother died. She sent her Harry Potter novel to 12 publishers, but they all rejected her novel.

continued

The Simple Past, The Habitual Past with *Used To* 83

A: Why _did they reject_ her novel?

B: They didn't think it would be successful. Finally a publisher agreed to publish it.

A: _Did they offer_ her a lot of money?

B: No, they _didn't_. They only offered her about $2,000. They printed only one thousand copies.

A: That's not very many books. _Did she accept_ their offer?

B: Yes, she _did_. She was happy to accept it.

A: _Did they print_ more copies?

B: Yes, they _did_. They had to print more copies because so many people wanted to read about Harry Potter. By 1999, her book went to the top of best-seller lists. When she wrote the fourth book, the publisher printed lots of copies.

A: How many copies _did they print_?

B: They printed over five million copies.

A: Wow! She wasn't a failure. She was a real success.

B: Besides writing, Rowling does other things. For example, she spoke to the graduating class of Harvard in 2008.

A: _Did she speak_ about her novels?

B: No, _she didn't_. She spoke about the benefits of failure. She said, "It is impossible to live without failing at something."

> **FUN WITH GRAMMAR**
>
> Play *Alibi*. Your teacher will tell you the time and place of a robbery. Two students are the suspects and leave the room. As a class, think of questions to ask the suspects, e.g., *Where were you at the time of the robbery? Who was with you?* The two suspects create an alibi (proof that they were not at the scene of the crime at the time it took place) together. They should try to anticipate what questions the class will ask them and think of answers. Then the class will interview the suspects one at a time. If their answers match, they are innocent. If their answers don't match, they are guilty.
>
> Class: Where were you at the time of the robbery?
>
> Suspect 1: I was at the Mexican restaurant down the street. Suspect 2 was with me.
>
> Class: What time did you leave the restaurant?
>
> Suspect 1: We left at around 9:30.

SUCCESS IN CHANGING LAWS

Martin Luther King, Jr., giving his famous "I Have a Dream" speech in Washington, DC, U.S.

Read the following article. Pay special attention to the words in bold.

Today all people in the United States have equal rights under the law. But this was not always the case, especially for African Americans. Even though slavery in the United States ended in 1865, blacks continued to suffer discrimination[1] and segregation[2], especially in the South. Many hotels and restaurants **used to serve** white customers only. Many businesses **used to have** signs in their windows that said, "Blacks Not Allowed." Black children **used to go** to separate, and often inferior, schools. Many professions were for whites only. Even in sports, blacks could not join the major baseball leagues[3]; there **used to be** separate leagues for them. In many places in the South, buses **used to reserve** the front seats for white people. But that all changed.

One evening in December of 1955, Rosa Parks, a 42-year-old woman, got on a bus in Montgomery, Alabama, to go home from work. She was tired and sat down. When some white people got on the crowded bus, the bus driver ordered Ms. Parks to stand up. Ms. Parks refused. The bus driver called the police, and they arrested Ms. Parks.

Martin Luther King, Jr., a black minister living in Montgomery, Alabama, wanted to put an end to discrimination. When King heard about Ms. Parks's arrest, he told African Americans in Montgomery to boycott[4] the bus company. People who **used to ride** the bus to work decided to walk instead. As a result of the boycott, the Supreme Court outlawed[5] discrimination on public transportation.

About 100 years after the end of slavery, Congress passed the Civil Rights Act of 1964. This law officially gave equality to all Americans. The law made discrimination in employment and education illegal. King won the Nobel Peace Prize for his work in creating a better world.

Martin Luther King, Rosa Parks, and other brave people succeeded in changing unfair laws.

---

[1] discrimination: unfair treatment, especially because of race, age, religion, etc.
[2] segregation: separation of the races
[3] league: a group of sports teams that compete against each other
[4] to boycott: to refuse to do business with a company
[5] to outlaw: to make an action illegal or against the law

The Simple Past. The Habitual Past with *Used To*

COMPREHENSION Based on the reading, write T for *true* or F for *false*.

1. __F__ When slavery ended, blacks gained equality.
2. __T__ Rosa Parks refused to obey the law on the bus.
3. __T__ The bus boycott in Montgomery was successful in helping change the law.

THINK ABOUT IT Discuss the questions with a partner or in a small group.

1. What do you think made Rosa Parks protest the way she did on that day? What might she have been feeling?

   She was tired and got upset about the situation, she might have been scared or nervous

2. What are some ways to protest that you know about? What are the pros and cons of each?

   People that leave to streets looking to anyone who listens to them.
   Pros: likely to be listen to. Cons: A lot of fights

3.7 The Habitual Past with *Used To*

EXAMPLES	EXPLANATION
Black children **used to attend** separate schools. Many professions **used to be** for white people only. There **used to be** separate baseball leagues for black people.	We use *used to* + a base form to show a habit or custom over a past period of time. It refers to a custom that no longer exists.

Notes:

1. *Used to* is not for an action that happened once or a few times.

   Many restaurants **used to serve** white people only. (This happened over a period of time.)

   In 1955, Rosa Parks **refused** to stand up. (This happened one time.)

2. For negatives and questions, we omit the *d* in *used to*.

   Some restaurants **didn't use to** serve African Americans.

   Where **did** they **use to** eat?

EXERCISE 11 Fill in the blanks with *use(d) to* + one of the verbs from the box. You will use two of the verbs twice.

| make | be ✓ | suffer | give up | ride | travel |
| consider | have | dream | wonder | support | |

1. J.K. Rowling __used to be__ poor. Now she's rich.
2. Rowling __used to have__ billions of dollars. But she gave away a lot of her money.
3. She didn't __use to consider__ herself a success. She thought she was a failure.
4. How did she __use to support__ herself and her daughter when she was poor?
5. Peter Athans, who climbed Mt. Everest several times, __used to make__ a lot of mistakes. Now he's much more experienced and careful.

86 Unit 3

6. People __used to wonder__ where the *Titanic* was. Thanks to Robert Ballard, now we know where it is.

7. Diana Nyad __used to dream__ of swimming from Cuba to Florida. She finally accomplished it.

8. Nyad __used to ride__ her bike 100 miles every Friday.

9. It __used to be__ difficult to arrive at the North Pole. Now it's easy.

10. People __used to travel__ from Europe to the U.S. by ship. Now people fly across the ocean.

11. Black people in the South __used to suffer__ discrimination in hotels and restaurants.

12. Black people in the South __used to give up__ their seats on buses to white people.

13. Baseball teams didn't __use to have__ black players. But that changed in 1947.

ABOUT YOU Compare the situation in your country in the past with the situation in your country today. Discuss your answers with a partner.

1. People used to have large families. Now most people have one or two children.
2.
3.
4.

ABOUT YOU Write sentences comparing the way you used to live with the way you live now. Discuss your answers with a partner. Use the ideas below for your sentences.

school   job   hobbies   apartment/house   family   friends

1. I used to live with my whole family. Now I live alone.
2. I didn't use to speak English at all. Now I speak English pretty well.
3.
4.
5.
6.
7.
8.

The Simple Past, The Habitual Past with *Used To* 87

SUMMARY OF UNIT 3

THE SIMPLE PAST OF BE

Affirmative Statement:	Dawson **was** happy.
Negative Statement:	He **wasn't** rich.
Yes/No Question:	**Was** he from a large family?
Short Answer:	Yes, he **was**.
Wh- Question:	Where **was** he born?
Negative Wh- Question:	Why **wasn't** he in school?

THE SIMPLE PAST OF REGULAR VERBS

Affirmative Statement:	Andrée **wanted** to go to the North Pole.
Negative Statement:	He **didn't want** to go over land.
Yes/No Question:	**Did** he **want** to go by balloon?
Short Answer:	Yes, he **did**.
Wh- Question:	Why **did** he **want** to go to the North Pole?
Negative Wh- Question:	Why **didn't** he **want** to go over land?

THE SIMPLE PAST OF IRREGULAR VERBS

Affirmative Statement:	Dawson **felt** happy.
Negative Statement:	He **didn't feel** lonely.
Yes/No Question:	**Did** he **feel** good when he learned to read?
Short Answer:	Yes, he **did**.
Wh- Question:	How **did** he **feel** about his life?
Negative Wh- Question:	Why **didn't** he **feel** lonely?

THE HABITUAL PAST WITH USED TO

Affirmative Statement:	Black children **used to attend** separate schools in some places.
Negative Statement:	They **didn't use to attend** schools with white children.
Yes/No Question:	**Did** baseball teams **use to have** black players?
Short Answer:	No, they **didn't**.
Wh- Question:	Why **did** schools **use to segregate** students?

REVIEW

Fill in the blanks to complete the conversation. Use the words given and context clues to help you. Use contractions wherever possible.

A: There ____was____ a good program on TV last night. ____Did you see____ it?
   1. be   2. you/see

B: No, I ____didn't____. What ____was it____ about?
   3.   4. be

A: It was about successful people who ____failed____ at first.
                                       5. fail

B: Who ____did they talk____ about?
       6. they/talk

A: One success was Bill Gates. Gates ____started____ a company with a friend when he
                                      7. start
   ____was____ 17 years old.
   8. be

B: What kind of company ____did they start____?
                         9. they/start

A: They ____built____ software to help regulate traffic. They ____tried____ to sell it to the city,
        10. build   11. try
   but they ____weren't____ successful.
            12. not/be

B: Why ____weren't they____ successful?
        13. they/not/be

A: The software ____did____ well in the lab, but it ____didn't____ well when they showed it
                 14. do   15. not/do
   to the city. Then Gates ____went____ to college, but he ____didn't finish____. He
                           16. go   17. not/finish
   ____left____ before graduation.
   18. leave

B: I ____didn't know____ that. Why ____did he leave____ college?
     19. not/know   20. he/leave

A: He ____was____ very interested in computers, and he ____started____ Microsoft with his
      21. be   22. start
   friend. They ____became____ successful. The program also talked about Thomas Edison. He
                23. become
   ____invented____ many things. He ____made____ 1,000 attempts
   24. invent   25. make
   before he ____succeeded____ with the light bulb. A reporter ____asked____ him
              26. succeed   27. ask
   how it ____felt____ to fail so many times. Edison ____replied____,
          28. feel   29. reply
   "I ____didn't fail____ 1,000 times. The light bulb was an invention with 1,000 steps."
      30. not/fail

B: I ____used to think____ that successful people succeeded right away.
     31. use to/think
   I ____didn't use to think____ of failure as a part of success.
     32. not/use to/think

FROM GRAMMAR TO WRITING

PART 1 Editing Advice

1. Use *was/were* with *born*.

                 was
   Dawson born in the South.

2. Don't use *was* or *were* with *die*.

   He ~~was~~ died in 2001.

3. Don't use a past form after *to*.

                     swim
   Nyad decided to ~~swam~~ from Cuba to Florida.

4. Don't use *was* or *were* to form the simple past.

            accomplished
   She ~~was accomplish~~ her goal.

5. Use a form of *be* before an adjective. Remember, some *-ed* words are adjectives.

            was
   Dawson excited about going to school.

6. Don't use *did* with an adjective. Use *was* or *were*.

                    weren't
   Andrée and his men ~~didn't~~ successful.

7. Form the past question correctly.

           didn't you
   Why ~~you didn't~~ read the article?

           did   write
   Why Dawson ~~wrote~~ a book?

8. Use the base form after *didn't*.

   He didn't learn~~ed~~ to read when he was a child.

9. Don't forget the *d* in *used to* in affirmative statements.

        d
   He use to live in the South.

10. Don't add the verb *be* before *used to* for habitual past.

    Nyad ~~is~~ used to be a sportscaster.

11. Use the correct past form.

           swam
    Nyad ~~swimmed~~ from Cuba to Florida.

PART 2 Editing Practice
Some of the shaded words and phrases have mistakes. Find the mistakes and correct them. If the shaded words are correct, write C.

          C   was
I recently **read** an article about Jackie Robinson. He **were** the first African American to play on
            1.   2.
a major league baseball team, the Brooklyn Dodgers. Major league baseball teams **use to** have only
                                                                                      3.
white players. Blacks **were used to** have their own teams.
                               4.

Robinson **born** in 1919 in the South. His family **was** very poor. When he was just a baby, his
father **leaved** the family, and his mother **decided** to **moved** the family to California. When he **were** in
high school and college, he **interested** in several different sports. After junior college, he **went** to the
University of California, where he **was won** awards in baseball, basketball, football, and track. He
didn't finished college. He **taked** a job as athletic director of a youth organization. Then he **enter** the
U.S. Army in 1942. After he left the Army in 1944, he **accepted** an offer to be the athletic director at a
college in Texas. In 1945, the Kansas City Monarchs, an African American baseball team, **sended** him an
offer to play professional baseball. In 1947, the Brooklyn Dodgers **offered** him a contract. The manager
of the team **knowed** that Robinson would face racial discrimination. He **didn't wanted** Robinson to fight
back. Some people in the crowds **yelled** racial insults to him. Even some of his teammates **objected** to
having an African American on their team. Robinson **didn't** surprised. He **knew** this would happen.
Some other teams **threatened** not to play against the Dodgers. **How the manager of the team reacted?**
The manager, Leo Durocher, **supported** Robinson. He **sayed** that he would rather keep Robinson than
some of them. In one game, when people yelled racial insults at Robinson, the team captain **come** over
and **putted** his arm around Robinson to show his support.
Robinson **succeeded** in breaking the racial barrier. He **become** the highest paid player in
Dodgers history. But more importantly, he **opened** the door for other African American athletes in
professional sports. He **retired** from baseball in 1957. He **was died** in 1972.

WRITING TIP
When writing about someone's life story, we use simple past forms. We often begin with information about when and where a person was born. Then it is common to provide details of his or her life chronologically; for example, the person's childhood, schooling, accomplishments, etc., in the simple past. Question forms may be used to bring attention to a particular detail, for example *Was George Lawson a success? He definitely was.*

PART 3 Write
Read the prompts. Choose one and write a paragraph about it.

1. Write about an ordinary person who did something extraordinary (like George Dawson). It can be someone you read about or someone you know.
2. Write about a time when you failed at something. What did you learn from your failure?

PART 4 Edit
Reread the Summary of Unit 3 and the editing advice. Edit your writing from Part 3.

UNIT 4

Possessives
Pronouns

WEDDINGS

Newlyweds Qu Shen and Liu Ge pose for wedding photos at the fire station where he works as a firefighter in Shangluo, Shaanxi Province of China.

A great marriage is not when the 'perfect couple' comes together. It is when an imperfect couple learns to enjoy their differences.

DAVE MEURER

A Traditional American WEDDING

Read the following article. Pay special attention to the words in bold. 4.1

Many young couples consider **their** wedding to be one of the most important days of **their** lives. They often spend a year planning for **it**: finding a place, selecting a menu, buying a wedding dress, ordering invitations and sending **them** to friends and relatives, selecting musicians, and more.

The bride chooses **her** bridesmaids[1] and maid of honor[2], and the groom chooses **his** groomsmen and best man. The bride and groom want to make this day special for **themselves** and for **their** guests. Sometimes the bride and groom use a professional wedding planner so they don't have to do everything by **themselves**.

When the day arrives, the groom doesn't usually see the bride before the wedding. It is considered bad luck for **him** to see **her** ahead of time. When the wedding begins, the groom and groomsmen enter first. Next, the maid of honor and bridesmaids enter. When the bride finally enters in **her** white dress, everyone turns around to look at **her**. Often the **bride's** father or both of **her** parents walk **her** down the aisle to the groom.

During the ceremony, the bride and groom take vows[3]. They promise to love and respect each other for the rest of their lives. The groom's best man holds the rings for **them** until they are ready to place **them** on each **other's** fingers. At the end of the ceremony, the groom lifts the **bride's** veil and kisses **her**.

There is a dinner and dance after the ceremony. The bride and groom usually dance the first dance alone. Then guests join **them**.

Before the bride and groom leave the party, the bride throws **her** bouquet over **her** head, and the single women try to catch **it**. It is believed that the woman who catches **it** will be the next one to get married.

The newlyweds[4] usually take a trip, called a honeymoon, immediately after the wedding.

---

[1] bridesmaid: one of a group of women (a good friend or close relative of the bride) who is part of the wedding ceremony
[2] maid of honor: one special woman (a good friend or close relative of the bride) who helps the bride during the wedding ceremony
[3] vow: a promise
[4] newlywed: a recently married person

A groom and his groomsmen

COMPREHENSION Based on the reading, write T for *true* or F for *false*.

1. _____ Some people use a wedding planner to help plan for the wedding.
2. _____ The bride usually enters with the groom.
3. _____ All the women try to catch the bouquet.

THINK ABOUT IT Discuss the questions with a partner or in a small group.

1. Are you familiar with American wedding customs? Are they similar to traditions in your culture?
2. Describe the perfect wedding. It can be a wedding you have been to or a wedding you imagine for yourself.

4.1 Overview of Possessive Forms and Pronouns

EXAMPLES	EXPLANATION
Your wedding was beautiful. **Her** mother looks happy.	A possessive adjective shows ownership or relationship.
You attended my wedding, and I attended **yours**.	A possessive pronoun also shows ownership or relationship.
The **bride's** dress is white.	A noun has a possessive form.
They sent **me** an invitation.	An object pronoun follows the verb.
They want to make the wedding special for **themselves** and their guests.	Some pronouns are reflexive.

EXERCISE 1 Listen to the conversation between a bride-to-be and a professional wedding planner. Then write T for *true* or F for *false*. 4.2

1. _____ The bride's mother suggested this wedding planner.
2. _____ Planning a wedding is actually pretty simple.
3. _____ The wedding planner costs between $1,000 and $3,500.

EXERCISE 2 Listen to the conversation again. Fill in the blanks with the words you hear. 4.2

A: My friend gave ___me your___(1) contact information. She said she used _____(2) services when she got married last year. My fiancé and _____(3) are planning _____(4) wedding now, and we want to know how _____(5) can help _____(6).

B: Some people try to plan _____(7) wedding _____(8), but the results are often not so good. So I'm glad you contacted _____(9). I can help _____(10) plan the perfect wedding. Planning a wedding by _____(11) is stressful. It's _____(12) special day, and I want _____(13) to enjoy _____(14). There are a lot of little details in planning a wedding, and it's my job to take care of _____(15) for _____(16).

continued

A: My _____ mother helped _____ plan _____ wedding, but
        17.   18.   19.

she was so busy that she didn't enjoy _____ very much. My cousin told
                                        20.

_____ that _____ wedding day was stressful for _____ and
   21.   22.   23.

_____ fiancé. I need help, but _____ budget is limited. How much is this
    24.   25.

going to cost _____?
                  26.

B: That depends. If you want _____ services for every step, it will be about $3,500. If you make
                                27.

_____ own arrangements and want _____ services for the two weeks before
    28.   29.

the wedding and on the wedding day, _____ fee is about $1,000. I have a list of all the
                                        30.

things I can do for a wedding. Please look at _____ and give _____ a call if
                                                  31.   32.

_____ have any questions. I would be happy to explain _____ options.
    33.   34.

4.2 Possessive Forms of Nouns

NOUN	RULE	EXAMPLES

Singular nouns:
    bride
    groom
	Add apostrophe + s.	The **bride's** dress is white.
		The **groom's** tuxedo is black.

Plural nouns ending in –s:
    parents
    guests
	Add apostrophe only.	She got married in her **parents'** house.
		The **guests'** coats are in the coat room.

Irregular plural nouns:
    men
    women
	Add apostrophe + s.	The **men's** suits are black.
		The **women's** dresses are beautiful.

Names that end in –s: Charles	Add apostrophe + s.	Do you know **Charles's** wife?

Inanimate objects:
    the church
    the dress
	Use *the* _____ *of the* _____.	New Hope is **the name of the church**.
		The front of the dress has pearls.

Time words:
    today
    this month
	Add apostrophe + s.	**Today's** weddings are very expensive.
		This month's assignment is easy.

Note:
Sometimes you will see only an apostrophe when a name ends in –s.
    Do you know **Charles'** wife?

EXERCISE 3 Fill in the blanks to make the possessive form of the noun given.

1. The _____bride's_____ grandfather looks very handsome.
   _{bride}

2. The _____ dresses are blue.
   _{bridesmaids}

3. They invited many guests to the wedding. Did they invite the _____ children?
   _{guests}

4. The _____ dresses are very elegant.
   _{women}

5. _____ sister is a bridesmaid.
   _{Ross}

6. _____ newspaper has the _____ photo.
   _{Today} _{newlyweds}

7. Do you know the _____ names?
   _{children}

EXERCISE 4 Fill in the blanks with the two nouns given. Put them in the correct order. Use the possessive form of one of the nouns, except with inanimate objects.

1. ___The bride's name___ is Lisa.
   _{name/the bride}

2. _____ is open.
   _{the door/the church}

3. _____ came to the wedding from London.
   _{the bride/grandmother}

4. _____ is June 1.
   _{the wedding/the date}

5. _____ is crying.
   _{the bride/mother}

6. _____ are black.
   _{the men/tuxedos}

7. _____ is white.
   _{the limousine/color}

8. _____ are pretty.
   _{dresses/girls}

9. Some people get married in their _____.
   _{house/parents}

10. What is _____?
    _{wedding/the cost}

11. _____ are put on a table in the reception room.
    _{the guests/gifts}

12. _____ helped him get ready before the ceremony.
    _{the groom/brother}

Possessives, Pronouns 97

4.3 Possessive Adjectives

EXAMPLES	EXPLANATION
I love **my** wife. Where did you buy **your** gift? He chose **his** brother to be **his** best man. She's wearing **her** sister's dress. It's a big restaurant with **its** own reception hall. We planned **our** wedding for over a year. They bought **their** rings at a jewelry store.	**Subject Pronoun** **Possessive Adjective** I my you your he his she her it its we our they their
My sister loves **her** husband. **My brother** loves **his** wife.	A possessive adjective refers to the noun before it. Be careful not to confuse *his* and *her*. NOT: My sister loves *his* husband. NOT: My brother loves *her* wife.
The **bride's mother's** dress is blue.	We can use two possessive nouns together.
My brother's wife didn't attend the wedding.	We can use a possessive adjective (*my*) before a possessive noun (*brother's*).

Note:
Don't confuse:
- *your* vs. *you're (you are)*.
- *their* vs. *they're (they are)*.
- *its* vs. *it's (it is)*.

EXERCISE 5 Fill in the blanks with a possessive adjective.

1. I love _____my_____ parents.

2. I have one sister. _____ sister got married five years ago.

3. She loves _____ husband very much.

4. He's an accountant. He has _____ own business.

5. They have one child. _____ son's name is Jason.

6. My sister and I visit _____ parents once a month. They live two hours away from us.

7. My sister said, "My car isn't working this week. Let's visit them in _____ car."

8. I agreed, but then my car wouldn't start. _____ battery had died.

EXERCISE 6 Fill in the blanks with a possessive adjective.

A: My sister, Nicole, is getting married next month.

B: Will your parents have the wedding at ____their____ home?
                                                1.

A: Oh, no. They live in an apartment. _____ apartment is too small. My sister invited more
                                              2.
than 200 guests. The wedding is going to be at a church. Afterwards, there's going to be a reception
nearby. The church has _____ own reception hall.
                          3.

B: Did she already buy _____ dress?
                              4.

A: Dresses are so expensive. We wear the same size, so my sister's going to wear _____
                                                                                        5.
dress. Nicole and _____ fiancé, Kevin, want to save money for _____
                      6.   7.
honeymoon. They're going to Paris.

B: Wow! Paris is beautiful—and expensive.

A: Yes, it is. But Kevin's aunt lives there. They're going to stay at _____ apartment.
                                                                            8.

B: Isn't she going to be at her apartment?

A: No. _____ aunt is coming here for _____ wedding. She's going to stay here
            9.   10.
an extra week to give Kevin and Nicole _____ apartment.
                                          11.

B: That's great! I'm sure they will enjoy _____ honeymoon in Paris.
                                                12.

4.4 Possessive Pronouns

We use a possessive pronoun to avoid repetition of a possessive adjective and noun.

EXAMPLE	EXPLANATION
We had our wedding in a church. They had **theirs** in a garden. (*theirs* = their wedding) Her dress is white. **Mine** is blue. (*Mine* = My dress) Their wedding was big. **Ours** was small. (*Ours* = Our wedding)	**Possessive Adjective** **Possessive Pronoun** my mine your yours his his her hers its — our ours their theirs
The groom's parents look happy. The **bride's** do, too. (*bride's* = bride's parents)	After a possessive noun, we can omit the noun to avoid repetition.

Possessives, Pronouns 99

EXERCISE 7 Circle the correct words to complete the conversation.

A: I heard your brother got married last month. How was the wedding? Was it anything like your wedding? I remember (*your*/*yours*) very well.
1.

B: (*My*/*Mine*) wedding was very different from my (*brother*/*brother's*). (*His*/*Hers*) was a very formal
2.   3.   4.
wedding in a church. (*My*/*Mine*) was very informal, in a garden.
5.

A: I enjoyed (*your*/*yours*) wedding. I prefer informal weddings. At most weddings, I have to get dressed up
6.
in a suit and tie. At (*your*/*yours*), I wore comfortable clothes. Where did your brother and his wife go for
7.
(*their*/*theirs*) honeymoon?
8.

B: They had a very different honeymoon from (*our*/*ours*). (*Our*/*Ours*) honeymoon was a two-day trip to
9.   10.
Chicago. (*Their*/*Theirs*) was a two-week trip to Hawaii.
11.

A: I remember your wife made (*her*/*hers*) own dress. You saved a lot of money.
12.

B: Yes. But my sister-in-law, Gina, bought (*hers*/*his*). Sarah made her dress for under $100. But
13.
(*Gina*/*Gina's*) cost over $1,000.
14.

A: The cost of a wedding isn't the most important thing. The most important thing is the happiness that follows. My (*uncle's*/*uncle*) wedding cost over $30,000, but his marriage lasted only eight months.
15.

B: That's too bad! (*My*/*Mine*) uncle had a short marriage, too. (*His*/*Hers*) only lasted a year.
16.   17.

A: Well, I hope your (*brother*/*brother's*) marriage is happy and long!
18.

ABOUT YOU Find a partner and discuss your answers to these questions.

1. What kind of clothes do a bride and groom wear in your native culture?
2. What kind of clothes do guests wear?
3. Do people use professional wedding planners in your country? Why or why not?

4.5 Questions with *Whose*

Whose + a noun asks a question about ownership or relationship.

WHOSE + NOUN	AUXILIARY VERB	SUBJECT	VERB	ANSWER
Whose dress	did	the bride	borrow?	She borrowed her sister's dress.
Whose flowers	are	those?		They're the bride's flowers.
Whose advice	will	the groom	take?	He'll take his mother's advice.

Note:
Don't confuse *whose* with *who's (who is)*.
    Who's that? That's the wedding planner.
    Whose mother is that? That's the bride's mother.

GRAMMAR IN USE

Whose can refer to possession of concrete objects (e.g., *Whose sweater is this? Whose computer did you use?*) as well as possession of abstract ideas (e.g., *Whose advice did you take in the end? Whose opinion matters to you the most?*). Even though you cannot touch the abstract ideas, they still belong to other people.

EXERCISE 8 Write a question with *whose*. The answer is given.

1. *Whose flowers are these?*

   They're the bride's flowers.

2. _____

   That's my father's car.

3. _____

   Those are the newlyweds' gifts.

4. _____

   She's wearing her sister's necklace.

5. _____

   They followed the wedding planner's advice.

6. _____

   They used their friend's house.

A DESTINATION Wedding

Read the following article. Pay special attention to the words in bold. 4.3

A year ago, Emily Reese and Josh Knoll got engaged[1]. The couple surfs, and one afternoon at the beach, Josh wrote "I love **you**. Will you marry **me**?" in the sand. "Of course, I told **him** yes," Emily laughs.

Later, Josh and Emily called their families. "When we told **them**, everyone was happy," Josh says. There was just one problem: Where would the couple get married?

"Josh's family is from Chicago," Emily explains. "They wanted **us** to have the wedding there. My family is in Miami, and they wanted **it** in that city. And Josh and I work in San Francisco."

Then the couple had an idea: have a destination wedding.

"We planned to honeymoon in Baja (Mexico) and go surfing," Josh explains. "So we said to **ourselves**, let's have the entire wedding in Baja on the beach."

Today, one in four couples in the U.S. has a destination wedding. The couple and their guests travel to an interesting place (in another city or country) for the event. Couples do **it** because it's fun, but there's another reason. The average American wedding costs around $35,000. Often, a destination wedding is several thousand dollars less, mainly because fewer people attend. The average number of guests at a destination wedding is 48, compared to 136. That's a big savings, especially for couples who pay for **it by themselves**.

Emily liked the idea for another reason. "I couldn't picture **myself** in a church in a formal dress," she says. "I wanted something casual and fun."

When Emily and Josh got married in Baja, only close family and friends came. "It was small, but we all enjoyed **ourselves**," Emily says. "Also, before the wedding, I didn't know Josh's sister. But she stayed in Baja for a few days, and I spent time with **her**. It was a great way to meet my new in-laws[2] and get to know **them**."

Top Destination Wedding Locations for Americans
Las Vegas, Nevada
Hawaii
Saint Thomas, U.S. Virgin Islands
Jamaica
The Bahamas
Mexico

[1] to get engaged: to agree formally that you will marry someone
[2] in-laws: your spouse's parents and siblings

COMPREHENSION Based on the reading, write T for *true* or F for *false*.

1. _____ Josh and Emily are from the city of Chicago.
2. _____ The average destination wedding costs about $35,000.
3. _____ Emily was very happy with her wedding.

THINK ABOUT IT Discuss the questions with a partner or in a small group.

1. What are some advantages of a destination wedding? Can you think of any disadvantages?
2. Look at the list of popular places for destination weddings. What do most of them have in common? Add one more idea to the list.

4.6 Object Pronouns

The object pronouns are *me, you, him, her, it, us,* and *them.*

EXAMPLES	EXPLANATION
"I love **you**," Josh said. We saw the wedding photos. We liked **them**.	We use object pronouns after a verb.
Did Emily's parents pay for the wedding? No, Josh and Emily paid for **it**.	An object pronoun can follow a preposition (*at, with, of, about, to, from, in,* etc.).
He invited my family and **me** to the wedding. My family and **I** went to the wedding.	Be careful with subjects and objects connected with *and*. After a verb, we use an object pronoun. Before a verb, we use a subject pronoun.

Notes:

1. An object can be direct or indirect.

    *I love **you**.* (A direct object receives the action of the verb.)

    *Emily showed **me** the wedding photos.* (An indirect object answers *to whom* or *for whom*, in this case, "Who did Emily show the wedding photos **to**?")

2. We can use *them* for plural people and things.

    *Emily met **Josh's sisters**, and she liked **them**.*

    *These are **the wedding photos**. Let's look at **them**.*

3. Compare subject pronouns (in the first column) and object pronouns (in the last column):

I				me.
You				you.
He	went to the wedding.	Emily	invited	him.
She				her.
We				us.
They				them.
It	was great.		loved	it.

Possessives, Pronouns 103

EXERCISE 9 Fill in the blanks with an object pronoun that corresponds to the underlined word(s).

1. Did <u>you</u> receive the wedding invitation? Josh and Emily want ____you____ to come.

2. Yes. I received <u>the invitation</u>. I put _____ on my refrigerator.

3. At the wedding, <u>Emily</u> didn't arrive at the ceremony with Josh. He arrived before _____.

4. During the ceremony, <u>Josh</u> promised to love Emily, and she promised to love _____.

5. <u>Emily</u> wore <u>a veil</u>. At the end, Josh lifted _____ to kiss _____.

6. Josh and Emily got <u>hotel rooms</u> for their guests, and the couple paid for _____.

7. <u>I</u> am going to give <u>the wedding toast</u>. Emily asked _____ to do _____.

8. You don't know <u>Josh's brothers</u>. I'll introduce you to _____.

9. <u>We</u> sent Josh and Emily <u>a wedding gift</u>. They sent a note to thank _____ for _____.

EXERCISE 10 Fill in the blanks with the correct subject pronoun, object pronoun, or possessive adjective.

A: How was Josh and Emily's wedding?

B: ____It____ was great.
       1.

A: How many guests were there?

B: About 40. I didn't count _____ all.
                                2.

A: Their wedding was in Mexico, right? How did they pay for _____?
                                                                3.

B: _____ used some of their savings. Also, _____ parents helped
       4.   5.

_____, too.
6.

A: Did Emily wear a traditional white dress?

B: No. The wedding was on the beach, so _____ wore an informal sun dress, but she looked
                                             7.

beautiful in _____.
             8.

A: I hope _____ 'll be happy. Sometimes marriage isn't easy.
             9.

B: I agree with _____. But I'm sure Emily and Josh will be happy. She loves
                   10.

_____ and _____ loves _____ very much.
11.   12.   13.

A: Did you take pictures at the wedding?

B: Yes. Do you want to see _____? I have some on _____ phone. Here's a
                               14.   15.

picture of Emily and _____.
                     16.

104 Unit 4

A: Who's that older woman between the two of you?

B: Emily is my cousin, and that's _____ grandmother. We were so happy she came to the
17.
wedding. It was a long trip for _____ because she lives in Australia.
18.

A: _____ grandmother looks so proud. Please tell Emily and Josh that I'm so happy for
19.
_____!
20.

EXERCISE 11 Circle the correct words to complete each sentence.

1. (*I*/*I'm*) have a wonderful fiancé, Katya.
2. I love (*her*/*hers*) very much, and she loves (*me*/*my*), too.
3. (*I*/*I'm*) so happy because (*we*/*we're*) going to get married.
4. (*Our*/*We're*) wedding will be in March.
5. My brother's wedding was small. (*Our*/*Ours*) is going to be big.
6. We invited all (*our*/*ours*) friends and relatives.
7. Some of (*them*/*they*) are coming from out of town.
8. (*They're*/*Their*) going to stay with relatives or in a hotel.
9. Katya has two sisters. (*Hers*/*Her*) sisters are going to be bridesmaids.
10. (*Their*/*They're*) dresses are blue.
11. There's one problem: Katya's father. (*I*/*I'm*) don't like (*his*/*her*) father very much.
12. I think (*he*/*he's*) doesn't like (*my*/*me*), either. (*He's*/*His*) very bossy.
13. But I like Katya's mother. (*Hers*/*Her*) mother is nice.
14. The wedding will be in a church. The church has (*it's*/*its*) own reception hall. (*Its*/*It's*) going to be a beautiful wedding.
15. Katya and (*me*/*I*) are going to have our honeymoon in Hawaii. My parents gave Katya and (*me*/*I*) money to help with the trip.
16. My fiancé and (*me*/*I*) will enjoy the wedding day with (*our*/*ours*) friends and family, and then (*we*/*we're*) going to relax on the beach for a week!

4.7 Reflexive Pronouns

EXAMPLES	EXPLANATION
"I can't see **myself** in a formal wedding dress," Emily said. They enjoyed **themselves** at the wedding. We said to **ourselves**, let's have the wedding in Mexico.	We use a **reflexive pronoun** when the object refers to the subject of the sentence. A reflexive pronoun can follow a verb or a preposition.
She made the invitations **all by herself**. They paid for the wedding **by themselves**.	We add *(all) by* before a reflexive pronoun to mean "alone," "without help."

SUBJECT	VERB	REFLEXIVE PRONOUN	
I		myself	
You		yourself	
He		himself	
She	enjoyed	herself	at the wedding.
We		ourselves	
You		yourselves	
They		themselves	

> **GRAMMAR IN USE**
>
> We use reflexive pronouns in a few idiomatic expressions.
>
> **Help yourself** (to more cake, to a drink, etc.).
>
> **Make yourself comfortable/at home.**
>
> If you don't believe me, come **see for yourself**.
>
> Relax and just **be yourself**.

EXERCISE 12 It is now a year after Josh and Emily's wedding, and their relationship has changed. Read each one's story and fill in the blanks with a reflexive pronoun.

Emily's Story:

Now that we're married, I don't have time for ___myself___ anymore. Josh and I
                                                    1.
used to go out every weekend. Now, there's never any time. It's hard because I'm in law school

and Josh works for _____. (He just started a small software company.) We're
                        2.

both busy, but Josh rarely helps with the housework or bills. I have to do everything by

_____. And I'm so tired. My friends are always saying, "You don't look well. You
      3.

need to take better care of _____." But how can I? I'm exhausted, and Josh
                                  4.

thinks only of _____. I tell _____ that things will get better, but
                    5.   6.

I'm not sure.

106   Unit 4

Josh's Story:

Emily never has time for me anymore. We used to do things together. Now I have to do everything by _____. She's always too busy or too tired. I try to help, but when I
                              7.
offer to do the housework, for example, she says "no" because she prefers to do everything

_____. My dad tells me, "Josh, don't blame _____." But it's hard.
     8.   9.

Our friends seem to enjoy _____.
                                  10.

I keep asking _____: Why can't Emily and I be happy?
                    11.

EXERCISE 13 Fill in the blanks with the correct object or reflexive pronoun.

Josh and Emily used to do a lot of things together. But now they are always too busy. Josh

works for _____; Emily is in law school. On the weekend, instead of sharing
             1.

household chores together, Emily does _____ by _____. When Josh
                                              2.   3.

offers to help, Emily tells _____ "No, I'll do it _____." And so Josh
                                 4.   5.

goes out by _____ or with others.
                 6.

Emily and Josh knew they had a problem, but they couldn't solve _____ by
                                                                              7.

_____. So they went to see a marriage counselor. At first, Josh didn't want to go.
      8.

He told Emily, "If you want to see a counselor, you can go by _____. I'm not going
                                                                          9.

with _____." To this, Emily said, "Josh, if you love _____, you'll
          10.   11.

come." And so Josh agreed.

During their meeting, the counselor said, "Emily, you spend your weekends doing

housework. Can Josh help _____?"
                                   12.

"Emily doesn't want _____ to help," Josh replied.
                              13.

"That's not true," Emily said. "I ask _____ to do the laundry, but he's always
                                            14.

busy, so I have to do _____."
                            15.

"OK, here's an idea," the counselor said. "Make a list of chores together. Then Josh, you take

some of _____ and Emily, you take some, too. You should make a schedule for
            16.

_____, too: time for work and time for you to go out *together*. When you have your
      17.

schedule, you have to follow _____. Try this, and then let's meet again in a month.
                                       18.

New Wedding Trends

Read the following article. Pay special attention to the words in bold. 4.4

Wedding traditions are changing. More and more couples are choosing to create a unique wedding experience for themselves and for their guests. In traditional weddings, a clergyperson[1] faces the bride and groom and **reads them their vows**. The bride and groom simply say, "I do" in response to the question of whether or not they agree to marry. But today, 43 percent of weddings are officiated by a friend or family member rather than a clergyperson. And more and more couples are writing their own vows and **saying them to each other** in their own words.

Following tradition, the bride and groom send their friends and relatives an invitation. But with today's busy schedules, the new norm is for the bride and groom to tell **their guests the date** at least five or six months in advance. They **send them "save-the-date" cards** so that their guests can make plans. Some couples are choosing to have a themed wedding—a central idea or style for their big day. Examples include a specific decade, a movie or television show, a book, a city, or a color. The cards give this information to guests so that they can dress appropriately.

Another new trend in weddings is to create a wedding based on the couple's ethnic background. For example, in an African-American wedding, some couples want to **show respect to their ancestors**[2] by jumping over a broom, a tradition from the time of slavery. The jumping of the broom symbolizes a new beginning by sweeping away the old and welcoming the new. Some African Americans use colorful clothing inspired by African costumes, rather than a white dress for the bride and a suit or tuxedo for the groom.

One thing stays the same. The newlyweds **send the guests thank-you cards** by mail to thank them for attending the wedding and for the gifts they gave.

An African-American couple jumps over a broom.

---

[1] clergyperson: a minister, rabbi, or other religious leader
[2] ancestor: the people from whom one is descended; great-grandparent, great-great-grandparent, etc.

COMPREHENSION Based on the reading, write T for *true* or F for *false*.

1. _____ More couples are choosing to have unique weddings.
2. _____ Both the couple and the guests need time to plan for a wedding.
3. _____ Jumping over a broom is part of some ethnic weddings.

THINK ABOUT IT Discuss the questions with a partner or in a small group.

1. Do you like the idea of modern weddings with an unusual theme, or do you prefer a more traditional celebration? Why?
2. What ethnic traditions have you seen in weddings? Which traditions would you like to have or did you have at your wedding?

4.8 Direct and Indirect Objects

Some verbs can have both a direct and an indirect object. The order of direct objects (DO) and indirect objects (IO) depends on the verb we use. With some verbs, it can also depend on whether we use a noun or a pronoun as the object.

With some verbs, pronouns affect word order.

POSSIBLE WORD ORDER	VERBS			
He gave his wife a present. (IO/DO) He gave a present to his wife. (DO *to* IO) He gave it to his wife. (DO *to* IO) He gave her a present. (IO/DO) He gave a present to her. (DO *to* IO) He gave it to her. (DO *to* IO)	bring email give	hand offer pay	read sell send	show tell write

Note:
When the direct object is a noun, not a pronoun, we usually put the indirect object before the direct object. However, we sometimes put the direct object before the indirect object for emphasis or contrast.

He didn't send you the invitation. He sent the invitation to me.

With some verbs, pronouns don't affect word order.

WORD ORDER = DO *TO* IO	VERBS			
He described the wedding to his friends. (DO *to* IO) He described it to them. (DO *to* IO) He described it to his friends. (DO *to* IO) He described the wedding to them. (DO *to* IO)	announce describe explain	introduce mention prove	recommend repeat report	say speak suggest

EXERCISE 14 Fill in the blanks with the words given. Put them in the correct order. Add *to* if necessary. In some cases, more than one answer is possible.

A: How was your cousin's wedding? Can you describe ___it to me___ ?
                                                    1. it/me

B: It was beautiful. The bride read _____, and then the groom read
                                    2. a lovely poem/the groom

_____, too.
3. a poem/her

A: Did they get married in a church?

B: No. They got married in a beautiful garden. Why didn't you go? I thought they sent

_____.
4. an invitation/you

A: They did. But I couldn't go. I wrote _____, and I explained
                                       5. an email/them

_____. I had to take an important exam for college that day.
6. my problem/them

But I sent _____.
           7. a present/them

B: I'm sure they'll appreciate it. It's too bad you couldn't go.

A: I'm sure I mentioned _____ a few weeks ago.
                        8. you/it

B: You probably did, but I forgot.

A: Do you have pictures from the wedding?

B: I took a lot of pictures. I'll email _____ tonight.
                                       9. you/them

A: Thanks.

4.9 Say and Tell

Say and *tell* have the same meaning, but we use them differently.

EXAMPLES	EXPLANATION
She **said** her name. She **told** me her name. She **said** her name to me. They **told** the musicians to start the music. She **said** (that) she wanted a big wedding.	We say something: *say* + DO. We tell someone something: *tell* + IO + DO. We say something to someone: *say* + DO *to* IO. We tell someone to do something: *tell* + IO *to* + verb. We say (that): *say* (+ *that*) + statement.
Tell the truth: do you love me?	We can use *tell the truth* or *tell a lie* without an indirect object.

EXERCISE 15 Fill in the blanks with the correct form of *say* or *tell*.

1. The bride ___said___ , "I love you."

2. They ___told___ us the date of the wedding.

3. You _____ me the groom's name, but I forgot it.

110 Unit 4

4. _____ the truth: do you like the bride's dress?

5. The bride hates to _____ goodbye to her family.

6. During the ceremony, the bride and groom _____, "I do."

7. We _____ the band to play romantic music.

8. My neighbor wants to come to my wedding. I wasn't planning on inviting her, but I can't _____ no.

9. We _____ our daughter to economize on her wedding, but she _____ that she wanted a fancy wedding.

ABOUT YOU Find a partner and discuss your answers to these questions.

1. Are wedding customs changing in your native culture? How?
2. In your native culture, what kind of vows do the bride and groom make to each other?

> **FUN WITH GRAMMAR**
>
> Create a story. Work with a partner. First, unscramble each sentence below. Then, put the story in order. The first team to complete the task, add a title, and tell the story to the class wins.
>
> told/was/she/him/it/delicious
> gave/she/a present/husband/her
> dinner/her/instead/cooked/an anniversary/for/he
> she/to him/explained/that it was/their anniversary/for
> buy/he/her/didn't/a gift

Throwing rice at the newlyweds is traditional.

QUESTIONS and ANSWERS about American Weddings

Read the following questions and answers. Pay special attention to the words in bold. 4.5

Q: **Who pays** for the wedding?

A: Usually the bride and groom do, especially if they are working and earning money. In some cases, their parents help.

Q: **What's** a shower?

A: A shower is a party for the bride (sometimes the bride and groom) before the wedding. Guests give the couple gifts to help them start their new home. Typical gifts are cookware, linens[1], and small kitchen appliances.

Q: **Who hosts**[2] the shower?

A: Usually the maid of honor hosts the shower.

Q: **When do** they **have** the shower?

A: Usually the shower is two to six weeks before the wedding.

Q: **How long does** it **take** to plan a wedding?

A: Most couples plan their wedding for seven to twelve months.

Q: **When do** the couples **send** invitations?

A: They usually send the invitations about eight weeks before the wedding.

Q: When guests come in from out of town, **who pays** for their hotel?

A: They pay for the hotel themselves. However, the groom pays for his groomsmen, and the bride pays for her bridesmaids.

Q: **Whom does** the groom **choose** as his best man?

A: He usually chooses a brother or best friend. The groom chooses other close friends or male relatives as the groomsmen.

Q: **When do** the bride and groom **open** their gifts?

A: They open their gifts at home, not at the wedding.

Q: **How do** the guests **know** what the bride and groom need as gifts?

A: The bride and groom usually register for gifts at stores. They list the gift items they want and need for their new home. When the guests go to buy a gift, they check the registry in the store. However, money is the most popular gift.

Q: **How do** I **know** how much money to give?

A: Most guests spend about $100 on a gift. People who are closer to the bride or groom often spend more.

---

[1] linens: sheets, pillowcases, and towels
[2] to host: to invite and entertain guests

COMPREHENSION Based on the reading, write T for *true* or F for *false*.

1. _____ In most cases, the bride's parents pay for the wedding.
2. _____ It takes about six weeks to plan for a wedding.
3. _____ A registry in a store lets guests know what kind of gifts the bride and groom want.

THINK ABOUT IT Discuss the questions with a partner or in a small group.

1. Which details about American weddings surprise you?
2. Imagine you are marrying an American man or woman. Which of the elements of an American wedding would you want to include? Which ones would you not include? Why?

4.10 Subject Questions

STATEMENT	SUBJECT QUESTION
The groom **paid** for the rings.	Who **paid** for the wedding dress?
The bride **has** a white dress.	Who **has** a blue dress?
Some women **plan** the shower.	Which women **plan** the shower?
Some people **send** money.	How many people **send** money?
The bride's mother **cried** at the wedding.	Whose mother **cried** at the wedding?

Notes:

1. Subject questions do not include *do, does,* or *did*.
   For the simple present:
   - We use the singular (*-s*) form after *who* and *which* + singular noun.
   - We use the base form after *which* and *how many* + plural noun.
2. **What happened** is a subject question. We answer with a different verb.
   What happened after the wedding?   Everyone **left**.
3. We often answer a subject question with a subject and an auxiliary verb.
   Who paid for the rings?   *The groom **did**.*
   Who likes a simple wedding?   *I **do**.*
4. Don't confuse *who's* (*who is*) and *whose*.
   Whose dresses are blue?   The bridesmaids' dresses are blue.
   Who's that woman?   She's the bride's grandmother.

EXERCISE 16 Read each statement. Then write a subject question with the words given.

1. Someone takes the bride to the groom. (*who*)

   <u>Who takes the bride to the groom?</u>

2. Someone holds the rings. (*who*)

   _____

continued

3. Someone's car has a "just married" sign. (*whose car*)

___

4. Some couples have a destination wedding. (*how many couples*)

___

5. One woman has a camera. (*which woman*)

___

6. Some guests stay at a hotel. (*which guests*)

___

7. Many people give money. (*how many people*)

___

4.11 Wh- Questions

STATEMENT	WH- QUESTION
The groom **paid** a lot of money for the wedding.	How much **did** he **pay**?
The bride **has** a white dress.	What color dress **does** her mother **have**?
The bride **borrowed** her dress.	Whose dress **did** she **borrow**?
The bride and groom **chose** a restaurant for the wedding dinner.	Which restaurant **did** they **choose**?
The bride and groom **will go** on a honeymoon.	Where **will** they **go**?

Notes:
1. Wh- questions include *do, does, did,* and other auxiliary verbs.
2. In a question about the object, *whom* is very formal. Informally, many people use *who.*
    FORMAL: **Whom** did your brother marry?
    INFORMAL: **Who** did your brother marry?

EXERCISE 17 Read each statement. Then write a *wh-* question with the words given.

1. The wedding will be in a church. (*where*)

   <u>Where will the wedding be?</u>

2. I bought a nice gift. (*what*)

___

3. The bride's brother lives in another state. (*where*)

___

4. I'm going to spend a lot of money. (*how much*)

___

114   Unit 4

5. I received an invitation. (*when*)

___

6. My brother needs to buy a new suit for the wedding. (*why*)

___

7. They didn't invite our children. (*why*)

___

EXERCISE 18 Read each statement. Then write a question with the words given. Some are subject questions, and some are *wh-* questions.

1. The bride wears a white dress. (*what/the groom*)

   What does the groom wear?

2. The bride enters last. (*who/first*)

   Who enters first?

3. The bride throws the bouquet. (*when*)

   ___

4. Some women try to catch the bouquet. (*which women*)

   ___

5. The bride chooses women for bridesmaids. (*which women*)

   ___

6. The band plays music. (*what kind of music*)

   ___

7. Someone dances with the bride. (*who*)

   ___

8. The guests give presents. (*what kind of presents*)

   ___

9. Some people cry at the wedding. (*who*)

   ___

10. The guests go to dinner after the ceremony. (*where/after the dinner*)

    ___

EXERCISE 19 Fill in the blanks to complete the questions in the conversation. Some are subject questions, and some are *wh-* questions. In some cases, more than one answer is possible.

A: How do you have time to work, go to school, and take care of a family?

B: I don't have to do everything myself.

A: Who ___helps you___ ?
1.

B: My husband helps me.

A: I usually cook in my house. Who _____ ?
2.

B: Sometimes my husband cooks; sometimes I cook. We take turns.

A: I usually clean. Who _____ ?
3.

B: I usually clean the house.

A: How many _____ ?
4.

B: I have five children.

A: How many _____ ?
5.

B: Three children go to school. The younger ones stay home.

A: Do you send them to public school or private school?

B: One of my sons goes to private school.

A: Which son _____ ?
6.

B: The oldest does. He's in high school now.

A: It's hard to take care of so many children. How do you find the time to go to class?

B: As I said, my husband helps me a lot. And sometimes I use a babysitter.

A: I'm looking for a sitter. Who _____ ?
7.

B: I recommend our neighbor, Sasha. She's sixteen years old, and she's very good with our children.

A: Maybe she's too busy to help me. How many families _____ ?
8.

B: I think she works for only one other family. I'll give you her phone number. If she's not busy, maybe she can work for you, too.

EXERCISE 20 Fill in the blanks with *who, whom, who's,* or *whose*.

1. _____Who's_____ that woman over there?

   That's my mother-in-law.

2. _____ did you invite to the wedding?

   I invited all my friends and relatives.

3. _____ took pictures?

   My brother did. He borrowed a camera because his is broken.

4. _____ camera did he borrow?

   He borrowed my aunt's camera. She has a fantastic camera.

5. _____ your aunt?

   She's that woman over there.

ABOUT YOU Find a partner. Use the questions to talk about weddings and marriages in your native culture and country.

1. Who pays for the wedding?
2. What happens at the wedding?
3. What happens after the wedding?
4. Do the guests bring gifts to the wedding?
5. What kind of gifts do they give?
6. Where do the bride and groom open the gifts?
7. How many people attend a wedding?
8. Where do people get married?
9. Do people dance at a wedding?
10. What color dress does the bride wear?
11. How long does a wedding last?
12. How do the bride and groom invite people? Do they send invitations?
13. Is there a shower before the wedding? Who hosts the shower? Who attends the shower?
14. Do the bride and groom send thank-you notes for the gifts?

SUMMARY OF UNIT 4

Possessive Forms and Pronouns

SUBJECT PRONOUN	OBJECT PRONOUN	POSSESSIVE ADJECTIVE	POSSESSIVE PRONOUN	REFLEXIVE PRONOUN
I	me	my	mine	myself
you	you	your	yours	yourself
he	him	his	his	himself
she	her	her	hers	herself
it	it	its	—	itself
we	us	our	ours	ourselves
you	you	your	yours	yourselves
they	them	their	theirs	themselves
who	whom	whose	whose	—

Order of Direct and Indirect Objects

EXAMPLE	EXPLANATION
I sent my grandmother the date. I sent her the date. I sent the date to my grandmother. I sent the date to her. I sent it to my grandmother. I sent it to her.	Some verbs have two possible word orders (*bring, give, send, show, tell, write*). Pronouns can affect the word order.
They announced their engagement to their parents. They announced it to them.	Some verbs have one possible word order (*announce, describe, explain, say, suggest*). Pronouns don't affect the word order.

Possessive Form of Nouns

SINGULAR NOUN	PLURAL NOUN	INANIMATE NOUN
the **bride's** dress my **father's** house the **child's** toy the **man's** hat **Charles's** wife **today's** topic	the **bridesmaids'** dresses my **parents'** house the **children's** toys the **men's** hats	the entrance of the building the name of the hotel

Questions

SUBJECT	WH-
Who **has** the rings? Which woman **wore** a red dress? How many people **came** to the wedding? What **happened** after the wedding? Who **will come** to the wedding?	Who(m) **do** you **know** at the wedding? Which women **did** you **meet**? How many people **did** they **invite**? What **did** they **serve** at the wedding? Who(m) **will** you **invite** to your wedding?

REVIEW

Circle the correct words to complete the conversation.

A: I know (**you**/*your*/*you're*) just got married. (*Tell*/*Say*/*Tell to*) me about (*you're*/*you*/*your*) wedding.
　　　　　　 1.　　　　　　　　　　　　　　　　2.　　　　　　　　　　　　3.

B: (*It's*/*It*/*Its*) was a small wedding. Sara wanted a big wedding, but a big wedding is so expensive.
　　　　4.

(*Hers*/*Her's*/*Her*) parents wanted to pay for (*it*/*its*/*it's*). (*Their*/*Their's*/*Theirs*) was a big wedding
　　5.　　　　　　　　　　　　　　　　　　　　6.　　　　　7.

because they have a big family. But we don't have a lot of money. We wanted to pay for it

(*ourself*/*ourselves*/*oneself*). We explained (*them the situation*/*the situation to them*/*the situation them*).
　　　　8.　　　　　　　　　　　　　　　　　　　　　　9.

We showed (*them our budget*/*to them our budget*/*our budget them*), and they didn't insist on a large
　　　　　　　　　　　　　　　　10.

wedding. We just invited (*our*/*ours*/*our's*) immediate families: parents, grandparents, sisters, brothers,
　　　　　　　　　　　　　　　11.

aunts, and uncles.

A: How many people (*did attend*/*attended*/*did attended*) the wedding?
　　　　　　　　　　　　　　　12.

B: Fifty. Unfortunately (*Sara's grandfather*/*grandfather Sara*/*grandfather of Sara*) didn't come.
　　　　　　　　　　　　　　　　　　　13.

A: Why not? What (*was happened*/*did happen*/*happened*) to (*him*/*his*/*he*)?
　　　　　　　　　　　　　14.　　　　　　　　　　　　　　15.

B: Nothing. (*His*/*Her*/*Her's*) grandfather lives in Peru. (*His*/*He*/*He's*) old and doesn't like to travel.
　　　　　　16.　　　　　　　　　　　　　　　　　　　17.

A: (*Your*/*You're*/*Yours*) grandparents are old, too, aren't they? Did they come?
　　　18.

B: Yes, they did. (*Mines*/*Mine*/*My*) live nearby.
　　　　　　　　　　19.

A: Where (*you got*/*you get*/*did you get*) married?
　　　　　　　　　20.

B: In a church. The (*name of the church*/*the church name*/*the church's name*) is St. John. We had a party
　　　　　　　　　　　　　　　21.

afterwards at (*my uncle's house*/*house my uncle*/*my uncle house*). (*He*/*He's*/*His*) house is big. We even
　　　　　　　　　　　　22.　　　　　　　　　　　　　　　　　　　23.

saved money on the wedding dress because Sara borrowed one.

A: (*Whose*/*Who's*/*Who*) dress (*did she borrow*/*she borrowed*/*borrowed she*)?
　　　24.　　　　　　　　　　25.

B: She borrowed her cousin's dress. We saved money on photos, too. My uncle took pictures, and he gave

(*them us*/*us them*/*them to us*) digitally. We printed (*they*/*them*/*its*) and made an album. We went to
　　　　　26.　　　　　　　　　　　　　　　　　　　　27.

Miami for our honeymoon. Sara's uncle has a home there. He let (*myself and Sara*/*Sara and me*/*Sara and I*)
　　　　　　　　　　　　　　　　　　　　　　　　　　　　　　　28.

use it. With the money we saved, we hope to buy a house soon.

A: (*You're*/*Your*/*You*) a wise man! When (*Lisa and I*/*me and Lisa*/*Lisa and me*) get married after we graduate,
　　　29.　　　　　　　　　　　　　　　　30.

I'd like to do the same thing. But I don't think Lisa will agree. She wants a big wedding.

B: Who (*know*/*does know*/*knows*)? Start to talk to (*hers*/*her*/*she*) about it now.
　　　　　　31.　　　　　　　　　　　　　　32.

FROM GRAMMAR TO WRITING

PART 1 Editing Advice

1. Don't confuse contractions with possessive forms.

   ~~Your~~ **You're** late for the wedding. ~~Its~~ **It's** almost 6 o'clock.

   ~~His~~ **He's** married. ~~He's~~ **His** wife is a doctor. ~~Their~~ **They're** from California.

2. Don't confuse *his* and *her*.

   My sister loves ~~his~~ **her** husband. My brother loves ~~her~~ **his** wife.

3. Be careful to choose the right pronoun in compound subjects and objects.

   ~~Me and my mother~~ **My mother and I** planned the wedding.

   My parents gave my husband and ~~I~~ **me** $500.

4. Don't use an apostrophe to make a plural form.

   They invited many ~~guest's~~ **guests** to the wedding.

5. Don't use an auxiliary verb in a subject question.

   Who ~~does~~ help**s** the bride?

6. Put the apostrophe after the *–s* of a plural noun that ends in *–s*.

   My ~~parent's~~ **parents'** house is too small for the wedding.

7. Don't use *–s* in a possessive adjective. (A possessive adjective has no plural form.)

   Their~~s~~ parents live in Canada.

8. Use the correct word order with direct and indirect objects.

   They explained ~~me their wedding customs~~ **their wedding customs to me**.

   Do you have the wedding present? Please give ~~them it~~ **it to them**.

9. Don't confuse *say* and *tell*.

   She ~~said~~ **told** me about her wedding.

PART 2 Editing Practice

Some of the shaded words and phrases have mistakes. Find the mistakes and correct them. If the shaded words are correct, write C.

Sometimes **we** (1. C) have an unrealistic view of marriage. We think that **its** (2. it's) all about love and nothing else. Some women especially think of the wedding as the **bride's** (3.) special day and don't think about the marriage that follows.

Me and my sister (4.) both wanted to get married. I got married when I was 27 years old. **My** (5.) husband was 30. We both had good careers. By the time I got married, many of my friends were already married. Some of **they** (6.) had small children.

120 Unit 4

My sister, Maya, got married right after high school. **Ours** **parents** wanted her to wait, but
                                                      7.   8.
she didn't want to. She was so in love with **his** boyfriend, Tony. My **parent's** were against it at
                                            9.   10.
first, and **Tony's** were, too, but they gave **to them** **permission** to get married. **Mine** sister wanted
           11.   12.   13.
to have a big wedding. But of course, Maya and Tony couldn't pay for it **themself**. Mom and Dad
                                                                         14.
said them they would pay for the wedding, but it would have to be small.
15.

Maya and Tony really loved each other, but **there** marriage didn't last more than three years.
                                            16.
What **went** wrong? Maya and Tony didn't understand **they're** responsibilities as a married couple.
     17.   18.
My parents told **to them** that marriage includes bills, laundry, and children, too. My father said,
                19.
"If **you're** going to stay in school, you have to budget not only **you're** money but **you** time, too." He
    20.   21.   22.
also warned **they**, "If you have kids while **you're** still in school, **their** going to need your attention.
            23.   24.   25.
Whose going to take care of them?" Tony and Maya soon had a baby girl.
26.

Maya wants to stay in school, but she can't. My mother can't help **her** because she works
                                                                   27.
full time. Tony loves **her** daughter. **His** a good father, and he works hard to support her, so he
                      28.   29.
can't finish college at this time. **Theirs** lives are so difficult now. I feel sorry for **them**. I'm happy
                                   30.   31.
my husband and me established **ourselves** as responsible adults before marriage.
32.   33.

If you compare **my sister and I**, you can see a big difference in our lives. Her life is very hard
                34.
as a single mother with no career. **Its** too bad my sister didn't listen to our **parent's** advice.
                                    35.   36.

> **WRITING TIP**
>
> When writing about differences between two things, it is important to use transition words to help connect ideas. Some examples are:
>
> | although | however | instead | in contrast | on the other hand | but | yet |
>
> Brides in the Unites States typically wear white wedding dresses. **In contrast**, brides in China often wear red.

PART 3 Write

Read the prompts. Choose one and write a paragraph about it.

1. How is a typical wedding in your native culture different from a typical American wedding?
2. What are some problems many married people have today?

PART 4 Edit

Read the Summary of Unit 4 and the editing advice. Edit your writing from Part 3.

UNIT
5

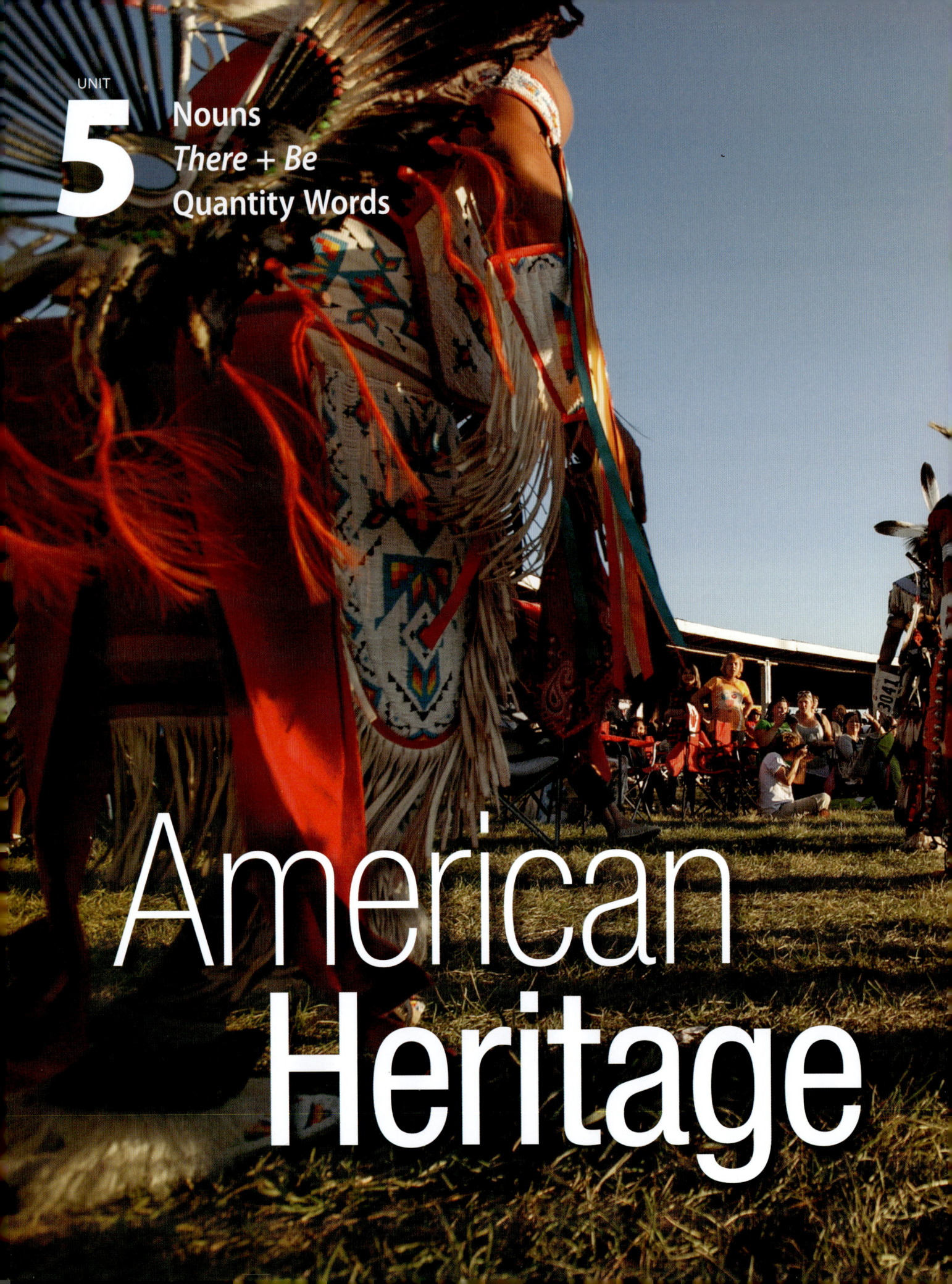

Nouns
There + Be
Quantity Words

American Heritage

Treat the Earth well: it was not given to you by your parents, it was loaned to you by your children. We do not inherit the Earth from our Ancestors, we borrow it from our Children.

ANCIENT AMERICAN INDIAN PROVERB

Dancers wear traditional clothing during the annual pow wow at the Crow Indian Reservation, Montana, U.S.

The Macy's Thanksgiving Day Parade in New York has been an annual event since 1924. Each year it draws millions of spectators.

THANKSGIVING

Read the following article. Pay special attention to the words in bold. 5.1

Thanksgiving is a very special American holiday. On the fourth Thursday in November, **Americans** come together with their **families** and **friends** to share a special meal and give **thanks** for all the good **things** in their **lives**. Typical **foods** on Thanksgiving are turkey, sweet **potatoes**, mashed **potatoes** and gravy, stuffing, cranberry sauce, **green beans**, and pumpkin pie for dessert.

What is the origin of this great day? In 1620, a group of **Pilgrims** left England and came to America in search of religious freedom. There were 120 of them: **men**, **women**, and **children**. They started their new life in a deserted[1] American Indian village in what is now the state of Massachusetts. But half of them did not survive their first cold, hard winter. In the spring, two American **Indians**[2] found the **people** from England in very bad condition. They didn't have enough food, and they were in bad health. Squanto, an English-speaking American Indian, stayed with them for several **months** and taught them how to survive in this new land. He brought them deer meat and animal **skins**; he showed them how to grow corn and other **vegetables**; he showed them how to use **plants** as medicine; he explained how to use **fish** for fertilizer[3]—he taught them many **skills** for survival in their new land. By the time their second fall arrived, the **Pilgrims** had enough food to get through their second winter. They were in better health. They decided to have a Thanksgiving feast[4] to celebrate their good fortune[5]. They invited Squanto and neighboring Indian **families** of the Wampanoag tribe to come to their dinner. The **Pilgrims** were surprised when 90 **Indians** showed up. The **Pilgrims** did not have enough food for so many **people**. Fortunately, the Indian chief sent some of his **people** to bring food to the celebration. They brought **deer**, **fish**, **beans**, squash, cornbread, **berries**, and wild **turkeys**. The feast lasted for three **days**. This was a short time of peace and friendship between the **Indians** and the **Pilgrims**.

Now on Thanksgiving, Americans eat some of the traditional **foods** from this period in American history.

---

[1] deserted: empty of people
[2] American Indians: the native people of America; American Indians are sometimes called Native Americans.
[3] fertilizer: something put into the earth to help plants grow
[4] feast: a large meal
[5] fortune: luck

COMPREHENSION Based on the reading, write T for *true* or F for *false*.

1. _____ American Indians helped the Pilgrims through their first winter in America.
2. _____ Squanto helped the Pilgrims learn about their new land.
3. _____ The Pilgrims invited 90 American Indians for a feast of Thanksgiving.

THINK ABOUT IT Discuss the questions with a partner or in a small group.

1. Reread the last line of the second paragraph. Why do you think there was a short time of peace between the Indians and Pilgrims? What do you think happened afterwards?
2. On Thanksgiving, Americans give thanks for all the good things in their lives. What things in your life are you thankful for?

5.1 Noun Plurals—Form

We use the plural to talk about more than one. To make regular noun plurals, we add -s or -es.

REGULAR NOUN PLURALS

WORD ENDING	EXAMPLE NOUN	PLURAL ADDITION	PLURAL FORM	PRONUNCIATION
Vowel	bee banana	+ s	bees bananas	/z/
ch sh x s	church dish box class	+ es	churches dishes boxes classes	/əz/
Voiceless consonants	snack month	+ s	snacks months	/s/
Voiced consonants	card pin	+ s	cards pins	/z/
Vowel + y	boy day	+ s	boys days	/z/
Consonant + y	lady story	~~y~~ + ies	ladies stories	/z/
Vowel + o	video radio	+ s	videos radios	/z/
Consonant + o	potato hero	+ es	potatoes heroes	/z/
Exceptions: altos, autos, avocados, photos, pianos, solos, sopranos, tuxedos					
f or fe	leaf knife	~~f~~ + ves	leaves knives	/z/
Exceptions: beliefs, chefs, chiefs, cliffs, roofs, sherriffs					

continued

IRREGULAR NOUN PLURALS			
SINGULAR	PLURAL	EXAMPLES	EXPLANATION
man woman tooth foot goose	men women teeth feet geese	The **women** cooked the dinner. The **men** washed the dishes.	Vowel change
sheep fish deer	sheep fish deer	There are many **fish** in the lake.	No change in word
child mouse person	children mice people	The **children** set the table. We invited a lot of **people** to dinner.	Different word form

Notes:
1. The plural of *person* can also be *persons*, but *people* is more common.
2. The pronunciation of *woman* is /ˈwʊ-mən/. The pronunciation of *women* is /ˈwɪ-mən/. We hear the difference between singular and plural in the first syllable.

EXERCISE 1 Fill in the blanks with the words you hear. 5.2

1. _____Airports_____ are often crowded right before Thanksgiving.

2. _____ want to get home to their _____.

3. On Thanksgiving, people eat a very big _____.

4. Before the big dinner, they often eat _____, such as _____ and potato _____, while waiting for other _____ to arrive.

5. The Thanksgiving meal usually includes turkey and sweet _____.

6. The typical Thanksgiving meal contains more than 3,000 _____.

7. Many _____ have a parade on Thanksgiving morning. _____ of people go to see the parade.

8. _____ like to watch the parade.

9. After the meal, it is a typical _____ to watch professional football on TV.

10. Some _____ play a friendly game of football before or after the big meal.

126 Unit 5

EXERCISE 2 Write the plural form of each noun. If the plural ends in -s or -es, indicate if the pronunciation is /s/, /z/, or /əz/. If not, write Ø.

1. hour — hours — /z/
2. turkey
3. cranberry
4. potato
5. child
6. family
7. guest
8. ship
9. man
10. woman
11. apple
12. peach
13. spice
14. pie
15. knife
16. deer
17. watch
18. tax
19. pot
20. goose
21. dish
22. month
23. life
24. plant

EXERCISE 3 Fill in the blanks with the plural form of the words.

A: Who prepares the Thanksgiving meal in your family?

B: As usual, the ___women___ in my family do most of the cooking. But the _____
   1. woman   2. man

help, too. My husband usually makes the mashed _____ and gravy. I always prepare the
                                                3. potato

turkey and stuffing. Even the _____ help. Last year, my son and daughter made the
                              4. child

cranberry sauce.

A: Did they use fresh _____ ?
                         5. cranberry

B: Yes, they did. They just boiled them with sugar and added fruit.

A: What kind of fruit did they use?

B: They used _____ .
              6. apple

A: What do you make for dessert?

continued

Nouns, *There + Be*, Quantity Words **127**

B: I don't make the dessert. I always invite my next-door _____. They bring several
7. neighbor

_____. They buy them at a bakery.
8. pie

A: It's nice when all the _____ help with the preparation.
9. guest

B: I agree. I love Thanksgiving. The only thing I don't like is washing the _____ afterwards.
10. dish

A: Same here. After all that cooking, I like to put my _____ up and relax by watching the
11. foot

football game.

5.2 Using the Plural for Generalizations

EXAMPLES	EXPLANATION
Football games last about three hours. **Sweet potatoes** are nutritious.	We can use the plural to make a generalization. We don't use the article *the* to make a generalization.

ABOUT YOU Make a generalization about the following nouns. Talk about holiday traditions in your country or native culture. You may talk about family members, schools, businesses, etc. Discuss your answers with a partner.

1. children *For Chinese New Year, children get money in red envelopes.*

2. men _____

3. women _____

4. games _____

5. grandparents _____

6. stores _____

7. schools _____

8. people _____

9. food _____

10. soccer games _____

128 Unit 5

5.3 Special Cases of Singular and Plural

EXAMPLES	EXPLANATION
The U.S. has more than 320 **million** people. **Millions** of people go shopping the day after Thanksgiving. My grandfather is in his **seventies**. He was born in the **1940s**.	We use the singular form for exact numbers. We use the plural form for inexact numbers. We use the plural form for an approximate age or year.
One of my **neighbors** brought a pie to our Thanksgiving dinner. One of the **men** helped with the dishes.	We use the plural form after the expression: *one of* (*the, my, his, her,* etc.).
Every **guest** brought something. Each **person** helped. We washed all the **dishes**.	We use a singular noun after *every* and *each*. We use a plural noun after *all*.
After dinner, the kids put on their **pajamas** and went to bed. We're wearing our best **clothes** today.	Some words have no singular form: *pajamas, clothes, pants, slacks, (eye)glasses, scissors*.
Let's watch the **news**. It's on after dinner. Let's not discuss **politics** during dinner. It's not a good subject.	Even though *news* and *politics* end in *-s*, they are singular.

EXERCISE 4 Fill in the blanks with the correct form of the word given.

1. Five ____**men**____ watched the football game.
   _{man}

2. One of the _____ helped make the cranberry sauce.
   _{child}

3. Each _____ gave a presentation to the class.
   _{student}

4. Ten _____ people pass through the airports before Thanksgiving.
   _{million}

5. _____ of people travel for Thanksgiving.
   _{million}

6. Every _____ stayed to watch the game.
   _{guest}

7. Thanksgiving is one of my favorite _____.
   _{holiday}

8. _____ of people saw the parade.
   _{thousand}

9. My grandmother came for Thanksgiving. She's in her _____.
   _{eighty}

10. The children should go to bed. Their _____ are on the bed.
    _{pajama}

11. English people started to come to America in the sixteen _____.
    _{hundred}

12. One _____ twenty Pilgrims came in 1620.
    _{hundred}

Nouns, *There + Be*, Quantity Words 129

Cranberry SAUCE

Read the following article. Pay special attention to the words in bold.
🎧 5.3

Cranberries are **a** very American **fruit**. They grow in the cooler **regions** of northeastern North America and are ready for harvest[1] in the fall. We see cranberry **juice** all year, but **packages** of fresh **cranberries** appear in **supermarkets** just before Thanksgiving.

American **Indians** introduced **cranberries** to the **Pilgrims** in 1621. The **Indians** used **cranberries** as **a food** and for different kinds of **medicines**. They also made **tea** from **cranberries** and used it to add color to their **jewelry**.

Cranberries are very sour, so a recipe for cranberry sauce uses **a lot of sugar** or **honey**. You prepare cranberry sauce by boiling **water** with **sugar** and then adding the **cranberries**. You continue cooking them until the **skins** pop[2] open. Before serving, you cool the mixture in the refrigerator. Some people add **pieces of fruit**, such as **apples** or **pears**, to the **cranberries**. Some people sprinkle chopped **walnuts** on top. This is the perfect side dish to go with **helpings of turkey**.

[1] harvest: a time for picking or gathering crops
[2] to pop: to break, burst

The Native American Superfood

Cranberries, **blueberries**, and Concord **grapes** are the three cultivated **fruits** that are native to North America. **Cranberries** in particular have **many** health **benefits**.

- **Cranberries** have **a lot of** fiber and **antioxidants**.
- **A glass of** cranberry **juice** may have up to a day's worth of Vitamin C.
- The **fruit** doesn't have **much sugar** or **many calories**. (**A cup of cranberries** has only 1 **teaspoon of** natural **sugar** and just 46 **calories**.)
- The **berries** are good for heart **health**.

130 Unit 5

COMPREHENSION Based on the reading, write T for *true* or F for *false*.

1. _____ Cranberries grow in all parts of the United States.
2. _____ The Indians used cranberries for medicine.
3. _____ The Pilgrims learned about cranberries from the American Indians.

THINK ABOUT IT Discuss the questions with a partner or in a small group.

1. What is a typical fruit in your country? How do people eat it?
2. Describe your favorite recipe that has fruits from your country. How is the dish made? When do you eat it?

5.4 Count and Noncount Nouns

A count noun is something we can count. It has a singular and plural form. A noncount noun has just one form.

EXAMPLES	EXPLANATION
We used one **apple** in the recipe. We used two **pears** in the recipe.	We use a count noun in the singular form or plural form. We can put *a, an*, or a number before a count noun.
Boil **water** and add **sugar**.	We use a noncount noun in the singular form only. We don't put *a, an*, or a number before a noncount noun.

There are several types of noncount nouns.

GROUP A: NOUNS THAT HAVE NO DISTINCT, SEPARATE PARTS. WE LOOK AT THE WHOLE.

milk	coffee	yogurt	soup	butter	lightning
oil	tea	beef	bread	paper	thunder
water	juice	honey	meat	air	blood

GROUP B: NOUNS THAT HAVE PARTS THAT ARE TOO SMALL OR INSIGNIFICANT TO COUNT.

| rice | hair | sand | salt |
| sugar | popcorn | grass | snow |

GROUP C: NOUNS THAT ARE CLASSES OR CATEGORIES OF THINGS. THE MEMBERS OF THE CATEGORY ARE NOT THE SAME.

money or cash (nickels, dimes, dollars)	mail (letters, packages, postcards, flyers)
furniture (chairs, tables, beds)	homework (essays, exercises, readings)
clothing (sweaters, pants, dresses)	jewelry (necklaces, bracelets, rings)
fruit (apples, peaches, pears)	produce (oranges, apples, corn)

GROUP D: NOUNS THAT ARE ABSTRACTIONS.

love	happiness	nutrition	patience	work	nature
truth	education	intelligence	poverty	health	help
beauty	advice	(un)employment	music	fun	energy
luck/fortune	knowledge	pollution	art	information	friendship

GROUP E: SOME FRUITS AND VEGETABLES ARE USUALLY NONCOUNT NOUNS.

| broccoli | celery | lettuce | kale | asparagus | spinach |
| corn | squash | cauliflower | grapefruit | cabbage | celery |

Note:

Count and *noncount* are grammatical terms, but they are not always logical. *Rice* and *beans* are both very small, but *rice* is a noncount noun and *bean* is a count noun.

EXERCISE 5 Fill in the blanks with a noncount noun from the box.

advice	snow	freedom✓	friendship
health	work	corn	honey

1. The Pilgrims wanted to find ____freedom____ in America.

2. They had poor _____ during their first winter in America.

3. The American Indians gave the Pilgrims a lot of _____ about how to grow food.

4. Squanto taught them to plant _____.

5. The first winter was hard. It was cold, and there was a lot of _____.

6. Learning American agriculture was hard _____ for the Pilgrims.

7. In the beginning, there was _____ between the Pilgrims and the American Indians.

8. Cranberries are very sour, so the Indians added _____.

5.5 Nouns That Can Be Both Count and Noncount

EXAMPLES	EXPLANATION
(NC) **Life** in America was difficult. (C) The Pilgrims had difficult **lives**. (NC) The Pilgrims had a lot of **trouble** their first winter. (C) The American Indians' **troubles** began when the Europeans arrived. (NC) I like to spend **time** with my family on the holidays. (C) My neighbors invited me for dinner many **times**. (NC) American Indians had **experience** with American winters. (C) The first winter for the Pilgrims was **a** bad **experience**.	The meaning or use of a noun determines whether it is count (C) or noncount (NC).
We put some **fruit** in the cranberry sauce. We prepare a lot of **food** for Thanksgiving.	When we talk about fruit or food in general, these words are noncount nouns.
Oranges and lemons are citrus **fruits**. American Indians used cranberries as **a food** and as a dye.	When we are referring to kinds or categories of food or fruit, these words are count nouns.
We ate some **pie** for dessert. We eat **turkey** on Thanksgiving.	When a noun refers to a part of the whole, it is a noncount noun.
My friend brought three **pies** to the Thanksgiving dinner. One **turkey** is enough for the whole family.	When a noun refers to the whole, it is a count noun.

EXERCISE 6 Decide if each noun given is count or noncount. If it is a count noun, change it to the plural form. If it is a noncount noun, do not change it.

1. The _____Pilgrims_____ wanted _____freedom_____.
     a. Pilgrim   b. freedom
2. American Indians have a lot of respect for _____.
                                              a. nature
3. They love _____, _____, and _____.
              a. tree   b. bird   c. fish
4. Thanksgiving is a celebration of _____ and _____.
                                     a. peace   b. friendship
5. On Thanksgiving, Americans eat a lot of _____.
                                            a. food
6. Americans sometimes eat _____ for dessert.
                           a. pie
7. Squanto gave the Pilgrims a lot of _____ about planting _____ and other
                                      a. advice   b. corn
   _____. He had a lot of _____ about the land.
   c. vegetable   d. knowledge
8. The Pilgrims didn't have any _____ with American agriculture.
                                a. experience
9. On the first Thanksgiving, American Indians brought _____, _____,
                                                       a. meat   b. bean
   _____, and _____.
   c. bread   d. berry
10. The Pilgrims celebrated because they had a lot of good _____.
                                                           a. fortune
11. American Indians use _____ for _____.
                         a. plant   b. medicine
12. I would like more _____ about American _____.
                      a. information   b. holiday

5.6 Units of Measure with Noncount Nouns

We don't usually put a number before a noncount noun. We use a unit of measure, which we can count—for example, two *cloves* of garlic.

BY CONTAINER	BY PORTION	BY MEASUREMENT	BY SHAPE OR WHOLE PIECE	OTHER
a bottle of water a carton of milk a jar of pickles a bag of flour a can of soda (pop) a cup of coffee a glass of water a bowl of soup a tube of toothpaste	a slice (piece) of bread a piece of meat a piece of cake a strip of bacon a slice of pizza a piece of candy	an ounce of sugar a teaspoon of salt a cup of oil a pound of meat a gallon of milk a pint of cream a scoop of ice cream a pinch of salt	a loaf of bread an ear of corn a piece of fruit a head of lettuce a bar of soap a clove of garlic a stalk of celery a candy bar a stick of butter	a piece of mail a piece of furniture a piece of advice a piece of information a work of art a homework assignment a piece (sheet) of paper

Note:
We can use *a helping of* or *a serving of* for almost any food.
   How many **helpings/servings of turkey** did you have?

EXERCISE 7 Listen to this list of ingredients for stuffing. Fill in the blanks with the unit of measure for each ingredient. 5.4

1. A half _____cup_____ of chopped onions

2. One _____ of butter

3. Two _____ of garlic

4. Three _____ of celery, chopped

5. Four _____ of dry bread, cut into cubes

6. One quarter _____ of salt

7. One _____ of dry parsley

8. One _____ of hot chicken broth

EXERCISE 8 Fill in the blanks with a specific quantity or unit of measure + *of*. Answers may vary.

1. We bought three ___loaves of___ bread for Thanksgiving.

2. Would you like a _____ water with dinner? There's a pitcher on the table. Help yourself.

3. You'll need a _____ butter to make the stuffing.

4. How many _____ garlic are in the stuffing?

5. After dinner, we served a _____ coffee to each guest.

6. Most guests ate a _____ pie after dinner.

7. Can I have your recipe for cranberry sauce? I need a pencil and a _____ paper to write it down.

8. Would you like a _____ fruit after dinner? How about an apple or a tangerine?

9. I bought two _____ lettuce to make a salad.

10. Let me give you a _____ advice about Thanksgiving: There's a lot of food. Try to eat just a little of everything. If you eat too much, you won't feel good afterwards.

ABOUT YOU Find a partner. Talk about the food you eat on a holiday or special day. Describe the ingredients using specific quantities or units of measure.

5.7 A Lot Of, Much, Many

Notice which quantity words go with count (C) and noncount (NC) nouns.

	EXAMPLES	EXPLANATION
Affirmative	(C) You need **a lot of cranberries** for this recipe. (NC) We use **a lot of sugar** to make cranberry sauce.	We can use *a lot of* with both count and noncount nouns in affirmative statements.

Affirmative	(C) I am thankful for **many things**.
	(NC) We eat **a lot of food** on Thanksgiving.
		In affirmative statements, we use:
		   many with count nouns.
		   a lot of with noncount nouns.
		Much is rare in affirmative statements.

Negative	(C) The Pilgrims didn't have **many skills** in American agriculture.
	(NC) Today American Indians don't have **much land**.
		In negative statements, we use:
		   many with count nouns.
		   much with noncount nouns.

Negative	(C) The Pilgrims didn't have **a lot of skills** in American agriculture. (NC) Today American Indians don't have **a lot of land**.	We can use *a lot of* with both count and noncount nouns in negative statements.

Question	(C) Did you invite **many people** for dinner?
	(NC) Did you eat **much turkey**?
		In questions, we use:
		   many with count nouns.
		   much with noncount nouns.

Question	(C) Did you invite **a lot of guests** for Thanksgiving? (NC) Did you eat **a lot of turkey**?	We can use *a lot of* with both count and noncount nouns in questions.

Question	(C) **How many hours** did you cook the turkey?
	(NC) **How much time** did you spend on food preparation?
		In questions, we use:
		   how many with count nouns.
		   how much with noncount nouns.

Note:
With a quantity word, we can sometimes omit (leave out) the noun when we know what the noun is.
   *I usually drink **a lot of water**, but I didn't drink **a lot** today.* (We know that *a lot* refers to *water*.)

GRAMMAR IN USE

We use quantity words often in speaking and in writing, so it's a good idea to recognize which one to use in different situations. Notice how these words express different levels of formality.

FORMAL:	many, much	We're having **many** problems at work.
LESS FORMAL:	a lot of	We're having **a lot of** problems at work.
LEAST FORMAL:	lots of	We're having **lots of** problems at work.

EXERCISE 9 Circle the correct words to complete this conversation. In some cases, more than one answer is correct. If so, circle both options.

A: Did you prepare (*a lot of*/*many*) food for Thanksgiving?
   1.

B: No, I didn't prepare (*a lot*/*a lot of*). This year I didn't invite (*much*/*many*) people. I just invited my
   2.   3.
immediate family.

A: How (*much*/*many*) people are there in your immediate family?
   4.

B: Just seven. I bought a 12-pound turkey. It was more than enough.

A: I don't know how to prepare a turkey. Is it (*a lot of*/*many*) work?
   5.

B: Not really. But if it's frozen, it takes (*a lot of*/*much*) time to defrost it. Cooking it is easy.
   6.

A: Did you make (*many*/*a lot of*) other dishes, like sweet potatoes and cranberry sauce?
   7.

B: No. Each person in my family made something. That way, I didn't have (*much*/*a lot of*) work. But we had
   8.
(*many*/*a lot of*) work cleaning up.
   9.

A: Have you thought about using paper plates? That way, you won't have (*many*/*much*) work cleaning up.
   10.

B: I know (*many*/*much*) people do that, but I want my dinner to look elegant. For me, paper plates are for
   11.
picnics.

A: That's true. Also paper plates aren't very environmentally friendly. It's better to have (*a lot*/*a lot of*) dishes
   12.
to clean, especially with (*a lot*/*a lot of*) people to help.
   13.

B: Right! With help, it wasn't too (*much*/*many*) work.
   14.

FUN WITH GRAMMAR

Play a game with units of measure. Form two or three teams. Your teacher will say a noncount noun and one team member will go to the board and write the noun with a unit of measure (e.g., *water—a glass of water; art—a work of art*). For each correct answer, the team earns a point. Every student has a turn. The team with the most points wins.

This map shows a land bridge between Asia and North America that humans crossed thousands of years ago.

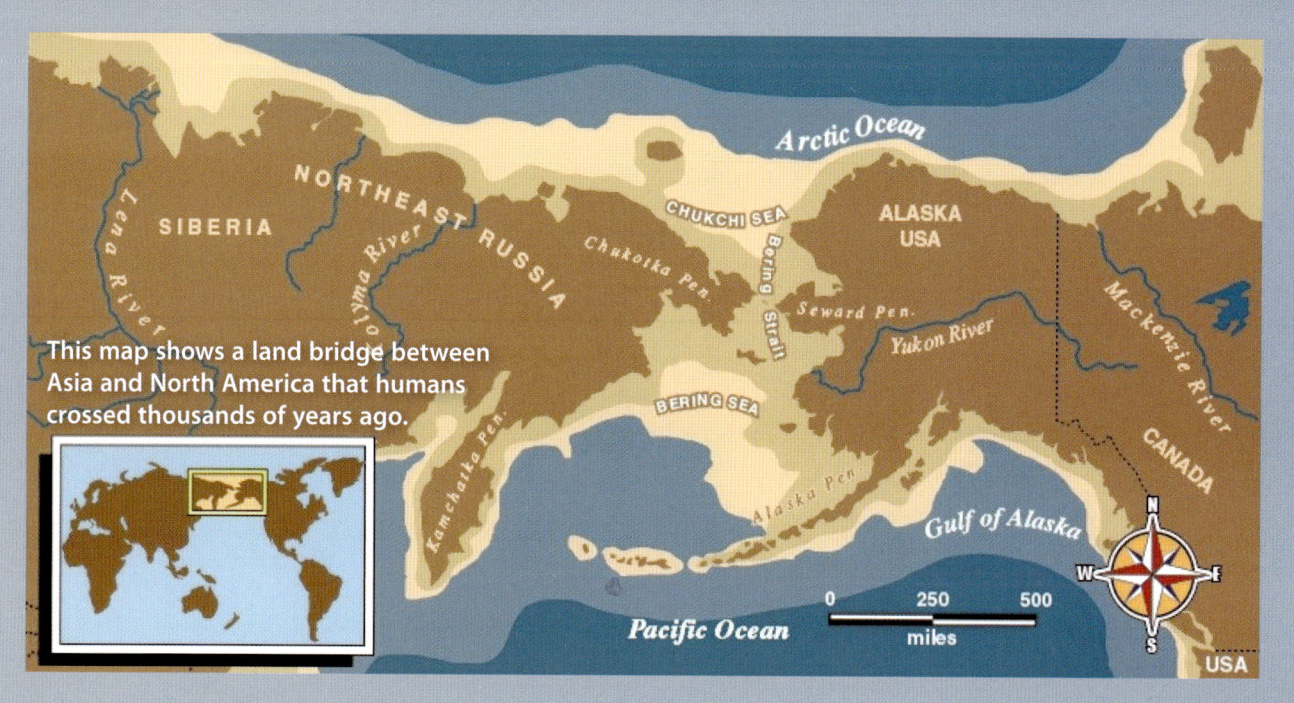

The First Americans

Read the following article. Pay special attention to the words in bold. 5.5

Who were the first Americans? Long before Europeans came to America starting about 500 years ago, Indians lived in the Americas. We refer to these people as American Indians. Where did these people come from, and how did they get here?

Thousands of years ago, **there was** a land bridge connecting Eastern Siberia to Alaska. For many years, scientists believed that Siberians crossed this bridge about 16,000 years ago and spread out over the Americas.

In 1968, the skeleton of a young boy was found in Montana. Recently scientists tested the DNA[1] of this child's bones and learned that he lived 12,600 years ago. Scientists refer to his ancient Indian culture as Clovis culture, and to the boy as Clovis Boy. **Is there** a connection between Clovis Boy and Siberians? Definitely. Scientists compared the DNA from Clovis Boy with the DNA of a 24,000-year-old Siberian boy, and **there is** enough genetic[2] evidence to show that Clovis Boy's ancestors were from Siberia.

But even more interesting is this: **There is** a genetic connection between Clovis Boy and about 80 percent of native North and South Americans today.

There were many tools and other objects buried with the boy. At that time, **there were** large mammals, such as mastodons, mammoths, horses, and camels in America. These early Americans used the tools to hunt these animals. These animals became extinct[3] in America, maybe because the Clovis people over-hunted[4].

Even though **there was** a lot to learn from this boy's bones, American Indians wanted to make sure that he was buried again. They saw him as a connection to their ancestors. Shane Doyle, a member of the Crow tribe of Montana, was satisfied to find the connection of his people to Clovis Boy. But, says Doyle, "now it is time to put him back to rest again." Clovis Boy was buried again in June of 2014 in a tribal ceremony. The tools from the first burial are at the Montana Historical Society in Helena, Montana.

[1] DNA: the genetic information in cells
[2] genetic: related to the traits that are transmitted from parents to offspring
[3] extinct: no longer in existence
[4] to over-hunt: to hunt and kill too many of an animal

Stone tools found with Clovis Boy

COMPREHENSION Based on the reading, write T for *true* or F for *false*.

1. _____ Most American Indians came to America from Siberia.
2. _____ Clovis Boy is about 24,000 years old.
3. _____ Most of today's American Indians are genetically connected to Clovis Boy.

THINK ABOUT IT Discuss the questions with a partner or in a small group.

1. Look at the map on the previous page. Reread the second paragraph and discuss with a partner how people might have arrived at the Clovis Boy site in Montana.
2. Look at the photograph of Clovis tools. How do you think Clovis people used the tools?

5.8 There + a Form of *Be*

We use *there* + a form of *be* to introduce a subject into the conversation.

EXAMPLES	EXPLANATION
There is a connection between Clovis Boy and today's American Indians. **There was peace** between the American Indians and the Pilgrims at first.	We use *there is/was* to introduce a singular noun.
There are American Indian tribes in Montana. **There were Indians** in America before Europeans.	We use *there are/were* to introduce a plural noun.
Were there any tools with Clovis Boy? Yes, **there were**.	For *yes/no* questions, we put *be* before *there*. For an affirmative short answer, we use: Yes, + *there* + form of *be*.
Were there other people with Clovis Boy? No, **there weren't**.	For a negative short answer, we use: No, + *there* + form of *be* + *not*.
How many tools **were there** with him? **There were** more than 100. How much time **is there** between now and Thanksgiving? **There are** about 28 days.	We often use *how many/how much* to ask a question with *there*. We put *be* before *there*.

Notes:
1. We can make a contraction with *there is*: *there's*. We don't make a contraction with *there are*.
2. If two nouns follow *there*, we use a singular verb if the first noun is singular. We use a plural verb if the first noun is plural.
   *There **was** a skeleton and tools at the burial site.*   *There **were** tools and a skeleton at the burial site.*
3. After we introduce a noun with *there*, we can use a pronoun (*they, it, she*, etc.) in place of the noun.
   *There is **information** in Clovis Boy's DNA.*   ***It's** very important to scientists.*
   *There were **tools** with Clovis Boy.*   ***They** give us information about his life.*
4. For the future, we use *there* + *will be*.
   *There **will be** a documentary about American Indians next week.*
   ***Will there be** a discussion after the movie? Yes, **there will**.*
5. In *How many* questions with a location, we sometimes omit *there*.
   How many tools were (there) at the Clovis Boy site?

138 Unit 5

EXERCISE 10 Listen to the conversation. Then write T for *true* or F for *false*. 🎧 5.6

1. _____ There are about 12 million American Indians in the United States today.
2. _____ The friendship and peace between Pilgrims and Indians during the first Thanksgiving did not last.
3. _____ American Indians didn't want to speak their own language when they moved to reservations.

EXERCISE 11 Listen again. Fill in the blanks with words you hear. 🎧 5.6

A: How many American Indians ___are there___ in the United States today?
              1.

B: _____ about five million. But before the arrival of Europeans, _____
      2.   3.
many more.

A: How many _____?
              4.

B: _____ at least 12 million. Some historians think _____ up to
      5.   6.
18 million.

A: In this unit, _____ an article about the first Thanksgiving. _____ a
                  7.   8.
beautiful story about peace. It says _____ friendship between the Pilgrims and the
                                         9.
American Indians.

B: Unfortunately, _____ didn't last. As more English people came to America,
                      10.
_____ started to take the land away from the Indians. In 1830, President Andrew Jackson
    11.
sent American Indians away from their lands. They had to live on reservations.

A: What's a reservation?

B: _____ land given to the American Indians. American Indian children had to learn
      12.
English. Often _____ weren't allowed to speak their own language. As a result,
                   13.
_____ very few American Indians today who speak the language of their ancestors.
    14.

A: How many reservations _____ in the United States today?
                             15.

B: _____ about 300.
      16.

Nouns, *There* + *Be*, Quantity Words   **139**

EXERCISE 12 Fill in the blanks to complete each conversation. Use *there, is, are, was, were, it, they, not,* or a combination of these words. Use contractions wherever possible.

1. **A:** What's Siberia?

    B: _____It's_____ a region of Russia.

a.

    A: How did people go from Siberia to Alaska thousands of years ago?

    B: Today _____ water between these two places. But thousands of years ago, there

b.

    _____ a land connection.

c.

2. **A:** Where's Montana?

    B: _____ in the northwest of the United States.

a.

    A: _____ any reservations in Montana?

b.

    B: Yes, there _____ .

c.

3. **A:** How many tribes _____ in the U.S. today?

a.

    B: There _____ about 560 tribes in the U.S. today. Some, like the Navajo tribe in the

b.

    Southwest, are very big.

    A: How many people _____ in the Navajo tribe?

c.

    B: There are about 300,000 members.

4. **A:** _____ a very small tribe in California. It's the Cahuilla tribe.

a.

    B: How many members does _____ have?

b.

    A: In 2010, _____ had only eleven members.

c.

5. **A:** _____ a reservation in every state?

a.

    B: No, there _____ .

b.

    A: _____ any reservations in Illinois?

c.

    B: No, there _____ .

d.

6. **A:** Less than half of today's American Indians live on reservations.

    B: Why?

    A: _____ a lot of unemployment on many reservations. When American Indians

a.

    need jobs, _____ sometimes go to big cities.

b.

7. **A:** Did Europeans kill Indians?

    B: Yes, _____ did. Also, there _____ many deaths from diseases that

a.   b.

    Europeans brought to America.

5.9 Some, Any, A, No

Compare words used with count nouns (C) and noncount nouns (NC).

	EXAMPLES	EXPLANATION
Affirmative	(C) There is **a** big **reservation** in the Southwest.	We use *a* or *an* with singular count nouns.
	(C) I put **some apples** in the cranberry sauce. (NC) I put **some orange juice** in the cranberry sauce.	We use *some* with both plural count nouns and noncount nouns.
Negative	(C) There are**n't any** American Indian **reservations** in Illinois. (C) There are **no** American Indian **reservations** in Illinois. (NC) There is**n't any information** about Clovis Boy's family. (NC) There is **no information** about Clovis Boy's family.	We use *not any* or *no* with both plural count nouns and noncount nouns.
Question	(C) Are there **any nuts** in the cranberry sauce? (NC) Is there **any honey** in the cranberry sauce?	We use *any* with both plural count nouns and noncount nouns.

Notes:

1. You will sometimes see *any* with a singular count noun.

    *Which tribe should I write about? You can write about **any** tribe.*

    Any, in this case, means "whichever you want." It doesn't matter which tribe.

2. Don't use a double negative.

    I don't have any information. (NOT: *I don't have no information.*)

EXERCISE 13 Fill in the blanks with *some, any, a, an,* or *no*.

1. **A:** There were _____some_____ bones near Clovis Boy.
   a.

   B: Were there _____any_____ tools with him?
   b.

2. **A:** Can you name _____ American Indian tribes?
   a.

   B: Yes, I can name _____ tribes: the Navajo and the Crow.
   b.

   A: Are there _____ Navajos in the Southwest today?
   c.

   B: Yes, there are. There's _____ big Navajo reservation in the Southwest.
   d.

3. **A:** I don't use sugar, so there's _____ sugar in this cranberry sauce.
   a.

   B: Is there _____ honey?
   b.

   A: Yes, there is. There's _____ fruit juice in it, too. And there are _____
   c.   d.
   pieces of apple, too.

Navajo Code Talkers

Read the following article. Pay special attention to the words in bold. 5.7

American Indian languages are very complicated. There are many different languages, and each one has **several** dialects[1]. One of these languages is the Navajo language. **Very few** non-Navajos can speak or understand it. One exception was Philip Johnston. Johnston was not an American Indian, but he grew up on the Navajo reservation and spoke the language fluently.

In World War II, the United States was at war with Japan. The Japanese were very skillful at breaking codes[2]. They got **too much** classified[3] information. The military needed a better solution. Johnston had an idea: to use Navajo Indians to create a code in their language.

In 1942, Johnston met with **several** American military men and explained his idea. At first, they weren't interested. Then Johnston met with Major James E. Jones of the Marines and spoke **a few** Navajo words to him. He convinced the major to give his idea a try.

The Marines recruited[4] 29 speakers of Navajo to create a code based on their language. There were only **a few** military words in the Navajo language, so the Navajos had to develop **a lot of** words for these things. For example, a commanding general was a "war chief," a battleship was a "whale," and a submarine was an "iron fish."

In the first two days of code talking, more than 800 messages were sent without any errors. About 400 Navajos participated in the code program. During and after the war, they got **little** recognition for their great help in World War II. **Too many** years went by before they were finally honored for their service. It wasn't until 1992 that the U.S. government honored the Navajo code talkers for their help in winning major battles of the war.

---

[1] dialect: a regional variety of language
[2] code: a system of hiding the real meaning of a message
[3] classified: secret; only meant to be seen by authorized people
[4] to recruit: to look for and choose people to join the military

A parade in Monument Valley, Arizona, U.S.

COMPREHENSION Based on the reading, write T for *true* or F for *false*.

1. _____ Philip Johnston learned the Navajo language as a child.
2. _____ The Navajo language had many military words.
3. _____ About 800 Navajos learned to use the code.

THINK ABOUT IT Discuss the questions with a partner or in a small group.

1. Why do you think that at first, the military men were not interested in Johnston's idea to create code using the Navajo language?
2. Why do you think the Navajo code would be difficult to break?

5.10 *A Few, Several, A Little*

	EXAMPLES	EXPLANATION
Count	Johnston spoke **a few words** of Navajo to Major Jones. The Navajo language has **several dialects**.	Use *a few* or *several* with count nouns.
Noncount	Johnston needed **a little time** to convince the major.	Use *a little* with noncount nouns.

EXERCISE 14 Choose the correct words to complete these sentences.

1. (*A few*/*A little*) American Indians came to help the Pilgrims in 1621.
2. They taught the Pilgrims (*a few/a little*) new skills for planting.
3. We read (*a little/several*) articles about American Indians.
4. Johnston met with (*several/a little*) military men.
5. He gave them (*a few/a little*) examples of the Navajo language.
6. (*A few/A little*) Navajo Indians developed a code.
7. It took (*a few/a little*) time to develop the code.

5.11 *A Few* vs. *Few*; *A Little* vs. *Little*

EXAMPLES	EXPLANATION
We read **a few** articles about American Indians. **Few** non-Navajos could speak the Navajo language. **Very few** young American Indians speak the language of their ancestors.	*A few* means "some" or "enough." *Few* and *very few* mean "not enough, almost none."
There's **a little** turkey left over. Let's make a sandwich. The Navajo code talkers got **little** recognition for their help in World War II. The Pilgrims had **very little** food the first winter.	*A little* means "some" or "enough." *Little* and *very little* mean "not enough, almost none."

Note:
Whether something is enough or not enough does not depend on the quantity. It depends on the perspective of the person.

EXERCISE 15 Fill in the blanks with *a little, very little, a few,* or *very few* in each conversation.

1. **A:** We read about American Indians in my English class. I'm starting to learn _____a little_____
   a.
   about that topic. Did you know that Eskimos are American Indians, too?

   B: Really? I know _____ about Eskimos. In fact, I know almost nothing.
   b.

   A: They live in Alaska, Canada, and Greenland. They make their houses out of ice.

   B: What do they eat? _____ plants grow in the cold regions.
   c.

   A: They use a lot of sea animals for food. They eat whale, seal, and fish.

   B: I like to eat _____ fish, but I can't imagine eating it all the time. How do you
   d.
   know so much about Eskimos?

   A: I saw the movie *Eskimo*. I learned _____ about Eskimos from the movie.
   e.
   And I read _____ books. Do you want to borrow my books?
   f.

   B: No, thanks. I have _____ time for reading now. I have a lot of schoolwork.
   g.

2. **A:** Let's prepare the Thanksgiving dinner together. I always like to get _____ help.
   a.

   B: I don't think I'm going to be much help. You know I have _____ experience
   b.
   in the kitchen.

   A: Don't worry. You can be my assistant. First, I need to put _____ oil on the turkey.
   c.

   B: There's _____ oil in the house. I don't think it's going to be enough.
   d.

   A: Don't worry. I have another bottle. Next, I need you to get the spices out of the cabinet for me. We're going
   to put _____ spices on the turkey. I also need _____ string to tie
   e.   f.
   the legs. Then the turkey will be ready to go into the oven. Lastly, I need you to go to the store and get
   _____ things for me. Here's a list.
   g.

   B: Shopping! That's something I can do well.

   A: Why is it that in this family, _____ men cook the turkey? I almost never see a man
   h.
   prepare the Thanksgiving dinner. In fact, _____ men even come into the kitchen unless
   i.
   they're hungry.

5.12 Too Much/Too Many vs. A Lot Of

EXAMPLES	EXPLANATION
My friend left the reservation because there was **too much** unemployment. If we invite **too many** people to dinner, we won't have enough food.	*Too much* and *too many* show an excessive quantity. A problem with the quantity is presented or implied.
A lot of Navajo Indians live in the Southwest.	*A lot of* shows a large quantity. No problem is presented.
I feel sick. I ate **too much**.	We can put *too much* at the end of a verb phrase. Note that the noun *food* is omitted. It is understood by the context.

Note:
Sometimes we use *a lot of* in place of *too much/too many*.

If we invite **a lot of** people to dinner, we won't have enough food.

EXERCISE 16 Fill in the blanks with *a lot of, too much,* or *too many*. In some cases, more than one answer is possible.

1. You put _____*too much*_____ pepper in the potatoes, and they taste terrible.

2. On Thanksgiving Day, most people eat _____ and don't feel well afterwards.

3. I'm so busy before Thanksgiving. I have no time to rest. I have _____ things to do.

4. I love garlic. This recipe calls for _____ garlic, so it's going to be delicious.

5. She's going to bake a cherry pie for Thanksgiving. She needs _____ cherries.

6. I think I ate _____ pieces of pie. Now I feel sick.

7. We had _____ food at the Thanksgiving dinner. We had to throw away a lot.

8. There are _____ American Indian languages.

9. The Navajo code talkers gave _____ help during World War II.

10. The code talkers sent _____ messages successfully.

SUMMARY OF UNIT 5

Words Used before Count and Noncount Nouns

SINGULAR COUNT	PLURAL COUNT	NONCOUNT
the apple	**the** apples	**the** sugar
an apple	**some** apples	**some** sugar
no apple	**no** apples	**no** sugar
	any apples (with questions and negatives)	**any** sugar (with questions and negatives)
	a lot of apples	**a lot of** sugar
	many apples	**much** sugar (with questions and negatives)
	a few apples	**a little** sugar
	two apples	**two** teaspoons of sugar
	several apples	
	How many apples?	**How much** sugar?

There + a Form of *Be*

COUNT	NONCOUNT
There's one onion in the recipe.	**There is** some celery in the soup.
There are two carrots in the recipe.	**There isn't** any garlic in the soup.
Is there a potato in the recipe?	**Is there** any rice in the soup?
No, **there isn't**.	No, **there isn't**.
Are there any nuts in the recipe?	How much salt **is there** in the soup?
Yes, **there are**.	
How many nuts **are there** in the recipe?	

A Few/(Very) Few; A Little/(Very) Little

	COUNT	NONCOUNT
some	**A few** people brought a pie to dinner.	Do you want **a little** sugar in your tea?
not enough	It's too bad that (**very**) **few** Navajos speak their language today.	The Navajo code talkers got (**very**) **little** recognition during World War II.

A Lot Of/Too Much/Too Many

NEUTRAL (COUNT AND NONCOUNT)	PROBLEMATIC (COUNT)	PROBLEMATIC (NONCOUNT)
I cooked **a lot of** potatoes. I put **a lot of** butter on the potatoes.	You put **too many** raisins in the stuffing. It's too sweet.	You put **too much** salt in the soup. I can't eat it.

REVIEW

Read this essay by an American Indian. Circle the correct words to complete it.

My name is Joseph Falling Snow. I'm (*an/a/any*) American Indian from a Sioux[1] reservation in South Dakota.
1.
There are (*a little/little/several*) Sioux reservations; I'm from the Pine Ridge reservation. I don't live
2.
in South Dakota anymore because I couldn't find (*a/any/no*) job. There's (*a little/a few/little/few*)
3. 4.
work on my reservation. There's a lot of (*unemployment/unemployments*) there. (*A poverty/Poverty*) is a
5. 6.
big problem on my reservation. My uncle gave me (*a/an/some/any*) good (*advice/advices*). He told me
7. 8.
to go to (*big city/a big city*) to find (*a/an/some/any*) job. I decided to go to Minneapolis. There are
9. 10.
(*much/many/any*) job opportunities there. I had (*no/not/any*) trouble finding a job because I have
11. 12.
(*a lot of/many/much*) (*experiences/experience*) as a carpenter.
13. 14.

The language of my tribe is Lakota, but I know (*any/a few/very few*) words in my language. Most of the
15.
(*people/person/peoples*) on my reservation speak only English. (*A few/Any/A little*) older people still speak our
16. 17.
tribal language, but the language is dying out as the older people die.

(*A few/A little/Few/Little*) times a year, I go back to the reservation for a celebration called a pow wow.
18.
It gets very crowded at these times because (*much/any/a lot of*) people from our reservation and nearby
19.
reservations attend this celebration. We have (*much/too much/a lot of*) fun. We dance to our (*music/musics*) and
20. 21.
socialize with our (*friend/friends*).
22.

---
[1] Sioux *is* pronounced /su/.

FROM GRAMMAR TO WRITING

PART 1 Editing Advice

1. Some plural forms are irregular and don't take -s.

    There were a lot of childre~~ns~~ at the Thanksgiving dinner.

2. Use a singular noun and verb after *every*.

    Every reading~~s~~ teach*es* us something new.

3. Use the plural form of the noun after *one of*.

    One of my neighbor*s* made a pumpkin pie.

4. Don't use *a* or *an* before a plural noun.

    The code talkers had to create ~~a~~ *(some)* new words.

5. Don't put *a* or *an* before a noncount noun.

    Clovis Boy's bones give us ~~a~~ *(some)* useful information about the past.

6. A noncount noun is always singular.

    The American Indians gave the Pilgrims a lot of advice~~s~~.

7. Use *there is* or *there are* to introduce a noun.

    ~~Are~~ *There are* a lot of Navajo Indians in the Southwest.

8. Don't use a specific noun after *there is/there are*.

    ~~There's~~ *T*he Grand Canyon *is* in Arizona.

9. Include *of* with a unit of measure.

    We used one cup *of* sugar in the cranberry sauce.

10. Omit *of* after *a lot* when the noun is omitted.

    You ate a lot of turkey, but I didn't eat a lot ~~of~~.

11. Use *a little/a few* to mean "some." Use *(very) little/(very) few* to mean "not enough."

    He went to a big city to find a job because there were ~~a~~ *(very)* few jobs on the reservation.

12. Don't use *too much* or *too many* if the quantity doesn't present a problem.

    She loves to go back to the reservation because she has ~~too many~~ *a lot of* friends there.

13. Don't confuse *too* and *too much/too many*.

    The potatoes are too ~~much~~ salty. I can't eat them.

14. Don't use a double negative.

    The Navajo language doesn't have ~~no~~ *a* word for "submarine."

    OR

    The Navajo language has no word for "submarine."

148 Unit 5

PART 2 Editing Practice

Some of the shaded words and phrases have mistakes. Find the mistakes and correct them. If the shaded words are correct, write C.

    I love Thanksgiving. Every years(1.), the whole family comes to our house for this holiday and a few(2. C) other holidays. But Thanksgiving is my favorite. There are(3.) a lot of childrens(4.) in my family, and they love to see each other on Thanksgiving. They don't have many(5.) time to see each other the rest of the year. It's so joyful to have too many(6.) children in the house few(7.) times a year. There's(8.) a lot of noise(9.) when they're here, but we don't mind. We all bring some foods(10.). One of my sister(11.) always makes a pumpkin pie(12.). Her husband always makes a cookies(13.) in the shape of turkeys. My other sister makes cranberry sauce. She uses a lot of sugars(14.), and sometimes it's too much(15.) sweet, but I never say anything. My brother doesn't like to cook, so he brings a lot fresh fruit(16.). My cousin brings about 10 big bottles soda(17.). I prepare the sweet potatoes(18.). My mother always makes the turkey. It takes much time(19.) to cook a big turkey.

    We have a lot(20.) to prepare before Thanksgiving. My mother has very little(21.) time the week before because of her job. But I have a lot of(22.) because I don't have no(23.) homeworks(24.) that week. So I clean the house. My father likes to help, but he has very few(25.) experience in the kitchen, so my mother asks him to do the shopping. He doesn't have much(26.) experience shopping either, so she always gives him an advice(27.) about shopping.

    It's always fun to spend Thanksgiving with too many(28.) people. But there's(29.) one thing I don't like: are(30.) always a lot of dishes(31.) to wash afterwards.

WRITING TIP

There is/There are is a useful structure when you write a description. If you choose prompt 1 below, you can use *there is/are* to introduce food, clothing, and other traditions (e.g., *There is one main food everyone prepares for Thanksgiving.*). If you choose prompt 2, you can use *there are* to introduce different ethnic minorities in your country and then focus on one (e.g., *There are many ethnic minorities in Vietnam. The largest ethnic group is. . .*).

PART 3 Write

Read the prompts. Choose one and write a paragraph about it.

1. Write about a holiday celebration in your country. You may write about food, clothing, preparations, customs, etc. Use expressions of quantity.
2. Write about an ethnic minority in your native country or another country you know about. Where and how do these people live? Use expressions of quantity.

PART 4 Edit

Reread the Summary of Unit 5 and the editing advice. Edit your writing from Part 3.

UNIT

6

Modifiers
Adverbs

Forest bathing in Jedediah Smith Redwoods State Park, California, U.S.

A HEALTHY PLANET, A HEALTHY BODY

> It is health that is real wealth and not pieces of gold and silver.
> MAHATMA GANDHI

Feeding the Planet

An increasing demand for meat and dairy puts pressure on the planet.

Read the following article. Pay special attention to the words in bold. 6.1

Can you name some things that harm our environment? If you said cars, you're **right**. If you said smoke from **large** factories, well, that's a **big** part of the problem, too. But maybe you didn't think of something in your **daily** life: your dinner. Agriculture, which produces your food, is more **harmful** to the environment than cars, trucks, trains, and airplanes combined. **Today's** farming uses our **water** supplies inefficiently[1]. Chemicals used on farms run into rivers and lakes and pollute[2] them. When **rain forests** and **grassland** are cleared for **farm** animals and crops, the result is often the extinction[3] of **wildlife**[4]. **Farming** methods release **harmful** gases into the air. These gases are an **enormous** contributor to **global** warming.

By 2050, the **world** population will be 9 billion, 2 billion more than it is today. Because of **population** growth, the problem of feeding so many people is **huge**. There will be a **growing** need for food all over the world. As countries such as China and India continue to become more **prosperous**[5], there is an **increasing** demand for meat, eggs, and dairy.

How can we increase the amount of food and maintain a **healthy** planet? Here are some solutions.

1. It is **important** to stop cutting down forests for agriculture. This is very **destructive** to the environment.
2. We don't need to eat so much meat. Producing meat wastes **valuable** resources and contributes to **global** warming.
3. We must stop wasting food. In **rich** countries, about 50 percent of food goes in the trash. In **poor** countries, a lot of food is lost between the farmer and the market because storage and transportation are not **efficient.**

It won't be **easy** to make these changes, but if we don't try, the result will be **terrible** for **future** generations. All of us have to be **thoughtful** about the connection between the food on our plates, the farmers that produce it, and the effect on the planet. As we push our **shopping** carts down the aisles of our supermarkets, our **food** choices will decide our future.

---

[1] inefficiently: in a way that is not productive or economical
[2] to pollute: to contaminate, make impure or dirty
[3] extinction: the state of no longer living or existing
[4] wildlife: animals living in their natural setting
[5] prosperous: wealthy

COMPREHENSION Based on the reading, write T for *true* or F for *false*.

1. _____ Agriculture can cause a lot of harm to the planet.
2. _____ Rain forests cause a lot of harm to the planet.
3. _____ If we eat less meat, this will be better for the planet.

THINK ABOUT IT Discuss the questions with a partner or in a small group.

1. In your opinion, which is more important: feeding the population or maintaining a healthy planet? Explain.
2. Read the last line of the article again. Think about how you eat and shop for food. What choices can you make to help the environment?

6.1 Modifying a Noun

EXAMPLES	EXPLANATION
Food is part of our **daily** life. We shouldn't waste **valuable** resources.	An adjective can modify or describe a noun. (*Daily* and *valuable* are adjectives.)
Population growth is a problem. Our **food** choices affect the environment.	A noun can modify or describe another noun. (*Population* and *food* are nouns.)

EXERCISE 1 Listen to the paragraphs. Then write T for *true* or F for *false*. 🎧 6.2

1. _____ One in ten American children is overweight.
2. _____ Today's lifestyle includes a lot of physical activity.
3. _____ More kids biked to school in the late 1960s than they do now.

EXERCISE 2 Listen again and fill in the blanks with the words you hear. 🎧 6.2

We know that it's ___important___ to eat well and get _____ exercise.
                                  1.   2.
Health clubs are _____ of people trying to get in shape. Sales of _____-
                             3.   4.
calorie foods show that Americans want to be _____. However, two-thirds of
                                                    5.
_____ adults are _____. One in three American children is
    6.   7.
overweight. Weight is becoming a _____ problem as _____ costs go
                                             8.   9.
up because of diseases related to obesity: _____ disease, stroke, diabetes, and
                                                      10.
_____ blood pressure.
    11.
What is the reason for this _____ problem? First, today's lifestyle does not include
                                       12.
enough _____ activity. When the United States was an _____
         13.   14.
society, farmers ate a _____ meal, but they also worked hard in the fields.
                            15.

continued

_____ technology removes _____ activity from our
        16.   17.
_____ lives. Most trips are _____, within _____
        18.   19.   20.
distance of home, but most Americans drive. Only 13 percent of schoolchildren walk or bike to a

school. Compare this to 48 percent in 1969. The _____ American child spends about
                                                        21.
35 hours a week watching TV. Kids are not _____ enough.
                                                22.
_____ kids may be the first generation to have a shorter _____
        23.   24.
expectancy than their parents.

6.2 Adjectives

EXAMPLES	EXPLANATION
Rich countries waste food. **Large** factories cause pollution.	An adjective can come before a noun.
We all want to have **healthy, active** kids. We all want to have **active, healthy** kids.	Two adjectives can come before a noun. We separate the adjectives with a comma when we can change the order of the adjectives without changing the meaning.
We don't do **hard physical** labor anymore. NOT: We don't do **physical hard** labor anymore.	We don't use a comma if we can't reverse the order of the adjectives.
The problem is **huge**. Feeding 9 billion people seems almost **impossible**.	An adjective can come after *be, seem*, and the sense-perception verbs: *look, sound, smell, taste,* and *feel*.
It is important to protect the planet. **It won't be easy** to solve the problem.	An adjective can come after impersonal expressions beginning with *it*.
Are you **concerned** about the future? Scientists are **interested** in finding a solution.	Some *-ed* words are adjectives: *tired, worried, located, crowded, married, divorced, excited, disappointed, finished,* and *frightened*.
We read an **interesting** article about farming. I learned **surprising** information about our food.	Some *-ing* words are adjectives: *amazing, exciting, boring, increasing, disappointing, frightening,* and *growing*.
It is **extremely** important to find a solution. This is a **very** difficult problem.	*Very, so, quite,* and *extremely* can come before adjectives.
Is farming a problem? Yes, it is a huge **one**. Do you have any ideas about how to protect the planet? There are some good **ones** in the article.	After an adjective, we can substitute a singular noun with *one* and a plural noun with *ones*.

Note:
We don't make an adjective plural.
    a **big** farm   **big** farms

GRAMMAR IN USE

In conversation, we often use informal modifiers before adjectives to express degree. Some of these words and phrases are: *pretty, sort of, kind of, really,* and *real*. It's better not to use these in academic writing.

    I was **kind of** surprised by the article.
    The food situation sounds **really** bad.

EXERCISE 3 Fill in blanks with one of the words from the box.

| growing | tired | healthy | greasy | worried | sweet | high ✓ |
| important | ones | sick | one | rich | busy | valuable |

1. Burgers and fries are _____high_____ in calories.
2. It is _____ to have a good diet.
3. Fries are cooked in oil. They are very _____.
4. If you don't eat a healthy diet, you can get _____.
5. Some people eat a big breakfast. Others eat a small _____.
6. Are you _____ about the future of the planet?
7. Children need to get enough sleep. It's not good to be _____ in school.
8. Cookies are very _____.
9. Most Americans have _____ lives and don't make the time to eat well.
10. Obesity is a _____ problem. It is a bigger problem today than it was years ago.
11. We need to have a _____ body.
12. In _____ countries, many people waste food. In poor _____, there is not enough food.
13. We shouldn't waste _____ resources.

Students at the 24th Street School in Los Angeles, California, U.S., learn the importance of fresh food.

EXERCISE 4 Circle the correct words to complete this conversation between a husband and wife.

A: We're gaining weight. When we were younger, we used to be (*thin*/thins), but now that we're
   1.

   (*marry*/*married*), we're getting fat.
   2.

B: Let's go jogging after work. There's a (*beautiful park*/*park beautiful*) where we can go.
   3.

   It's (*locate*/*located*) just a few blocks from our apartment.
   4.

A: But after work I'm always too (*tire*/*tired*). I just want to eat dinner and watch TV.
   5.

B: It's not good to eat a big meal so late at night. In many countries, people eat a big meal during the day and

   (*a small one*/*a small*) at night. If we do that, we have the rest of the day to burn off the calories.
   6.

A: I'm sure that's (*an idea very good*/*a very good idea*), but I don't have time to eat a big meal in the middle
   7.

   of the day.

B: We're always eating out in (*expensive*/*expensives*) restaurants. We should cook more at home. And we
   8.

   should go for a walk after dinner.

A: Good idea. Let's cook steaks tonight.

B: We need to eat less meat. Meat production is (*harm*/*harmful*) to the planet. It contributes to
   9.

   (*globe*/*global*) warming. I read (*an article very interesting*/*a very interesting article*) about it today.
   10.   11.

A: You're right. Let's eat fish tonight.

Preparing food yourself gives you more control over your health.

156 Unit 6

6.3 Noun Modifiers

EXAMPLES	EXPLANATION
The **world** population is increasing. **Population** growth is a problem.	A noun can modify (describe) another noun. When two nouns come together, the first one modifies the second.
We use a **shopping** cart in a supermarket. **Farming** methods produce gas.	Sometimes a gerund (-ing word) describes a noun.
Potato chips have a lot of grease. My **five-year-old** son prefers candy to fruit.	The first noun is always singular. When we use a number before the noun, we usually attach it to the noun with a hyphen.
Very few **schoolchildren** walk to school. Do you have a healthy **lifestyle**?	Sometimes we write the two nouns as one word. The noun modifier and the noun become a compound word.
Today's lifestyle doesn't include much physical activity. Everyone needs a good **night's** sleep.	Sometimes a possessive noun describes a noun, especially with time words.

Pronunciation Note:

When a noun describes another noun, the first noun usually receives the greater emphasis in speaking.

I wear my <u>running</u> shoes when I go to the <u>health</u> club and use the <u>exercise</u> machines.

EXERCISE 5 Fill in the blanks with one of the words from the box.

rain	world	population✓	health	shopping
farm	walking	heart	food	cow

1. ___Population___ growth is a big problem.
2. The _____ population will be 9 billion in 2050.
3. When we shop at the supermarket, we need to make healthy _____ choices.
4. When we shop, we usually use a _____ cart.
5. Some people go to _____ clubs to exercise.
6. One result of a poor diet is _____ disease.
7. Many children live within _____ distance from their schools, but they go by bus or car.
8. Cows and pigs are _____ animals.
9. Cutting down _____ forests is harmful to the environment.
10. Some people are allergic to _____ milk.

EXERCISE 6 Fill in the blanks to complete this conversation between a mother and her son. Put the words given in the correct order. Remember to use the singular form for the first noun. Some answers are compound words.

A: We need a lot of things today. Let's take a _____shopping cart_____.
  1. cart/shopping

B: Can I sit in the _____?
  2. child/seat

A: You're much too big. You're a six- _____ boy.
  3. years/old

B: Mom, please buy me that cereal. It looks good. I saw it on a _____.
  4. commercial/TV

A: Let's read the ingredients on the _____ first. I want to see the
  5. cereal/box

_____ before we buy it. Let me put on my _____.
  6. content/sugar   7. glasses/eyes

Oh, dear. This cereal has 20 grams of sugar.

B: But I like sugar, Mom.

A: You know sugar is bad for your teeth. Remember what the dentist told you?

B: But I brush my teeth once a day.

A: I want you to use your _____ after every meal, not just once a day.
  8. teeth/brush

B: Mom, can we buy those _____?
  9. chips/potatoes

A: They have too much fat.

B: How about some soda?

A: You should drink more juice. How about some _____?
  10. juice/oranges

B: I don't like juice.

A: Let's get in the _____ and pay now. Maybe we should shop at the
  11. line/check-out

_____ store next time.
  12. food/health

ABOUT YOU Make a list of things you usually have in your refrigerator. Compare your list to a partner's.

  orange juice, low-fat milk
  _____
  _____

> **FUN WITH GRAMMAR**
>
> Describe your world. Write these words on a sheet of paper, numbered 1–10: *bag, building, daily, food, hard, health, room, school, shopping, world*. Then write sentences using the words as modifiers, e.g., *health* → *My brother has health problems*. You will have 10 minutes for this task. It is not a race to see who is fastest. The goal is to get the most correct answers.

The Happiest City in the U.S.

Read the following article. Pay special attention to the words in bold. 6.3

A recent study identified Boulder, Colorado, as the happiest city in the United States. Why are people in Boulder **mostly** happy with their lives? Here are three reasons.

❶ They are healthy.

When people eat **well** and exercise **regularly**, their health improves and their happiness increases, studies show.

In Boulder, there are many ways to eat **healthily**. The city has weekly farmers' markets which sell fresh fruit and vegetables. There are lots of healthy restaurants and food stores to choose from, too.

People in Boulder are also **physically** active. There are walking and bike paths throughout the city, so people can get around **easily** on foot or by bike. The city is also surrounded by a lot of natural beauty, including the Rocky Mountains, which are great for hiking, biking, and skiing. And the weather is **rarely** bad in Boulder, so people can spend a lot of time outside. Access to fresh air and sunshine can **greatly** improve people's health and happiness.

❷ They live in a small, friendly community.

The city of Boulder has about 107,000 people. Many residents know each other, and they socialize **regularly**. People in shops and cafes often greet you **in a friendly way**, too. Also, there is **hardly** any crime in Boulder, so people can walk the streets **safely** day and night.

❸ They can live **comfortably**.

In Boulder, many jobs pay **well**. People work **hard**, but **occasionally** they can take vacations and relax. This is good for their health and happiness.

Things are changing **fast**, though. Until **recently**, people could live **very cheaply** in Boulder. But today, more big companies are moving into the area, and the cost of living (housing, food, and education) has increased **dramatically**[1]. As a result, almost half of Boulder's residents feel stressed more **frequently** now.

---

[1] dramatically: a lot, greatly

Many of Boulder's residents are happy because they are able to spend a lot of time outdoors.

COMPREHENSION Based on the reading, write T for *true* or F for *false*.

1. _____ The weather in Boulder is good, so people can be outside often.
2. _____ Because Boulder isn't very big, many people know each other, and crime is low.
3. _____ You can live very cheaply in Boulder.

THINK ABOUT IT Discuss the questions with a partner or in a small group.

1. People are happy in Boulder for three reasons. What are they? Explain each reason. Are these things true about your city?
2. What do you think of Boulder? Complete the sentence with your opinion. Then explain it.
   I would/wouldn't like to live in Boulder because…

6.4 Adverbs

EXAMPLES	EXPLANATION
subject / **verb phrase** / **adverb of manner** You / can walk at night / **safely**. People / can live / **comfortably**. Costs / have increased / **dramatically**.	An adverb of manner tells *how* or *in what way* the subject does something. We form most adverbs of manner by putting *-ly* at the end of an adjective. An adverb of manner usually follows the verb phrase.
Fresh air and sunshine **greatly** improve your health. Boulder residents socialize **regularly**. Many people feel stressed **frequently** now.	Other common *-ly* adverbs are: *eventually, annually, (in)frequently, certainly, greatly, suddenly, recently, directly, completely, generally, repeatedly, naturally, finally, probably, (un)fortunately, extremely, constantly.*
In Boulder, many jobs pay **well**.	The adverb for *good* is *well*.
People in Boulder are **physically** active. The weather is **rarely** bad in Boulder.	An adverb can come before an adjective.
adjective / **adverb** Residents are **hard** workers. / They work **hard**. He has a **fast** car. / His car goes **fast**. We had a **late** lunch. / We at lunch **late**. We went for an **early** hike. / We went for a hike **early**.	Some adjectives and adverbs have the same form: *hard, fast, early,* and *late*. (The *-ly* in *early* is not an adverb ending.)
She worked **hard** so she could live in Boulder. I **hardly** know my neighbors. There is **hardly** any crime in Boulder.	*Hard* and *hardly* are both adverbs, but they have completely different meanings. *She worked hard* means she put a lot of effort into the work. *Hard* comes after the verb phrase. *Hardly* means "very little" or "almost no." *Hardly* comes before many verbs, but it comes after a *be* verb.
He came home **late** from school. **Lately**, people are feeling more stress in Boulder. People are feeling more stress in Boulder **lately**.	*Late* and *lately* are both adverbs, but they have completely different meanings. *Late* means "not on time." It comes after the verb phrase. *Lately* means "recently." It comes at the beginning or end of the sentence.

160 Unit 6

She is a **friendly** person. She behaves **in a friendly manner**. He is a **lively** person. He dances **in a lively way**.	Some adjectives end in -ly: lovely, lonely, friendly, lively, and ugly. They have no adverb form. With these adjectives, we use an adverbial phrase (in a _____-ly way/manner) to describe the action.
We gain weight **very** easily. She cooks **extremely** well. He eats **so** fast. She exercises **really** hard. You eat **quite** slowly.	Very, extremely, so, really, and quite can come before an adverb.

Note:
Though not grammatically correct, in conversation people often shorten *really* to *real*.
　　She exercises **real** hard.

EXERCISE 7 Complete the sentences with an adverb from the box. Use each word only once.

hard	hardly ✓	honestly	neatly
quickly	regularly	very	well

A Tidy* and Happy Home

Our homes are filled with things we ____hardly____ ever use: old clothes, books,
                                          1.
papers, electronics. We try _____ to throw away these items, but it's difficult. As a
                                2.
result, our homes become messy _____ _____.
                                       3.   4.

What can we do? Marie Kondo, the author of the book *The Life-Changing Magic of Tidying Up,* has a suggestion. Begin with your clothes. Look at each item in your closet and drawers. First, ask yourself: Do I use this item _____? (For example, do I wear this sweater
                                                        5.
often?) Also ask: Does this item make me happy? Then answer _____. If you say
                                                                    6.
yes, keep the item. If you say *no*, donate it or throw it away. For the clothes you keep, fold or hang

them _____. When you are done, you will only have clothes that look good and fit
       7.

_____ — and you will be happier.
    8.

―――――――
*tidy: clean and organized

ABOUT YOU Write the adverb form of the word given. Then check (✓) the activities that you do in this way. Make statements telling how you do these activities, and explain them to a partner.

Ten Ways to Be Happy

1. ✓ exercise <u>regularly</u>
   _{regular}

   <u>I exercise regularly. I go to the gym three times a week. OR</u>

   <u>I don't exercise regularly. I sit a lot. I hardly ever go to the gym.</u>

2. ___ eat _____
   _{good}

3. ___ socialize with others _____
   _{frequent}

4. ___ spend time in nature _____
   _{occasional}

5. ___ sleep seven or eight hours a night; don't stay up _____ often
   _{late}

6. ___ think _____ about most things
   _{positive}

7. ___ treat others _____
   _{nice}

8. ___ work _____ but take breaks, too
   _{hard}

9. ___ smile _____ at least once a day
   _{happy}

10. ___ disconnect _____ from digital devices for an hour a day
    _{complete}

6.5 Adjectives vs. Adverbs

An adjective describes a noun. An adverb describes a verb (phrase), an adjective, or another adverb.

EXAMPLES	EXPLANATION
Boulder is **easy** to get around on foot. You can get around **easily** on foot.	*Easy* is an adjective. It describes a noun—in this case, *Boulder*. *Easily* is an adverb of manner. It tells how you can go from place to place.
People in Boulder **seem happy**. I **felt great** after the hike. People always smile **happily**. The hike **greatly** improved my mood.	We use an adjective, not an adverb, after the following verbs if we are describing the subject: *smell, sound, taste, look, seem, appear,* and *feel*. We use an adverb of manner if we are describing *how* the action (the verb phrase) is done.
If you don't eat well, you can **get sick**. They **got hungry** during the hike.	We use an adjective, not an adverb, in expressions with *get*. Some expressions with *get* are *get hungry, get tired, get sick,* and *get rich*.
He's sick. He doesn't feel **well** today.	For health, we use *well*.
Boulder residents are **really** healthy. They exercise and eat **very** well.	We use an adverb before an adjective or another adverb.
As usual, they went to the farmers' market on Saturday.	We use the adjective, not the adverb, in the expression *as usual*.

> **GRAMMAR IN USE**
> In conversational English, people sometimes use *good* for health.
>
> A: *How do you feel?*
> B: *Good.*

EXERCISE 8 Fill in the blanks with the correct adjective or adverb form of the word given.

Here are three tips for living a ____happy____ and _____ life.
　　　　　　　　　　　　　　　　　　1. happy　　　　　　　　2. healthy

Tip 1: Exercise _____. Being _____ active can _____ improve
　　　　　　　　　　3. regular　　　　　4. physical　　　　　5. great

how you look and feel. _____ exercise also helps you sleep better.
　　　　　　　　　　　　6. Regular

Tip 2: When you get _____ between meals, skip the junk food (like potato chips and
　　　　　　　　　　　　7. hungry

cookies). Instead, eat fruit or some nuts. Junk food tastes _____, and it's OK to eat
　　　　　　　　　　　　　　　　　　　　　　　　　　　　　　　　　　8. good

_____. But in large amounts, it is _____ for your health.
9. occasional　　　　　　　　　　　　　10. bad

Tip 3: Learn to cook. At one university, nutritionists _____ interviewed students about their
　　　　　　　　　　　　　　　　　　　　　　　　　　　　11. recent

diets. Many students said they _____ ate any vegetables each week because they work
　　　　　　　　　　　　　　　12. hard

_____ all day, and they are too _____ to shop or cook. These students
13. hard　　　　　　　　　　　　　　　14. tired

_____ ate fast foods (such as instant noodles or pizza). Because they didn't eat
15. frequent

_____, they got _____ often. But then the students started cooking
16. good　　　　　　　17. sick

their own meals, and their health improved _____.
　　　　　　　　　　　　　　　　　　　　　18. dramatic

ABOUT YOU Answer the questions. Discuss your answers with a partner.

1. How often do you exercise (hardly ever, occasionally, regularly)?

2. When you get hungry and want a snack, what do you eat? Is it healthy? How do you feel after eating it?

3. In your country, do people generally eat well or poorly? How about in the United States?

Modifiers, Adverbs **163**

A GOOD NIGHT'S SLEEP

Mike Wallace takes part in a sleep study at Johns Hopkins University in Baltimore, Maryland, U.S.

Read the following article. Pay special attention to the words in bold. 6.4

Most people need seven to nine hours of sleep. But most Americans sleep less than seven hours a night. When people aren't **rested enough**, there may be a bad result. For example, if people drive when they're **too tired**, they can cause serious accidents on the road. According to the National Transportation Administration, sleepy drivers cause 100,000 accidents each year. Airplane safety also depends on well-rested pilots. An airplane crash in 2009 killed all the passengers. The National Transportation Safety Board concluded that the pilots were **too sleepy** to make good decisions.

Sleep is **very** important to our health. In experiments with rats, where the rats were not allowed to sleep, all of them were dead in about two weeks. More studies on sleep are needed, but scientists complain that they don't receive **enough money** for sleep research.

If sleep is so important, why don't we try to go to bed earlier and get at least eight hours of sleep? About 20 percent of Americans say that they don't get **enough sleep**. Are we **too busy**? Not always. Besides job and family responsibilities, Americans have a lot of other things that keep them out of bed. Twenty-four-hour-a-day Internet and TV and all-night supermarkets can take away from our sleep time.

What can we do to improve our sleep? Sleep experts have some recommendations:
- Don't nap during the day.
- Sleep in a dark room. **Too much light** in a room can harm sleep.
- Try not to have **too much stress** in your life.
- Don't get **too stimulated** before going to bed. Avoid activities such as watching TV or eating before bed.
- Go to bed at the same time every night.
- Avoid caffeine after lunchtime. If you drink **too much coffee** during the day, don't expect to get a good night's sleep.
- Exercise. Physical activity is **very good** for sleep. But if you exercise **too late** in the day, it will interfere with your sleep.

A good night's sleep is **very important**, so turn off the TV, shut down the computer, put away your devices, and sleep well.

COMPREHENSION Based on the reading, write T for *true* or F for *false*.

1. _____ Most people get seven to nine hours of sleep.
2. _____ Scientists did sleep experiments with rats.
3. _____ A lot of money goes into research for sleep experiments.

THINK ABOUT IT Discuss the questions with a partner or in a small group.

1. What do you think scientists measure in a sleep study?
2. Do you do any of the things that sleep experts recommend that you don't do? How could you improve your sleep habits?

6.6 *Too, Too Much, Too Many,* and *Enough*

EXAMPLES	EXPLANATION
The pilot was **too sleepy** to fly the airplane. You work **too hard** and don't relax.	We put *too* before adjectives and adverbs. *Too* indicates a problem.
You spend **too much time** on the computer.	We put *too much* before a noncount noun.
You spend **too many hours** watching TV.	We put *too many* before a count noun.
He doesn't sleep well because he worries **too much**.	We put *too much* at the end of the verb phrase.
Five hours of sleep is not **good enough**. You worked **hard enough**. Get some rest now.	We put *enough* after adjectives and adverbs.
Some people don't get **enough exercise**. Do you get **enough hours** of sleep?	We put *enough* before noncount and count nouns.

Note:
An infinitive can follow a phrase with *too* and *enough*.
  I'm too tired **to drive**.
  I don't have enough time **to exercise**.

> **GRAMMAR IN USE**
>
> *Too* + adjective indicates that there is too much of something and usually has a negative connotation (e.g., *That watch is too expensive.*). Sometimes we use *too* with certain positive adjectives to emphasize the feeling (e.g., *You're too kind. She's too generous.*). Such statements don't suggest a problem. They just bring attention to a large amount of something.

EXERCISE 9 Fill in the blanks with *too, too much, too many,* or *enough*.

1. Are Americans _____too_____ busy to get a good night's sleep?

2. Some people don't get _____ exercise because of their busy lives.

3. It's hard to sleep if you exercise _____ late in the evening.

4. If you're _____ tired when you drive, you can cause an accident.

5. Some people spend _____ time on the Internet. They should put away their electronic devices and go to bed.

6. If you drink _____ coffee, it can affect your sleep.

7. People drive everywhere. They don't walk _____.

8. Try not to eat _____ before you go to bed.

9. Children shouldn't drink so much soda because it contains _____ sugar.

10. We need to think about the future. We need to make sure there is _____ food for the nine billion people on the planet in 2050.

11. Don't eat _____ meat. Try eating fish or chicken a few times a week.

ABOUT YOU Find a partner and discuss your answers to these questions.

1. How many hours do you sleep a night?

2. How many hours is enough for you?

6.7 Too and Very

EXAMPLES	EXPLANATION
We ate dinner **very** late last night. We arrived at the theater **too** late. We missed the beginning of the movie. My grandmother is 85. She's **very** old, but she's in great health. The child is six years old. He's **too** old to sit in a shopping cart.	Don't confuse *very* and *too*. *Too* indicates a problem. The problem can be stated or implied. *Very* is a neutral word. It does not indicate a problem.

Note:
We can use *a little* before *too*.
    You woke up **a little too** late. You missed a great breakfast.

EXERCISE 10 Fill in the blanks with *too* or *very* in this conversation between a husband and his wife.

A: I enjoyed the dinner _____very_____ much.

B: I'm glad you liked it. I worked _____ hard to prepare your favorite dishes.

A: Thanks! Everything was great. But the soup was a little _____ salty.

B: Oh. I thought you liked everything.

A: I did. Other than the salt, it was _____ good. And I especially liked the potatoes.

B: I'm glad.

A: They were a little _____ greasy, but I ate them anyway.

B: I'm afraid the meat was overcooked. I left it in the oven _____ long.

A: Well, no one's perfect. I gave some to the dog.

B: What about the cake I made? Did you like that?

A: Yes. It was _____ good. The only problem was it was _____ small. I was hoping to have another piece, but there was nothing left.

B: I thought you wanted to lose weight. You always say you're _____ fat and need to lose weight.

A: Fat? I'm not fat. I'm just right. But my clothes are _____ small. When I washed them, the water I used was _____ hot, and they shrank.

B: They didn't shrink. You gained weight.

ABOUT YOU Write about some habits you wish to change to improve your health. Discuss your sentences with a partner.

1. I don't get enough exercise.
2. I spend too much time online.
3. _____
4. _____
5. _____

SUMMARY OF UNIT 6

Adjectives and Adverbs

ADJECTIVES	ADVERBS
We had a **quick** lunch. We had a **late** dinner. She is a **good** cook. She looks **serious**. As **usual**, he drank a cup of coffee.	We ate **quickly**. We ate **late**. She cooks **well**. She is looking at the label **seriously**. He **usually** drinks coffee in the morning.

Adjective Modifiers and Noun Modifiers

ADJECTIVE MODIFIER	NOUN MODIFIER
a **new** machine **old** shoes a **short** vacation **big** problems	an **exercise** machine **running** shoes a **two-week** vacation **today's** problems

Very/Too/Enough/Too Much/Too Many

EXAMPLES	EXPLANATION
He's **very** healthy.	*very* + adjective
I slept **very** well.	*very* + adverb
I'm **too** sleepy.	*too* + adjective
It's **too** late to drive.	*too* + adverb
I'm rested **enough** to do my work.	verb + *enough*
Did you get **enough** sleep last night?	*enough* + noun
She doesn't eat ice cream because it has **too much** fat.	*too much* + noncount noun
She doesn't eat ice cream because it has **too many** calories.	*too many* + count noun
He loves coffee, but when he drinks **too much**, he can't sleep.	verb + *too much*

REVIEW

Choose the correct words to complete these sentences.

1. It's (too/*very*) important to get a good (*night/night's*) sleep.
2. Parents want their kids to eat (*good/well*).
3. We use a lot of resources to raise (*farm/farms*) animals.
4. Some farmers use chemicals to make cows grow (*fast/fastly*).
5. Farmers work very (*hard/hardly*).
6. If we use too (*much/many*) chemicals, we can harm the environment.
7. The (*world population/population world*) is increasing.
8. You seem (*sleepy/sleepily*). You shouldn't drive.
9. Did you get (*sleep enough/enough sleep*) last night?
10. I slept (*good/well*) last night.
11. I feel (*great/greatly*) today.
12. I took a two-(*hour/hours*) nap this afternoon.
13. Do you exercise (*regular/regularly*)?
14. Are you (*alert enough/enough alert*) to drive?
15. We ate dinner (*late/lately*) last night.
16. My grandfather's health is (*too/very*) good.
17. He's 75, but he looks like a 50-(*year/years*)-old man.
18. I'm always (*very/too*) tired to exercise after work.
19. Yesterday was an (*extreme/extremely*) hard day for me.
20. We like to go for a walk in the park near my house. It's (*very/too*) beautiful there.
21. Are you (*too/too much*) busy to exercise?

Modifiers, Adverbs   169

FROM GRAMMAR TO WRITING

PART 1 Editing Advice

1. Adjectives are always singular.

    People in ~~poors~~ countries don't eat a lot of meat.

2. Certain adjectives end with -ed.

    We're interest_ed_ in taking care of the planet.

3. Put an adjective before the noun or after a linking verb, like *be*.

    She is a ~~woman very healthy~~ *very healthy woman*. OR The woman is very healthy.

4. Use *one(s)* after an adjective to take the place of a noun.

    Do you prefer to sleep on a hard bed or a soft _one_?

5. Put a specific noun before a general noun.

    We have to be careful about our ~~supply water~~ *water supply*.

6. A noun modifier is always singular.

    Don't eat so many potato~~es~~ chips.

7. An adverb of manner describes the action of a verb. An adjective describes a noun.

    I choose my food careful_ly_.

    You seem serious~~ly~~ about exercise.

8. Don't put an -*ly* adverb of manner between the verb and the object.

    He read ~~carefully~~ the ingredients _carefully_.

9. Adverbs of manner that don't end in -*ly* follow the verb phrase.

    He ~~late~~ came home _late_.

10. *Too* indicates a problem. If there is no problem, use *very*.

    Your father is ~~too~~ _very_ healthy.

11. Don't use *too much* and *too many* before an adjective or adverb. Use *too*.

    She's too ~~much~~ tired to drive.

12. Put *enough* after the adjective.

    I'm ~~enough rested~~ _rested enough_ to drive.

13. Don't confuse *hard* and *hardly*.

    I'm tired. I worked hard~~ly~~ all day.

    He's lazy. He hard_ly_ worked at all.

170 Unit 6

PART 2 Editing Practice

Some of the shaded words and phrases have mistakes. Find the mistakes and correct them. If the shaded words are correct, write C.

              C   well

I exercise regularly, and I eat very good most of the time. Luckily, I'm too healthy. I try to
             1.   2.   3.

eat a lot of fresh fruits and vegetables every day. I also eat a lot of wholes grains. I rarely eat
                                                                                     4.

red meat. I eat fish or chicken. But I rarely eat chicken fried because it's too much greasy. Most
 5.   6.   7.

mornings, I have a glass of juice orange and cereal. For lunch, I have a small meal, usually a
                                      8.   9.

tuna sandwich. For dinner, I like to eat a nice meal slowly. Most of the time, I cook dinner. But
    10.   11.

on Fridays, I have a three-hours biology course, and I late get home, so I'm too much tire to
                       12.   13.   14.   15.

cook. Then I'm not very carefully about what I eat. My roommate offers me food, but he eats
                              16.

very poorly. He often eats hamburgers and greasy fries from a fast-food place, or he brings home
      17.   18.

a sausage pizza. He eats quickly his food, and he drinks a lot of sweets drinks. He thinks it's
   19.   20.   21.

enough good, but I don't agree. When I eat with him, I don't eat very careful, and then I don't feel
 22.   23.

well the next day. I think it's important to have a diet very healthy. I'm going to try hardly to have
 24.   25.   26.

a better meal on Friday nights.

WRITING TIP

When comparing or contrasting, it is useful to use transition words to help connect ideas.

To show similarity, you can use transitions such as: *similarly, also, in comparison, as well, likewise,* and *like*.

    There is a lot of diverse food in the United States. **Likewise**, in Canada people enjoy many different cuisines.

To show difference, you can use transitions such as: *but, however, on the other hand, on the contrary, nevertheless,* and *unlike*.

    In the U.S., I eat bread every day. In China, **however**, *I ate rice instead.*

PART 3 Write

Read the prompts. Choose one and write a paragraph about it.

1. Compare food in your native culture to food in the United States.
2. Describe your eating habits today with your eating habits in your native country.

PART 4 Edit

Reread the Summary of Unit 6 and the editing advice. Edit your writing from Part 3.

UNIT

7

Time Words
The Past Continuous

Chef José Andrés (in blue) moved to the U.S. from Spain and became an American citizen in 2013. He and his nonprofit organization, World Central Kitchen, along with local chefs served more than 3.6 million meals after Hurricane Maria devastated Puerto Rico in 2017.

> America was born as a nation of immigrants who have always contributed to its greatness.
> CHARLES B. RANGEL

A NEW START

Ellis Island

Immigrants arrive from Europe to Ellis Island around 1880.

Read the following article. Pay special attention to the words in bold.

In the 1800s, the United States experienced the largest human migration in the history of the world. As more and more immigrants came to the United States, it soon became clear that the original processing center was too small to handle such a large number. Ellis Island, in New York Harbor, was opened **on** January 1, 1892, as the new processing center. **When** the first passengers approached Ellis Island, they saw the new Statue of Liberty, which was only six years old.

The first person to enter Ellis Island was Annie Moore, a teenager from Ireland. **When** she got off the ship **after** traveling for 12 days with her two younger brothers, reporters were waiting to interview her. **After** she went through the registration process, an official gave her a 10-dollar gold coin. That day, 700 immigrants passed through Ellis Island.

During the early 1900s, immigration continued to grow. The largest number of immigrants came **in** 1907. Approximately 1.25 million immigrants came through that year.

For 62 years, Ellis Island was the main door through which millions of immigrants entered the United States. **From** the time it opened **in** 1892 **until** the time it closed **in** 1954, Ellis Island processed 12 million immigrants. Sometimes more than 10,000 people passed through the registry room **in** one 24-hour period. New arrivals often waited **for** many hours **while** inspectors checked to see if they met legal and medical standards. Most did not speak English, and they were tired, hungry, and confused. Two percent (250,000 people) did not meet the requirements to enter the United States and had to return to their countries.

After it closed down, Ellis Island remained abandoned[1] **until** 1965, **when** President Lyndon Johnson decided to restore[2] it as a monument. Restoration of Ellis Island was finished **by** 1990. Visitors to this monument could see the building as it looked **from** 1918 **to** 1920. Almost two million people visited the Ellis Island monument each year **until** a storm damaged the building **in** 2012. Luckily, the exhibits did not suffer damage.

Almost half of Americans are descendants of immigrants who passed through Ellis Island many years **ago**.

---
[1] abandoned: empty
[2] to restore: to make something look like it did when it was new

COMPREHENSION Based on the reading, write T for *true* or F for *false*.

1. __F__ Ellis Island was the first immigrant processing center in the United States.
2. __T__ On the day Annie Moore arrived from Ireland, 700 immigrants passed through Ellis Island.
3. __F__ Ellis Island processed 12 million immigrants in 1954.

THINK ABOUT IT Discuss the questions with a partner or in a small group.

1. What challenges did workers at Ellis Island face when ships arrived with large numbers of potential immigrants?
2. Imagine being a passenger on a ship approaching Ellis Island. You see the Statue of Liberty growing larger as you approach shore. Share how you feel. Include details of how old you are and why you are making this journey to America.

7.1 Time Words

TIME WORD	EXAMPLES	EXPLANATION
on	Ellis Island opened its doors **on** January 1, 1892.	We use *on* with a specific date or day.
in	Ellis Island opened **in** January. Ellis Island opened **in** 1892. **In** the early 1900s, many immigrants came to the U.S. My brother will come to the U.S. **in** two months.	We use *in*: • with a month. • with a year. • with a group of years. • to mean after a period of time.
during	**During** the early 1900s, many immigrants came to the U.S. The building at Ellis Island suffered damage **during** a storm in 2012.	We use *during* with a period of time (*the 1900s, the month of May,* etc.). We use *during* with an event (*the storm, the trip, the movie,* etc.).
for	**For** 62 years, Ellis Island was the main entrance for immigrants to the U.S.	We use *for* with a quantity of years, months, weeks, days, etc.
by	**By** 1990, restoration of Ellis Island was complete.	We use *by* to mean *up to and including a specific time.*
from . . . . . . to . . . till . . . until	Ellis Island was open **from** 1892 **to** 1954. Ellis Island was open **from** 1892 **till** 1954. Ellis Island was open **from** 1892 **until** 1954.	We use *from* with the starting time. We use *to, till,* or *until* with the ending time.
while	**While** they were restoring Ellis Island, it was closed.	We use *while* to mean *during that time.*
when	**When** Ellis Island opened on January 1, 1892, 700 people passed through.	We use *when* to mean *at that time* or *starting at that time.*
while *versus* during	New arrivals waited **while** inspectors checked their documents. New arrivals waited **during** the inspection.	We use *while* with a clause. (Clause = subject + verb) We use *during* with a noun (phrase).
until	Ellis Island remained closed **until** 1990.	We use *until* to mean *before that time and ending at that time.*
in *versus* after	I will become a citizen **in** two months. The plane will arrive **after** 9 p.m. My brother will come to the U.S. **after** he gets his visa.	We use *in* to mean *after a period of time.* We use *after* with a date, time, or action.
ago *versus* before	She got married three years **ago**. She got married **before** she came to the U.S. **Before** 1892, there was a different processing center.	We use *ago* to mean *before now.* We use *before* with an event, a date, or a time.

EXERCISE 1 Listen to this article about the Immigration Act of 1965. Fill in the blanks with the words you hear.

_____Until_____ 1892, the United States did not restrict any group of foreigners from
          1.
coming as immigrants. But _____In_____ 1924, Congress passed a law to limit
                                 2.
immigration. _____from_____ 1924 _____to_____ 1965, the United States had a quota
             3.   4.
system. That means only a limited number of people could come from each country.
_____For_____ all those years, this system discriminated against certain foreigners.
    5.
Northern and Western Europeans received preference over other nationalities. Asians, in
particular, were not welcome.

_____In_____ the 1960s, Americans started to see the quota system as a form of
    6.
discrimination. _____While_____ President Kennedy was in office, he gave a speech about
                      7.
immigration restrictions. He called this system "intolerable." Members of Congress invited
experts to give their opinions. _____During_____ their discussions, they said that very little
                                      8.
would change as a result of changing the law. Congress passed a bill to eliminate the quota
system. When President Johnson signed the bill into law _____on_____ October 3, 1965,
                                                               9.
he said, "It does not affect the lives of millions." But he was completely wrong.

_____In_____ the first five years _____after_____ the bill passed, immigration
    10.   11.
from Asian countries increased by 400 percent _____In_____ the 1950s, six percent of
                                                      12.
immigrants were Asian. _____By_____ the 1990s, 31 percent of immigrants were from
                             13.
Asian countries. Other immigrants and political refugees started coming from Africa and Latin
America. _____By_____ the end of the twentieth century, there was a great change in the
              14.
American population.

When we see the diversity in the United States today, it is hard to imagine that many years
_____ago_____, certain groups of people were not allowed into the United States.
    15.

EXERCISE 2 Circle the correct time word to fill in the blanks.

1. I stayed in my country (**until**/by) I got a visa.

2. I applied for my visa (in/**on**) January.

3. I waited (**for**/from) January (**till**/at) June to get my visa.

176 Unit 7

4. I was very excited (*when*/while) I got my visa.

5. I got my visa five years (before/*ago*).

6. (While/*During*) my trip to the U.S., I couldn't sleep.

7. (*While*/During) I was on the airplane, I couldn't sleep.

8. I never thought about learning English (by/*until*) I applied for my visa.

9. I arrived in New York (*on*/in) July 4, 2014.

10. I was at the airport (during/*for*) three hours.

11. (Until/*By*) 3:30 p.m., I passed through immigration and customs and was ready to start my life in the U.S.

12. I hope my parents will come here (*in*/after) a few years.

13. I hope my parents will come here (during/*after*) they get their visas.

EXERCISE 3 Fill in the blanks with one of the time words from chart 7.1.

1. My grandfather came to the U.S. ____when____ he was 36 years old.

2. My grandfather came to the U.S. many years ____ago____.

3. He lived in Poland ____until____ 1911.

4. He arrived at Ellis Island ____in____ May of 1911.

5. He was alone and scared. He was nervous ____while____ he was in line.

6. In Poland, he didn't study English. He didn't speak a word of English ____until____ he started to work in the U.S. Then he learned a little.

7. My grandmother was without her husband ____from____ 1911 ____to____ 1921.

8. My grandfather worked ____for____ ten years to save money to bring his wife and children to the U.S. Finally, ____in____ 1921, he sent money to bring his family.

9. ____During____ the long trip, my aunt became sick.

10. My grandmother arrived with my mother and her siblings ____on____ August 13, 1921.

11. ____When____ the inspectors examined them, they decided to put my aunt in the hospital. My grandmother was afraid the officials would send them back.

12. ____By____ the end of the week, my aunt was better.

13. ____When____ my aunt felt better, she passed the health inspection. They all took a train to Chicago and started their new life there.

ABOUT YOU Complete each statement about leaving your country. Share your answers with a partner.

1. I stayed in my country until **I won the diversity lottery.**
2. During my trip to the U.S., **I had some funny experiences.**
3. I traveled for **3 hours, when I went to US.**
4. While I was on the airplane/boat/road, **I was tired and hungry.**
5. I arrived on **September 11, 2021**
6. When I arrived, **I was confused, everything was in English and I didn't know too much English at that day.**
7. I never knew **how good the food of different countries was** until I came to the U.S.

7.2 When and Whenever

EXAMPLES	EXPLANATION
When I went to New York a few years ago, I visited Ellis Island.	*When* means *at that time* or *after that time*.
Whenever I go to New York, I enjoy myself.	*Whenever* means *any time* or *every time*.

Note:
In the present, *when* and *whenever* are often interchangeable.
　　When/Whenever my grandfather tells me about his life, I find it very interesting.

EXERCISE 4 Add a main clause to complete each statement. Share your answers with a partner.

1. Whenever people travel by airplane, **they have to pass through security.**
2. Whenever passengers pass through security, **they have to take off their shoes**
3. Whenever passengers are on an airplane, **they have to be kind and neat.**
4. Whenever people fly to another country, **they have to learn a bit of its culture.**
5. Whenever immigrants come to the U.S., **they have to adapt to the language and lifestyle**
6. Whenever I'm on an airplane, **I want to be in peace and full of food.**
7. When I got my visa, **I traveled to US right away**
8. When I arrived in the U.S., **I saw my mom and family.**

> **FUN WITH GRAMMAR**
>
> Create a story. Form groups of three. Your teacher will write five time words on the board. Each team will write a brief story correctly using those time words (e.g., *for*: Martin worked at the company for ten years.). Be creative! The group with the most interesting story and the most correct sentences wins. Be careful: some of these words can have an additional use other than a time word (e.g., This gift is *for* Mike.).

IMMIGRANTS:
Building Businesses and Communities

Read the following article. Pay special attention to the words in bold.

The United States is home to many immigrants and refugees who have come for different reasons. In 1994, Hamdi Ulukaya immigrated to the United States. **When** he **arrived** from Turkey with $3,000, he **was hoping** to learn English and find work. Today his Greek yogurt company, Chobani, has annual sales of about $1.5 billion and employs more than 2,000 people.

Mr. Ulukaya grew up in a small village in eastern Turkey. Many of the villagers were shepherds[1] who took their sheep, goats, and cows into the mountains when the weather was warm. They made yogurt and cheese from the milk. **When** he **was studying** business and English in New York state, he **had** the idea to start a feta cheese[2] company, making cheese from his family's recipe. Then he saw an ad for a yogurt factory for sale. He bought the factory and started a new company, Chobani, which means *shepherd* in Turkish.

In 2010, the company **was growing** and Ulukaya needed more employees. It was important to him to support the community around his factory. Many immigrants and refugees from Africa, Asia, and Eastern Europe **were living** in the area. They needed work and he needed workers. He gave them help with language, training, and transportation, and in return they worked hard. Years later, he opened the world's largest yogurt factory in Twin Falls, Idaho. He hired refugees from the community to work at the new factory. Today approximately 30 percent of his employees are immigrants or refugees. Ulukaya said, "The minute that they got the job, that's the minute they stopped being refugees." There are people from 19 different countries working at Chobani.

Ulukaya knew his employees **were working** hard, but they **were** still **struggling** to support their families. In 2016 he announced a profit-sharing program for employees, which is very rare in manufacturing. Mr. Ulukaya said, "I've built something I never thought would be such a success, but I cannot think of Chobani being built without all these people. Now they'll be working to build the company even more and building their future at the same time." **When** he **immigrated**, Ulukaya **was looking** for work. He created it not only for himself, but for many other immigrants, too.

---
[1] shepherd: a person who takes care of sheep
[2] feta cheese: cheese made from the milk of a goat or sheep

Hamdi Ulukaya, left, with employees in Twin Falls, Idaho, U.S.

Time Words, The Past Continuous   179

COMPREHENSION Based on the reading, write T for *true* or F for *false*.

1. __F__ Ulukaya came to the U.S. to start a business.
2. __T__ Chobani employs many immigrants and refugees.
3. __T__ Ulukaya shares his success with his employees.

THINK ABOUT IT Discuss the questions with a partner or in a small group.

1. What do you think Ulukaya's quote about refugees means?
2. Would you like to work at a company like Chobani? Complete the sentence with your opinion. Then explain it.

    I would/wouldn't like to work for Chobani because...

7.3 The Past Continuous—Form

To form the past continuous, we use *was* or *were* + the present participle (*-ing* form of the verb).

SUBJECT	WAS/WERE (+ NOT)	PRESENT PARTICIPLE	
I	was	reading	about immigrants.
He	was	studying	business.
You	were	asking	about Turkey.
They	were not	living	in Turkey.

Notes:
1. The contraction for *was not* is *wasn't*. The contraction for *were not* is *weren't*.
2. We can put an adverb between *was/were* and the present participle.

    *He was **already** studying English at that time.*
3. The past continuous is also called the past progressive.

Compare statements, *yes/no* questions, short answers, and *wh-* questions.

STATEMENT	YES/NO QUESTION & SHORT ANSWER	WH- QUESTION
They **were living** in Turkey in 2003.	**Were** they **living** in a home? No, they **weren't**.	Where **were** they **living**?
They **weren't living** in their country.	**Were** they **living** in a refugee camp? Yes, they **were**.	Why **were** they **living** in a refugee camp? Why **weren't** they **living** in their country?
A volunteer **was helping** them in the U.S.	**Was** the volunteer **helping** them with English? Yes, she **was**.	Who else **was helping** them?

EXERCISE 5 Listen to the conversation. Then write T for *true* or F for *false*. 7.4

1. __T__ The man was studying medicine when the war broke out.
2. __F__ He needed permission from the refugee agency to go to America.
3. __F__ The man was in the same refugee camp as his parents.

EXERCISE 6 Listen to the conversation again. Fill in the blanks with the words you hear. 7.4

A: Before you came to the U.S., __were you living__ with your parents?
                                        1.
B: No, I __wasn't__ . I __was studying__ at a university in another city.
              2.   3.
A: What __were__ you __studying__ ?
              4.   5.
B: I __was planning__ to become a doctor, but a war broke out. I ran to a refugee camp in
          6.
Kenya. While I __was living__ in the refugee camp, I tried to get information about my
                  7.
family back home, but I couldn't.

A: That's terrible. While you __were living__ in the refugee camp,
                                      8.
__were__ you __planning__ to come to the U.S.?
  9.   10.
B: Of course, I __was thinking__ about it. I __was studying__ English with the hope
                      11.   12.
of coming to the U.S. I didn't know if I would get permission. But finally the United Nations gave me permission.

A: Who __was waiting__ for you at the airport when you arrived?
            13.
B: A man from a refugee agency. When I arrived, he __was holding__ a sign with my name on
                                                          14.
it. He could easily identify me because I __was wearing__ a name tag.
                                              15.
A: Did you ever find your family?

B: Yes, I did. They __were living__ in a refugee camp in Zambia.
                          16.

EXERCISE 7 Fill in the blanks with the past continuous form of the verb given. In some cases, you just need to complete the short answer.

1.
A: I read an article about Annie Moore, the first immigrant to come to Ellis Island. Did you read it, too?

B: Yes. She __was traveling__ to the U.S. with her younger brothers.
                  a. travel
A: __Were they traveling__ with their parents, too?
          b. they/travel
B: No, they __weren't__ .
                  c.
A: Why __weren't they traveling__ with their parents?
              d. they/not/travel
B: Their parents came to the U.S. first. They __were waiting__ for their children at Ellis Island.
                                                    e. wait

continued

Time Words, The Past Continuous **181**

2.
A: What <u>were you doing</u> at about nine o'clock last night?
          <small>a. you/do</small>

<u>Were you sleeping</u>? I called you and texted you, but you didn't answer.
<small>b. you/sleep</small>

B: I <u>was watching</u> a program on TV about immigration.
     <small>c. watch</small>

I <u>was taking</u> notes because I want to write an essay about it.
   <small>d. take</small>

3.
A: My great-grandmother came through Ellis Island.

B: <u>Was she traveling</u> alone?
    <small>a. she/travel</small>

A: No, she <u>wasn't</u>. She was just a little girl. She
           <small>b.</small>

<u>was immigrating</u> to the U.S. with her parents and her brother. Her aunt
<small>c. immigrate</small>

<u>was already living</u> in the U.S.
<small>d. already/live</small>

4.
A: Where <u>were you living</u> when you heard about the assassination of the
         <small>a. you/live</small>

president?

B: We <u>were living</u> in Rwanda.
      <small>b. live</small>

A: <u>Were you working</u>?
   <small>c. you/work</small>

B: Yes, I <u>was</u>.
        <small>d.</small>

A: Where <u>were you working</u>?
         <small>e. you/work</small>

B: At a hospital. My wife was at home. She <u>was taking</u> care of the children.
                                                           <small>f. take</small>

7.4 The Past Continuous with a Specific Time

EXAMPLES	EXPLANATION
In 1993, he **was working** in a hospital.	We use the past continuous to show what was in progress at a specific time in the past.

182 Unit 7

ABOUT YOU Find a partner. Tell your partner if the following things were happening in your life in January, 2019.

1. go to school

    I was (not) going to school in January 2019.

2. work

    I wasn't working anything in January 2019.

3. exercise

    I wasn't exercising, instead I was playing videogames in January 2019.

4. study English

    I was studying English in January 2019.

5. live in the U.S.

    I wasn't living in the US in January 2019.

6. live with my parents

    I was living with my father and grandparents in January 2019.

7. look for a new apartment

    I wasn't looking for a new apartment in January 2019.

8. go out every night with friends

    I wasn't going out every night with friends in January 2019.

9. travel

    I was traveling to small towns in January 2019.

10. celebrate the New Year with friends

    I wasn't celebrating the New Year with friends, I was with my family in January 2019.

ABOUT YOU Find a partner. Ask each other questions with *What were you doing . . . ?* at these times.

1. at six o'clock this morning

    A: What were you doing at six o'clock this morning?
    B: I was sleeping.

2. at ten o'clock last night

3. at nine o'clock this morning

4. at five o'clock yesterday afternoon — What were you doing at five o'clock yesterday ft?
   I was having a dinner with my family
5. at this time yesterday — What were you doing at this time yesterday?
   I was sleeping.
6. at this time last year

    What were you doing at this time last year?
    I was in high school.

7.5 The Past Continuous with a *When* Clause

EXAMPLE	EXPLANATION
He **was working** in a hospital **when** he **heard** the news.	We use the past continuous with the simple past in the same sentence to show the relationship of a longer past action to a shorter past action.
When Annie Moore **arrived** at Ellis Island in 1892, her parents **were waiting** for her.	We use *when* + the simple past in the clause with the shorter action. We use the past continuous in the clause with the longer action.

Note:
If the main clause precedes the time clause, do not separate the two clauses with a comma.
   He was working in a hospital when he heard the news.
If the time clause precedes the main clause, separate the two clauses with a comma.
   When he heard the news, he was working in a hospital.

GRAMMAR IN USE
The past continuous is used to recount events or tell stories. It helps set the scene and portray the mood. The past continuous can also build suspense, which then may be interrupted by an action in the story in the simple past.

*The wind **was howling**, and a fresh layer of snow **was** quickly **covering** everything in sight. One lonely car **was inching** along on the slippery road. Suddenly the car stopped . . .*

EXERCISE 8 Use the past continuous for the longer action and the simple past for the shorter action.

1. She __was traveling__ to the U.S. when she __met__ her future husband.
   (travel) (meet)

2. When I _____ at the airport, my uncle _____ for me.
   (arrive) (wait)

3. They _____ in a refugee camp when they _____ permission to come to the U.S.
   (live) (get)

4. I _____ a program on TV about immigration when I _____ asleep.
   (watch) (fall)

5. We _____ in the U.S. when a war _____ out in our country.
   (live) (break)

6. My wife _____ care of the kids at home when we _____ the news about the president.
   (take) (hear)

7. When the first ship _____ at Ellis Island in 1892, reporters _____ to write about the arrival of the first immigrants there.
   (arrive) (wait)

8. I _____ to the airport to pick up my aunt and uncle when I _____ a flat tire.
   (drive) (get)

184 Unit 7

ALBERT EINSTEIN
Refugee from Germany

Albert Einstein takes the oath during his citizenship ceremony.

Read the following article. Pay special attention to the words in bold.

Of the many refugees who came to the United States, one will always be remembered throughout the world: Albert Einstein. Einstein changed our understanding of the universe.

Einstein was born in Germany in 1879 to Jewish parents. When he graduated from college in Switzerland in 1900, he was planning to become a teacher of physics and math, but he couldn't find a job in those fields. Instead, he went to work in a patent[1] office as a technical expert from 1902 to 1909. **While** he **was working** at this job, he **studied** and **wrote** in his spare[2] time. In 1905, when he was only 26 years old, he published three papers about the basic structure of the universe. His theory of relativity explained the relationship of space and time. He returned to Germany to accept a research position at the University of Berlin. However, in 1920, **while** he **was lecturing** at the university, anti-Jewish groups often **interrupted** his lectures, saying they were "un-German."

In 1921, Einstein visited the United States for the first time. During his visit, he talked not only about his scientific theories, but also about world peace. **While** he **was traveling** outside the country in 1933, the Nazis **came** to power in Germany. They took his property, burned his books, and removed him from his university job.

The United States offered Einstein refugee status, and, in 1940, he became a U.S. citizen. He received many job offers from all over the world, but he decided to accept a position at Princeton University in New Jersey. He lived and worked there until he died in 1955.

---
[1] patent: a document that identifies the owner of a new invention. Only the person or company who has the patent can sell the invention.
[2] spare: free

COMPREHENSION Based on the reading, write T for *true* or F for *false*.

1. _____ Einstein taught math and physics while he was living in Switzerland.
2. _____ In 1933, Einstein returned to his university job in Germany.
3. _____ Einstein developed his theory of relativity while he was living in the United States.

THINK ABOUT IT Discuss the questions with a partner or in a small group.

1. Do you think Einstein faced the same difficulties as other refugees who came to the United States? Why or why not?
2. Look at the photo of the citizenship ceremony. What does it make you think about?

7.6 The Past Continuous with a *While* Clause

EXAMPLES	EXPLANATION
While Einstein **was living** in Switzerland, he **developed** his theory of relativity. **While** Einstein **was traveling** outside of Germany, the Nazis **came** to power.	We use the past continuous with the simple past in the same sentence to show the relationship of a longer past action to a shorter past action. We use *while* + the past continuous in the clause with the longer action. We use the simple past in the clause with the shorter action.
Einstein was living in the U.S. **when** he **died**. **While** he **was living** in the U.S., he wrote many papers.	We use *when* + the simple past with the shorter action. We use *while* + the past continuous with the longer action.

Notes:
1. We can use *when* in place of *while* with a continuous action.
   While Einstein was living in Switzerland, he developed his theory.
   When Einstein was living in Switzerland, he developed his theory.
2. We cannot use *while* with an action that is not continuous.
   NOT: Einstein was living in the U.S. while he died.
3. The simple past form of *be* often has a continuous meaning.
   While Einstein **was** outside the country, the Nazis took his property.
4. We use the past continuous in both clauses if the two actions occurred at the same time.
   While Einstein **was working** at the patent office, he **was thinking** about his theory.

EXERCISE 9 Use the past continuous for the longer action and the simple past for the shorter action.

1. While I __was traveling__ to the U.S., I __met__ a nice man on the airplane.
   (travel) (meet)
2. Einstein __wrote__ about his theory of relativity while he __was working__
   (write) (work)
   in a patent office.
3. While he __was teaching__, some people __interrupted__ his lectures.
   (teach) (interrupt)
4. While I __was reading__ the story about Einstein, I __had__ to use my
   (read) (have)
   dictionary to look up the word "patent."

186 Unit 7

5. While I __was waiting__ (wait) for permission to come to the U.S., I __started__ (start) to study English.

6. While the teacher __was talking__ (talk) about immigration, one of the students __asked__ (ask) an interesting question.

7. I __watched__ (watch) a movie on the airplane while I __was traveling__ (travel) to the U.S.

EXERCISE 10 Fill in the blanks with the simple past or the past continuous of the verb given to complete this conversation.

A: I __was looking__ (1. look) through some old boxes when I __found__ (2. find) this picture of you and Grandpa when you were young. How did you meet Grandpa?

B: One day I __was walking__ (3. walk) in the park in my hometown in Poland when he __stopped__ (4. stop) me to ask what time it was. We started to talk, and then he asked me to go for a cup of coffee with him. We dated, but a few months later his family applied for the green card lottery in the U.S. While we __were dating__ (5. date), they __received__ (6. receive) a letter that gave them permission to immigrate to the U.S.

A: What happened next?

B: At first, I was worried that I'd never see your grandfather again. But he __wrote__ (7. write) to me often and __called__ (8. call) me whenever he could. About a year later, he went back to Poland to visit me. While we __were eating__ (9. eat) in a restaurant, he __asked__ (10. ask) me to marry him.

A: Did you get married right away?

B: Yes. We got married a few weeks later, but then he had to return to the U.S. I couldn't go to the U.S. with him. I had to wait several years.

A: That's awful. What did you do while you __were waiting__ (11. wait)?

B: I took English classes. Finally, I got permission to come. When I __arrived__ (12. arrive) at the airport, he __was waiting__ (13. wait) with roses and balloons.

7.7 The Simple Past vs. The Past Continuous with *When*

Both the simple past and the past continuous can be used in a sentence that has a *when* clause. However, the time sequence is completely different.

EXAMPLES	EXPLANATION
When Einstein **graduated** from college, he **tried** to get a job as a teacher. Einstein **came** to live in the U.S. **when** he **lost** his German citizenship.	If we use the simple past in both clauses, *when* means *after*.
When Einstein **entered** college, he **was living** in Switzerland. Einstein **was living** in the U.S. **when** he **died**.	If we use the simple past after *when* and the past continuous in the main clause, *when* means *at the same time*.

EXERCISE 11 Fill in the blanks with the simple past or the past continuous of the verb given.

1. Henri ___was living___ in a refugee camp when he got his visa.
   live

   When he got to the U.S., he ___needed___ to find a job.
   need

2. He ___was working___ in a hospital when he heard the news about the president.
   work

   When he ___got___ permission, he came to the United States.
   get

3. When they arrived in the U.S., volunteers ___helped___ them.
   help

   When they arrived in the U.S., a volunteer ___was waiting___ for them at the airport.
   wait

4. They ___were living___ in the U.S. when their fourth child was born.
   live

   When their fourth child was born, they ___moved___ to a bigger apartment.
   move

5. When Henri learned enough English, he ___started___ to work in a hotel.
   start

   He ___was working___ in a hotel when his daughter was born.
   work

6. Henri ___was taking___ morning English classes when he found a job.
   take

   Henri ___changed___ to night classes when he found a job.
   change

7. When Einstein entered college, he ___studied___ to become a teacher.
   study

   When Einstein entered college, he ___was living___ in Switzerland.
   live

8. Einstein ___became___ a resident of the U.S. when he lost his German citizenship.
   become

   Einstein ___was living___ in the U.S. when he died.
   live

188 Unit 7

7.8 Using the -ing Form after Time Words

When the main clause and the time clause have the same subject, we can delete the subject of the time clause and use a present participle (verb + -ing) after the time word.

EXAMPLES

1. Einstein left high school **before he finished** his studies.

   Einstein left high school **before finishing** his studies.

2. **After Einstein left** high school, he studied mathematics and physics.

   After leaving high school, Einstein studied mathematics and physics.

Note:
In the second set of examples above, notice that the subject (Einstein) becomes part of the main clause.

EXERCISE 12 Change these sentences. Use a present participle after the time word. Make any other necessary changes.

1. After ~~Einstein entered~~ *entering* the university, ~~he~~ *Einstein* developed his theory.

2. Einstein passed an exam before he entered the university.
   Before entering the university, Einstein passed an exam

3. He left high school before he received his diploma.
   Receiving

4. After Einstein developed his theory of relativity, he became famous.
   developing   *Einstein*

5. He became interested in physics after he received books on science.
   receiving

6. After Einstein came to the U.S., he got a job at Princeton.
   coming   *Einstein*

7. Before he came to the U.S., Hamdi Ulukaya lived in Turkey.
   coming

8. While the children were living in the refugee camp, they didn't go to school.
   The Children

9. The parents were working while they were raising a family.

SUMMARY OF UNIT 7

Time with Dates, Days, Time Periods, etc.

TIME WORD	EXAMPLES

from . . .
  to
  till
  until
	From 1892 **to** 1954, Ellis Island was an immigrant processing center.
	From 1892 **till** 1954, Ellis Island was an immigrant processing center.
	From 1892 **until** 1954, Ellis Island was an immigrant processing center.

during	**During** that time, 12 million immigrants passed through Ellis Island.
for	New arrivals had to wait **for** many hours.
in	**In** 1905, Einstein wrote about relativity. I became a resident **in** March. He'll take his citizenship test **in** six months.
by	Restoration of Ellis Island was finished **by** 1990.
ago	One hundred years **ago**, new arrivals passed through Ellis Island.
on	We came to the U.S. **on** Wednesday.
until	Ellis Island remained closed **until** 1990.
after	**After** class, I saw a movie about immigration.
before	He became a citizen **before** his twentieth birthday.

Time Words with Clauses

TIME WORD	EXAMPLES
when	**When** my grandfather came to the U.S., he passed through Ellis Island. Henri was working in a hospital **when** he heard the news about the president.
while	**While** Einstein was traveling, the Nazis took his property in Germany.
whenever	**Whenever** you enter the U.S., you have to make a declaration of things you're bringing in.
until	Ellis Island remained closed **until** the restoration was complete.

Uses of the Past Continuous

USE	EXAMPLES
To describe a past action that was in progress at a specific moment	At 9:45 a.m., I **was driving** to the airport to pick up my brother. Where **were** you **living** in December, 2013?
With the simple past, to show the relationship of a longer past action to a shorter past action	Einstein **was living** in New Jersey when he died. While Einstein **was living** in Switzerland, he developed his theory of relativity.

REVIEW

Circle the correct words to complete each statement.

1. (While/**When**) Ellis Island opened (**on**/in) January 1, 1892, 700 immigrants passed through.

2. (**During**/For) the early 1900s, immigration was high.

3. Ellis Island closed as an immigrant processing center (**in**/at) 1954.

4. (**When**/While) Annie Moore arrived with her two brothers, her parents (waited/**were waiting**) for them.

5. (While/**For**) many years, immigrants from Asian countries weren't welcome.

6. The immigration law didn't change (**until**/by) 1965 (**when**/while) President Johnson (**signed**/was signing) a new law.

7. President Johnson started restoration of Ellis Island. It was finished (until/**by**) 1990.

8. (While/**Whenever**) people enter another country, they have to pass through customs.

9. (During/**While**) we were visiting New York last year, we (**decided**/were deciding) to see the Statue of Liberty.

10. You can visit the Statue of Liberty (of/**from**) 8:30 a.m. (**till**/at) 5 p.m.

11. Einstein died while he (**was living**/lived) in Princeton, New Jersey.

12. He lived in the U.S. (**for**/during) 22 years.

13. I came to the U.S. five years (before/**ago**).

14. When I (**arrived**/was arriving) in the U.S., I was so happy.

15. Before (to come/**coming**) to the U.S., I studied English.

16. I will become a citizen (after/**in**) five years.

FROM GRAMMAR TO WRITING

PART 1 Editing Advice

1. Put the subject before the verb in all clauses.

   When ~~came my mother~~ *my mother came* to the U.S., our family was so happy.

2. Use *when,* not *while,* if the action has no duration.

   ~~While~~ *When* she arrived, we were waiting for her.

3. Be careful to choose the correct time word.

   She traveled ~~during~~ *for* 10 hours.

   She arrived ~~in~~ *on* May 2.

4. Don't confuse *before* and *ago.*

   I came to the U.S. three years ~~before~~ *ago*.

5. After a time word, use an *-ing* form, not a base form.

   After ~~learn~~ *learning* English, she found a job.

6. Don't forget *be* and *-ing* with the past continuous.

   At 9:30 last night, I was watch*ing* a program about immigration.

   They *were* talking about famous immigrants on this program.

7. Don't forget to use a comma if the time clause precedes the main clause.

   When he heard the news*,* he was studying at the university.

PART 2 Editing Practice

Some of the shaded words and phrases have mistakes. Find the mistakes and correct them. If the shaded words are correct, write C.

I left my country three years **ago** [C]. But my husband didn't come with me. (1.)
He wanted to stay in our country **during** [for] two more years **until** (2.) (3.) he
finished college. **While** (4.) I got here, I started to study English right away.
While (5.) I **going** (6.) to school, I worked in the school library.
My husband **was plan** (7.) to get a degree in engineering **when** (8.) a war **broke** (9.)
out in our country. When **started the war** (10.), he left the country quickly
and went to a neighboring country. He was in a refugee camp **during** (11.) one

192 Unit 7

year. While he was living in the camp, he started to study English. He applied
        12.
for permission to come to the United States. After wait for one year, he finally got
                                                      13.
permission. When he was getting here, we were so excited to see each other again.
            14.   15.

He's learning English quickly. After he learns English well enough, he's

going to enter an engineering program. I know he'll be happy until he gets
                                                              16.
his engineering degree. Until then, he will continue to work and study. While he
                        17.   18.
finishes his program, we will celebrate.

> **WRITING TIP**
> Use time words (*before, after, while*) to combine short simple sentences into more sophisticated sentences.
>
> *I graduated from college in 2001. I wasn't sure what to do with my life.*
>
> **When** *I graduated from college in 2001, I wasn't sure what to do with my life.*
>
> Make your writing smoother by using present participles after time words when each clause has the same subject.
>
> *After Jack moved to Boston, he decided to pursue a career in politics.*
>
> ***After moving*** *to Boston, Jack decided to pursue a career in politics.*

PART 3 Write

Read the prompts. Choose one and write a paragraph about it.

1. Write about a major historical event that took place in your country or in another part of the world. What was happening when this event took place? What happened afterwards? If you research your paragraph, provide your sources.
2. Write about an important event that took place in your life or in the life of a famous person.

PART 4 Edit

Reread the Summary of Unit 7 and the editing advice. Edit your writing from Part 3.

UNIT

8

Modals

Where We Live

> Quality of life actually begins at home - it's in your street, around your community.
> CHARLES KENNEDY

Friends gather on a rooftop in Bulgaria.

An Apartment Lease

Read the following article. Pay special attention to the words in bold. 8.1

Do you live in an apartment? **Did** you **have to sign** a lease? **Could** you **understand** what you signed? A lease, or rental agreement, **can be** hard to read, but you **should try** to understand what you are signing.

Your lease is a legal agreement between the owner (landlord[1]) and you, the renter (tenant). A lease states the period of time for the rental, the amount of the rent, when the tenant **must pay** it, who pays for utilities[2], and any rules the renter and the landlord **must follow**. Some leases contain the following rules:

- Pets **are not permitted**.
- Renters **may not change** the locks without the owner's permission.
- Renters **must pay** a late fee if they don't pay their rent on time.

The lease **might** even **state** how many overnight guests you **may have** and where you **can** or **cannot park**.

Many of the rules in the lease are for the benefit of the owner. The owner protects his or her property by requiring a security deposit. Usually a renter **has to pay** one to two months' rent as a deposit. The owner **can use** part or all of the money to repair any damage the renter causes. However, the landlord **may not keep** the renter's money for normal wear and tear[3].

There are also rules that protect the renter. For example, owners **must provide** heat during the winter months. In most cities, they **must put** a smoke detector in each apartment and in the halls. The owner **may not raise** the rent during the period of the lease.

When the landlord gives the renter the lease, it looks like an unchangeable document, but it isn't. Renters **don't have to accept** and sign the lease as is. If they don't agree to all the terms, they **can ask** for changes before they sign. For example, if you **would like to have** a pet, you **can ask** for permission by offering to pay a higher security deposit.

There **has to be** trust between the landlord and the renter. When looking for a new apartment, if you have a bad feeling about the landlord, you probably **ought to look** elsewhere.

---

[1] landlord: the owner of a rental property. If the owner is a woman, she is called "landlady."
[2] utilities: basic services such as water, electricity, or gas
[3] normal wear and tear: the normal use of something

A young woman takes a break from unpacking to video chat with family.

COMPREHENSION Based on the reading, write T for *true* or F for *false*.

1. __F__ A renter cannot ask for changes to a lease.
2. __T__ The owner can use the security deposit to pay for a renter's damages.
3. __F__ The owner can raise the rent during the term of the lease.

THINK ABOUT IT Discuss the questions with a partner or in a small group.

1. Imagine the following situation. You are a tenant with a one-year lease. After two months, you receive a letter from the landlord that rent is increasing by $100. What would you say or do?
2. What are some issues that a tenant and landlord might need to negotiate? You can use ideas from the article or your own experience.

8.1 Overview of Modals

Modals add meaning to the verbs that follow them. The modal verbs are *can, could, should, would, may, might,* and *must*.

EXAMPLES	EXPLANATION
A renter **must sign** a lease. A tenant **can ask** for changes before signing the lease.	The base form of the verb follows a modal. A modal never has an *-s* ending.
You **should not pay** your rent late. I **cannot understand** my lease.	To form the negative, we put *not* after the modal. The negative of *can* is written as one word: *cannot*. The contraction for *cannot* is *can't*.
If you don't trust the landlord, you **should probably look** for another apartment.	We can put an adverb between the modal and the main verb.

Notice these seven patterns with a modal:

AFFIRMATIVE STATEMENT:	We **can have** a cat in the apartment.
NEGATIVE STATEMENT:	We **can't have** a dog.
YES/NO QUESTION:	**Can** we **have** a bird?
SHORT ANSWER:	Yes, you **can**.
WH- QUESTION:	Why **can** we **have** a cat?
NEGATIVE WH- QUESTION:	Why **can't** we **have** a dog?
SUBJECT QUESTION:	Who **can have** a dog?

8.2 Phrasal Modals

Phrasal modals are expressions that are like modals in meaning.

EXPRESSIONS	EXAMPLES
have to	He **has to sign** the lease.
have got to	He **has got to return** the security deposit.
be able to	He **is able to pay** the rent.
be supposed to	I'm **supposed to pay** my rent by the first of the month.
be permitted to	You **are not permitted to park** on the side of the building.
be allowed to	You **are not allowed to change** the locks in your apartment.
ought to	You **ought to respect** your neighbors.
had better	You **had better read** your lease carefully before signing it.

EXERCISE 1 Listen to the statements. Then write T for *true* or F for *false*. 8.2

1. __T__ It is possible that a landlord will let you out of your lease early.
2. __T__ If there is damage to the apartment, the landlord probably won't return the security deposit.
3. __T__ A landlord cannot refuse to rent to a person based on sex, race, or religion.

EXERCISE 2 Listen again to these sentences about renting an apartment. Fill in the blanks with the words you hear. 8.2

1. When a lease is up for renewal, the owner ___can___ offer the renter a new lease, or he ___might___ ask the renter to leave.
2. The owner ___supposed to___ notify the renter if he or she wants the renter to leave.
3. If you pay your rent late, you ___might___ have to pay a late fee.
4. If you want to make changes to the lease, you and the landlord ___should___ initial the changes.
5. What if you ___have to___ move before the lease is up? What ___should___ you do? You ___ought to___ inform the landlord as soon as possible.
6. ___Can___ the landlord make you pay until the end of your lease? Yes, he ___can___.
7. Some landlords ___may___ let you out of your lease by keeping your security deposit. Or a landlord ___can___ make you pay until the end of your lease.
8. The landlord ___must___ return your security deposit if there is no damage to the apartment.
9. The landlord ___has___ obey the law. He ___can't___ refuse to rent to a person because of sex, race, religion, nationality, or disability.
10. If the landlord doesn't keep his end of the agreement, you ___might___ need a lawyer.

EXERCISE 3 Read each statement. Fill in the blanks to complete the question.

1. You should read the lease before you sign it. Why ___should I___ read the lease before I sign it?
2. You can't have a dog. Why _____ a dog?
3. We must pay a security deposit. How much _____?
4. Someone must install a smoke detector. Who _____ a smoke detector?
5. The landlord must return the security deposit. When _____ it?
6. The landlord said I can pick up the key tomorrow. What time _____ the key?

198   Unit 8

8.3 Obligation/Necessity—*Must* and Phrasal Modals

MUST	PHRASAL MODAL	EXPLANATION
The landlord **must provide** smoke detectors.	The landlord **has to provide** smoke detectors.	We use *must* and *have to* for rules and obligations. *Must* is more formal than *have to*.
	I've **got to call** my landlord today. I **have to tell** him about a problem in my bathroom.	We use *have to* or *have got to* for personal obligations or necessities.
	At the end of my lease last June, I **had to move**. I **had to find** a bigger apartment.	*Must* has no past form. The past of both *must* and *have to* is *had to*.

Notes:
1. *Have got to* is usually contracted with a subject pronoun.
   I have got to = I've got to   He has got to = He's got to
2. We don't use *have got to* for questions or negatives.
3. Many legal documents use *shall* for obligation.
   If the security deposit does not cover the cost to repair any damages, the tenant shall pay the additional costs to the owner.

Pronunciation Note:
In informal speech, *have to* is often pronounced "hafta." *Has to* is often pronounced "hasta." *Got to* is often pronounced "gotta." In informal speech and writing, people often say or write "gotta." (I gotta go now.)

EXERCISE 4 Fill in the blanks with one of the items from the box. Use the correct form of *have*.

have to notify	have to move	must put	must give ✓
have got to obey	have to sign	have to return	have got to clean

1. The landlord ___must give___ you heat in cold weather.
2. You ___have to sign___ the lease with a pen. A pencil is not acceptable.
3. The landlord ___has to return___ your security deposit if you leave your apartment in good condition.
4. The landlord ___has to notify___ you if he wants you to leave at the end of your lease.
5. The landlord ___must put___ a smoke detector in each apartment and in the hallways.
6. I ___have got to obey___ the rules of the lease.
7. My new apartment is dirty. I ___have got to clean___ it before I move in.
8. My old apartment was too expensive, so I ___have to move___ last month.

ABOUT YOU Make a list of personal obligations you, your roommate, or your family members have in your apartment or house. Practice *have to* and *have got to*. Share your answers with a partner.

1. I've got to throw out the garbage twice a week.
2. My roommate has to clean the kitchen on the weekend.
3. I've got to keep my bedroom neat and clean.
4. I have to clean my shower frequently.
5. My mom has to clean the living room.

ABOUT YOU Make a list of things you had to do last weekend. Share your answers with a partner.

1. I had to do my laundry.
2. I had to organize my shoes.
3. I had to wash the garage.
4. I had to clean the cars sits.
5. I had to organize my clean clothes.

8.4 Permission/Prohibition—*May* and Phrasal Modals

MAY	PHRASAL MODALS	EXPLANATION
The landlord **may enter** the apartment in case of emergency.	The landlord **is permitted to enter** the apartment in case of emergency.	We can use *may*, *be permitted to*, and *be allowed to* for permission or prohibition. We often see *may* in legal documents.
The tenant **may not leave** items in the hallway.	The tenant **is not allowed to leave** items in the hallway.	

Notes:
1. *May not* and *must not* have the same meaning—prohibition.
    Tenants **may not park** behind the building.
    Tenants **must not park** behind the building.
2. Many legal documents use *shall (not)* for permission or prohibition.
    The tenant **shall have** one parking space behind the building.
    The tenant **shall not change** the locks without the owner's permission.

200 Unit 8

EXERCISE 5 The rules for driving in the United States are similar in most states. Fill in the blanks with one of the phrases from the box to complete each sentence.

aren't allowed to ride	must reduce	may not go	have to go
aren't permitted to hold	may drive	must have	must wear ✓
may not pass	have to get	may not park	may use

1. You _____must wear_____ a seatbelt.

2. If you are from another state or another country, you _____may get_____ with a valid license. However, you _____have to get_____ a license in the state where you're living (usually within 90 days).

3. You _____may not park_____ in a disabled parking space unless your vehicle has a disabled license plate or a removable windshield card.

4. Bicycle riders _____aren't allowed to ride_____ against traffic. They _____have to go_____ in the same direction as traffic.

5. A driver _____must have_____ insurance.

6. You _____may not pass_____ on a hill or curve if you are not able to see the oncoming vehicles.

7. In many places, you _____aren't permitted to hold_____ a cell phone in your hand while driving. However, you _____have to get_____ a hands-free device.

8. Drivers _____must reduce_____ their speed in a school zone during school hours.

9. When a school bus stops for children to get on or off, you _____may not go_____ around it.

8.5 Expectation—Be Supposed To

EXAMPLES	EXPLANATION
The landlord **is supposed to give** you a copy of the lease. When **am I supposed to pay** the rent? My friend **is supposed to help** me move.	*Be supposed to* expresses an expectation. We expect something because of: 　a law or a requirement. 　a personal obligation.
We're not supposed to have cats in my building, but my neighbor has one. **I was supposed to pay** my rent yesterday, but I forgot.	We use *be supposed to* when someone broke a rule or did not meet an expectation.

Pronunciation Note:
We don't pronounce the *d* in *supposed to*.

Modals 201

EXERCISE 6 Finish these statements. Use *be supposed to* (present or past, affirmative or negative) and one of the verbs from the box. Use contractions wherever possible.

use	paint	provide	pay ✓	clean	take out
return	fix	replace	wash	have	

1. I 'm supposed to pay my rent on the first of the month.
2. Pets are not permitted in my apartment. I 'm not supposed to have a pet.
3. In which months is the landlord supposed to provide heat?
4. The tenants are supposed to clean the apartment before they move out.
5. My stove isn't working. My landlord is supposed to fix it tomorrow.
6. We're going to move out next week. Our apartment is clean and in good condition. The landlord is supposed to return our security deposit.
7. The janitor is supposed to take out the garbage every day.
8. When we moved in, we were supposed to use the back stairs, not the front stairs.
9. My smoke detector doesn't work. The landlord is supposed to replace it.
10. My landlord was supposed to paint the walls of my apartment last month, but he didn't do it. I'm still waiting.
11. My roommate was supposed to wash the dishes last night, but she forgot.

8.6 Ability/Permission—*Can, Could,* and Phrasal Modals

CAN/COULD	PHRASAL MODALS	EXPLANATION
I **can clean** the apartment by Friday. I **can't understand** the lease.	I **am able to clean** the apartment by Friday. I **am not able to understand** the lease.	Ability/ Inability
I **could understand** the first page of the lease. I **couldn't understand** the rest of the lease.	I **was able to understand** the first page of the lease. I **wasn't able to understand** the rest of the lease.	Past Ability/ Inability
I **can have** a cat in my apartment. I **can't have** a dog.	I **am permitted to have** a cat in my apartment. I **am not allowed to have** a dog.	Permission/ Prohibition
I **could have** a cat in my last apartment, but I **couldn't have** a dog.	I **was permitted to have** a cat in my last apartment, but I **wasn't allowed to have** a dog.	Past Permission/ Prohibition

Notes:
1. We also use *may* for permission. *May* is more formal than *can*.
2. A common expression with *can* is *can(not) afford*.

   I **can afford** a one-bedroom apartment. I **can't afford** a two-bedroom apartment.

Pronunciation Note:

Can is not usually stressed in affirmative statements. In negative statements, *can't* is stressed, but it can be hard to hear the final *t*. So we must pay attention to the vowel sound and stress to hear the difference between *can* and *can't*.

    I "can" go. (kIn)   I "can't" go. (kænt)

In a short answer, we pronounce *can* as /kæn/.

    "Can" you help me later?   Yes, I "can." (kæn)

EXERCISE 7 Fill in the blanks with one of the words from the box to complete this conversation.

can't carry	can give	can't do	couldn't reach
wasn't able to find	're not allowed to use ✓	can you put	can cook
'm not allowed to leave	're not permitted to use	are you able to wash	can't afford

A: How do you like your new apartment?

B: The apartment is great. But I don't like some of the rules. For example, we **'re not allowed to use** (1.) the laundry room after 11 p.m. I work late, and I **can't do** (2.) my laundry in the daytime.

A: **Are you able to wash** (3.) your clothes on Sundays?

B: Yes, but that's when most people do their laundry. Also, I like to barbecue on the porch. But we **'re not permitted to use** (4.) a fire grill. We **can cook** (5.) on a gas grill, but I prefer a fire grill. Here's another problem: I use my bike every day, but I **'m not allowed to leave** (6.) it in the hallway. I'm on the third floor, and there's no elevator. I **can't carry** (7.) my bike upstairs every day.

A: **Can you put** (8.) your bike in the basement?

B: I don't know. I don't have a key to the basement. I called the landlord yesterday to ask him about it, but I **couldn't reach** (9.) him.

A: Try again. Is your roommate happy with the apartment?

B: I don't have a roommate. I **wasn't able to find** (10.) one. But the rent is high, and I **can't afford** (11.) it on my own.

A: I have a friend who's looking for a roommate. I **can give** (12.) you his phone number.

B: Thanks.

Modals **203**

In the U.S., people buy over a billion plastic bottles every year. We recycle only 25% of them.

FREQUENTLY ASKED QUESTIONS:
Recycling Plastic in Your Home

Read the following FAQs. Pay special attention to the words in bold. 8.3

Q: Why **should** I **recycle** plastic?

A: In the United States, we produce tons of plastic waste every year, but we recycle only about nine percent of it. A lot of this plastic goes into the ocean, and it is killing sea animals. Plastic is appearing in our food and drinking water now, too. As one expert said recently: We**'d better do** something about this problem. . . before it's too late. Everyone **ought to recycle** and **use** less plastic.

Q: Where **should** I **recycle** plastic items?

A: If your city has a recycling program, your dorm or home will have a bin. (It's usually blue or gray.) You **should put** your plastic items here.

Note: In many U.S. cities, all recyclable items (plastic, glass, paper, metal) go in the same bin. However, in some cities (e.g., New York City), plastic, glass, and metal items go in one bin and paper in another. If you aren't sure what to do, you**'d better check** online. Residents can be fined[1] for not putting items in the correct bin.

Q: **Should** I **put** plastic bags in the recycling bin?

A: **No,** you **shouldn't**. Many recycling centers do not take them. If possible, you **ought to keep** the plastic bags and take them to a supermarket. Many stores recycle them.

Q: **Should** I **clean** plastic containers first?

A: **Yes,** you **should**. Dirty bottles and other containers cannot be recycled, so you **shouldn't leave** food or liquid in them. Also, you **ought to remove** the caps[2] from bottles and jars. (The cap and container are usually different kinds of plastic.)

Q: I want to use less plastic, but it's hard. What **should** I **do**?

A: Over 40 percent of all plastic waste comes from single-use plastics (shopping bags, cups, bottles). You **ought to stop** using these items. Instead, you **should buy** and **use** your own bag or bottle. Many coffeeshops and stores give a discount[3] when you bring your own bottle or bag. By doing this, you can make a big difference—and you'll save money, too!

---

[1] fined: charged money as a punishment for breaking a rule
[2] cap: the cover on top of a bottle, jar, or other container
[3] discount: a little bit of money subtracted from the regular price

COMPREHENSION Based on the reading, write T for *true* or F for *false*.

1. _F_ In many U.S. cities, you should put plastic in one bin and glass, metal, and paper in another.
2. _F_ In many U.S. cities, plastic bags go in the recycling bin.
3. _F_ It is OK to put a dirty container in the recycling bin with the cap on.

THINK ABOUT IT Discuss the questions with a partner or in a small group.

1. According to the reading, why should we reduce and recycle? Explain in your own words.
2. The reading gives tips for using less plastic. What are they? Do you do these things? What else should you do? Think of at least one more idea.

8.7 Advice—*Should, Ought To, Had Better*

EXAMPLES	EXPLANATION
You **should bring** your own shopping bag to the store. You **shouldn't put** plastic bags in the recycling bin.	For advice, we use *should*. *Should* = It's a good idea. *Shouldn't* = It's a bad idea.
Everyone **ought to recycle** plastic.	*Ought to* means the same as *should*. We don't usually use *ought to* in questions or negatives.
Plastic is in our food and drinking water. We **had better do** something about this problem before it's too late. We**'d better not wait** much longer.	When it is probable that something bad or unpleasant will happen, we use *had better (not)*. The contraction for *had* (in *had better*) is *'d*. I'd you'd he'd she'd we'd they'd

Note:
Should is for advice. *Must* is for obligation or necessity.
Compare:
  You **should bring** your own shopping bags to the store. (advice)
  You **must pay** 10 cents for each new bag at the store. (obligation)

Pronunciation Note:
Native speakers often don't pronounce *had* or the *'d* in *had better*. You will hear people say:
  If you are unsure about the recycling rules, **you better ask**.

EXERCISE 8 Complete each sentence with *should/ought to, shouldn't,* or *'d better*.

1. The blue bin is for recycling. You ___shouldn't___ put garbage in there.
2. All glass and plastic bottles ___should___ go in the recycling bin.
3. You ___'d better___ not pour cooking oil down the sink. It can block the drain.
4. Everyone ___ought to___ use less plastic. It's good for the environment.
5. You ___shouldn't___ put broken glass in recycling. It goes in the garbage bin.
6. You ___should___ bring your own cup to a coffeeshop. You'll get a discount.

EXERCISE 9 It is the end of the school year, and two college students are cleaning their dorm room. Unscramble the words to complete the dialogue.

A: OK, we packed our clothes. ___What should we do___ next?
     1. should/we/what/do

B: I think ___we should throw out___ the trash.
     2. should/we/throw out

A: OK. ___Should I put___ all these plastic bottles in the garbage?
     3. put/I/should

B: No. ___Those ought to go___ in recycling.
     4. go/those/ought to

A: Oh, right. And these old batteries? ___Where should I put___ them?
     5. I/where/put/should

B: I'm not sure. ___You'd better check___ online.
     6. better/check/you'd

A: Good idea. It says ___we shouldn't put___ batteries in the garbage.
     7. shouldn't/we/put

___We should take them___ to the campus recycling center.
     8. them/we/take/should

B: OK. What about this microwave oven? It doesn't work anymore. ___Should we leave it___ here?
     9. we/it/leave/should

A: ___We'd better not___. The school charges money if we leave things in the room. I'll take
     10. better/not/we'd

it with me.

EXERCISE 10 Read about the recycling rules in one community. For each item, write a sentence that explains the rule. Use *should/ought to* and *shouldn't*.

SHOULD THESE ITEMS GO IN THE RECYCLING BIN?			
ITEM	RECYCLING	GARBAGE	OTHER
1. plastic bags		✓	✓(recycle at a supermarket)
2. milk cartons	✓		
3. paper napkins			✓(put in the compost bin; use cloth)
4. laundry soap bottles	✓		
5. light bulbs		✓(regular bulbs)	✓(CFLs: take to a recycling center)
6. magazines	✓		
7. old pens		✓	
8. an old phone			✓(take to a recycling center or donate)
9. takeout containers	✓		
10. batteries			✓(put in a bag on top of the garbage bin)

1. Plastic bags shouldn't go in the recycling bin. You should put them in the garbage bin or recycle them at a supermarket.

2. _____

3. _____
4. _____
5. _____
6. _____
7. _____
8. _____
9. _____
10. _____

8.8 Negatives of Modals

EXAMPLES	EXPLANATION
Tenants **are not supposed to leave** bikes near the door, but someone always does.	*Be not supposed to* shows that something is not acceptable by rule or custom.
Renters **must not change** the locks. Renters **may not change** the locks. Renters **cannot change** the locks. Renters **are not allowed to change** the locks. Renters **are not permitted to change** the locks.	*Must not, may not, cannot, be not allowed to,* and *be not permitted to* show prohibition.
I **cannot** open this water bottle. I **am not able to** open this water bottle.	*Cannot* and *be not able to* show inability.
You **shouldn't put** plastic bottles in the garbage bin. They go in recycling.	*Shouldn't* shows that something is not advisable.
Renters **don't have to accept** the lease as is. They can ask for changes.	*Don't have to* shows that something is not necessary. It often means that there is an option.
You **had better not make** noise at night. You will disturb your neighbors.	*Had better not* shows that a negative consequence can result.

Note:
Even though *have to* and *must* have basically the same meaning in the affirmative, in the negative they are completely different.

You **must sign** the lease. = You **have to sign** the lease.

The landlord **doesn't have to renew** the lease. (He has a choice.)

He **must not enter** your apartment without your permission. (This is prohibited.)

Modals 207

EXERCISE 11 Circle the correct words to complete this list of advice on living in the United States. In some cases, both answers are possible, so circle both options.

1. Americans are generally on time for appointments. You (*can't*/**shouldn't**) keep people waiting.

2. You (***shouldn't/must not***) visit friends without an invitation. If someone says, "Let's get together sometime," wait for a specific invitation.

3. Americans don't like to wait in line, but if they have to, they're usually courteous. You (***shouldn't***/*don't have to*) push to try to get ahead of someone.

4. Bribing[1] an official is against the law. You (***must not***/*don't have to*) offer a bribe if a police officer gives you a ticket or a government official turns down your application.

5. When you buy new items in a store, you (***had better not/shouldn't***) try to negotiate the price. Prices in stores are fixed. However, a major exception is when buying a new car. You (***don't have to***/*must not*) pay the asking price. The price is negotiable.

6. You (***may not/must not***) drive without insurance in the U.S. You (***must/have to***) have insurance to protect the other car and driver. You (***don't have to***/*must not*) have insurance to protect your own car.

7. In most places, you (***may not/can't***) use a hand-held cell phone while driving.

---

[1] bribing: the illegal act of offering money in exchange for something

Americans generally don't dress up for casual house parties.

8. A driver's license is often used for identification, but you (*must not/don't have to*) have a driver's license. You can get a state ID. A state ID looks like a driver's license, but you (*can't/aren't allowed to*) drive a car with it.

9. If you have a Social Security number, you (*shouldn't/can't*) give it to strangers over the phone. Someone can steal your identity and cause you a lot of problems.

10. Americans are generally very casual. If you're invited to an informal party at someone's house, you (*don't have to/may not*) dress up.

11. If you are invited to a party, you (*aren't supposed to/don't have to*) bring anything, but many guests will come with something to eat, such as a dessert or something to drink. When you leave, you (*shouldn't/may not*) take that food or drink home. It's the custom to leave it there.

12. If you are invited to a formal wedding, you (*aren't supposed to/must not*) take children unless the invitation specifically invites them.

EXERCISE 12 Fill in the blanks with the negative of *have to, should, be supposed to, must, had better, can,* or *may* to complete the conversation between students (A) and their teacher (B). In some cases, more than one answer is possible.

A: Do I have to sit in a specific seat for the test?

B: No, you _____don't have to_____ . You can choose any seat you want.
   1.

A: Is it OK if I talk to another student during a test?

B: No. Absolutely not. You _____might not_____ talk to another student during a test.
   2.

A: Is it OK if I use my book?

B: Sorry. You _____might not_____ use your book.
   3.

A: What if I don't understand something on the test?

B: Please ask me if you have a question.

A: What happens if I'm late for the test? Will you let me in?

B: Of course I'll let you in. But you _____shouldn't_____ come late. You'll need a lot of
   4.
time for the test.

A: Do I have to bring my computer for the final test?

B: If you want to, you can. But you _____don't have to_____ bring it.
   5.
There will be school computers you can use.

continued

A: Do I have to write my final essay on the computer? Or can I use a pen and paper?

B: You can use whatever you want. You ___don't have to___ use a computer.
6.

A: Do you have any advice on test-taking?

B: Yes. On the grammar section, if you see an item that is difficult for you, go on to the next item. You ___shouldn't___ spend too much time on a difficult item, or you won't finish the test.
7.

A: Can I bring coffee into the classroom?

B: The school has a rule about eating or drinking in the classroom. You ___may not___ bring food or drinks into the classroom.
8.

A: How long will we have for the test?

B: You'll have two hours. That's usually enough time. If you finish early, you ___don't have to___ stay. You can leave.
9.

A: If we need more time, can we keep working?

B: You ___might not___ need more time. But I will give you 10 extra minutes if you do.
10.

A: Will we get our test results tomorrow?

B: You ___can't___ expect me to grade 25 tests overnight! You'll get the results by the end of the week.
11.

> **FUN WITH GRAMMAR**
>
> Imagine a new student is joining your class. Work with a partner to write a list of class regulations and advice. They can be serious or silly and may include both things you should do and things you shouldn't or can't do.
>
> *Students are not permitted to have pizza delivered during class.*
>
> *You should have two notebooks—one for general notes and one for vocabulary.*

Starting Life in a NEW COUNTRY

A neighborhood party

Read the following article. Pay special attention to the words in bold. 8.4

You're about to go to college in the United States. Or your family just moved to the United States. Your friends back home tell you, "It **must be** so exciting to live in a new country." But there are so many new rules and customs to learn. After the excitement wears off[1], there are many questions you'll have and decisions you have to make.

Now you're here, and you find yourself in situations that are completely new to you. You **might ask** yourself: "Should I buy a car or use public transportation? Should I get a roommate? If so, how and where? How do I find a doctor? Where do I get insurance? How do I find a job? When and where do I tip?" There **must be** hundreds of things you never thought about before.

In addition to those practical things, you **might** also **wonder** about social differences. You **might ask** yourself: "What topics are appropriate for making small talk here? What topics **might not be** so good? Why did the person I am talking to step back from me? Did I say something wrong?" It **might be** that you are standing too close. People in the U.S. like their personal space. This is one of many unspoken rules that **might be** new to you.

Besides questions you have about life in the United States, you're probably discovering that many Americans are curious about you. Of course, they'll ask you where you're from. Keep in mind that they **might not know** much about your country or culture. If you say Sri Lanka, for example, they **may have** no idea where this is. They **might not understand** the differences between different Asian countries. If you're from Brazil, people **might think** you speak Spanish. People who think that **must not know** that Portuguese is the language of Brazil. Just explain where you're from and what language you speak.

With time, you'll learn more about American behaviors, and others will learn more about you and your native culture.

---

[1] to wear off: to go away, little by little

Modals 211

COMPREHENSION Based on the reading, write T for *true* or F for *false*.

1. __T__ Americans are often curious about foreigners.
2. __T__ Some Americans might not know a lot about different Asian countries.
3. __T__ Everyone knows that Portuguese is the language of Brazil.

THINK ABOUT IT Discuss the questions with a partner or in a small group.

1. Describe a situation in the U.S. that was new or confusing for you. Explain how you handled it.
2. Talk about the questions you wanted answers to when you first moved to the United States. How did you find the answers?

8.9 Conclusions or Deductions—*Must*

EXAMPLES	EXPLANATION
It **must be** exciting to live in another country. You're from Mexico? You **must speak** Spanish, then.	We often make a deduction or come to a conclusion using *must*. We think our assumption is probably true. (We may be wrong.)
I told a classmate that I'm from Brazil. He thinks I speak Spanish. He **must not know** much about Brazil.	For a negative deduction/conclusion, we use *must not*. We don't use a contraction.

Note:
Remember, we also use *must* to express necessity.
    Students must register for classes.

EXERCISE 13 Fill in the blanks with an appropriate verb phrase from the box to complete the conversation between two neighbors. You may use an answer more than once.

must spend	must have	must get	must not like
must know	must not be	must be	

A: Hi. My name's Alma. I live on the third floor. You ___must be___ new in this building.
                                               1.

B: I am. We just moved in last week. My name's Eva.

A: I noticed your last name on the mailbox. It's Gonzalez. Are you from Mexico?

B: No. Actually I'm from the Philippines.

A: I'm so sorry. You ___must get___ that mistake all the time. Are you going to school now?
                                 2.

B: Yes, I'm taking English classes at Washington College. I'm in Level 5.

A: You ___must know___ my husband, Hasan. He's also in the Level 5 class there.
               3.

B: Oh, yes, I know him. I didn't know he lived in the same building. I never see him here. He ___must not be___ home very much.
               4.

A: He isn't. He has two jobs. By the way, I saw the movers carrying in a crib.

You __must have__ a baby.
5.

B: We do. We have a 10-month-old son. He's sleeping now. Do you have any kids?

A: Yes. I have a 16-year-old daughter and an 18-year-old son. I __must spend__ half my time
6.

worrying about them. My daughter texts her friends all day.

B: Kids today __must not like__ to talk much. They rely more on texting.
7.

A: You're right. Listen, I don't want to take up any more of your time. You __must have__ a
8.

lot to do. I just wanted to bring you these cookies.

B: That's very nice of you. They're still warm. They __must be__ right out of the oven.
9.

A: They are. Maybe we can talk some other time when you're all unpacked.

EXERCISE 14 Use *must* + base form to show Eva's conclusions about Alma's life when she is visiting Alma in her apartment. Answers may vary.

1. There is a bowl of food on the kitchen floor.

   Alma's family must have a pet.

2. There is a nursing certificate on the wall with Alma's name on it.

   Alma must be a nurse

3. There are many different kinds of coffee on a kitchen shelf.

   Alma must enjoy different kind of coffee

4. There are a lot of classical music CDs.

   Alma must listen to a lot of classical music.

5. In Alma's bedroom, there's a sewing machine.

   Alma must like to make clothes alteration

6. There's a piano in the living room.

   Someone in the family must like to play piano.

7. On the kitchen calendar, there's an activity filled in for almost every day of the week.

   Alma's family must be an active family

8.10 Possibility—May/Might

EXAMPLES	EXPLANATION
Americans **might ask** you some strange questions. They **may have** little or no knowledge of your country.	*May* and *might* both have about the same meaning: possibility or uncertainty about the present.
They **may not know** much about your country. They **might not know** the difference between a Spanish person and a Spanish-speaking person.	For the negative, we use *may not* or *might not*. We don't use a contraction for these negatives.
I **may get** a roommate next semester. I **might get** a roommate next semester.	*May* and *might* can give a future meaning.

Notes:

1. *Maybe* is an adverb. It is one word. It usually comes at the beginning of the sentence and means *possibly* or *perhaps*. *May* and *might* are modals. They follow the subject and precede the verb.

    Maybe he is Mexican. = He **may be** Mexican. = He **might be** Mexican.
    Maybe I will get a roommate next semester. = I **may get** a roommate next semester. = I **might get** a roommate next semester.

2. Remember, *must* shows a conclusion, an assumption, or a deduction. Compare:

    You're from Mexico. You **must speak** Spanish. (assumption)
    He speaks Spanish. He **might be** from Guatemala or Peru. (possibility)

EXERCISE 15 Remove *maybe* from each of the following sentences and rewrite the sentences using the modal given.

1. Maybe some questions seem silly to you. (*may*)

    <u>Some questions may seem silly to you.</u>

2. Maybe Americans don't know much about your country. (*may*)

    <u>Americans mayn't know about your country</u>

3. Maybe you will become impatient with some questions. (*might*)

    <u>You might become impatient with some questions.</u>

4. If you say you speak Spanish, maybe an American will say, "Oh, you're Spanish." (*may*)

    <u>If you say you speak Spanish, American may say, "Oh, you're Spanish".</u>

5. Maybe you will be confused at times. (*may*)

    <u>You may be confused at times.</u>

6. Maybe Americans ask you some strange questions. (*might*)

   Americans might ask you some strange questions.

7. Maybe you will learn about Americans from their questions. (*might*)

   You might learn about Americans from their questions.

EXERCISE 16 Fill in the blanks with a verb to show possibility. Answers may vary.

1. **A:** I'm going to move on Saturday. I'm going to need help. Can you help me?

   B: I'm not sure. I may ____go____ away this weekend.

2. **A:** My next-door neighbor's name is Terry Karson. I see her name on the doorbell, but I never see her.

   B: Your neighbor may ____be____ a man. *Terry* is sometimes a man's name.

3. **A:** I need coins for the laundry room. Do you have any?

   B: Let me look. I might ____have____ some. No, I don't have any. Look in the laundry room.

   There might ____be____ a dollar-bill changer there.

4. **A:** Do you know the landlord's address?

   B: No, I don't. Ask the manager. She might ____know____.

5. **A:** Do they allow cats in this building?

   B: I know they don't allow dogs, but they might ____allow____ cats.

6. **A:** Are you going to stay in this apartment for another year?

   B: I'm not sure. I may ____move____. The landlord might ____increase____ the rent. If the rent goes up more than 25 percent, I'll move.

7. **A:** I have so much stuff in my closet. There's not enough room for my clothes.

   B: There might ____be____ lockers in the basement where you can store your things.

   A: Really? I didn't know that.

   B: Let's look. I may ____have____ a key to the basement with me.

   A: That would be great.

8. **A:** When I tell people I'm from Korea, they ask me if I speak Chinese. I get so mad.

   B: Don't get mad. Be patient and teach them something about your culture. They may ____learn____ something new from you.

How to Furnish YOUR NEW APARTMENT Cheaply

There are ways to furnish a new apartment without spending a lot of money.

Read the following conversation. Pay special attention to the words in bold. 8.5

Many people need to furnish their home, apartment, or room, but they don't want to spend a lot of money. In this conversation, Student B gives his friend Student A (who moved to the U.S. recently) some tips for furnishing a new place cheaply.

A: The first thing I need for my new place is a bed.

B: OK, **would you rather get** a twin- or full-sized bed?

A: I know it's more expensive, but **I'd rather get** a full. A twin is too small.

B: OK. Look, this discount website has a full bed set for $250. They deliver for free, too.

A: Great. **Could you text** that information to me? And **can I use** your pen? I want to do some quick math.

B: Sure, here you go. What else do you need?

A: Some things for the kitchen—plates, glasses, pots.

B: **Why don't you buy** them at a second-hand store? There's one nearby. It sells lots of gently used, inexpensive household items.

A: Good idea. But I'll need help bringing things home. **Will you come** with me?

B: Sure. **Would you like** to go this afternoon?

A: Yeah, that'd be great.

B: Is there anything else?

A: **I'd like to get** a desk and chair, but I don't have enough money.

B: Try Craigslist.org or Freecycle.org. You can find free stuff[1] on those sites. And people often put unwanted items on the sidewalk, too—especially furniture.

A: I can take stuff on the street?

B: Yeah. Many people **would rather give** away unwanted items **than** put them in the garbage. Actually, I have a small desk that I don't use anymore. **Why don't I bring** it to your place later?

A: Really? Thank you!

---
[1] stuff: an informal word for *things*

COMPREHENSION Based on the reading, write T for *true* or F for *false*.

1. __F__ Student A wants to get a twin-sized bed.
2. __T__ Student B suggests buying the bed at a second-hand store.
3. __T__ In the U.S., people often put unwanted items on the sidewalk for others to take.

THINK ABOUT IT Discuss the questions with a partner or in a small group.

1. Imagine you are renting a new apartment. What furniture do you buy first? Where do you buy it?
2. Do you like to shop at second-hand stores? Why or why not?

8.11 Using Modals for Politeness

EXAMPLES	EXPLANATION
May / Can / Could **I use** your pen?	We use *may*, *can*, or *could* + *I* to ask for permission.
Can / Could / Will / Would **you text** that information to me?	We use *can*, *could*, *will*, or *would* + *you* to make a request.
Would you **like to go** shopping today? Yes. I'**d like to**.	*Would like* has the same meaning as *want*. *Would like* is more polite than *want*. The contraction for *would* after a pronoun is *'d*.
Would you **rather get** a twin- **or** full-sized bed? I **would rather get** a full-sized bed (**than** a twin bed).	*Would rather* shows a preference of choices. We use *or* in questions. We use *than* in statements. The second choice can be omitted if it's obvious.
I'**d rather get** a full-sized bed. I'**d rather not spend** a lot of money.	The contraction for *would* after a pronoun is *'d*. The negative is *would rather not*.
Why don't you buy your bed online? **Why don't I bring** the desk to your place?	We can use a negative question to offer a polite suggestion.
May I help you? **Can I help** you?	In a shopping situation, the salesperson often uses these questions.

Notes:
1. When asking for permission, it is more polite to use *may* or *could* rather than *can*.
2. When making a request, it is more polite to use *could* or *would* rather than *can* or *will*.

GRAMMAR IN USE

Choosing the correct level of politeness for a situation will make your English sound more natural. In formal situations, use these modal phrases:

> *May I please speak to …?*
> *Could you please tell me where …?*
> *I would like to make an appointment.*

In less formal contexts, you can use other phrases:

> *Can I speak to …?*
> *Can you tell me where …?*
> *I want to make an appointment.*

If you are uncertain of the situation, it's better to be too polite than not polite enough.

EXERCISE 17 The conversation takes place in a second-hand store. Person A is a shopper; Person B is a salesperson. Make the language more polite by using modals and other expressions in place of the underlined words. Answers may vary.

A: Excuse me.

B: Yes? ~~Do you need help?~~ *[May I help you?]*
1.

A: Yes. <u>I want to see</u> that lamp—the one on the shelf. <u>Show it to me</u>, please. *[I would like to see]* *[Could you please show it to me]*
2.   3.

B: Sure. <u>Wait a minute</u>. I have to get a ladder. *(A moment later)* OK, here's the lamp. *[Please wait a moment]*
4.

A: Thanks. It's nice, but does it work?

B: I think so, but <u>let's check</u>. I'll plug it in. Yes, it works. *[let's make sure]*
5.

A: Great. <u>Tell me how much it is</u>. *[Could you tell me how much it is]*
6.

B: Let's see. It's 15 dollars.

A: OK, I'll take it.

B: <u>Do you want to see</u> any other lamps? *[Would you like to see any other lamps?]*
7.

A: Yes, <u>show me</u> that blue one, please. *[Could you show me]*
8.

B: Sure, here you go.

A: It's nice, but it's 30 dollars, and <u>I don't want to spend</u> that much money. *[I'd prefer not to spend]*
9.

B: Sure, I understand. <u>Do you want to see</u> anything else? *[Would you like to see]*
10.

A: No, thanks. I'm done shopping. I'll just pay for this lamp.

B: <u>Do you want to pay</u> by debit or credit card? *[Would you prefer to pay]*
11.

218   Unit 8

A: Is it OK to pay in cash?
   12.
B: Yes, of course. Your total with tax is $15.75.

ABOUT YOU Work with a partner. Use *would rather* to ask and answer questions. Take notes on your partner's answers.

1. own a house/a condominium
   A: Would you rather own a house or a condominium?
   B: I'd rather own a condominium (than a house).
2. live in the United States/in another country
3. own a condominium/rent an apartment
4. have young neighbors/old neighbors
5. have wood floors/carpeted floors
6. live in the center of the city/in a suburb
7. drive to work/take public transportation
8. buy new/used items for your home

EXERCISE 18 Tell a new classmate about your partner's answers in the exercise above.
   A: Yusef was my partner. He'd rather own a condo than a house because he's single. But I'd rather own a house. A house has more space.
   B: My partner was Sofia. Our answer to number one was the same. We'd both rather own a condo.

Some people prefer an apartment to a house.

SUMMARY OF UNIT 8

Modals

MODAL	EXAMPLES	EXPLANATION
can	I **can** stay in this apartment until March. I **can** carry my bicycle up to my apartment. **Can** I write you a check? **Can** you plug in the microwave, please? You **can't** paint the walls without the landlord's permission.	Permission Ability/Possibility Asking permission Request Prohibition
should	You **should** change the batteries in the smoke detector. You **shouldn't** leave matches in the reach of small children.	A good idea A bad idea
may	**May** I borrow your pen? You **may** leave the room. The tenant **may not** leave things in the hallway. I **may** move next month. The landlord **may** have an extra key.	Asking permission Giving permission Prohibition Future possibility Present possibility
might	I **might** move next month. The landlord **might** have an extra key.	Future possibility Present possibility
must	The landlord **must** install smoke detectors. The tenant **must not** change the locks. The new neighbors have a crib. They **must** have a baby.	Necessity—Formal Prohibition—Formal Conclusion/Deduction
would	**Would** you help me move?	Request
would like	I **would like** to buy your used TV.	Want
would rather	I **would rather** have a roommate than live alone.	Preference
could	In my last apartment, I **couldn't** have a pet. In my country, I **could** attend college for free. **Could** you help me move? **Could** I borrow your car?	Past permission Past ability Request Asking permission

Phrasal Modals

PHRASAL MODAL	EXAMPLES	EXPLANATION
have to	She **has to** find a roommate. I **had to** move last month.	Necessity Past necessity
have got to	She **has got to** sign the lease. I'**ve got to** pay my rent tomorrow.	Necessity
not have to	You **don't have to** pay with cash. You can pay by check.	Lack of necessity
had better	You **had better** get permission before changing the locks.	Warning / Personal interest
be supposed to	We **are not supposed to** have a dog here. I **was supposed to** pay my rent by the fifth of the month, but I forgot.	Expectation by rule or custom Past: reporting an unmet expectation
be able to	I **am able to** carry my bike to my apartment. Everyone **was able to** get out of the apartment during the fire.	Ability Past ability
be permitted to be allowed to	We **are not permitted/allowed to** park here overnight. In my last apartment, I **was not permitted/allowed to** leave my bike in the hallway.	Permission Past permission
ought to	You **ought to** change the batteries in your smoke detector.	A good idea / Moral value

REVIEW

Circle the correct expression to complete the conversation.

A: I'm moving on Saturday. (**Could**/May) you help me?
                                    1.

B: I (should/*would*) like to help you, but I have a bad back. I went to my doctor last week, and she told me
       2.

that I (*shouldn't*/don't have to) lift anything heavy for a while. (*Can*/Would) I help you any other way
       3.   4.

besides lifting things?

A: Yes. I don't have enough boxes. (Should/*Would*) you help me find some?
                                            5.

B: Sure. I (*have to*/must) go shopping this afternoon. I'll pick up some boxes while I'm at the supermarket.
              6.

A: Boxes can be heavy. You (would/*had*) better not lift them yourself.
                                    7.

B: Don't worry. I'll have someone put them in my car for me.

A: Thanks. I don't have a free minute. I (*couldn't go*/can't go) to class all last week. There's so much to do.
                                             8.

B: I know what you mean. You (might/*must*) be tired.
                                      9.

A: I am. I have another favor to ask. (*Can*/Would) I borrow your van on Saturday?
                                            10.

B: I (should/*have to*) work on Saturday. How about Sunday? I (must not/*don't have to*) work on Sunday.
         11.   12.

A: Sunday's too late. I (*'ve got to*/should) move out on Saturday. The new tenants are moving
                              13.

in on Sunday morning.

B: Oh, I see. My brother has a van, too. He (*has to*/should) work Saturday, but only for half a day.
                                                  14.

He (must/*might*) be able to let you use his van.
        15.

A: Thanks. (*Could*/May) you ask him for me? I'd appreciate it.
                 16.

B: Sure. I (should/*can*) ask him later this evening. Why are you moving? You have a great apartment.
                  17.

A: We (*'d rather*/'d better) live in the suburbs. And I want to have a dog.
            18.

I (shouldn't/*'m not supposed to*) have a dog in my present apartment. But my new landlord says
        19.

I (might/*can*) have one.
    20.

Modals 221

FROM GRAMMAR TO WRITING

PART 1 Editing Advice

1. After a modal, use the base form.

    You must ~~to~~ pay your rent on time.

2. A modal has no -s form.

    He can~~s~~ carry his bike upstairs.

3. Don't forget *to* after *be permitted, be allowed, be supposed, be able,* and *ought*.

    We're not permitted ^to^ leave a bicycle in the hallway.

    I don't like my apartment. I ought ^to^ look for a new one.

4. Don't forget *be* before *permitted to, allowed to, supposed to,* and *able to*.

    I ^am^ not supposed to have a pet in my apartment.

5. Use the correct word order in a question.

    What ^should I^ ~~I should~~ do in case of fire?

6. Don't use *can* for past. Use *could* + a base form.

    I ^couldn't find^ ~~can't found~~ a roommate, so I live alone.

7. Don't forget *would* before *rather*.

    I ^would^ rather live with my parents than live alone.

8. Don't forget *had* before *better*.

    You ^had^ better not park here. You can get a ticket.

9. Don't forget *have* before *got to*.

    I ^'ve^ got to change the batteries in the smoke detectors.

10. Don't use *maybe* before a verb.

    I ^may^ ~~maybe will~~ move next month.

11. Use *not* for negative modals.

    I don't like garage sales. I'd rather ^not^ ~~don't~~ buy used things.

PART 2 Editing Practice

Some of the shaded words and phrases have mistakes. Find the mistakes and correct them. If the shaded words are correct, write *C*.

I am renting an apartment, and I **would like to give** (1) [C] you some advice. First, before you move in, you **should ~~to~~ take** (2) pictures of the empty apartment, keep a copy of the pictures for yourself, and email a copy to the landlord. The pictures will show the condition of the apartment before you moved in, so the landlord **can't ~~to~~ blame** (3) [couldn't] you for damage you didn't do. Test everything, like

222 Unit 8

light switches, toilets, and faucets. You maybe will find that something isn't working properly.
Make a list of these things. You better show this list to the landlord immediately. He should fix these things before you move in. If not, he ought give you a credit on your rent so that you can fix them yourself, if you rather do it that way. You can finding checklists online. You can search for "rental condition checklist." This list may help you identify many common problems.

Second, you got to take your lease seriously. If the lease says "no pets," that means no pets. If you not allowed to have a pet, it's for a good reason. A pet cans cause damage. Dogs make noise, too, so this rule protects other tenants. If you are not supposed use the laundry room during certain hours, this might be because of the noise.

Third, before you sign a lease, you should try to find out something about the landlord, the neighbors, and the neighborhood. How you can do that? You can waiting outside the building during a busy afternoon or on a weekend and talk to the tenants walking in and out. Interview them. Are they happy? Are there any problems? What should you know before signing the lease? In my last apartment, I didn't do this. I was surprised to find that I couldn't park my car on the street overnight, so I must to park far away. This is not the fault of the landlord or the lease, but this was inconvenient for me. I'd rather don't have this situation again. Find out what you can before signing a lease for a place where you may don't be happy.

WRITING TIP

When comparing things, there are different ways to organize your ideas. One option is to write about the first topic, for example, apartment life in the United States. You cover that topic completely and then write about the next topic you are comparing, for example, apartment life in Brazil.

Another option is to write about one point of similarity or difference between the two topics, for example, *In the United States, neighbors aren't typically friendly with each other. In Brazil, however, neighbors usually know one another well.* Then you would write about another point of similarity or difference between the two topics.

PART 3 Write

Read the prompts. Choose one and write a paragraph or two about it.

1. Compare apartment life in the United States with apartment life in another country.
2. Compare driving rules in the United States with driving rules in another country.

PART 4 Edit

Reread the Summary of Unit 8 and the editing advice. Edit your writing from Part 3.

UNIT
9
The Present Perfect
The Present Perfect Continuous

VIRTUAL COMMUNITIES

National Geographic's Space Projection Helmets allow participants to look at Earth from an astronaut's perspective.

> Technology is nothing. What's important is that you have a faith in people, that they're basically good and smart, and if you give them tools, they'll do wonderful things with them.
>
> STEVE JOBS

Google

Larry Page and Sergey Brin

Read the following article. Pay special attention to the words in bold.

How many times **have** you **wanted** a quick answer to something and **gone** to your computer to google it? The word *google* **has become** synonymous[1] with "search". Since its start in 1998, Google **has been** one of the most popular search engines. It **has grown** from a research project of two college students to a business that now employs approximately 85 thousand people.

Google's founders, Larry Page and Sergey Brin, **have known** each other since 1995, when they were graduate students[2] in computer science at Stanford University in California. They realized that Internet search was an important field and began working to make searching easier. Both Page and Brin left their studies at Stanford to work on their project and **have** never **returned** to finish their degrees. In 2014, when they were 41 years old, *Forbes* magazine listed Page's and Brin's net worth at about $30 billion each. Today, they are each worth more than $50 billion.

Brin was born in Russia, but he **has lived** in the United States since he was five. His father was a mathematician in Russia. Page, whose parents were computer experts, **has been** interested in computers since he was six years old.

When Google started in 1998, it did ten thousand searches a day. Today it does more than five billion a day in 40 languages. It indexes[3] 130 trillion Web pages.

How is Google different from other search engines? **Have** you ever **noticed** how many ads there are on other search engines? News, sports scores, links for shopping, and more fill other search engines. Brin and Page wanted a clean home page. They believed that people come to the Internet to search for information, not to see unwanted data. The success of Google over its competitors **has proven** that this is true.

Over the years, Google **has added** other features to its Web site: Google Images, Google Drive, Google Calendar, Google Earth, and more. But one thing **hasn't changed**: the clean opening page that Google offers its users.

---
[1] synonymous: having the same meaning as
[2] graduate student: a student who studies for a higher degree such as a Master's or Doctorate
[3] to index: to sort, categorize, and organize information

COMPREHENSION Based on the reading, write T for *true* or F for *false*.

1. _F_ Larry Page and Sergey Brin have known each other since they were children.
2. _T_ Larry Page has been interested in computers since he was a child.
3. _F_ Brin and Page have finished their graduate degrees.

THINK ABOUT IT Discuss the questions with a partner or in a small group.

1. What do you know about Google's features such as Google Search, Google Earth, or Google Drive? What have you used them for?
2. If a friend or family member had an idea for a project, would you support their decision to leave school to pursue their project? Why or why not?

9.1 The Present Perfect—Forms

SUBJECT	HAVE/HAS (+ NOT)	PAST PARTICIPLE		EXPLANATION
I	have	used	Google.	We use *have* with the subjects *I, you, we, they*, a plural subject, or *there* + a plural subject.
You	have not	heard of	Larry Page.	
We	have	read	about Sergey Brin.	
Brin and Page	have	become	billionaires.	
There	have	been	many changes in computers.	
Brin	has	lived	in the U.S. most of his life.	We use *has* with the subjects *he, she, it*, a singular subject, or *there* + a singular subject.
Google	has not	used	ads on its opening page.	
There	has	been	a lot of interest in search.	

Notes:
1. Contractions: have not → haven't, has not → hasn't, he has → he's, we have → we've, there has → there's
2. The apostrophe + s can mean *has* or *is*. The verb form following the contraction tells you what the contraction means.

> He**'s worked** with computers. (He's = He has)
> He**'s working** with computers. (He's = He is)

> **GRAMMAR IN USE**
>
> Contractions are common in speaking, both formally and informally. They make your speech sound more fluent and natural. We also use them in informal writing, such as in emails to friends or personal letters. However, many teachers do not want students to use contractions in formal academic writing (essays, research papers).

EXERCISE 1 Fill in the blanks with the words you hear. 9.2

The Internet <u>has made</u> it easy to get information. But it <u>has</u>
1.   2.

also <u>become</u> easy for cybercriminals, people who commit crimes through the
3.

Internet, to steal your personal data. About 32 percent of Internet users in the United States

<u>have been</u> victims of online crime.
4.

Cybercriminals steal important information such as Social Security or credit card numbers.

According to a Consumer Report survey, 62 percent of responders <u>have done</u> nothing
5.

to protect their online privacy.

<u>have</u> you ever <u>gone</u> to a coffee shop and <u>used</u>
6.   7.   8.

the Wi-Fi there? If so, other customers can easily gain access to your private information. Also, the

cloud seems like a good place to store data, but it <u>has made</u> it easy for criminals to steal
9.

information.

Without knowing it, it is possible that you <u>have given</u> ordinary thieves too much
10.

information. <u>Have</u> you ever <u>posted</u> news about an upcoming
11.   12.

trip on a social media site? <u>Have</u> you ever <u>mentioned</u> where you're
13.   14.

going on your next vacation, when you're leaving, and how long you'll be gone? Then you

<u>have</u> also <u>let</u> thieves know when your house will be empty.
15.   16.

In addition to stealing private information from your computer, hackers—people

who illegally get into computer systems— <u>have broken</u> into bank websites and
17.

<u>have stolen</u> large amounts of money. In 2018, hackers stole nearly $1 billion.
18.

Hackers <u>have gotten</u> information from government sites, too. Since the beginning
19.

of the Internet, security <u>has been</u> a problem. <u>Have</u> you ever
20.   21.

<u>been</u> a victim?
22.

228   Unit 9

9.2 The Past Participle

BASE FORM	SIMPLE PAST FORM	PAST PARTICIPLE	EXPLANATION
work wonder change	worked wondered changed	worked wondered changed	The past participle is the same as the simple past form for all regular verbs.
hear make let	heard made let	heard made let	For some irregular verbs, the past participle is the same as the simple past form.
break grow go	broke grew went	broken grown gone	For other irregular verbs, the simple past and the past participle are different.

For the following verbs, the past form and past participle are different.

BASE FORM	PAST FORM	PAST PARTICIPLE
become	became	become
come	came	come
run	ran	run
blow	blew	blown
draw	drew	drawn
fly	flew	flown
grow	grew	grown
know	knew	known
throw	threw	thrown
tear	tore	torn
wear	wore	worn
break	broke	broken
choose	chose	chosen
freeze	froze	frozen
speak	spoke	spoken
steal	stole	stolen
begin	began	begun
drink	drank	drunk
ring	rang	rung
sing	sang	sung
sink	sank	sunk
swim	swam	swum

BASE FORM	PAST FORM	PAST PARTICIPLE
bite	bit	bitten
drive	drove	driven
ride	rode	ridden
rise	rose	risen
write	wrote	written
be	was/were	been
eat	ate	eaten
fall	fell	fallen
forgive	forgave	forgiven
give	gave	given
mistake	mistook	mistaken
see	saw	seen
shake	shook	shaken
take	took	taken
do	did	done
forget	forgot	forgotten
get	got	gotten
go	went	gone
lie	lay	lain
prove	proved	proven (or proved)
show	showed	shown (or showed)

*For a complete list of irregular past participles, see Appendix C.

EXERCISE 2 Write the base form and the simple past form for each past participle in the chart. If the simple past and the past participle are the same, write S. If they are different, write D.

BASE FORM	SIMPLE PAST FORM	PAST PARTICIPLE	SAME (S) OR DIFFERENT (D)
want	wanted	wanted	S
be	was/were	been	D
grow	grew	grown	D
know	knew	known	D
steal	stole	stolen	D
return	returned	returned	S
become	became	become	D
notice	noticed	noticed	S
add	added	added	S
change	changed	changed	S
make	made	made	S
have	had	had	S
go	went	gone	D
do	did	done	D
think	thought	thought	S
tell	told	told	S
choose	chose	chosen	D
break	broke	broken	S
get	got	gotten	D
live	lived	lived	S

EXERCISE 3 Write the past participle of these verbs.

1. eat ____eaten____
2. go ____gone____
3. see ____seen____
4. look ____looked____
5. study ____studied____
6. bring ____brought____
7. take ____taken____
8. say ____said____
9. be ____been____
10. find ____found____
11. give ____given____
12. leave _____
13. live ____lived____
14. know ____known____
15. like ____liked____
16. fall ____fallen____
17. feel ____felt____
18. come ____came____
19. break ____broken____
20. wear ____worn____
21. let ____let____
22. grow ____grown____
23. drive ____driven____
24. write ____written____
25. put ____put____
26. begin ____begun____
27. want ____wanted____
28. get ____gotten____
29. fly ____flown____
30. drink ____drank____

230 Unit 9

EXERCISE 4 Fill in the blanks with the present perfect form of a verb from the box. You can use one verb more than once. Make a contraction with *have* or *has* where possible.

do	read	know	use	be
finish	go	have	steal	

1. I _'ve read_ several articles about Internet security.
2. You _'ve used_ Wi-Fi in coffee shops.
3. _Have_ you _done_ anything to protect your personal information?
4. _Has_ your friend _been_ careful with Wi-Fi at coffee shops?
5. Larry Page _'s known_ Sergey Brin since they were students at Stanford University.
6. _Have_ they _finished_ graduate school? No. They left their graduate program to start Google.
7. It _'s been_ easy for hackers to steal information.
8. Some hackers _'ve stolen_ a lot of money.
9. Some hackers _'ve gone_ to jail for stealing money online.
10. _Has_ your computer ever _had_ a virus?

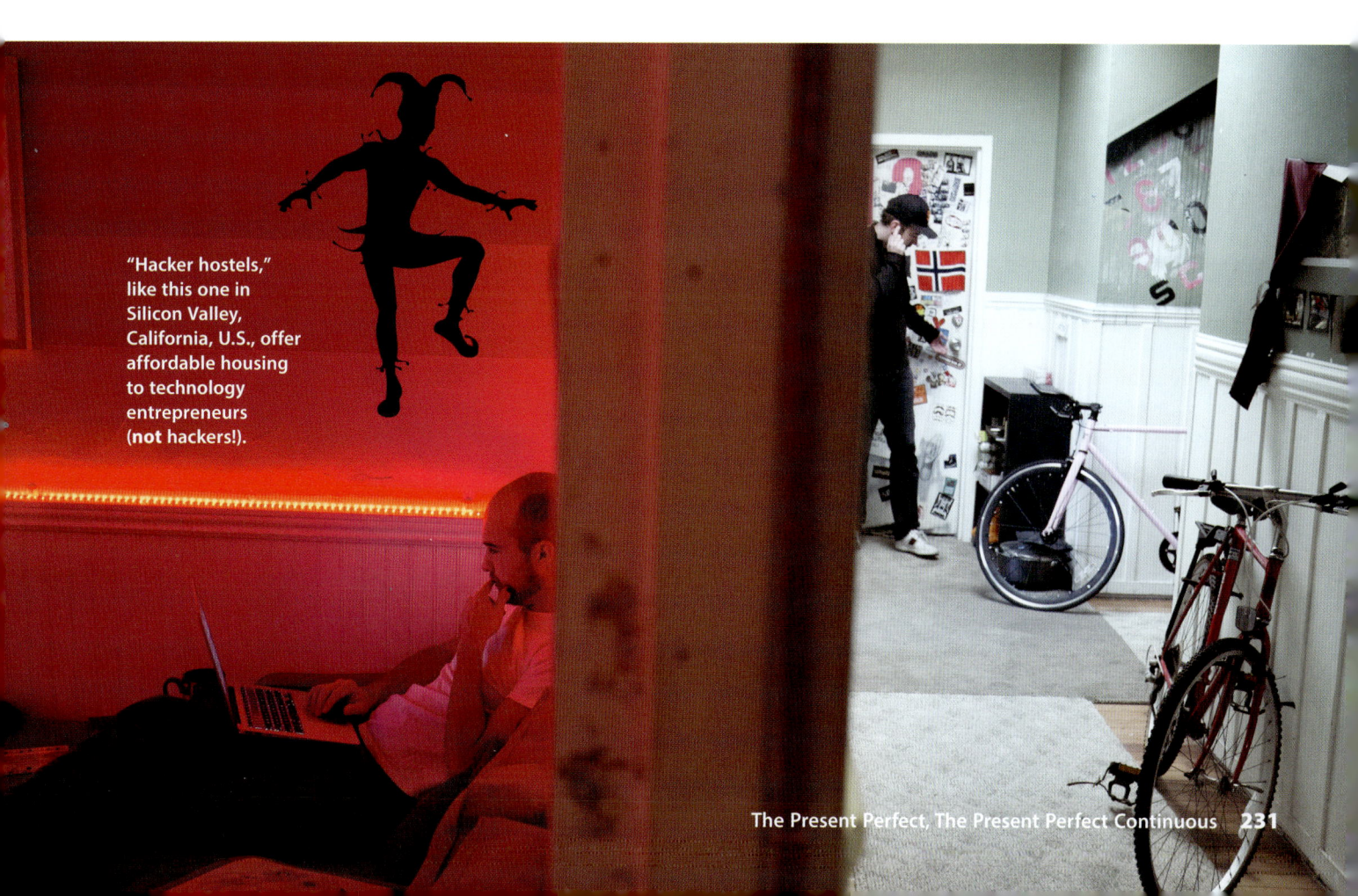

"Hacker hostels," like this one in Silicon Valley, California, U.S., offer affordable housing to technology entrepreneurs (not hackers!).

EXERCISE 5 Use the words in parentheses to write a question about each statement.

1. Google has changed the way people search. (*how*)

    How has Google changed the way people search?

2. I have used several search engines. (*which ones*)

    Which ones search engines have you used?

3. Brin and Page haven't finished their graduate degree. (*why*)

    Why haven't Brin and Page finished their graduate degree?

4. They have made a lot of money. (*how much*)

    How much money have they made?

5. Brin has been in the United States for many years. (*how long*)

    How long has he been in the US?

6. You haven't been careful about Internet security in coffee shops. (*why*)

    Why haven't you been careful about Internet security in coffee shops?

7. Internet security has become a big problem. (*why*)

    Why has internet security become a big problem?

8. Hackers have stolen money from banks. (*how much*)

    How much money have hackers stolen from banks?

ABOUT YOU Use the words to write present perfect questions. Then take turns asking and answering your questions with a partner. Use contractions. Share what you learned with your class.

1. (Internet security/be/problem/for you) Has Internet security been a problem for you?

2. (which/music apps/use) _____

3. (try/VR) _____

4. (what/change/in the last 20 years) _____

232 Unit 9

9.3 The Present Perfect with an Adverb

SUBJECT	HAS/HAVE (+ NOT)	ADVERB	PAST PARTICIPLE		EXPLANATION
Page and Brin	have	never	finished	their graduate degree.	We can put an adverb between the auxiliary verb (*have/has*) and the past participle.
Internet security	has	often	been	a problem.	
I	haven't	always	been	careful in a coffee shop.	
You	have	probably	used	Wi-Fi in a coffee shop.	

Note:
The adverb *already* can come between the auxiliary verb and the main verb or after the verb phrase.
   They have **already** become billionaires.
   They have become billionaires **already**.

EXERCISE 6 Add the word in parentheses to each sentence.

1. You have used your laptop in a coffee shop. (*probably*)

   You have probably used your laptop in a coffee shop.

2. I have installed an anti-virus program. (*already*)

3. We have heard of Larry Page. (*never*)

4. Page and Brin have been interested in search technology. (*always*)

5. You have used Google. (*probably*)

6. He hasn't finished his college degree. (*even*)

7. I have read the article about Internet security. (*already*)

FUN WITH GRAMMAR

Race to write. Form three teams. One person from each team goes to the board. Your teacher will say an irregular verb, and you will write the past participle of that verb on the board. Every student has a turn. The first to finish writing the word correctly wins a point.

For an extra challenge, the first to write a sentence using the verb in the present perfect wins another point.

CROWDFUNDING

Read the following article. Pay special attention to the words in bold. 🎧 9.3

Have you ever **had** an idea for a business but no way to fund it? **Have** you **asked** relatives and friends for money to help you? If you **have done** these things, you know it isn't easy to get people interested in investing in your dream. After getting money from relatives and friends, it's hard to find more people willing to invest. Lately, people **have found** a different way to raise cash: through crowdfunding. Crowdfunding is a method of "collecting small amounts of money from a lot of different people, usually by using the Internet." While the idea **has been** around for possibly hundreds of years, the word *crowdfunding* **has** only **existed** since 2006.

Crowdfunding websites, which started to appear on the Internet in 2010, **have helped** individuals raise billions of dollars worldwide. So how does it work? A person demonstrates his idea in a short video and states his financial goal and the time frame for raising money. Usually the first investors are family and friends. Little by little, strangers become interested and donate money.

Not all crowdfunding plans are for profit. Some people **have used** crowdfunding websites that are specifically for philanthropic[1] projects. These sites **have attracted** people who want to make the world a better place. The 97 Supermarket in Changchun, China, is one example of this. Jiang Naijun used crowdfunding to get the money to open a supermarket. She named her market 97 because that was her age when she did this. Since she became profitable, she **has given** at least half the money she earns to charity[2], to help children in need. "I wanted to do more for society," she said.

If you want more information, just google "crowdfunding" and you will find a number of different sites specializing in different types of projects.

[1] philanthropic: intended to help others
[2] charity: an organization that helps people in need

Crowdfunding has become one of the most popular ways for people to raise money for a cause, project, or event. In 2017, $34 billion was raised globally. This number is expected to grow to more than $300 billion by 2025.

98-year-old Jiang Naijun used crowdfunding to start her supermarket and donates the profits to charity.

COMPREHENSION Based on the reading, write T for *true* or F for *false*.

1. __T__ Sometimes strangers help fund a crowdfunding project.
2. __T__ The idea of crowdfunding is old, but it has become easier to do with the Internet.
3. __F__ The "97 Supermarket" project didn't reach its financial goal.

THINK ABOUT IT Discuss the questions with a partner or in a small group.

1. What would you like to crowdfund for? Why?
2. What might be some challenges with crowdfunding? Explain.

9.4 The Present Perfect—Overview of Uses

EXAMPLES	EXPLANATION
People **have used** crowdfunding since 2010. Google **has been** in existence for over 20 years.	We use the present perfect to show that an action or state started in the past and continues to the present.
I **have used** my laptop in coffee shops many times. How many articles about crowdfunding **have** you **read**?	We use the present perfect to show that an action repeated during a period of time that started in the past and includes the present.
Have you ever **asked** relatives for money?	We use the present perfect to show that an action occurred at an indefinite time in the past.

EXERCISE 7 Tell if the sentences show continuation from past to present (**C**), repetition from past to present (**R**), or an indefinite time in the past (**I**).

1. Larry Page has been interested in computers since he was a child. __C__
2. How many emails have you received today? __R__
3. I've had my laptop for one year. __C__
4. The word *crowdfunding* has been in existence since 2006. __C__
5. Internet security has become a big problem. __I__
6. Has your computer ever had a virus? __I__
7. My cousin has used crowdfunding two times. __R__
8. Have you ever used your laptop in a coffee shop? __I__

GRAMMAR IN USE

When an event happened in the recent past, and the effect is still felt, we often use the present perfect. This is especially common for speakers of British English. In American English, we use either the present perfect or the simple past.

Someone **has** just **donated** $10,000!	Someone just donated $10,000.
I **have forgotten** my password again.	I forgot my password again.
Have you **heard** the news?	Did you hear the news?

9.5 The Present Perfect with Continuation from Past to Present

We use the present perfect to show that an action or state started in the past and continues to the present.

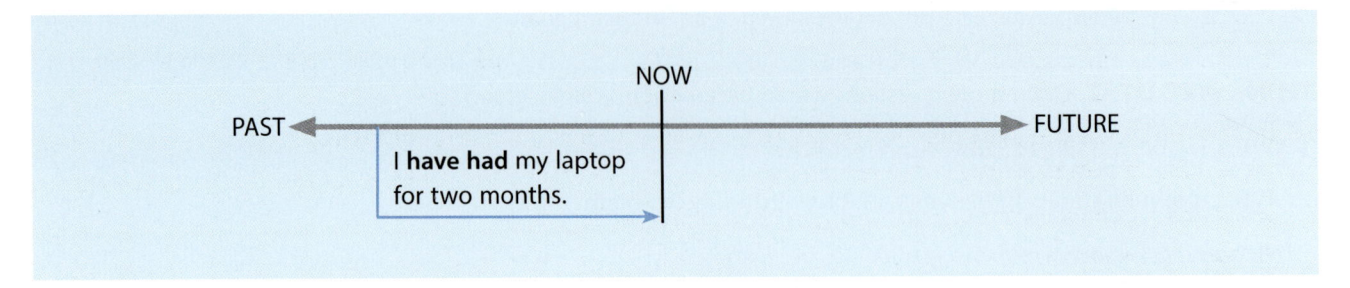

```
                        NOW
PAST ◄──────────────────┼──────────────────► FUTURE
         I have had my laptop
         for two months.
```

EXAMPLES	EXPLANATION
Crowdfunding **has been** around **for about** 10 years.	We use *for* + an amount of time: *for two months, for three years, for a long time,* etc.
Crowdfunding sites **have been** on the Internet **since** 2006.	We use *since* with a date, month, year, etc., to show when the action began.
I **have been** interested in computers (**ever**) **since** I **was** a child.	We use *since* or *ever since* with the beginning of a continuous action or state. The verb in the *since* clause is simple past.
How long have you **had** your computer?	We use *how long* to ask about the amount of time from the past to the present.
I **have always dreamed** of starting a business.	We use the present perfect with *always* to show that an action or state began in the past and continues to the present.
I **have never heard** of crowdfunding.	We use the present perfect with *never* to show that something has not occurred any time before now.

EXERCISE 8 Fill in the blanks with the words from the box. You may use an item more than once.

've been interested	ever since	've always wanted	had	since
how long	for	has never used	have	was
graduated	has	've had	have been	has been

1. I've been interested in computers _____since_____ I _____was_____ in high school.
2. I __'ve always wanted__ to start my own business. Maybe now I can do it with crowdfunding.
3. The word *crowdfunding* _____has_____ existed _____since_____ 2006.
4. I __'ve been interested__ in crowdfunding _____since_____ I read the article about it.
5. Crowdfunding websites ____have been____ around _____for_____ over 10 years.
6. My grandmother __has never used__ a computer. She doesn't like computers.

7. I _**'ve had**_ my tablet _**for**_ three months.

8. _**How long**_ _**have**_ you _**had**_ your tablet?

9. I've had my laptop ever since I _**graduated**_ from high school.

10. _**Ever since**_ 1998, Google _**has been**_ one of the most popular search engines.

ABOUT YOU Write true statements using the present perfect form of the verbs given and *for, since, always,* or *never*. If possible, write about technology. Share your sentences with a partner.

  A: I've had my phone since March. How long have you had yours?
  B: Really? I've had mine for two years.

1. (have) I've had my smartphone since March.
2. (like) _**I've liked the grammar class since the beginning**_
3. (be) _**I've been working since I was 16**_
4. (want) _**I've wanted to learn English since I come to US**_
5. (know) _**I've known Royner for a few months**_
6. (have) _**I've had to drive all day for 2 years**_

EXERCISE 9 Fill in the blanks with the present perfect and other missing words to complete this conversation. Use context clues to help you.

A: I see you have a new tablet. How _**long**_ (1) _**have you had**_ (2) it?

B: I _**'ve had**_ (3) it _**for**_ (4) just one week. I love it. What kind of tablet do you have?

A: I don't have a tablet. I _**have**_ (5) never _**had**_ (6) one. I don't like them.

B: Why not? I think they're wonderful.

A: They're great for some things, but they're not computers. I need a real computer. I'm a writer, and I need a good word processing program.

B: A writer? _**How**_ (7) long _**have you been**_ (8) a writer?

A: I _**'ve been**_ (9) a writer ever _**since**_ (10) I graduated from college.

B: What do you write? Novels?

A: No. I _**'ve**_ (11) never _**written**_ (12) a novel. I write poetry. Do you like poetry?

B: Yes. I _**'ve**_ (13) always _**written**_ (14) poetry.

A: I'll give you a copy of my latest book.

The Present Perfect, The Present Perfect Continuous   237

9.6 The Simple Past, the Present Perfect, the Simple Present

EXAMPLES	EXPLANATION
Sergey Brin **came** to the U.S. in 1979. Brin **has been** in the U.S. since 1979. Brin **lives** in California.	We use the simple past with an action that is completely past. We use the present perfect to connect the past to the present. We use the simple present to refer only to the present.
When **did** you **learn** about crowdfunding? How long **have** you **known** about crowdfunding?	We use *when* to ask about the past. We use *how long* to ask about the connection of past to present.

EXERCISE 10 Fill in the blanks with the simple past, the present perfect, or the simple present form of the verb given. Include any other words you see.

A: I __have__ a great idea for a business but no way of funding it.
   1. have

B: What about crowdfunding?

A: I __'ve never heard__ of it. What is it?
   2. never hear

B: It's a way of getting money from friends, relatives, and strangers. Look it up online, and you'll find a lot of crowdfunding websites.

A: This is terrific! How __did you know__ about it?
   3. you/know

B: I __knew__ about it ever since I __'ve read__ an article about
   4. know   5. read
it a few years ago.

A: So it __'s been__ around for a long time?
   6. be

B: The idea __has been__ around for a long time but on the Internet only since 2010. A
   7. be
friend of mine __used__ it last year to start a small business. In a short time, he
   8. use
__collected__ $25,000.
   9. collect

A: Wow! I __'m__ so happy you told me about it. I'm going to look it up right now.
   10. be

GRAMMAR IN USE

The news is typically about things important today. Often, a news story begins with the present perfect to give important information, and then it continues in the simple past to tell what happened, or the simple present to describe current feelings or thoughts.

*Twelve boys and their coach **have disappeared** in Thailand. No one **has seen** them since their soccer game on June 23rd. A bypasser **found** their bikes and bags near a cave entrance. A teammate **said** the boys **went** into the cave after their game. Unfortunately, it **rained** heavily soon after. Officials **fear** they **are** lost in the cave, unable to get out.*

EXERCISE 11 Circle the correct word to complete this conversation between a teacher (A) and students (B) and (C).

A: I (**like**/have liked) to know about my students' lives. Let's start with Bernard. Where are you from?
　　　1.

B: I'm from Rwanda.

A: Maybe some of the other students (never hear/**have never heard**) of Rwanda. Let's google it so everyone
　　　　　　　　　　　　　　　　　　　　　　　　2.
can see where it is in Africa. OK. Here it is. (**Have you been**/Are you) in the United States for a long time?
　　　　　　　　　　　　　　　　　　　　　　　　　　　3.

B: No, (I'm not/**I haven't**).
　　　　　　　4.

A: How long (are you/**have you been**) in the United States?
　　　　　　　　　　5.

B: I (**came**/have come) to the United States in 2018.
　　　6.

A: Thanks, Bernard. What about you, Carlos? Where are you from?

C: I'm from Puerto Rico.

A: Can you tell us a little about your country?

C: Puerto Rico isn't a country. It(**'s**/'s been) a territory of the United States. Puerto Ricans (**are**/have been)
　　　　　　　　　　　　　　　　7.　　　　　　　　　　　　　　　　　　　　　　　　　　8.
American citizens.

A: Let's google "Puerto Rico." When (**did Puerto Rico become**/has Puerto Rico become) a territory of
　　　　　　　　　　　　　　　　　　　　9.
the United States?

C: In 1898. Puerto Rico used to belong to Spain. The U.S. (**fought**/has fought) a war with Spain
　　　　　　　　　　　　　　　　　　　　　　　　　　　　　　　　10.
and the United States (**won**/has won).
　　　　　　　　　　　　11.

A: Thank you for this information. Please tell the class what language you speak in Puerto Rico.

C: We speak Spanish, but I (**'ve had**/had) English lessons since I was in high school.
　　　　　　　　　　　　　　12.

A: Thanks, Carlos.

FUN WITH GRAMMAR

Get to know your classmate. You have five minutes to practice a conversation with a partner similar to the one above, discussing where you are from, one interesting piece of information about your countries, and your length of time in the United States. When you are finished, try to perform your conversation for the class without any notes.

　　A: Where are you from?
　　B: I'm from China. How about you?
　　A: I'm from Peru.

Khan Academy

Salman Khan records one of his tutorials for the Khan Academy.

Read the following article. Pay special attention to the words in bold. 9.4

Have you ever **had** trouble keeping up with a class? **Have** you **been** bored because your class moves too slowly for you? Either way, learning in a group can sometimes be frustrating.

Khan Academy, created by Salman Khan in 2006, **has** quickly **become** the largest "school" in the world. Students learn online at their own pace with short videos. With over 10,000 lectures in many different subjects, it **has attracted** about 18 million students a month, from kindergarten through high school. Amazingly, Khan **has** never **charged** any money for his videos. They are available to anyone anywhere in the world with a computer and an Internet connection.

Salman Khan didn't start out to create a revolution in instruction. In 2004, his niece asked him for help in math. He started to create math videos for her to view online. Then he decided to make his videos available to anyone who wanted to get math help. One day, he received an email from a stranger who improved his math grade by using Khan's videos. The email said, "You **have changed** my life and the lives of everyone in my family."

Khan's life **has changed**, too. In 2009, he quit his job and started making more instructional videos. At first he focused on math, but over the past few years, he **has added** many other subjects, including history, science, and art. Volunteers **have helped** translate his videos into at least 25 different languages. Khan **has** personally **created** over 3,000 videos.

At first Khan had no funding for his project. Since he started to appear on TV, he **has attracted** financial support from many people, including Bill Gates. So far, he **has raised** more than 40 million dollars.

Many teachers **have started** to use Khan's lectures to supplement[1] their classroom instruction. Because most of today's students are digital natives, it is not surprising that Khan Academy **has become** so popular with today's students.

---

[1] to supplement: to add to

COMPREHENSION Based on the reading, write T for *true* or F for *false*.

1. __F__ Khan Academy is available only in the United States.
2. __T__ Khan Academy is mostly for elementary and high school students.
3. __T__ Salman Khan has created many of the videos himself.

THINK ABOUT IT Discuss the questions with a partner or in a small group.

1. What video courses would you be interested in taking?
2. What is a challenge of studying alone?

9.7 The Present Perfect with Repetition from Past to Present

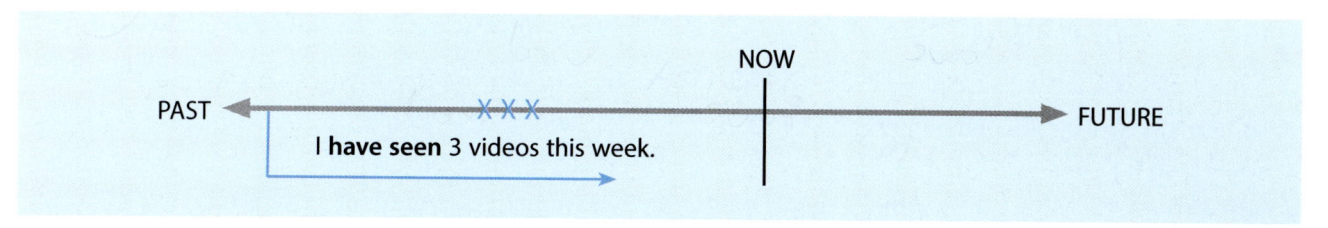

PAST ←——— x x x ——————— NOW ———————→ FUTURE
I **have seen** 3 videos this week.

EXAMPLES	EXPLANATION
Khan **has appeared** on TV many times. **Up to now**, Khan Academy **has created** over 5,000 videos. I **have watched** 10 videos on Khan Academy **so far**.	We use the present perfect to talk about repetition in a time period that includes the present. We expect more repetition. Adding the words *so far* and *up to now* indicate that we are counting up to the present moment.
How many times **has** Khan **been** on TV? How much money **has** he **charged** for his videos? He **hasn't charged** any money **at all** for his videos.	We can ask a question about repetition from past to present with *how much* and *how many*. To indicate zero times, we can use a negative verb + *at all*.

Notes:
We use the present perfect in a time period that is open. There is a possibility of more repetition.

   Khan **has made** over 3,000 videos so far. (possibility for more videos)

   Khan **has added** new subjects over the years. (possibility for adding more subjects)

We use the simple past with a time period that is finished or closed: *in 2004, 50 years ago, last week,* etc. There is no possibility of more repetition.

   Khan **made** a few videos in 2004 for his niece. (2004 ends the time period)

GRAMMAR IN USE

When you consider the action finished, use the simple past.

   I **read** many great books in high school.

When you know that the action might happen again in the future, use the present perfect.

   I'**ve read** many great books.

EXERCISE 12 Fill in the blanks with the present perfect form of one of the verbs from the box.

| add | read | help ✓ | not charge | translate | use | attract | have | appear | be |

1. Salman Khan _____has helped_____ a lot of students improve their math skills.
2. Khan Academy _____has attracted_____ millions of students.
3. So far, Khan _____has not charged_____ any money for his instructional videos.
4. Khan started with math, but he _____has added_____ many other subjects.
5. Volunteers _____have translated_____ Khan's lectures into about 25 different languages so far.
6. Khan _____has appeared_____ on many TV programs.
7. How many times _____have_____ you _____used_____ instructional videos?
8. How many articles about the Internet _____have_____ we _____read_____ so far?

EXERCISE 13 Fill in the blanks with the simple past or the present perfect form of the verb given.

1. A magazine _____chose_____ Salman Khan as one of the 100 most influential people.

choose
2. He _____has been_____ on the cover of several magazines.

be
3. Several news programs _____have interviewed_____ Salman Khan over the past few years.

interview
4. Khan _____has started_____ Khan Academy in 2006.

start
5. Sergey Brin and Larry Page _____met_____ each other in graduate school in 1995.

meet
6. So far they _____haven't changed_____ Google's clean home page.

not change
7. I _____'ve used_____ my laptop in coffee shops many times.

use
8. Yesterday I _____went_____ to a coffee shop to work on my laptop.

go
9. So far my cousin _____has recieved_____ 80 percent of his crowdfunding goal.

receive

EXERCISE 14 Fill in the blanks with the simple past or the present perfect form of the verb given. Use contractions wherever possible.

A: Do you have any hobbies?

B: Yes. I love to read.

A: How many books _____have you read_____ this year?

1. you/read

B: I _____'ve read_____ about 20 books so far this year. Last month I

2. read
_____went_____ on vacation, and I _____'ve read_____ 10 books while I

3. go   4. read
_____was_____ at the beach.

5. be

242   Unit 9

A: How <u>did you carry</u> so many books on your vacation? They're heavy.
   6. you/carry

B: I <u>carried</u> only one: my tablet. Before I left on my trip, I <u>downloaded</u> 20 books.
   7. carry   8. download

A: Are book downloads expensive?

B: I pay about $10 a book. But I <u>'ve spent</u> much more than that on print books over the
                                   9. spend
   years. My public library <u>has made</u> about 5,000 books available for download so far, and
                             10. make
   those are free. Every month, they add new electronic books.

A: I <u>'ve never tried</u> to download books from my library.
     11. never/try

9.8 The Present Perfect with an Indefinite Time in the Past

EXAMPLES	EXPLANATION
A: **Have** you **ever heard** of Khan Academy? B: Yes, I **have**. A: **Have** you **ever seen** Khan's history videos? B: No, I never **have**. But I**'ve used** several of his math videos this semester.	We use the present perfect with *ever* to ask a question about any time from past to present. We can answer an *ever* question with the present perfect when there is no reference to time. The time is indefinite or repeated in an open time frame.
A: I know your brother is using crowdfunding to raise money. **Has** he **raised** enough money **yet** for his project? B: No, **not yet**. But he **has already raised** over $5,000.	We use the present perfect in a question with *yet* to ask about an expected action. We use *yet* with questions and negative statements. We use *already* with affirmative statements.
A stranger wrote to Salman Khan, "You **have changed** my life." Khan Academy **has become** the largest "school" in the world.	We can use the present perfect to talk about the past without any reference to time when the time is not important, not known, or imprecise. Using the present perfect, rather than the simple past, shows that the past is relevant to a present situation or discussion.

ABOUT YOU Write questions in the present perfect. Use *How much* or *How many* and the words. Take turns asking and answering your questions with a partner.

1. (ebooks) <u>How many ebooks have you bought?</u>
2. (money) <u>How much have you had the last month?</u>
3. (YouTube) <u>Have you ever tried to see YouTube videos before?</u>
4. (online classes) <u>How many online classes have you taken in high school</u>
5. (smartphones) <u>How many smartphones have you had in the last 5 years?</u>

GRAMMAR IN USE

The present perfect is commonly used to talk about accomplishments or achievements, especially when they were completed in the indefinite past. It is often necessary to talk about these things in job interviews or university applications.

I **have won** three awards for my work.

He **has produced** thousands of videos.

Have you **graduated** from high school?

She **has written** two novels, a dozen short stories, and numerous poems.

EXERCISE 15 Fill in the blanks to complete each conversation using the correct form of the verb and *yet* or *already*.

1. **A:** <u>Has your grandmother bought</u> a computer <u>yet</u>?
   a. your grandmother/buy   b.

   B: No, not <u>yet</u>. She<u>'s gone</u> to several stores <u>already</u>, but she
   c.   d. go   e.

   <u>hasn't decided</u> <u>yet</u>. She needs me to help her.
   f. not/decide   g.

2. **A:** The teacher gave us an assignment to write about crowdfunding. <u>Have you done</u> it
   a. you/do

   <u>yet</u>?
   b.

   B: No, not <u>yet</u>. But I <u>'ve read</u> several articles about it.
   c.   d. read

   I <u>haven't decided</u> what to write about <u>yet</u>.
   e. not/decide   f.

3. **A:** I just bought a new computer. My daughter helped me.

   B: <u>Has your daughter installed</u> an anti-virus program for you <u>yet</u>?
   a. your daughter/install   b.

   A: Yes. She <u>'s already</u> <u>   </u>.
   c.   d.

4. **A:** I just read the article about Khan Academy. <u>Have you read</u> it <u>yet</u>?
   a. you/read   b.

   B: Yes, I <u>'ve already read it</u>.
   c.

   A: I know Salman Khan <u>'s made</u> mostly math videos.
   d. make

   <u>He's made</u> any other kind of videos <u>yet</u>?
   e. he/make   f.

   B: Yes. He <u>'s created</u> videos on many subjects. And volunteers
   g. create

   <u>have translated</u> them into many different languages.
   h. translate

   A: My language is Urdu. <u>Have they translated</u> videos into my language <u>yet</u>?
   i. they/translate   j.

   B: Yes, they <u>have</u>.
   k.

5. **A:** I have trouble with math. I can't keep up with the teacher.

   B: <u>Have you asked</u> the teacher for help?
   a. you/ask

244 Unit 9

A: Yes, I _already have_ . But she only has time once a week. I need help after every class.
b.

B: _Have you tried_ Khan Academy _yet_ ?
c. you/try   d.

A: No. Where's Khan Academy? Is it in this city?

B: It's not a physical location. It's on the Internet.

A: I've _already_ looked for help on the Internet, but it wasn't very good.
e.

B: But you _haven't tried_ Khan Academy _yet_ . Try it.
f. not/try   g.

I'm sure you'll get the help you need.

ABOUT YOU Write statements about yourself. Then find a partner and ask questions with *Have you ever…* Answer with: *Yes, I have; No, I haven't;* or *No, I never have.*

A: *Have you ever studied computer programming?*
B: *No, I never have.*

1. (*study*) computer programming

   I've never studied computer programming.

2. (*google*) your own name

   I've googled my name once.

3. (*use*) the Internet to look for a person you haven't seen in a long time

   I've hardly ever used

4. (*download*) music from the Internet

   I've often downloaded

5. (*use*) a search engine in your native language

   I've frequently used

6. (*buy*) something online

   I've often bought

7. (*edit*) photos on your computer

   I've never edited

8. (*take*) a selfie with your selfie stick

   I've never taken

9. (*see*) the movie *The Social Network*

   I've never seen

The Present Perfect, The Present Perfect Continuous

9.9 The Present Perfect vs. the Simple Past

EXAMPLES	EXPLANATION
A: You were talking about getting a new computer. **Have** you **gotten** one **yet**? B: Yes. I **got** a new one **last week**. A: **Have** you **seen** any of Khan's videos? B: Yes. I **saw** one this morning. A: **Have** you **ever taken** a chemistry class? B: Yes. **Last semester**, I **took** Chemistry 101.	We can answer a present perfect question with the simple past and a definite time. Some definite times expressions are: • last week, month, year, semester • in 2008 • two weeks ago • when I was 18 years old
How long **have** you **had** your computer? **When did** you **buy** your computer?	For a question with *how long* that connects the past to the present, we use the present perfect. For a question with *when* about a specific time before now, we use the simple past.

EXERCISE 16 Fill in the blanks with the correct form of the verb given and any other words you see.

1. A: <u>Have you ever sent</u> money to help pay for a crowdfunding project?
   a. you/ever/send
   B: No, I _<u>haven't</u>_ . But last week, my sister _<u>saw</u>_ a project
   b.   c. see
   that she's interested in, so she _<u>is sent</u>_ money to help fund it.
   d. send

2. A: I need money for a new project I'm working on.
   B: _<u>Have you ever asked</u>_ your friends for money?
   a. you/ever/ask
   A: No, I never _<u>asked before</u>_ . I don't like to borrow money from friends. Last year, a friend
   b.
   of mine _<u>borrowed</u>_ money from me and never paid me back.
   c. borrow
   B: _<u>Have you ever mentioned</u>_ it to him?
   d. you/ever/mention
   A: No, I _<u>haven't</u>_ . I don't like to talk to friends about money.
   e.
   B: _<u>Have you ever heard</u>_ of crowdfunding?
   f. you/ever/hear
   A: Yes, I _<u>heard about it</u>_ . But I don't know how to use it.
   g.

3. A: You asked me for a suggestion for math help, and I told you about Khan Academy.
   <u>Have you tried</u> it yet?
   a. you/try
   B: Yes. Thanks for your suggestion. I _<u>looked</u>_ for it immediately.
   b. look
   A: _<u>Did it help</u>_ you?
   c. help

246 Unit 9

B: Oh, yes. I _____got_____ an A on my last calculus test. How long
d. get

_____have you known_____ about Khan Academy?
e. you/know

A: For about a year. My cousin _____told_____ me about it.
f. tell

4. A: _____Have you ever heard_____ of Sergey Brin and Larry Page?
a. you/ever/hear

B: No, I never _____have_____. Who are they?
b.

A: They're the creators of Google.

B: When _____did they create_____ Google?
c. they/create

A: They _____worked_____ on it when they _____were_____ in graduate
d. work   e. be

school. They _____put_____ it on the Internet in 1998.
f. put

B: "Sergey" sounds like a Russian name.

A: He is Russian. He _____came_____ to the United States when he
g. come

_____was_____ a child.
h. be

5. A: _____Has your computer ever gotten_____ a virus?
a. your computer/ever/get

B: Yes, it _____has_____. Yesterday someone _____used_____ my email to
b.   c. use

send a message to everyone in my address book. I don't know how that happened.

A: _____Have you ever used_____ your laptop or tablet in a coffee shop to connect to the Internet?
d. you/ever/use

B: Yes, I _____have_____. In fact, I _____went_____ to a coffee shop a few
e.   f. go

days ago to use the Wi-Fi there.

A: Maybe someone in the coffee shop _____stole_____ your personal information.
g. steal

B: Is that possible?

A: Yes, it is. Actually, it's not uncommon. I sent you an article about Internet security.
_____Have you read_____ it yet?
h. you/read

B: No, I _____haven't_____. I _____haven't had_____ time.
i.   j. have

A: I suggest you read it.

The Present Perfect, The Present Perfect Continuous   **247**

Genealogy and the Genographic Project

Read the following article. Pay special attention to the words in bold. 9.5

Genealogy[1] is one of the most popular hobbies in the United States. The percentage of Americans interested in family history **has been increasing** steadily. This increase has to do with the ease of searching on the Internet.

Cyndi Howells quit her job in 1992 and **has been working** on her family tree ever since. To help other family historians, she created a website called Cyndi's List. Over the years, this site **has been growing**.

Although the Internet has made research easier, it is only the beginning for serious family historians. Genealogists[2] still need to go to libraries to find public records, such as the U.S. Census. Since 1790, the U.S. Census Bureau **has been conducting** a census every 10 years.

But genealogy research on the Internet and in libraries can only go back a couple of hundred years. Then it stops. In the past, that meant the end of one's family search. But since the beginning of the twenty-first century, serious family historians **have been using** genetics to trace their backgrounds. This technology shows the relationship between people, going back thousands of years.

In 2005, National Geographic started the Genographic Project. Since then, it **has been collecting** and **analyzing** DNA[3] from people all over the world. Dr. Spencer Wells, founder of the project, **has been using** this information to understand how we are all related to each other.

How does this project work? People get a DNA kit, put in a bit of saliva, and send it back. Dr. Wells has concluded that all humans alive today descended from early humans who lived in Eastern Africa around two hundred thousand years ago. Dr. Wells **has been studying** human migration[4] from Africa to other parts of the world. Dr. Wells thinks that by understanding who we are and where we came from, we will have a better sense of where we are going.

---

[1] genealogy: the study of family history
[2] genealogist: family historian
[3] DNA: the molecules that carry genetic information and define the traits of a person, plant, or animal
[4] migration: movement from one place to another, usually in large groups

Dr. Spencer Wells, director of National Geographic's Genographic Project

COMPREHENSION Based on the reading, write T for *true* or F for *false*.

1. __F__ Library and Internet research for genealogy can help us find family information from thousands of years ago.
2. __T__ DNA analysis can show us the relationship of people all over the world.
3. __T__ The U.S. Census provides family historians with useful information.

THINK ABOUT IT Discuss the questions with a partner or in a small group.

1. What do you know about your family's genealogy? How did you learn what you know?
2. What more would you like to know about it?

9.10 The Present Perfect Continuous—Forms

SUBJECT	HAVE/HAS (+ NOT)	BEEN	PRESENT PARTICIPLE	
Cyndi Howells	has	been	working	on her family history since 1992.
The Genographic Project	has	been	analyzing	information since 2005.
Family historians	have	been	using	DNA to trace their backgrounds.
The U.S. Census Bureau	hasn't	been	keeping	detailed records for more than 150 years.

Observe statements, *yes/no* questions, short answers, and *wh-* questions.

STATEMENT	YES/NO QUESTION & SHORT ANSWER	WH- QUESTION
Dr. Wells **has been studying** DNA for several years.	**Has** he **been studying** the DNA of people all over the world? Yes, he **has**.	How long **has** he **been studying** human DNA?
You **have been thinking** about researching your family history.	**Have** you **been thinking** about DNA testing? No, I **haven't**.	Why **haven't** you **been thinking** about DNA testing?
Cyndi Howells **has been working** on her family history.	**Have** you **been working** on your family history? No, I **haven't**.	Who **has been working** on your family history?

Note:
The present perfect continuous is sometimes called the present perfect progressive.

EXERCISE 17 Listen to the information about the U.S. Census. Write T for *true*, F for *false*, or NS for *not stated*. 🎧 9.6

1. __T__ At first, children were not counted in the census.
2. __F__ All census information is available to everyone.
3. __NS__ Most Americans complete the census questionnaire.

EXERCISE 18 Listen to the information again. Fill in the blanks with the words you hear. 🎧 9.6

The U.S. Census __has been collecting__ information every 10 years since 1790.
                         1.
Family historians __have been taking__ advantage of census records to trace their family history.
                         2.
What is the difference between the early census and the census today?

In 1790, when the population was less than four million, the government wanted to find out how many men were eligible for military service, so census workers didn't even count children. In more recent years, the government __has been using__ this information to give citizens representation in Congress and
                    3.
to decide how to use federal money for schools, hospitals, roads, and more.

At first the census results were available to everyone. More recently, the government __has been protecting__ the privacy of individuals. Census information is only available after
         4.
72 years. Genealogists were excited when the 1940 census information became available in 2012.

Since 1950, the government __has been using__ computers to compile census data, making
                               5.
the information available much faster.

Before 1960, census takers went door to door. Since 1960, the government __has been sending__
                                                                                    6.
census forms to people through the U.S. mail.

For many years, the census forms were only in English. In recent years, the U.S. government __has been making__ census forms available in several languages besides English.
        7.

The government found that it needed data between the 10-year intervals. Since 2005, the census bureau __has been collecting__ information every year from a sample of Americans. Each year, 3.5 million
        8.
households receive a questionnaire.

EXERCISE 19 Fill in the blanks with the present perfect continuous form of the verb given. Include any other words you see.

1. How long __has Cyndi been managing__ a genealogy website?
              Cyndi/manage
2. Interest in genealogy __has been growing__.
                                  grow
3. Cyndi Howells __has been working__ on her family history since 1992.
                           work
4. Cyndi __has been lecturing__ all over the United States to genealogy groups.
                lecture
5. The number of genealogy websites __has been increasing__.
                                              increase
6. How long __has U.S. Census Bureau been keeping__ records?
                  U.S. Census Bureau/keep

250 Unit 9

7. How _has US Census been collecting_ information?
   _{U.S. Census Bureau/collect}
8. _Have you been working_ on a family tree? Yes, I _have_.
   _{you/work}
9. Family historians _have been using_ the Internet to do family research since the 1990s.
   _{use}
10. How long _has Dr. Wells been studying_ human DNA?
    _{Dr. Wells/study}

9.11 The Present Perfect Continuous—Use

We use the present perfect continuous to show that an action started in the past and continues to the present.

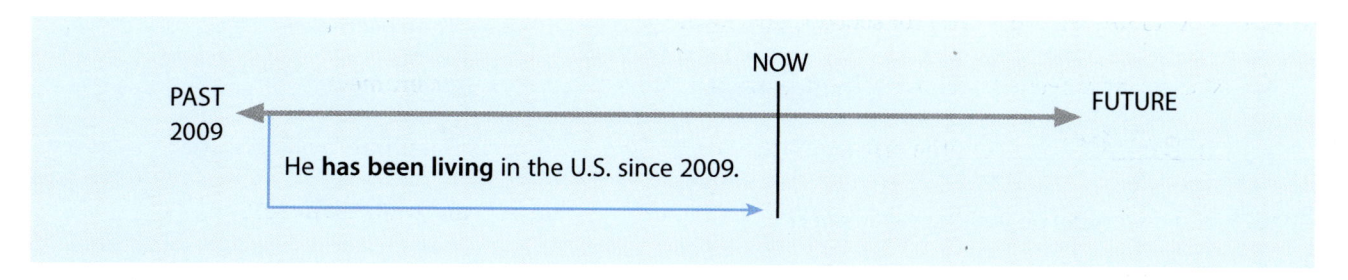

PAST 2009 ←———— He **has been living** in the U.S. since 2009. ————| **NOW** ————→ **FUTURE**

EXAMPLES	EXPLANATION
The U.S. Census **has been collecting** information **for** over 200 years.	We use *for* with the amount of time.
Cyndi's website **has been helping** family historians **since** 1996.	We use *since* with the beginning time.
Cyndi **has been working** full-time on her website **since** she **quit** her job.	We use the simple past in the *since* clause.
I **have been studying** my family history since 2010. OR I **have studied** my family history since 2010.	With some verbs (*live, work, study, teach,* and *wear*), we can use either the present perfect or the present perfect continuous with actions that began in the past and continue to the present. The meaning is the same.
My father is working on our family tree right now. He **has been working** on it since 9 a.m.	If an action is still happening, we use the present perfect continuous, not the present perfect.
I **have been** interested in genealogy for 10 years. She **has wanted** to learn about her family history since she was in high school.	We do not use the continuous form with nonaction verbs, such as *be, like, want, have, know, remember,* and *see*.
I **have been** *thinking about* sending my DNA for analysis. I **have** always *thought that* genealogy is an interesting hobby.	*Think* can be an action or nonaction verb, depending on its meaning. *Think about* = action verb *Think that* = nonaction verb

Note:
We do not use the continuous form with *always* and *never*.

   I have **always** lived in this country.
   NOT: I have always been living in this country.

EXERCISE 20 Fill in the blanks to complete the conversations.

1. **A:** _____Are_____ you studying your family history?
   B: Yes, I __am__.
   A: How long __have you been studying__ your family history?
   B: __For__ about five years.

2. **A:** __Is__ Spencer Wells working on the Genographic Project?
   B: Yes, he __is__.
   A: __How__ long __has__ he been __working__ on this project?
   B: __Since__ 2005.

3. **A:** Are you working on your family history?
   B: Yes, I __m__.
   A: How long __have__ you __working__ on your family history?
   B: I __have been working__ on it __for__ about 10 years.

4. **A:** Is your sister using your computer now?
   B: Yes, she __is__.
   A: __How__ long __has she been using__ it?
   B: __Since__ she woke up this morning!

5. **A:** __Does__ the U.S. Census Bureau collect information about Americans?
   B: Yes, it __does__.
   A: How __long__ the U.S. Census Bureau __has been collecting__ information about Americans?
   B: __For__ over 200 years.

6. **A:** __Do__ your grandparents live in the U.S.?
   B: Yes, they __do__.
   A: How __long have they been living__ in the U.S.?
   B: Since they __were__ born.

252 Unit 9

ABOUT YOU Write true statements using the present perfect with the words given and *for* or *since*. Share your sentences with a partner.

1. work My brother has been working as an engineer for six years.
2. study I've studied English for several years. / How long have you been studying English?
3. live I've lived in my new house since last year. / How long
4. use I've used my old computer for 5 years
5. try I've tried to ask more questions since I graduate from HS

EXERCISE 21 Fill in the blanks with the correct form of the verb given. Use the present perfect, present perfect continuous, or the simple past. Fill in any other missing words.

A: Hi. My name is Ana. I'm from Guatemala.

B: Hi, Ana. My name is Jimmy. My family is from Cuba. How _long have you been living_ here?
   1. you/live

A: I _'ve only been_ here for about six months. What about you?
   2. only/be

B: I _was_ born in the U.S. My family _left_ Cuba in
   3. be   **4.** leave

   1962. Lately I _'ve been trying_ to trace my family history.
   5. try

A: Me, too. I've been _working_ on a family tree _for_ many years.
   6. work   **7.**

B: When _did you start_ ?
   8. you/start

A: I _started_ when I _was_ 16 years old. Over the
   9. start   **10.** be

   years, I _'ve found_ a lot of interesting information about my family. Some of my
   11. find

   ancestors were Mayans, and some were from Spain and France.

B: Where _did you find_ all that information?
   12. you/find

A: There's a wonderful site called Cyndi's List. I _'ve been using_ it
   13. use

   since around 2001. Last summer, I _went_
   14.   **15.** go

   to Spain to look for information there.

B: How many ancestors _have you found_ so far?
   16. you/find

A: So far, I _found_ about 50 in four generations. I'm still looking.
   17. find

B: _Have you ever heard_ of the Genographic Project?
   18. you/ever/hear

A: No, I _haven't_ . What is it?
   19.

B: It connects people from all over the world, going back thousands of years.

SUMMARY OF UNIT 9

The Present Perfect and the Simple Past

PRESENT PERFECT	SIMPLE PAST
The action of the sentence began in the past and includes the present.	The action of the sentence is completely past.
Sergey Brin **has been** in the U.S. since 1979.	Sergey Brin **came** to the U.S. in 1979.
Khan's videos **have been** available for many years.	Khan **created** his first math videos in 2004.
I**'ve** always **wanted** to learn more about my family's history.	When I was a child, I always **wanted** to spend time with my grandparents.
How long **have** you **been** interested in genealogy?	When **did** you **start** your family tree?

PRESENT PERFECT	SIMPLE PAST
Repetition from past to present	Repetition in a past time period
Khan Academy **has created** over 5,000 videos so far.	Khan **created** several videos for his niece in 2004.

PRESENT PERFECT	SIMPLE PAST
The action took place at an indefinite time between the past and the present.	The action took place at a definite time in the past.
Have you ever **used** Cyndi's list?	**Did** you **use** the 1940 census in 2012?
My brother **has raised** $5,000 on a crowdfunding site already.	He **put** his project on a crowdfunding site six months ago.
I'm interested in the DNA project. I**'ve received** my kit, but I **haven't sent** the sample back yet.	My friend **sent** her DNA sample to the Genographic Project last month.

The Present Perfect and the Present Perfect Continuous

PRESENT PERFECT	PRESENT PERFECT CONTINUOUS
A continuous action (nonaction verbs)	A continuous action (action verbs)
I **have been** interested in genealogy for five years.	I**'ve been working** on my family tree for five years.
A repeated action	A nonstop action
Cyndi Howell's website **has won** several awards.	The U.S. Census Bureau **has been keeping** records since the 1880s.
Question with *how many/how much*	Question with *how long*
How many times **has** Khan **been** on the cover of a magazine? How much time **has** he **spent** on Khan Academy?	How long **has** Khan **been living** in Boston?
An action that is at an indefinite time, completely in the past	An action that started in the past and is still happening
Many teachers **have started** to use Khan lectures in their classrooms.	Dr. Wells **has been collecting** DNA for several years.

REVIEW

Fill in the blanks with the simple present, the simple past, the present perfect, or the present perfect continuous form of the verbs given. Include any other words you see. In some cases, more than one answer is possible.

A: What do you do for a living?

B: I __work__ as a programmer. I __'ve been working__ as a
  1. work   2. work

programmer for five years. But my job is boring.

A: __have you ever thought__ about changing jobs?
  3. you/think/ever

B: Yes. Since I __was__ a child, I __'ve always wanted__ to be an actor.
  4. be   5. always/want

When I was in college, I __was__ in a few plays. But since I
  6. be

__graduated__, I __haven't had__ time to act. What about you?
  7. graduate   8. not/have

A: I __work__ in computer security.
  9. work

B: How long __have you been doing__ that?
  10. you/do

A: For about six years.

B: I __think__ the field of computer security is very important.
  11. think

A: Yes, it is. But lately I __have been using__ the computer for other things, too. My hobby is
  12. use

genealogy. I __'ve been working__ on my family tree for about a year. Last month, I
  13. work

__found__ information about my father's ancestors. My grandfather
  14. find

__lives__ with us now, and he likes to tell us about his past. He
  15. live

__was__ born in Italy, but he __came__ here when he
  16. be   17. come

was very young, so he __lived__ here most of his life. He
  18. live

__doesn't remember__ much about Italy. I __haven't found__ any information
  19. not/remember   20. not/find

about my mother's ancestors yet.

FROM GRAMMAR TO WRITING

PART 1 Editing Advice

1. Don't confuse the *-ing* form and the past participle.

   I've been ~~taken~~ *taking* a course in genealogy.

   My parents have ~~giving~~ *given* me family photos.

2. Use the present perfect, not the simple present or present continuous, to describe an action or state that started in the past and continues to the present.

   He has *had* his laptop for two years.   How long ~~are you~~ *have you been* studying math?

3. Use *for*, not *since*, with the amount of time.

   I've been interested in my family's history ~~since~~ *for* three years.

4. Use the simple past, not the present perfect, with a specific past time.

   He ~~has studied~~ *studied* algebra when he was in high school.

   When ~~have~~ *did* you ~~studied~~ *study* algebra?

5. Use the simple past, not the present perfect, in a *since* clause.

   He has collected $5,000 since he ~~has put~~ *put* his project on a crowdfunding site.

6. Use the correct word order with adverbs.

   I have ~~studied never~~ *never studied* my family history. Have you ~~heard ever~~ *ever heard* of Dr. Spencer Wells?

7. Use the correct word order in questions.

   How long ~~your family has~~ *has your family* been in this country?

8. Use *yet* for negative statements; use *already* for affirmative statements.

   I haven't taken advanced algebra ~~already~~ *yet*.

9. Don't forget the verb *have* in the present perfect (continuous).

   I *have* been studying my family history for two years.

10. Don't forget the *-ed* of the past participle.

    He's watch*ed* a math video several times.

PART 2 Editing Practice

Some of the shaded words and phrases have mistakes. Find the mistakes and correct them. If the shaded words are correct, write C.

How many changes ~~you have~~ *have you* made since you came to the U.S.? For our journal, our teacher
                     1.   2. C
asked us to answer this question. I have come to the U.S. two and a half years ago. Things have
                                      3.
change a lot for me since I've come here. Here are some of the changes:
  4.   5.

256 Unit 9

First, since the past two years, I am studying to be a software engineer. I knew a little about this subject before I came here, but my knowledge has improve a lot. I started to work part-time in a computer company three months ago. Since I have started my job, I haven't have much time for fun.

Second, I have a driver's permit, and I'm learning how to drive. I haven't took the driver's test yet because I'm not ready. I haven't practiced enough already.

Third, I've been eaten a lot of different foods like hamburgers and pizza. I never ate those in my country. Unfortunately, I been gaining weight.

Fourth, I've gone to several museums in this city. But I've taken never a trip to another American city. I'd like to visit New York, but I haven't saved enough money yet.

Fifth, I've been living in three apartments so far. In my country, I lived in the same house with my family all my life.

One thing that bothers me is this: I've answered the following questions about a thousand times so far: "Where do you come from?" and "How long time you have been in the U.S.?" I'm getting tired of always answering the same question. But in general, I been happy since I came to the U.S.

WRITING TIP

When you write a paragraph or essay about a change in your life, start your paper with a sentence that states how the new situation (technology, for example) has changed your life.

*Since I got a cell phone, my life **has** greatly **improved**.*

Then use the simple past to talk about what you used to do and the simple present to talk about what you do habitually now.

*Before I got a cell phone, I **went** to work in the morning and only **talked** to my family at night. Now, I **call** before I **go** home to **ask** if they need anything.*

PART 3 Write

Read the prompts. Choose one and write a paragraph or two about it.

1. Write about the changes that you have made since you came to this country, city, or school.
2. Write about new technology that you've started using recently. How has that made your life different?

PART 4 Edit

Reread the Summary of Unit 9 and the editing advice. Edit your writing from Part 3.

UNIT

10

**Gerunds
Infinitives**

A worker maintains the
paint on a ship at sea.

JOBS

> Choose a job you love, and you will never have to work a day in your life.
>
> CONFUCIUS

Job seekers attend the Big East Career Fair at Madison Square Garden in New York, U.S. The fair is for students and alumni from ten specific schools on the east coast.

FINDING a JOB

Read the following article. Pay special attention to the words in bold. 10.1

Finding a job in the United States takes time and effort. Here are some tips[1] to help you:

- Write a good résumé. Include only relevant[2] experience. Describe your accomplishments[3]. Avoid **including** unnecessary information. Consider **asking** a friend to read your résumé to check it for grammar and spelling mistakes.

- Find out about available jobs. One way is by **looking** on the Internet. Another way is by **networking**. **Networking** means **exchanging** information with anyone you know who might know of a job. These people might be able to give you insider information about a company, such as who is in charge of **hiring** and what it is like to work at their company. You can find out about a job before it is even advertised. *The Wall Street Journal* reports that 94 percent of people who succeed in **finding** a job say that **networking** was a big help.

- Practice before you go for an interview. The more prepared you are, the more relaxed you will feel and the more you will convey[4] confidence. If you are worried about **saying** or **doing** the wrong thing, practice will help.

- Learn something about the company by **going** to the company's website.

- Arrive at least 15 minutes before the scheduled time of your interview. **Feeling** relaxed is important. **Arriving** on time or just a few minutes before the interview doesn't give you time to relax.

---

[1] tip: useful information
[2] relevant: closely connected
[3] accomplishment: a difficult thing done well
[4] to convey: to communicate

- Behave professionally during the interview. Avoid **chewing** gum. Turn off your cell phone completely.

- Avoid **saying** anything negative about your current job or employer.

- One question might be, "Tell me something about yourself." Instead of **talking** about your personal life, focus on your skills and work experience. Answer each question concisely[5]. Avoid **giving** long answers.

- At the end of the interview, offer a firm handshake. **Thanking** the interviewer by letter or email a few days later is a good idea.

Some people send out hundreds of résumés and go on dozens of interviews before **finding** a job. **Looking** for a job isn't something you do just once or twice in your lifetime.

---

[5] concisely: using few words to communicate

COMPREHENSION Based on the reading, write T for *true* or F for *false*.

1. _____ *Networking* means getting information from the Internet.
2. _____ Arriving right on time to an interview is a good idea.
3. _____ Thanking the interviewer with a handshake is enough.

THINK ABOUT IT Discuss the questions with a partner or in a small group.

1. What networking opportunities exist today for people who are looking for work?
2. If an interviewer asked you to describe your greatest weakness, what could you say that would also show something positive about you?

10.1 Gerunds—An Overview

A gerund is the *–ing* form of a verb.

EXAMPLES	EXPLANATION
Finding a job is hard. I recommend **talking** to a job counselor. Are you thinking about **changing** careers?	A gerund (phrase) can be: • the subject of a sentence. • the object of the verb. • the object of a preposition.
I'm worried about **not getting** a good job.	We put *not* in front of a gerund to make it negative.

Note:
A gerund phrase is a gerund + a noun or noun phrase.
- *finding a job*
- *exchanging information*
- *preparing for a job interview*

EXERCISE 1 Listen to these tips about how to be successful at your job. Then write T for *true* or F for *false*. 🎧 10.2

1. _____ You should speak up if you are unhappy about working on a project.

2. _____ If you practice talking confidently, you can become better at it.

3. _____ You should be direct about your weaknesses.

EXERCISE 2 Listen to the tips again. Fill in the blanks with the words you hear. 🎧 10.2

You care __*about keeping*__(1) your job. You may not be aware _____(2) things that can make your supervisor think less of you. So here are a few tips:

- Avoid _____(3) about things you have to do. If you dislike _____(4) on a project, keep it to yourself. Don't say, "It's not my job." Even if you don't like _____(5) it, do it anyway _____(6).

- Practice _____(7) positive words to show confidence and a good attitude. _____(8) "It's not fair" makes you sound like a child.

- Get used _____(9) strong words. Instead _____(10), "I think I can do the job," simply say, "I can do the job. When do you need the work done?" Most people don't know how they sound. Consider _____(11) a friend listen to the way you talk. Or try _____(12) yourself and analyzing what you say.

- Don't point out your weaknesses. "I'm not good _____(13) reports" sounds bad. Instead say, "I want to do a good job. I'd like to work with someone who can help me learn to write better reports."

- _____(14) a coworker that you don't like a supervisor is not a good idea. You never know what this person might say to the supervisor.

- If you're interested _____(15) more tips on good job behavior, there are books and online sources that can give you more information.

262 Unit 10

10.2 Gerunds as Subjects

EXAMPLES	EXPLANATION
Using positive words conveys confidence. **Not dressing** appropriately gives a bad impression.	We can use a gerund or gerund phrase as the subject of the sentence.
Exchanging ideas with friends **is** helpful. **Visiting** company websites **pays** off.	A gerund subject takes a singular verb.

EXERCISE 3 Use the gerund form of one of the verbs from the box to complete each sentence.

| arrive | wear | feel | know | get ✓ | network | prepare | select |

1. _____Getting_____ a good night's sleep will help you feel rested and alert for an interview.
2. _____ with other people will improve your chances of finding a job.
3. _____ your clothes the night before the interview is a good idea.
4. _____ a good résumé is very important. Some people use a résumé service.
5. _____ something about the company will help you make a good impression.
6. Not _____ serious clothes to the interview will give a very bad impression.
7. _____ early for an interview will give you time to relax.
8. _____ relaxed before an interview is important.

ABOUT YOU Fill in the blanks with the gerund form of the verb given. Then tell if this behavior is or isn't common in a work situation in your country.

1. _____Socializing_____ with the boss (is/*isn't*) common.
   socialize
2. _____ the boss by his or her first name (*is/isn't*) acceptable.
   call
3. _____ with coworkers (*is/isn't*) common.
   socialize
4. _____ on time (*is/isn't*) very important.
   arrive
5. _____ a personal computer at a job (*is/isn't*) common.
   use
6. _____ jeans to the office (*is/isn't*) acceptable.
   wear
7. _____ a long lunch break (*is/isn't*) the custom.
   take
8. _____ from home (*is/isn't*) common.
   work
9. _____ coffee or tea while working (*is/isn't*) acceptable.
   drink
10. _____ early on Friday afternoons (*is/isn't*) common.
    leave

ABOUT YOU In preparing for an interview, it is good to think about the following questions. Give some thought to your answers and compare them with a partner's answers.

1. What are your strengths?

   working well with others; learning quickly; thinking fast in difficult situations

2. What are some of your weaknesses?

3. List your accomplishments and achievements. (They can be achievements in jobs, sports, school, etc.)

4. What are your short-term goals?

5. What are your long-term goals?

6. What are some things you like in a job situation? (personalities, tasks, environments, types of work)

7. What are some things you dislike? (personalities, tasks, environments, types of work)

EXERCISE 4 Work with a partner to write sentences about behaviors during an interview that would hurt your chances of getting a job.

1. Chewing gum during the interview looks bad.
2.
3.
4.
5.
6.

10.3 Gerunds as Objects

EXAMPLES	EXPLANATION
Do you **enjoy working** on a team? **Avoid complaining** about your supervisor.	A gerund (phrase) can be the object of many verbs.
I **went shopping** for work clothes last weekend. After work, I like to **go swimming**.	We use *go* + gerund in expressions of recreational activities.

A gerund (phrase) can follow these verbs:

admit	dislike	love	quit
appreciate	enjoy	mind	recommend
avoid	finish	miss	start
begin	hate	postpone	stop
consider	imagine	practice	suggest
continue	keep (on)	prefer	
discuss	like	put off	

We use *go* + gerund in the following expressions:

go boating	go camping	go fishing	go hunting
go jogging	go shopping	go skating	go swimming
go bowling	go dancing	go hiking	go skiing

Notes:

1. *I mind* means that something bothers me. *I don't mind* means that something is OK with me; it doesn't bother me.

    Do you **mind wearing** a suit to work? No, I don't **mind**.

2. *Put off* means "postpone."

    Don't **put off writing** your résumé. Do it now.

*For a list of verbs followed by gerunds, see Appendix D.

EXERCISE 5 Use the gerund form of a verb from the box to complete each conversation.

| answer | shop | find | say | get | be | do ✓ |
| work | wear | go | act | discuss | talk | read |

1. **A:** I want to quit my boring job. I dislike _____*doing*_____ the same thing every day.
    a.

   B: I suggest _____ another job before you quit. I can't imagine _____
    b.   c.

   without a job.

2. **A:** Interviewing for a job scares me. I hate _____ about my strengths.
    a.

   B: Have you considered _____ help from a job counselor? You can practice _____
    b.   c.

   common interview questions. I have a good book about job hunting. When I finish _____
    d.

   it, you can borrow it.

continued

3. **A:** I have to wear a suit for my new job.

   B: I dislike _____ anything but jeans.
   　　　　　　　　a.

   A: Me, too. I have to go _____ for some new clothes. Can you help me pick something out?
   　　　　　　　　　　　　　　　　　b.

   B: Sorry. I don't have time. I suggest _____ to a store and asking the salesperson to help you.
   　　　　　　　　　　　　　　　　　　　　　　　c.

4. **A:** I really like my job.

   B: What do you like about it?

   A: I enjoy _____ on a team. The people on my team are smart and creative. I like
   　　　　　　　　a.

   _____ how to do a project with them.
   　　b.

5. **A:** My boss always asks me to do something that isn't my job. Sometimes I have to tell her, "It's not fair."

   B: Stop _____ "It's not fair" and just do it. Quit _____ like a child.
   　　　　　　a.　　　　　　　　　　　　　　　　　　　　　　　b.

ABOUT YOU Use the words below to make statements about yourself regarding jobs. Share your answers with a partner.

1. I hate *getting up every morning at 5 for my job.*

2. I enjoy _____

3. I don't mind _____

4. I've considered _____

5. I can't imagine _____

6. I avoid _____

7. I began _____

EXERCISE 6 Make a list of suggestions and recommendations for someone looking for a job or about to go on a job interview. Discuss your list with a partner.

1. *I recommend getting a good night's sleep the night before the interview.*

2. _____

3. _____

4. _____

5. _____

6. _____

10.4 Preposition + Gerund

A gerund can follow certain verb + preposition or adjective + preposition combinations.

COMMON VERB + PREPOSITION COMBINATIONS		EXAMPLES
verb + *about*	care about complain about dream about forget about know about talk about think about worry about	My sister **dreams about becoming** an engineer.
verb + *to*	look forward to object to	I **look forward to getting** a job and **saving** money.
verb + *on*	depend on insist on plan on	I **plan on going** to a career counselor.
verb + *in*	believe in succeed in	My father **succeeded in finding** a good job.
verb + object + *from*	stop + . . . + from	No one can **stop** you **from following** your dream.
COMMON ADJECTIVE + PREPOSITION COMBINATIONS		**EXAMPLES**
adjective + *of*	afraid of capable of guilty of proud of tired of	I'm **afraid of losing** my job.
adjective + *about*	concerned about excited about upset about worried about sad about	He is **upset about not getting** the job.
adjective + *for*	responsible for famous for	Who is **responsible for hiring** in this company?
adjective + *to* + object + *for*	grateful to . . . for	I'm **grateful to** you **for helping** me find a job.
adjective + *at*	good at successful at	I'm not very **good at writing** a résumé.
adjective + *to*	accustomed to used to	I'm not **accustomed to talking** about my strengths.
adjective + *in*	interested in successful in	Are you **interested in getting** a better job?

Note:
In general, you can use a gerund after any preposition.

*What is your method **of preparing** for an interview?*
*It's hard to do well at an interview **without practicing**.*

---

*For a list of verbs and adjectives followed by a preposition, see Appendix E.

EXERCISE 7 Fill in the blanks with a preposition and the gerund form of a verb from the box.

talk	do	work	complain	get	help
be	practice	tell	hear	go ✓	connect

1. **A:** I plan ___on going___ to India for a year to work in a clinic as a physician assistant.
   a.

   B: That's great. You've talked a lot _____ other people. This is your chance.
   b.

   A: When I get back, I'd like to go to medical school, but it's so expensive. I'm worried _____ not
   c.

   _____ financial aid.
   d.

   B: With your experience in India, you're a good candidate for financial aid.

2. **A:** I have an interview next week. I'm afraid _____ not _____ well.
   a.   b.

   B: Have you thought _____ for the interview?
   c.

   A: No, I haven't. I don't know how to do that.

   B: I have a friend who has a lot of experience with job interviews. Are you interested _____
   d.

   with her? She can give you good tips. I can set up a meeting for you. (*A few weeks later…*)

   A: I'm grateful to you _____ me with your friend. She helped me a lot.
   e.

3. **A:** Some people complain _____ long hours. But I don't even have a job.
   a.

   I'm upset _____ unemployed for so long.
   b.

   B: How long have you been unemployed?

   A: For almost six months. I'm worried _____ the interviewer about my long
   c.

   unemployment. It might hurt my chances of getting a job.

4. **A:** A coworker of mine always insists _____ about the boss. She hates the boss.
   a.

   B: Tell her you're not interested _____ her complaints.
   b.

ABOUT YOU Fill in the blanks with a preposition + gerund or noun phrase to complete each statement about jobs. Share your answers with a partner.

1. I'm afraid ___of losing my job.___

2. I'm not accustomed _____

3. Coworkers often talk _____

4. After work, I'm (not) interested _____

5. I worry _____

6. I'm proud _____

7. I'm not used _____

8. On Fridays, most workers look forward _____

EXERCISE 8 Fill in the blanks with the gerund form of the verb given. Some of the blanks need a preposition before the gerund. If so, add the preposition.

A: I need to find a job. I've had 10 interviews, but so far no job.

B: Have you thought <u>about practicing</u> for the interview? You can practice _____
                                             1. practice   2. answer
questions that the interviewer might ask you. Many interviewers ask the same general questions. For example, the interviewer will probably ask you to name your strengths.

A: I dislike _____ about myself.
              3. talk

B: But it's necessary. And she'll probably ask you to name your weaknesses, too.

A: What should I say? I'm afraid _____ the truth about my weaknesses.
                                        4. tell

B: There's a way to make your answer sound positive. For example, "I'm a perfectionist. I worry _____ in a project with mistakes. But I plan _____ careful so that
                   5. turn   6. be
I meet deadlines."

A: Wow! That sounds more like a strength than a weakness.

B: That's the idea. Here's another possible question: "Do you mind _____ overtime to finish
                                                                                      7. stay
a project?"

A: Will I have to work overtime? I'll have to get a babysitter for my son.

B: Don't complain _____ a babysitter. Don't mention personal problems.
                                  8. get

A: It feels like I'm never going to find a job. I'm tired _____ .
                                                                              9. look

B: Be patient. If you keep _____ , you'll succeed _____ a job.
                                 10. try   11. find

I suggest _____ a book that gives you sample interview questions.
               12. get

A: Thanks so much. I'm grateful to you _____ me so much help.
                                                    13. give

EMPLOYEE ENGAGEMENT

Employees gather for a group cheer just before opening a store during a busy holiday shopping weekend.

Read the following article. Pay special attention to the words in bold. 10.3

Do you like **to go** to work? Or are you glad **to leave** at the end of the day? If you have a full-time job, you probably spend most of your waking hours at work. It would be nice **to spend** that time in a pleasant atmosphere, right?

According to a survey, 70 percent of Americans are not happy at work. They often feel job burnout: physical and mental stress. Some of them can't wait **to get** home, but they often take their stress home with them to their families.

When workers are happy, they do a better job, and the company gains from this. What makes workers happy? The answer is "employee engagement." Researchers have been studying what makes a worker feel engaged. Engaged employees are enthusiastic about their work. Researchers have found that it takes a combination of things **to build** an engaged workforce:

1. Employees need **to feel** that the boss appreciates their work.
2. Workers need **to take** breaks during the day. When people work continuously, they feel worse physically. More work is not necessarily better work. Some experts believe that workers need a break every 90 minutes. Some companies have fitness facilities and nap rooms for their employees.
3. Workers want **to be** able to focus on one thing at a time. Too often, managers want them **to do** several things at once. The result is workers get stressed out, and their work suffers.
4. Workers want **to feel** that they are doing something meaningful. They want **to be** excited about what they're doing.

Employers need **to choose** a job candidate who fits the company's mission[1]. A worker who doesn't fit in is likely[2] **to quit**. It takes time and costs money **to train** a new employee. So it's important for a company **to hire** the right people and **make** the work atmosphere fun and meaningful.

---
[1] mission: purpose
[2] is likely: is probably going to

COMPREHENSION Based on the reading, write T for *true* or F for *false*.

1. _____ One way to promote employee engagement is for the employer to show the employee appreciation.
2. _____ The majority of Americans are happy to go to work.
3. _____ It is expensive for a company to train a new employee.

THINK ABOUT IT Discuss the questions with a partner or in a small group.

1. What type of job do you think would make you feel engaged? For example, would you like a job that encourages teamwork? Or would you feel more engaged in a job that requires mostly independent work?
2. Reread point 2 in the reading. What are some creative ways employers could offer employees breaks at work?

10.5 Infinitives—An Overview

An infinitive is *to* + the base form of a verb.

EXAMPLES	EXPLANATION
Are you happy **to go** to work? I need **to take** a break. It's important **to hire** the right people.	We can use an infinitive after: • certain adjectives. • certain verbs. • expressions beginning with *it*.
They decided **not to hire** me.	To make an infinitive negative, we put *not* before the infinitive.

Note:
When we connect two infinitives with *and*, we usually omit *to* after *and*.

   He wants **to take** a break and **rest**.

EXERCISE 9 Fill in the blanks with the words you hear. 🎧 10.4

It's important ___to write___ a good, clear résumé. It's only necessary
                      1.

_____ your most recent and related work. Employers are busy people. Don't
        2.

expect them _____ long résumés.
                    3.

You need _____ your abilities in your résumé. Employers expect you
                4.

_____ action verbs _____ your experience. Don't begin your
        5.   6.

sentences with *I*. Use past tense verbs such as: *managed, designed, created,* and *developed*. It's

not enough _____ you improved something. Be specific. How did you improve it?
                    7.

Before making copies of your résumé, it's important _____ the grammar and
                                                                    8.

spelling. Employers want _____ if you have good communication skills. Ask a
                                9.

friend or teacher _____ your résumé and check for mistakes.
                          10.

continued

It isn't necessary _____ references. If the employer wants you
                        11.

_____ references, he or she will ask you _____ so during or
    12.   13.

after the interview.

Don't include personal information such as marital status, age, race, family information, or hobbies.

Be honest in your résumé. Employers can check your information. No one wants

_____ a liar.
   14.

10.6 Infinitives after Expressions with *It*

EXAMPLES	EXPLANATION
It's important to write a good résumé. **It isn't necessary to include** all your experience. **It's a good idea to practice** before an interview.	An infinitive phrase can follow certain expressions beginning with *it*.
It's important **for managers to show** appreciation. It was hard **for me to leave** my last job.	We use *for* + a noun or object pronoun to make a statement that is true of a specific person or people.
It **takes patience to find** a job. It **took me** three weeks **to finish** my project.	We can use an infinitive after *take* + *time*, *patience*, or *money*. We can add an object before the infinitive.
It **costs** a lot of money **to train** a new worker. It **cost me** $100 **to use** a résumé service.	We can use an infinitive after *cost* + (object) + *money*.
It's important **to do** a good job. **Doing** a good job is important.	There is no difference in meaning between an infinitive after an *it* expression and a gerund subject.

We often use an infinitive after *it* + *be* + these words:

dangerous	expensive	a good/bad idea	impossible/possible
difficult	fun	hard	necessary
easy	a good/bad experience	important	a pleasure

EXERCISE 10 Fill in the blanks with the infinitive form of a verb from the box.

| practice | check | have ✓ | describe | arrive | write | include | dress |

1. It's necessary _____*to have*_____ a Social Security card.

2. When you write a résumé, it isn't necessary _____ all your previous experience.

   Choose only the most recent and related experience.

272   Unit 10

3. It's important _____ your spelling and grammar before sending a résumé.

4. It's important _____ your past work experience in detail, using words like *managed, designed, supervised,* and *built.*

5. It takes time _____ a good résumé.

6. It's a good idea _____ interview questions before going to an interview.

7. It's important _____ your best when you go to an interview, so choose your clothes carefully.

8. It's a good idea _____ early for your interview.

EXERCISE 11 Complete each statement with an infinitive phrase to talk about work. You can add an object, if you like.

1. It's easy to get information about a company online.

2. It's necessary for me to work overtime once a month.

3. It's important _____

4. It's impossible _____

5. It's possible _____

6. It's a pleasure _____

7. It isn't a good idea _____

8. It's hard _____

10.7 Infinitives after Adjectives

EXAMPLES	EXPLANATION
Are you **available to work** overtime? A happy worker is **likely to stay** with the company.	An infinitive (phrase) can follow certain adjectives. |//
An infinitive can follow these adjectives:	
afraid glad lucky proud sorry available happy prepared ready surprised	

*For a list of adjectives followed by infinitives, see Appendix D.

Gerunds, Infinitives 273

EXERCISE 12 Complete the conversation with the appropriate infinitive form of a verb from the box.

| help | talk | show | go ✓ | have | answer | wait | say |

A: I have my first interview tomorrow. I'm afraid ____to go____ alone. Would you go with me?
1.

B: I'd be happy _____ in the car. But nobody can go with you to an interview.
2.

You have to do it alone. It sounds like you're not ready _____ a job interview.
3.

You should see a job counselor and get some practice before you have an interview.

A: I don't have time. Maybe you can help me.

B: I'd be happy _____ you. We can go over some basic questions. Here's one question you
4.

should be ready _____: "Why are you leaving your present job?"
5.

A: I'm afraid _____ anything about my present job. I don't like my supervisor.
6.

B: Never say that! I'd be happy _____ you a few good websites that will give you typical
7.

questions and good answers.

A: Thanks. I'm glad you were available _____ to me this afternoon. I feel better already.
8.

10.8 Infinitives after Verbs

EXAMPLES	EXPLANATION
I **need to find** a better job. I **want to make** more money.	An infinitive (phrase) can follow certain verbs.

An infinitive can follow these verbs:

agree	decide	learn	remember	begin*	love*
attempt	expect	need	try	continue*	prefer*
begin	forget	plan	want	hate*	start*
choose	hope	promise	would like	like*	

Notes:
1. A gerund can also follow these verbs* with little or no difference in meaning. See chart 10.3.
   *I **love to work** with children. = I **love working** with children.*
2. *Plan on* + gerund is the same as *plan* + infinitive.
   *I **plan on seeing** a counselor. = I **plan to see** a counselor.*
3. Remember that in some expressions, *to* is part of a verb phrase, not part of an infinitive.
   *I **look forward to starting** my new job. (verb + to + gerund)*
   *I **need to write** a résumé. (verb + infinitive)*

*For a list of verbs followed by infinitives, see Appendix D.

EXERCISE 13 Fill in the blanks with the infinitive form of a verb from the box.

| feel | take | go | ask | find | sleep ✓ |
| work | get | be | hear | have | |

A: How's your new job?

B: I really like it. It's a great company. We can take a break every two hours. And we even have a nap room. Sometimes people need ____to sleep____ for a few minutes.
                                                                    1.

A: I've never heard of a nap room. I would like _____ a nap in the middle of the
                                                                    2.
day. I usually start _____ tired around two o'clock, but I have to keep working.
                          3.
How's your boss?

B: She's wonderful. She includes us on company decisions. Employees want _____
                                                                                    4.
like their opinion is important, don't you think?

A: Yes, I do.

B: It's fun for me _____ to work. After six months on the job, we can choose
                          5.
_____ from home, too. But I prefer _____
      6.   7.
with my team members at the office.

A: You're lucky _____ such a good job. My job is terrible.
                          8.

B: I'm sorry _____ that.
                    9.

A: I need _____ a new job. Do you know if your company is hiring?
                    10.

B: I don't know. But I promise _____ on Monday morning.
                                              11.

ABOUT YOU Work with a partner who has a job. Use the phrases to ask a question. Your partner will answer.

1. afraid/give your boss your opinion

    A: *Are you afraid to give your boss your opinion?*

    B: *Yes, I am.* OR *No, I'm not.*

2. like/go to work every day
3. plan/stay at your job for a long time
4. expect/make a lot of money
5. need/work at home
6. hope/get a better position within the company

continued

7. like/socialize with your coworkers
8. try/keep up with changes in technology
9. want/work overtime
10. hate/get up in the morning to go to work

10.9 Objects before Infinitives

EXAMPLES	EXPLANATION
I **want my boss to appreciate** my work. My boss **expects me to work** overtime.	We can use an object noun or pronoun between some verbs and an infinitive.

We can use an object between these verbs and an infinitive:

advise	expect	need	want
allow	help	permit	would like
ask	invite	tell	

Note:
We can follow *help* by either an object + base form or an object + infinitive.

> He helped me **find** a job.
> He helped me **to find** a job.

EXERCISE 14 Fill in the blanks with pronouns and infinitives to complete the conversation.

A: I want to quit my job.

B: Why?

A: I don't like my supervisor. He expects ___me to work___ at night and on weekends.
   1. work

B: But you get extra pay for that, don't you?

A: No. I asked _____ me a raise, but he said the company can't afford it.
   2. give

B: Is that the only problem?

A: No. My coworkers and I like to go out for lunch. But he doesn't want _____ out. He
   3. go

   expects _____ in the company cafeteria.
   4. eat

B: That's awful. He should permit _____ wherever you want to.
   5. eat

A: That's what I think. I also have a problem with my team manager. She never gives anyone a

   compliment. When I do a good job, I expect _____ something nice. But she
   6. say

   only says something when I make a mistake.

276   Unit 10

10.10 Infinitives to Show Purpose

EXAMPLES	EXPLANATION
You can use the Internet **in order to find** job information. I need a car **in order to get** to work.	We use *in order to* + verb to show purpose.
You can use the Internet **to find** job information. I need a car **to get** to work.	*To* is the short form of *in order to*.

Note:
The purpose phrase can come before the main clause. If so, we often use a comma after the purpose phrase.

> I need a car **to get** to work.
> **To get** to work, I need a car.

GRAMMAR IN USE

To + verb is used to say why we do something. It gives the reason or purpose for an action. It can be used in any tense.

> Marilyn is calling **to invite** us for dinner.
> Jeff has gone to the store **to buy** some milk.
> I will call you tomorrow **to see** how you are.

All these statements answer the question *Why?*

EXERCISE 15 Fill in the blanks with an infinitive to show purpose. Answers will vary.

1. I bought the Sunday newspaper _____(in order) to look for_____ a job.

2. I called the company _____ an appointment.

3. She wants to work overtime _____ more money.

4. You can use a résumé writing service _____ your résumé.

5. My job is in a distant suburb. I need a car _____ to work.

6. In the United States, you need experience _____ a job, and you need a job _____ experience.

7. You need to practice _____ well in an interview.

8. You should ask someone to read your résumé for you _____ sure you didn't make any mistakes in grammar or spelling.

9. You should try networking _____ your chances of finding a job.

10.11 Infinitives or Gerunds after Verbs

EXAMPLES	EXPLANATION
I started **looking** for a job a month ago. I started **to look** for a job a month ago.	We can follow these verbs with either a gerund or an infinitive with almost no difference in meaning: *begin, continue, like, love, prefer,* and *start*.
I was sleepy, so I **stopped (in order) to get** a cup of coffee. I **stopped driving** to work. Now I take public transportation.	Following *stop* with a gerund or infinitive affects the meaning. *Stop* + infinitive means "stop one activity in order to start something different." *Stop* + gerund means "quit."
I **used to be** a teacher. Now I work in a hotel. I'm **not used to talking** about my strengths, but that's what you have to do to find a job. At first it was hard for me, but I finally **got used to working** at night.	*Used to* + base form tells about a past habit or custom. This habit or custom has been discontinued. *Be used to* + gerund, noun, or pronoun means *be accustomed to*. Something is or was familiar to a person. *Get used to* + gerund, noun, or pronoun means "become accustomed to."

Notes:

1. The negative of *used to* + base form is *didn't use to*. (We remove the *d*.)

    I **didn't use to** drive to work.

2. The negative of *be* + *used to* + gerund, noun, or pronoun is *isn't/aren't/wasn't/weren't used to*. (We do not remove the *d*.)

    I'm **not used to** working on Saturdays.

3. The negative of *get/got used to* is usually *can't/couldn't get used to*.

    He **can't get used to** working at night.

---

* For a list of verbs followed by either gerunds or infinitives, see Appendix D.

EXERCISE 16 Circle the correct words to complete this story. In some cases, both choices are possible. If that's the case, circle both choices.

I was tired of driving to the office every day, so I started (*to use/using*) public transportation.
                                                                                    1.

But I was still wasting two hours a day. So my boss agreed to let me work from home a few days a

week. At first I had some difficulty. I (*wasn't used to being/didn't use to be*) alone all day, so I felt
                                                                  2.

a bit lonely.

I had to get used to (*stick/sticking*) to a schedule. Every time the phone rang, I stopped
                                    3.

(*to answer/answering*) it. Because I had a lot of work to do, I had to find a way to deal with
    4.

personal phone calls. I decided to stop (*to answer/answering*) the phone completely until I was
                                                        5.
finished with my day's work. Now I return calls only in the evening.

I had the same problem with email and text messages. I usually prefer (*to answer/answering*) an
                                                                                    6.
email or text as soon as it comes in. But I was losing concentration. Now I stop (*to work/working*)
                                                                                        7.
every two hours, get a little exercise, answer my personal emails and texts, and then get back

to work.

Now (*I used to work/I'm used to working*) at home. I save time by not traveling, I save money
            8.
on gas or public transportation, and I love (*to set/setting*) my own schedule.
                                                    9.

> **FUN WITH GRAMMAR**
>
> Write sentences with infinitives and gerunds. Get into teams. Your teacher will say a verb. Write a sentence using the verb + an infinitive or the verb + a gerund. The team with the most creative sentence wins the point.
>
> stop — We **stopped** on the way to school **to get** donuts for everyone.
> **Stop eating** my fries and get your own!

Working from home requires discipline, but can save you time and money.

Gerunds, Infinitives 279

SUMMARY OF UNIT 10

Gerunds

EXAMPLES	USE OF GERUNDS
Working all day is hard.	As the subject of the sentence
I **like working** on a team.	As the object of the verb
I don't **enjoy working** as a taxi driver.	After certain verbs
I **go shopping** after work.	In many idiomatic expressions with *go*
I'm worried **about losing** my job.	After prepositions

Infinitives

EXAMPLES	USE OF INFINITIVES
I **need to find** a new job.	After certain verbs
My boss wants **me to work** overtime.	After an object
I'm **ready to quit**.	After certain adjectives
It's **important to have** some free time.	After certain expressions beginning with *it*
I work **(in order) to support** my family.	To show purpose

Gerund or Infinitive—No Difference in Meaning

GERUND	INFINITIVE
I like **working** with computers. She began **working** at 8:30.	I like **to work** with computers. She began **to work** at 8:30.
Writing a good résumé is important.	It's important **to write** a good résumé.

Gerund or Infinitive—Difference in Meaning

EXAMPLES	USES
I **used to work** at night. Now I work in the day.	Past habit
I'm **used to working** at night. It's not a problem for me.	Customary activity
I stopped **to make** a personal phone call.	Stop in order to do something else
Stop **making** personal phone calls at work. The boss won't like it.	Quit completely

REVIEW

Fill in the blanks with the gerund or infinitive form of the verb given. In some cases, both a gerund and an infinitive are possible. Add a preposition where needed.

A: Hi, Molly. I haven't seen you in ages. What's going on in your life?

B: I've made many changes. First, I quit ___working___ in a factory. I disliked
1. work

_____ the same thing every day. And I wasn't used
2. do

_____ on my feet all day. My boss often wanted me _____
3. stand   4. work

overtime on Saturdays. I need _____ with my children on Saturdays.
5. be

A: So what do you plan _____?
6. do

B: I've started _____ some general courses at the community college.
7. take

A: What career are you planning?

B: I'm not sure. I'm interested _____ with children. Maybe I'll become a teacher's
8. work

aide. I've also thought _____ in a day-care center. I care
9. work

_____ people.
10. help

A: It's important _____ a job that you like. So you're starting a whole new career.
11. have

B: It's not new, really. I used _____ a kindergarten teacher back in my country.
12. be

But my English wasn't very good when I came here, so I found a job in a factory. I look

forward _____ back to my former profession.
13. go

A: How did you learn English so fast?

B: By _____ with people at work and _____ TV. But it
14. talk   15. watch

hasn't been easy for me _____ English. I studied formal English in my country,
16. understand

but here I have to get used _____ things like "gonna" and "wanna." I've had to
17. say

make a lot of changes.

A: Let's get together sometime and talk some more.

B: I'd love to. Maybe we can go _____ together sometime.
18. shop

Gerunds, Infinitives   281

FROM GRAMMAR TO WRITING

PART 1 Editing Advice

1. Use a gerund after a preposition.

   He succeeded in ~~to get~~ *getting* a good job.

2. Use the correct preposition.

   She insisted ~~in~~ *on* helping me with my résumé.

3. Use a gerund after certain verbs.

   I enjoy ~~to~~ work*ing* with children.

4. Use an infinitive after certain verbs.

   I decided *to* quit my job.

5. Use a gerund, not a base form, as a subject.

   ~~Find~~ *Finding* a good job is important.

6. Don't forget to include *it* before certain adjectives.

   ~~Is~~ *It's* important to find a good job.

7. Don't use the past form after *to*.

   I decided to ~~saw~~ *see* a job counselor.

8. After *want, expect, need, advise,* and *ask,* use an object pronoun, not a subject pronoun, before the infinitive. Don't use *that* as a connector.

   He wants ~~that I~~ *me to* check the spelling on his résumé.

9. Use *for*, not *to*, when introducing an object after impersonal expressions beginning with *it*. Use the object pronoun after *for*.

   It's important ~~to they~~ *for them* to finish their project on time.

10. Use *to* + base form, not *for*, to show purpose.

    I called the company ~~for~~ *to* make an appointment.

11. Don't put *be* before *used to* for the habitual past.

    I ~~am~~ used to work in an office. Now I work in a hospital.

12. Don't use the *-ing* form after *used to* for the habitual past.

    She used to work~~ing~~ on Saturdays, but now she has Saturdays off.

13. Don't forget the *d* in *used to*.

    I use*d* to drive to work. Now I take public transportation.

PART 2 Editing Practice

Some of the shaded words and phrases have mistakes. Find the mistakes and correct them. If the shaded words are correct, write C.

       to   C
 I'm planning ˄ be a nurse. I'd love to be a doctor, but I don't want be in school for so many
     1.   2.   3.
years. My mother is a doctor, and she wanted that I study medicine, too. I know that you're never
                  4.
too old to learn something new, but I'm 35 years old, and start something new at my age is not
                     5.
easy. Study medicine takes too long. It would take me eight years become a doctor. I went to my
   6.   7.
college counselor to get advice. She advised me take biology and chemistry this semester as well
        8.   9.
as English and math. It's hard to me to take so many courses, but I have no choice.
           10.

 In my country, I'm used to work in a nursing home. I enjoyed to help older people, but I
         11.   12.
didn't make enough money. When I decided to came to the U.S., I had to think about my future.
                13.
People say that is not hard to find a job as a nurse in the U.S. It's important for me to be in a
      14.   15.   16.
profession where I can help people. I can do that more quickly by going into a nursing program.
                     17.

WRITING TIP

Gerunds and infinitives are very common in writing. Gerunds are used as subjects and as objects of prepositions. Infinitives are most often used as objects of verbs. Be sure to include them in your writing.

If you choose prompt 1 below, you may use a gerund subject for your topic sentence and use prepositions + gerunds in your examples.

> *Working in Italy is very different from working in the United States. In the U.S., people are* **used to working** *all the time. In Italy, people are* **good about leaving** *work at work and relaxing when home.*

For prompt 2, recall that *like/not like* can take a gerund or infinitive.

> *At my last job, the work day started at 6:00 a.m. I* **didn't like waking up** *at 5:00 every morning, but I* **liked to walk** *to work while the city was still quiet.*

Incorporate a variety of verbs to express preferences (*enjoy, hate, dislike, prefer, appreciate*) but remember to check whether gerunds or infinitives or both can follow.

PART 3 Write

Read the prompts. Choose one and write a paragraph about it.

1. Write about the differences between working in the U.S. and working in another country. You may write about coworkers, salary, vacation time, relationships with superiors, punctuality, or another topic about work that interests you.
2. Write about your current job or a job you had in the past. Tell what you like(d) or don't (didn't) like about that job.

PART 4 Edit

Reread the Summary of Unit 10 and the editing advice. Edit your writing from Part 3.

UNIT
11
Adjective Clauses

MAKING CONNECTIONS

Participants of the Millennial Trains Project ride from Chicago to New York City, U.S.

> Many people will walk in and out of your life, but only true friends will leave footprints in your heart.
>
> ELEANOR ROOSEVELT

Reconnecting with Old Friends

The North High School class of 1936 gathered for their 75th reunion in St. Louis Park, Minnesota, U.S.

Read the following article. Pay special attention to the words in bold. 11.1

Estimates show that Americans move about 11.3 times in their lifetimes. As a result, they often lose touch with old friends. Usually, during their twenties and thirties, people are too busy building their careers and starting their families to think much about the past. However, as people get older, they often start to wonder about the best friend **they had in high school**, the soldier **with whom they served in the military**, or the person **who lived next door** when they were growing up.

Before the Internet, finding an old friend required going to libraries to search through old phone books of different cities. It was hard work, and you needed a lot of luck. It was especially hard to find women **who changed their names when they got married**.

Then came the Web, **which made it possible to find someone in seconds**. A quick search on various social media sites, such as Facebook or Instagram, can help you find that old classmate or neighbor. In addition, there are several sites **where alumni[1] of a specific high school can include themselves according to the year they graduated**. Married women **who chose to change their names** list themselves by their maiden names[2] so that others can find them easily.

Another way **that people make connections with old friends** is through class reunions. Often people come from out of town for a reunion, **which can last for a whole weekend**: Friday evening in the high school **that they attended**, Saturday evening for a dinner in a restaurant or hotel, and a Sunday brunch. They remember the time **when they were young** and exchange information about what they are doing today. They sometimes bring their high school yearbooks, **which have photos of the graduates**, other students, and school activities.

It takes some effort to connect with old friends. Looking back at fond memories, renewing old friendships, making new friends, and even starting a new romance with an old love can be the reward.

---
[1] alumni: graduates or former students of a school
[2] maiden name: a woman's family name which she may or may not change when she marries

COMPREHENSION Based on the reading, write T for *true* or F for *false*.

1. _____ Americans in their twenties and thirties often reconnect with old friends.
2. _____ Women usually list their maiden names on high school websites.
3. _____ A yearbook is a book that shows the people who attended the reunion.

THINK ABOUT IT Discuss the questions with a partner or in a small group.

1. Think of a close friend from childhood that you have lost touch with. How could you find him or her again?
2. In your culture, do you have organized reunions with former classmates? Do you enjoy such events? Or would you enjoy such events if your schools had them?

11.1 Adjective Clauses—Overview

EXAMPLES	EXPLANATION
Today it is common to find married women **who have not changed their names**. What is the name of the high school **that you attended**?	An adjective clause is a group of words that contains a subject and verb. It describes or identifies the noun before it (*women, high school*).

Notes:

1. *Who, whom, that, which, whose, where,* and *when* mark the beginning of an adjective clause. Sometimes an adjective clause begins with no marker.

    *I have a lot of friends **who moved away after we graduated**.*

    *The friends **I had in high school** are married now.* (no marker)

2. Some adjective clauses are set apart from the rest of the sentence with commas.

    *I like to look at my yearbook, **which has photos of my classmates**.*

3. An adjective clause can identify any noun in a sentence.

    *Von Steuben High School, **which is located in Chicago**, is a science academy.*

    *I attended Von Steuben High School, **which is located in Chicago**.*

4. Compare adjectives and adjective clauses. An adjective precedes a noun. An adjective clause follows a noun.

    *I attended a **big** high school.*

    *I attended a high school **that has over 5,000 students**.*

EXERCISE 1 Listen to the article. Then write T for *true* or F for *false*. 11.2

1. _____ Americans don't typically move from location to location.
2. _____ Older people prefer to live in states with warmer climates.
3. _____ San Francisco doesn't need lower paid workers.

EXERCISE 2 Listen again. Fill in the blanks with the words you hear. 🎧 11.2

Why do so many Americans lose touch with old friends ___that___ they had when they were
                                                        1.
younger? One reason is mobility. The average American will probably move more than 11 times in his or

her lifetime. Even though the number of people _____ move to a different state has gone
                                                     2.
down considerably since the 1950s, _____ 3.5 percent of households moved from state to
                                        3.
state, there are still a lot of people _____ move across state lines.
                                          4.

Some people move to states _____ the climate is better. The states _____
                              5.   6.
are losing the most population are in cold climates: New York, Illinois, New Jersey, and Connecticut. One

exception to this is North Dakota, _____ has very cold winter weather. It has a growing oil
                                       7.
industry and low unemployment, so it attracts young people who are looking for jobs. However, older

people usually want to live in states _____ have a good climate.
                                          8.

Some cities, such as San Francisco, attract high-paid professionals, _____ drive up the
                                                                         9.
cost of living. This makes it hard to attract lower-paid workers, such as construction workers,

_____ skills are just as important, but _____ don't earn enough to live in cities
    10.   11.
like San Francisco.

Washington, DC, is another place _____ attracts new residents. Washington was the
                                     12.
number one city Americans moved to in 2018. Most of them were young professionals _____
                                                                                        13.
were looking for work.

11.2 Relative Pronouns as Subjects

A relative pronoun can be the subject of the adjective clause.

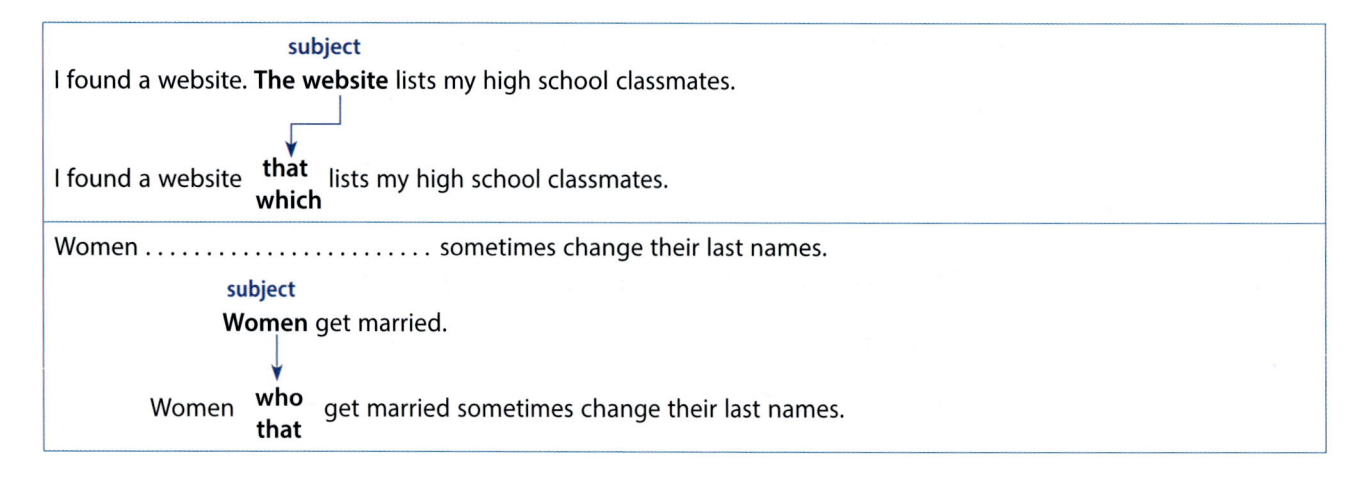

subject I found a website. **The website** lists my high school classmates. I found a website **that / which** lists my high school classmates.

Women . . . . sometimes change their last names.
           subject
      Women get married.
 	
Women **who / that** get married sometimes change their last names.

Notes:
1. The relative pronouns *who, that,* and *which* can be the subject of the adjective clause. Use *who* or *that* for people. Use *that* or *which* for things.
2. The verb in the adjective clause must agree in number with its subject.
    A **website** that **has** statistics needs to update its data frequently.
    Websites that **have** statistics need to update their data frequently.

Punctuation Note:
When the noun is unique, we set the adjective clause apart from the rest of the sentence with commas. We use only *who* and *which*; we don't use *that*.
   *I want to move to a state **that has low unemployment**.* (no comma)
   *I want to move to North Dakota, **which has low unemployment**.* (North Dakota is unique.)

GRAMMAR IN USE

Adjective clauses are common in both written and spoken English. They make your writing and speech more fluent. Instead of using short, simple sentences to express an idea, try to combine ideas using adjective clauses. For example:

   Juan comes from a small village. The village has only 210 residents.
   ↓
   Juan comes from a small village that has only 210 residents.

EXERCISE 3 Fill in the blanks with an adjective clause from the box.

who have moved	that allows	who plan ✓	who live	who have changed
who plays	that is convenient	that was popular	that will cover	
that is different	who can create	who have died	who graduated	

Planning a reunion takes time and effort. People ____who plan____ a reunion start at least a
                                                    1.
year in advance. They form a committee of about 10 people. Each committee member has a task

_____ from the tasks of other committee members. For example, one
            2.

committe member needs to calculate a budget for the reunion activities. The reunion committee

will charge an amount of money _____ the cost of attending the various
                                              3.

activities. Another committee member is in charge of locating classmates. This is the hardest part,

so all members of the committee help. To find classmates, the committee uses phone books, word

of mouth, social media sites, and other websites to search. It is especially hard to find women

_____ their names. The committee has to find classmates
            4.

_____ nearby and classmates _____ away. Sadly,
            5.   6.

sometimes they even find some classmates _____.
                                                        7.

continued

The committee chooses someone _____ a reunion website. A
                                        8.
reunion website is something _____ classmates to read about each
                              9.
others' lives.

The committee tries to set a date _____ for most people. The
                                   10.
committee hopes to find about 50 percent of the people _____ with their
                                                        11.
class, but 25 percent is a more realistic number.

At the reunion dinner, there's often a DJ. This is a person _____ recorded
                                                             12.
music. The DJ plays music _____ when the students were in
                           13.
high school.

ABOUT YOU Fill in the blanks with *who* or *that* + a form of the verb given. Then complete the statement. Answers will vary.

1. most of the students *who graduated* from my high school
                         graduate

   Most of the students who graduated from my high school went to college.

2. friends *who moved* to another state
            move

   I have several friends who moved to another state.

3. a classmate of mine _____ in life
                        succeed

   _____

4. a social media site _____ photos of my friends
                        have

   _____

5. the music _____ popular when I was in high school
              be

   _____

6. a person _____ next door to me when I was growing up
             live

   _____

7. classmates _____ to college
               go

   _____

8. a teacher _____ me
              inspire

   _____

11.3 Relative Pronouns as Objects

The relative pronoun can be the object of the adjective clause.

```
I contacted an old friend.
                object
         I found my friend on a social media site.
                         who
I contacted an old friend  whom  I found on a social media site.
                         that
                           Ø
```

```
                object
         She attended a high school.
The high school . . . . . . . . . . . . . . is in New York City.
                which
The high school that she attended is in New York City.
                  Ø
```

Notes:

1. The relative pronouns *who(m), that,* and *which* can be the object of the adjective clause. In conversation, we usually omit the relative pronoun when it is the object of the adjective clause.

   I contacted an old friend I found on a social media site.

   The high school she attended is in New York City.

2. *Whom* is more formal than *who*. However, the relative pronoun is usually omitted altogether in conversation.

   I reconnected with an old friend who(m) I saw at the reunion.

   I reconnected with an old friend I saw at the reunion.

Punctuation Note:

When the noun is unique, we set the adjective clause apart from the rest of the sentence with commas. We use only *who* and *which*; we don't use *that*.

*The high school **(that) she attended** is very small.* (no comma)

*Taft High School, **which I attended from 1998–2002**, is very small.* (Taft High School is unique.)

EXERCISE 4 Underline the adjective clause in each sentence.

1. I've lost touch with some of the friends <u>I had in high school</u>.

2. The high school I attended is in another city.

3. The teachers I had in high school are all old now.

4. We didn't have to buy the textbooks we used in high school.

5. My best friend married a man she met in college.

6. The friends I've made in this country don't know much about my country.

7. At the reunion, she saw a guy she dated in high school.

EXERCISE 5 Fill in the blanks with a phrase from the box to complete the conversation between a mother and her teenage daughter.

| she hasn't seen | I had ✓ | she put | she wrote | she married | I have for them |
| they attended | we had | I made | you take | they graduated | |

A: I'd like to contact an old friend ____I had____ in high school. I wish I could find her. I'll never
1.
forget the good times _____ back then. When we graduated, we said we'd always
2.
stay in touch. But then we went to different colleges.

B: Didn't you keep in touch by email?

A: When I was in college, email didn't exist. At first we wrote letters. But little by little, we wrote less and less
until, eventually, we stopped writing. I still have the letters _____ to me in a box in
3.
the basement.

B: Why don't you write to the address on the letters?

A: That wouldn't work. The address _____ on the letters was of the college town where
4.
she lived. I don't know what happened to her after she left college.

B: Have you tried calling her parents?

A: The phone number _____ is now disconnected. Maybe her parents have died.
5.

B: Why don't you try one of those classmates websites? There are websites with names of students categorized
by the high school _____ and the date _____.
6. 7.

A: But my friend probably got married. I don't know the last name of the man _____.
8.

B: That's not a problem. You can search for her by her maiden name on these sites.

A: If I find her, she'll probably think I'm crazy for contacting her almost 25 years later.

B: I'm sure she'll be happy to receive communication from a good friend _____ in
9.
years. When I graduate from high school, I'm never going to lose contact with the friends
_____. We'll always stay in touch.
10.

A: That's what you think. But as time passes, your lives go in different directions, and you lose touch.

B: But today we have all kinds of social media.

A: Well, that's a help. Even so, the direction _____ in life is different from the direction
11.
your friends choose.

292 Unit 11

EXERCISE 6 Fill in the blanks with appropriate words to complete the conversation. Answers may vary. You may use both subject and object relative pronouns. Remember: You can omit an object relative pronoun.

A: I'm lonely. I have a lot of friends in my native country, but I don't have enough friends here. The friends <u>(that) I have there</u> send me email and photos all the time, but that's not enough. I need to make new friends here.
  1.

B: Haven't you met any people here?

A: Of course. But the people _____ here don't share my interests. I like reading,
  2.
meditating, and going for quiet walks. Americans seem to like parties, TV, sports, movies, and going to restaurants.

B: You're never going to meet people with the interests _____. Your interests don't
  3.
include other people. You need some interests _____ other people, like tennis or
  4.
dancing, to mention just a few.

A: The activities _____ cost money, and I don't have much.
  5.

B: There are many parks in this city _____ free tennis courts. If you like to dance, I
  6.
know of a park district near here _____ free dance classes. In fact, there are a lot of
  7.
things _____ in this city. I can give you a list, if you want.
  8.

A: Thanks. I appreciate the suggestions _____ me.
  9.

B: Tomorrow I'll email you a list of interesting activities. I'm sure you'll find something
_____ on that list.
  10.

ABOUT YOU Use the words given to write a sentence. Discuss your answers with a partner.

1. the high school I attended

   <u>The high school I attended was very small.</u>

   OR

   <u>I can show you a photo of the high school I attended.</u>

2. the kids I knew in high school

   _____

continued

3. the teachers I had in high school

　

4. the subject I liked best in high school

　

5. the way I stay in touch with old friends

　

6. the best friend I had in high school

　

7. the social media I use

　

8. the friends I had when I was a child

　

9. the activities I liked in high school

　

10. the way I meet people now

　

FUN WITH GRAMMAR

Define people, places, and things. Form two teams. Team A thinks of a person, place, or thing. Team B works together to define it using an adjective clause. Then switch roles. For each correct sentence, the team earns a point. The team with the most points wins.

Team A: a giraffe
Team B: A giraffe is an animal that has a long neck and eats leaves.

MAKING CONNECTIONS USING MEETUP

Members of a Meetup group gather to watch birds.

Read the following article. Pay special attention to the words in bold.

Would you like to meet people **whose** interests are the same as yours? Maybe you like to knit and would like to meet with other knitters. Or maybe you're interested in the theater and want to find people **with whom** you can attend a play. A website called Meetup lets you do that. Unlike most social networking groups, **whose** members communicate with each other online, Meetup members actually meet each other in person. Most Meetup members want to get together just for fun: to play chess, discuss books, ride their bikes, practice French, etc. Some Meetups are support groups: people get together with others who have the same problem. For example, there are Meetups of people who have lost a spouse, or parents **whose** children have a serious disease. Other Meetup groups are for the purpose of career networking. As of 2019, there were about 39 million Meetup members in almost 200 countries.

Meetup was the brainchild[1] of Scott Heiferman, **whose** idea for creating these communities came as a result of the September 11, 2001 attacks in the United States. Heiferman stated that the manner **in which** the people of New York City came together in the aftermath[2] of that traumatic[3] event inspired him. He wanted to make it easy for people to connect with strangers in their own community. He created Meetup in 2002.

Meetup connects people online so that they can meet offline. Anyone can start a Meetup. Meetup believes that "people can change their personal world, or the whole world, by organizing themselves into groups that are powerful enough to make a difference."

---

[1] brainchild: an important idea or project of a person
[2] aftermath: the result of a tragic event
[3] traumatic: psychologically harmful

Adjective Clauses   295

COMPREHENSION Based on the reading, write T for *true* or F for *false*.

1. _____ Meetup members first make contact online.

2. _____ All Meetup groups are for the purpose of having fun together.

3. _____ Scott Heiferman got his idea for Meetup after the tragedy of September 11, 2001.

THINK ABOUT IT Discuss the questions with a partner or in a small group.

1. Think of an interest or hobby you have. Do you think there is a Meetup for that? Would you be interested in joining such a Meetup? If there isn't such a Meetup, would you like to create such a group? Why or why not?

2. Read the quote at the end of the article. In what ways do you think Meetup members are able to make a difference?

11.4 Relative Pronouns as Objects of Prepositions

A relative pronoun can be the object of a preposition.

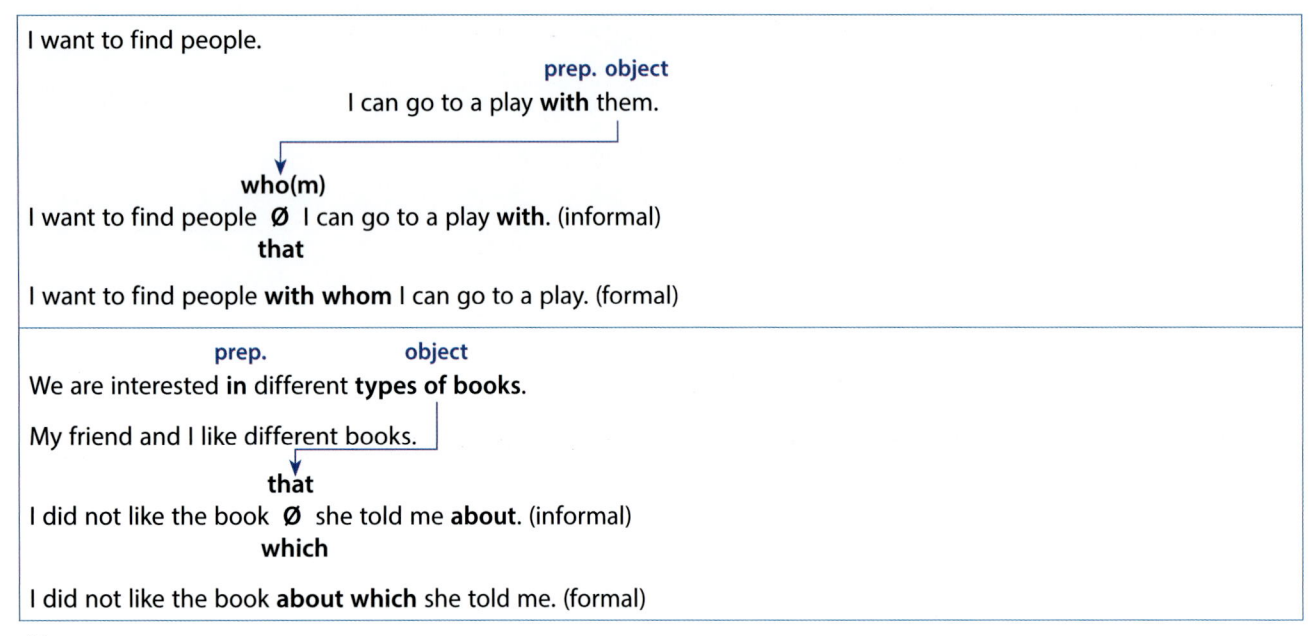

I want to find people.   **prep. object**
I can go to a play **with** them.
 	
                who(m)
I want to find people Ø I can go to a play **with**. (informal)
                that
I want to find people **with whom** I can go to a play. (formal)

prep.   **object**
We are interested **in** different **types of books**.
My friend and I like different books.
                that
I did not like the book Ø she told me **about**. (informal)
                which
I did not like the book **about which** she told me. (formal)

Notes:

1. Informally, we put the preposition at the end of the adjective clause. The relative pronoun is usually omitted. The most common way to say the above sentences is:

   I want to find people I can go to a play with.   *I did not enjoy the book you told me about.*

2. In very formal English, the preposition comes before the relative pronoun, and only *whom* and *which* may be used. *That* and *who* are not used directly after a preposition.

   I want to find people with whom I can go to a play. (NOT *with who* or *with that*)

   I did not enjoy the book about which you told me. (NOT *about that*)

Punctuation Notes:

1. When the adjective clause is not essential to identify the noun, we set it apart from the rest of the sentence with commas.

   Heiferman, who(m) we read about, is a member of a Meetup. (We know who Heiferman is without the adjective clause.)

2. A nonessential adjective clause begins with *who, whom, which, where, when,* or *whose*. We don't use *that*.

296   Unit 11

EXERCISE 7 Change these sentences to make them more informal.

1. I'd like to find people with whom I can go hiking.

   I'd like to find people I can go hiking with.

2. A woman with whom I work started a Meetup for young Hispanic professionals.

3. Scott Heiferman, about whom we read, is a member of a parents' Meetup.

4. He pays attention to the Meetups for which people are signing up.

5. People want to get together with others with whom they share a common interest.

6. The office in which Scott works is located in New York City.

EXERCISE 8 Change these sentences to make them more formal.

1. What is the name of the high school you graduated from?

   What is the name of the high school from which you graduated?

2. He found a friend that he served in the military with.

3. I can't find the friend I was looking for.

4. The high school she graduated from was torn down.

5. Do you remember the teacher I was talking about?

6. In high school, the activities I was interested in were baseball and band.

11.5 Whose + Noun

Whose is the possessive form of *who*. It represents *his, her, its, their,* or the possessive form of the noun.

I want to meet people.
Their interests are the same as mine.
I want to meet people **whose** interests are the same as mine.
Scott . . . . gets together with other parents of small children.
Scott's children are small.
Scott, **whose** children are small, gets together with other parents of small children.

Note:
We use *who* to substitute for a person. We use *whose* for possession or relationship.
    I want to meet people **who** are interested in sports.
    I want to meet people **whose** interests are the same as mine.

Punctuation Note:
When the adjective clause is not essential to identify the noun, we set it apart from the rest of the sentence with commas.
    Heiferman, **whose office is in New York,** created Meetup after September 11th. (We know who Heiferman is without the adjective clause.)

EXERCISE 9 Fill in the blanks with *whose* + a word from the box.

jobs	last name	inspiration
family	interests ✓	members

1. Do you want to meet people ___*whose interests*___ are the same as yours?

2. I joined a French Meetup _____ speak French very well.

3. People _____ keep them busy don't always have the time or energy to get together with friends.

4. I lost touch with an old friend _____ moved to another state.

5. I'm looking for a woman _____ used to be Carter. She changed it when she got married.

6. Scott Heiferman, _____ came from the way people came together after the 9/11 tragedy, started Meetup in 2002.

EXERCISE 10 Some people were asked what kind of friends they'd like to meet. Fill in the blanks with a response, using the words given.

1. I'd like to meet people __whose values are the same as mine__.
   Their values are the same as mine.

2. My math group is a club _____.
   I found it through Meetup.

3. I'd like to find a friend _____.
   I can trust that friend.

4. I don't want to be with people _____.
   They don't take life seriously.

5. I want to meet people _____.
   They like to play soccer.

6. I joined a Spanish Meetup _____.
   Its members speak Spanish very well.

7. We meet in a coffee shop _____.
   It isn't crowded in the morning.

8. I go to a book club Meetup _____.
   It meets at my local library.

9. There's a Meetup for divorced people _____.
   They have children.

10. I go to a Meetup for parents _____.
    Their children are deaf.

11. The Meetup _____ has about 50 members.
    I go to it.

12. The person _____ is a nice woman I met at a Meetup.
    I play tennis with her.

13. People _____ interest me.
    Their political views are similar to mine.

14. Neighbors _____ have a lot in common with me.
    The neighbors have small children.

GRAMMAR IN USE

We don't use an adjective clause when we can simply use an adjective.

*I like books **that are educational**.* (not needed: *I like educational books.*)
*We met many people **who were interesting**.* (not needed: *We met many interesting people.*)

When you cannot use an adjective, use an adjective clause.

*I like books **that have beautiful photos**.* (needed)

The SCIENCE of FRIENDSHIP

Read the following article. Pay special attention to the words in bold. 11.4

"I still remember the day **when we met**," says Alexa Martinez of her best friend Gabby Rivero. "It was in 2014, **when we were in high school**. Gabby sat in front of me in math class. At first, we didn't talk much. But later that year, **when we were both in the school play**, we became friends."

Like many people, Alexa and Gabby became friends for two main reasons. One was proximity. Research shows that we make friends with people who are nearby. (The person might be in a class with you at school or in the same office **where you work**.) Later, Alexa and Gabby were both in the school play, and they discovered a shared interest: acting. If two people have something in common[1], this also increases the possibility that they will be friends.

To become *close* friends with another person, though, two other factors are important. First, the two people should be able to share personal feelings and information with each other. A good friend will also be there to listen and offer help at times **when the other person needs it**.

Alexa recalls how she and Gabby became close friends. "Acting in the play was really hard," she says. "There were times **when I thought about quitting**. I never told other people this, but I could always talk to Gabby. She was very supportive[2]. She said things like, 'Acting is hard, but you're really good at it. I get nervous, too.'"

Both Alexa and Gabby needed extra practice, so they decided to meet and study their lines together after school. "There was a café **where we went** every day," Alexa recalls. "In time, we became good friends. After the school play ended, we continued to hang out[3]—and even now, we're still very close."

---

[1] to have something in common: to have similar interests or beliefs as another person
[2] supportive: helpful and kind
[3] to hang out: to spend time relaxing and enjoying oneself

COMPREHENSION Based on the reading, write T for *true* or F for *false*.

1. _____ Alexa and Gabby met and became friends in a high school math class.
2. _____ Most people become friends with another person because they don't want to be alone.
3. _____ According to the reading, a *close friend* is someone that we can talk to about personal things and who helps us in hard times.

THINK ABOUT IT Discuss the questions with a partner or in a small group.

1. Think of one of your good friends. How did you meet and become friends?
2. How does this person fit the definition of a close friend given in the passage? Give an example.

11.6 Adjective Clauses with *Where* and *When*

Some adjective clauses begin with the relative adverbs *where* and *when*.

EXAMPLES	EXPLANATION
Alexa met Gabby at Woodside High, **where they went to high school**. There was a café **where they went every day**.	*Where* means "in that place."
"I still remember the day **(when) we met**," says Alexa. "It was in 2014, **when we were in high school**."	*When* means "at that time."

Punctuation Note:
When the adjective clause is not essential to identify the noun, we set it apart from the rest of the sentence with commas.

They went to Java House, **where they studied**. (We don't need the adjective clause to identify the place.)

We met on the first day of school, **when we were in high school**. (We don't need the adjective clause to identify the day.)

We can omit *when* in a sentence with no comma. We cannot omit *where*.

EXERCISE 11 Two friends are talking about how they met. Write each adjective clause in the correct place to complete the dialogue.

when we were studying　　　when we met ✓
where we took that class　　where we could buy hot tea
when it was very cold　　　　when I passed the TOEFL
where we're going to college

A: I still remember the day ___when we met___.
　　　　　　　　　　　　　　　　1.

B: Me, too. It was in 2016, _____ for the TOEFL. You sat next to me in a test prep class.
　　　　　　　　　　　　　　　2.

continued

A: That's right! Do you remember the school _____?
　　　　　　　　　　　　　　　　　　　　　　　　　　　　　　　　　3.

B: Yeah, it was terrible. The rooms had no heating, and we were there in the winter, _____.
　　4.

A: I know. Luckily the school had a café _____. It was the only way to stay warm.
　　　　　　　　　　　　　　　　　　　　　　　　　　　　　5.

B: You know, I'll never forget the day _____. I was so happy.
　　　　　　　　　　　　　　　　　　　　　　　　　　　6.

A: I know. And now we're both in the U.S. _____!
　　　　　　　　　　　　　　　　　　　　　　　　　　　　　　7.

EXERCISE 12 Fill in the blanks with *who, whom, that, which, when, where, whose,* or Ø for no word. Sometimes more than one answer is possible.

A: I'm getting married next month.

B: Congratulations! Are you marrying the woman ___*that or Ø*___ you met at Mark's party last year?
　　　　　　　　　　　　　　　　　　　　　　　　　　　　　　　　1.

A: Oh, no. My fiancée is the woman _____ I introduced you to last week.
　　　　　　　　　　　　　　　　　　　　　　　　　2.

B: Oh, yeah. Now I remember. What's her name again?

A: Sara Liston.

B: I know someone _____ last name is Liston. I wonder if they're related. So how did you meet?
　　　　　　　　　　　　　　　3.

A: Actually, we met in 2012 _____ we were in college. We were just friends.
　　　　　　　　　　　　　　　　　　　　　4.

Then earlier this year, I saw Sara at a Meetup _____ we reconnected.
　　　　　　　　　　　　　　　　　　　　　　　　　　　　　　　　5.

B: What kind of Meetup was it?

A: It's for people _____ like movies. We watch a film, and then we have a meal after and discuss it.
　　　　　　　　　　　6.

B: Sounds fun.

A: You should join. I'll send you a text _____ has information about the next movie
　　　　　　　　　　　　　　　　　　　　　　　　　　　　　　7.

_____ we're going to see and the time _____ we're going to get together.
　　　8.　　　　　　　　　　　　　　　　　　　　　　　　　　　　　　9.

302　Unit 11

ABOUT YOU Use the words given to form an adjective clause. Then tell a partner if you agree or disagree. Give your reasons.

1. My friends are people <u>(whom) I can trust with all my secrets</u>.
   I can trust them with all my secrets.

2. A good friend is a person _____ almost every day.
   I see him.

3. My best friend is a person _____.
   He knows everything about me.

4. Most of my friends are people _____.
   They speak my native language.

5. This school is a place _____.
   I can make many new friends easily here.

6. It is hard to be friends with a person _____.
   His political views are different from mine.

7. Childhood is the only time _____.
   It is easy to make friends then.

8. I still remember the place _____.
   I met my best friend there.

9. I don't remember the day _____.
   I met my best friend then.

10. I want to return to the country _____.
    I was born there.

FUN WITH GRAMMAR

Play *Find Someone Who…* Complete these sentences using adjective clauses. Then go around your classroom and find someone who agrees with each statement. Write his or her name on the line under the statement. The person to finish first wins the game.

1. My closest friends are people _____.
   _____

2. My favorite activity is one _____.
   _____

3. My favorite childhood memory is one _____.
   _____

4. The café I go to most often is one _____.
   _____

5. I like a school _____.
   _____

6. My favorite kind of movies are ones _____.
   _____

SUMMARY OF UNIT 11

Adjective Clauses with:

RELATIVE PRONOUNS AS SUBJECTS

I lost touch with a friend **who/that moved to Alaska**.
A high school **that/which has a strong science program** attracts good students.
Scott Heiferman, **who created Meetup**, wants to connect people.
North Dakota, **which has cold winters**, has attracted people looking for jobs.

RELATIVE PRONOUNS AS OBJECTS

I have a new friend **who/whom/that/Ø I met at a Meetup**.
The high school **that/which/Ø I attended** is not very big.
My wife, **who/whom I met at a math Meetup**, is a teacher.
My tenth high school reunion, **which I attended last year**, was at a hotel.

RELATIVE PRONOUNS AS OBJECTS OF PREPOSITIONS

FORMAL:	Some of the friends **with whom I went to high school** moved away.
INFORMAL:	Some of the friends **who(m)/that/Ø I went to high school with** moved away.
FORMAL:	The Meetup **about which I told you** meets at a neighborhood café.
INFORMAL:	The Meetup **that/which/Ø I told you about** meets at a neighborhood café.

RELATIVE PRONOUNS FOR POSSESSION

I have a friend **whose brother lives in Japan**.
Scott Heiferman, **whose inspiration came from the aftermath of 9/11**, created Meetup to bring people together.

RELATIVE ADVERBS FOR PLACE

I like to visit the city **where I went** to college.
Boston, **where I went to college**, is cold in the winter.

RELATIVE ADVERBS FOR TIME

My friends and I get together in a café at a time **when/Ø it isn't crowded**.
We get together on Monday at 4 o'clock, **when the café isn't crowded**.

REVIEW

Fill in the blanks with *who, whom, that, which, whose, where, when,* or *Ø*. In some cases, more than one answer is possible.

1. I'm still friends with the people __who or whom or that or Ø__ I met in high school.

2. The high school _____ I attended is in Poland.

3. Most of the people with _____ I went to high school still live in our hometown.

4. Childhood is the time _____ it's easiest to make friends.

5. There are some teachers _____ names I've forgotten.

6. A coffee shop near my house is the place _____ my chess Meetup gets together.

7. I use several social networking sites _____ allow me to exchange information with my friends.

8. Scott Heiferman, _____ started his first company when he was 23, worked at a fast-food restaurant to get back in touch with real people.

9. Heiferman started Meetup in 2002, _____ he was 30 years old.

10. Silicon Valley, _____ is the center of technology, is in California.

11. The high school from _____ I graduated has around 5,000 students.

12. My sister married Mark Peters, _____ she met at a Meetup.

Adjective Clauses 305

FROM GRAMMAR TO WRITING

PART 1 Editing Advice

1. Use *who* or *that* to introduce a person. Use *that* or *which* to introduce a thing.

   The states ~~what~~ **that** are losing the most population are in cold climates.

   I have many friends ~~which~~ **who** go to Meetups.

2. If the relative pronoun is the subject of the adjective clause, don't omit it.

   She started a group **that** now has 100 members.

3. Use *whose* to substitute for a possessive form.

   Gabby, ~~her~~ **whose** father was an actor, hopes to find work in movies.

4. If the relative pronoun is used as the object of the adjective clause, don't put an object after the verb of the adjective clause.

   There are a lot of interesting Meetups that I found ~~them~~.

5. Use subject-verb agreement in the adjective clause.

   I have a friend who live**s** in Madrid.

6. Put a noun before an adjective clause.

   A person who ~~Who~~ has a few good friends is lucky.

7. Use *where*, not *that*, to mean "in a place."

   She moved to North Dakota, ~~that~~ **where** she found a good job.

8. Use *whom* and *which*, not *who* and *that*, if the preposition precedes the relative pronoun.

   He found a group in ~~that~~ **which** he's interested.

   I've never met the person about ~~who~~ **whom** you are talking.

9. Use the correct word order in an adjective clause (subject before verb).

   The first play that ~~acted in Gabby~~ **Gabby acted in** was at her high school.

10. Don't confuse *whose* (possessive form) and *who's* (who is).

    A woman ~~whose~~ **who's** in my science Meetup teaches biology at a high school.

PART 2 Editing Practice

Some of the shaded words and phrases have mistakes. Find the mistakes and correct them. If the shaded words are correct, write *C*.

I would like to find one of the friends that I had in college. **C** (1.) I found a website that **where** (2.) I can look for old friends. My friend, whose **(3.)** name is Linda Gast, got married shortly after we graduated. The man which **(4.)** she married is Bart Reed. I tried googling the names "Linda Gast" and "Linda Reed," but I had no luck. I found a woman with who **(5.)** she shared a room in college, and she gave

306 Unit 11

me a phone number. The phone number that gave me her roommate is not in service anymore.
                                        6.   7.

I called a man what used to be her neighbor, but he said that she moved away a long time ago.
                  8.

The last reunion that I attended it was four years ago, but she wasn't there. The people were our
                  9.   10.   11.
friends in high school didn't know anything about her. I looked in the phone book and found

some people their name is the same as hers, but they weren't the right people. I went back to the
            12.

high school that she was a student, but they had no information about her.
              13.

   Because of the Internet, now is a time when it's easier than ever to find people. But my
                                          14.
search, which have taken me almost five years, has produced no result. Recently I met someone
       15.   16.

whose a friend of her brother, and he told me that Linda's now living in South America. He's
   17.

going to try to find Linda's current address. Looking for Linda is hard, but I'm determined to find

her. Who tries hard enough usually succeeds.
     18.

> **WRITING TIP**
> Using a variety of adjectives and adjective clauses to describe nouns will make your writing more interesting. If you are writing about friendships (prompt 1), you might want to describe the kinds of people you were friends with when you were younger compared to now:
>
> *When I was younger, my friends were people **who were in the drama club**. Now my friends are people **who have young children like me**.*
>
> If you are writing about two types of relationships (prompt 2), you could describe the differences between the two:
>
> *At work, I'm friendly with people **who are serious and reliable**. When I'm away from work, I prefer to spend time with people **who are relaxed and fun to be around**.*

PART 3 Write
Read the prompts. Choose one and write a paragraph about it.

1. Compare the friendships you have today with the friendships you had when you were younger.
2. Compare your social relationships with your work relationships.

PART 4 Edit
Reread the Summary of Unit 11 and the editing advice. Edit your writing from Part 3.

UNIT
12
**Superlatives
Comparatives**

SPORTS and ATHLETES

2,300 athletes, and one green sea turtle, await the start of the 140.6-mile race at the Ironman World Championship triathlon in Kailua Kona, Hawaii, U.S.

> Obstacles don't have to stop you. If you run into a wall, don't turn around and give up. Figure out how to climb it, go through it, or work around it.
>
> MICHAEL JORDAN

GREGG TREINISH Extreme Athlete and Conservationist

Read the following article. Pay special attention to the words in bold. 12.1

Gregg Treinish is an adventurer who turned his love of physical challenges into something more.

In 2004, Treinish hiked the Appalachian Trail, one of **the longest** footpaths in the world, measuring about 2,180 miles (3,508 km) in length. This path follows through 14 states from Maine to Georgia. Maryland and West Virginia are **the easiest** states to hike. New Hampshire and Maine are **the most difficult**. While Treinish was hiking one of **the hardest** parts, he kept slipping and cutting his legs on the sharp rock. In frustration[1], he picked up a rock and threw it at a tree. "I felt like **the lowest** person on earth," he said, for being on this adventure purely for his own experience. He knew he wanted to do something more, but he didn't know what that was.

Then he and his friend, Deia Schlosberg, spent two years hiking 7,800 miles from Ecuador to Tierra del Fuego, following along the Andes Mountains, **the longest** mountain chain in the world. When they arrived, they commented that Tierra del Fuego was one of **the most spectacular** places on Earth.

In 2008, National Geographic named Gregg Treinish Adventurer of the Year. But he wasn't fulfilled[2]. He felt his **biggest** challenge was in his mind. He began asking himself: Is it enough to hike **the longest, most difficult** trails? Am I doing anything to help the world? How can I turn my adventures into something more beneficial?

Treinish had an idea: He thought that scientists might need information from hard-to-reach places where only **the bravest** adventurers go. And he was right. Scientists want data, samples, and photographs from **the most remote** places on Earth—places that they can't go to themselves. Treinish founded Adventurers and Scientists for Conservation (ASC) to connect scientists with extreme adventurers. Now, when athletes go to these unusual places, they can do something to benefit the world by collecting information for scientists. Several thousand adventurers have collected data with ASC.

ASC mountain climbers have discovered Earth's **highest** known plant life on Mount Everest and have brought back samples for researchers to study. These samples help farmers learn to grow crops in extreme conditions.

For Treinish, connecting science and outdoor adventure is **the most satisfying** kind of adventure. "Adventurers tell me these chances to give back have changed their whole perspective[3]. Now, being **the strongest** or summiting **the coolest** peak[4] isn't what's important. Trying to contribute and make a difference is what matters. And there's so much more we can do."

[1] frustration: a feeling of disappointment or anger at not being able to accomplish something
[2] fulfilled: satisfied
[3] perspective: a way of seeing things; point of view
[4] to summit a peak: to reach the top of a mountain

Gregg Treinish takes measurements while Jason Wilmot records them. They concluded that these tracks in Mongolia were made by a snow leopard.

COMPREHENSION Based on the reading, write T for *true* or F for *false*.

1. _____ The difficulty of the Appalachian Trail changes as a hiker goes from state to state.
2. _____ Gregg Treinish hiked along the Andes Mountains alone.
3. _____ Gregg's goal is to connect adventurers with each other.

THINK ABOUT IT Discuss the questions with a partner or in a small group.

1. Reread Gregg's questions: "Am I doing anything to help the world? How can I turn my adventures into something more beneficial?" Is there something in your life you could do to benefit the world?
2. What jobs might Gregg's organization have? Which ones would you be interested in?

12.1 The Superlative Forms of Adjectives and Adverbs

	SIMPLE	SUPERLATIVE
One-syllable adjectives and adverbs	long big	the longest the biggest
Two-syllable adjectives that end in *y*	easy happy	the easiest the happiest
Other two-syllable adjectives	remote extreme	the most remote the most extreme
Some two-syllable adjectives have two forms	simple polite	the simplest the most simple the politest the most polite
Adjectives with three or more syllables	spectacular difficult	the most spectacular the most difficult
-ly adverbs	quickly directly	the most quickly the most directly
Irregular superlatives	good/well bad/badly far	the best the worst the farthest
Quantity words	little few	the least the fewest
	a lot much many	the most

Notes:

1. Other two-syllable adjectives that have two forms are:

    handsome, quiet, gentle, narrow, clever, friendly, angry, common, stupid

2. Adjectives that are past participles use *the most*.

    tired—the most tired
    fulfilled—the most fulfilled
    worried—the most worried

EXERCISE 1 Listen to the conversation about Emma Gatewood, another amazing athlete. Then write T for *true* or F for *false*. 12.2

1. _____ Emma Gatewood was never in the Olympics.

2. _____ Emma Gatewood's grandmother hiked the Appalachian Trail.

3. _____ Emma Gatewood relied on wild food in addition to the dried food she carried with her.

EXERCISE 2 Listen to the conversation again. Fill in the blanks with the words you hear. 12.2

A: I just read an article about one of _the most interesting_ athletes.
                                          1.

B: Was it about Michael Phelps? He's one of _____ swimmers in the world.
                                              2.

A: No. It was about a woman.

B: Was it Katie Ledecky? She was one of _____ female swimmers at the 2016
                                            3.

   Olympics. I liked her _____ of all the female swimmers that year.
                         4.

A: No. This woman was never at the Olympics. Her name was Emma Gatewood. She was the first woman to

   hike the Appalachian Trail solo—at the age of 67! People often called her "Grandma Gatewood." She

   believed that hikers should carry _____ equipment possible. She wasn't
                                     5.

   interested in taking _____ equipment for her hike. She took a homemade bag
                        6.

   and carried a blanket, a raincoat, and a shower curtain.

B: A shower curtain? What for?

A: She used it to make a tent.

B: That's _____ thing I've ever heard!
              7.

A: She believed in doing things _____ way possible.
                                    8.

B: And _____ way possible, too. What about food?
           9.

A: She carried some dried food, but she did _____ she could to find wild food.
                                                10.

B: She was quite a woman!

A: Yes, she was. She hiked the Appalachian Trail again at the age of 75. At that time, she was

   _____ woman to hike the trail.
   11.

B: I've read stories of several athletes, but I like her story _____.
                                                                    12.

   She inspires me _____.
                   13.

A: Me, too. She's one of _____ athletes I've ever read about.
                             14.

312 Unit 12

EXERCISE 3 Write the superlative of each word.

1. fat — _the fattest_
2. important — _the most important_
3. interesting _____
4. good _____
5. responsible _____
6. thin _____
7. carefully _____
8. bad _____
9. famous _____
10. lucky _____
11. simple _____
12. extreme _____
13. far _____
14. bored _____

12.2 Superlatives—Use

EXAMPLES	EXPLANATION
The Andes is **the longest** mountain chain in the world. What is **the most difficult** part of the Appalachian Trail?	We use the superlative form to point out the number one item(s) of a group of three or more.
Treinish hiked **some of the most difficult** trails. Gatewood was **one of the most remarkable** hikers.	We often say *one/some of the* before a superlative form. The noun that follows is plural.
Mt. Everest is **the highest** mountain **in the world**. The Appalachian Trail is not **the longest** trail **in the United States**.	We often put a prepositional phrase after a superlative phrase: *in the world, of all time, in the U.S.,* etc.
The north part of the Appalachian Trail is **the least challenging**.	You can use *the least* to make a superlative.
What is the most spectacular place **(that) you've ever seen**?	An adjective clause with the present perfect and *ever* often completes a superlative statement.
In 2016, **one of the fastest swimmers** in the world was Katie Ledecky. Michael Phelps won **the most medals** at the 2016 Olympics.	A superlative form can precede any noun in the sentence.
Grandma Gatewood inspires me **the most**. I like her story **the best**.	A superlative form can follow a verb (phrase).

Notes:
1. Use *the* before a superlative form. Omit *the* if there is a possessive form before a superlative.
    What was **your most challenging** adventure? (NOT: *your the most challenging*)
2. When the verb *be* connects a noun to a superlative adjective + noun, there are two possible word orders:
    Football is the most popular sport in the U.S.
    The most popular sport in the U.S. is football.

EXERCISE 4 Write the superlative form of the word given.

1. At age 15, Michael Phelps was __the youngest__ American male swimmer in 68 years to make
   _{young}
   an Olympic team.

2. At the 2008 Olympics, he broke a record set in 1972, making him _____ swimmer
   _{fast}
   ever for that event.

3. Many people think Michael Phelps was _____ athlete at the 2012 Olympics.
   _{exciting}

4. A popular sports magazine named Phelps _____ sportsman of the year in 2008.
   _{good}

5. At the 2012 Olympics in London, he was _____ swimmer.
   _{successful}

6. He won _____ medals at the 2012 Olympics.
   _{a lot}

7. Will anyone take his place? Or will he always be _____ swimmer of all time?
   _{great}

ABOUT YOU Give your opinion. Write a superlative sentence about each of the following items. Then compare your answers to a partner's.

1. popular athlete in my country

   Manny Pacquiao is one of the most popular athletes in my country.

2. boring sport

3. interesting sport

4. good athlete

5. bad thing about (*name a sport*)

6. popular sport in my country

7. easy sport for children

8. challenging sport

9. dangerous adventure

314   Unit 12

ABOUT YOU Use the words to write superlative sentences about your experiences. Use the present perfect form with *ever* after the superlative. Share your answers with a partner.

1. long/distance/walk

   <u>My hike through the Alps was the longest distance I've ever walked.</u>

2. interesting/sporting event/see

3. dangerous/thing/do

4. difficult/sport/play

5. good/athlete/see

6. challenging/thing/do

> **FUN WITH GRAMMAR**
>
> Describe your classmates. Form groups of at least three. Take five minutes to write as many superlative sentences as you can to describe the people in your group (e.g., *This person is the most adventurous. This person is the tallest. This person is the funniest.*). Then share them with the class. The class will try to guess which person each sentence describes.

At age 35, Norway's Aksel Lund Svindal became the oldest Olympic alpine skiing champion with his win in 2018. Norway won the most medals (39) at the 2018 Winter Olympics in PyeongChang, South Korea.

Americans' Attitude toward Soccer

Fans cheer on the U.S. Women's National Team in Los Angeles, California. This was the seventh "Countdown to the Cup" game ahead of the 2019 FIFA Women's World Cup in France.

Read the following article. Pay special attention to the words in bold.

Almost everyone in the world calls it "football." Americans call it "soccer." Whatever you call it, it is by far the most popular sport in the world. In many countries, top international soccer players are as well-known as rock stars or actors—but not in the United States.

In 1999, when the Women's World Cup was played in the United States, there was **more excitement** about soccer **than** ever before. It seemed as if the United States might start to become **more interested** in this international sport. In 2014, when the World Cup was held in Brazil, a record number of people in the United States (an average of 24.7 million), watched the game in which the U.S. team tied with Portugal in the first round. Soccer seemed to be getting **more popular**. But for the next World Cup in 2018, the men's team did not even qualify to play. The number of viewers in the United States went down by nearly one half.

Some statistics show that interest in soccer is **higher than** before. Certainly, during the World Cup, there is a **larger** audience for soccer **than** at other times. But soccer is still much **less popular** in the United States **than** in the rest of the world.

Experts believe that to increase interest in soccer, professional teams have to produce **better** players and capture kids' interest at a **younger** age. Many American parents enroll their kids in soccer programs because they consider soccer **safer than** other sports, such as football or hockey. Between 1990 and 2010, the number of young soccer players doubled. **More recently**, however, that number has been dropping. Between 2015 and 2018, the percentage of 6- to 12-year-olds playing soccer dropped nearly 14 percent. With **more** time spent on electronics, **fewer** American kids are playing youth sports **than** ever before. But while soccer numbers are down, baseball and basketball numbers are up. For American soccer to be on a level with the rest of the world, **a lot more** children need to play, and these developmental programs need to be **more rigorous**[1].

The record number of viewers who tuned in to watch the women play in 2019 is encouraging. Will the 2019 World Cup win by the United States' women's national team lead to **more** interest in the sport? Only time will tell.

---

[1] rigorous: difficult; having high standards

COMPREHENSION Based on the reading, write T for *true* or F for *false*.

1. _____ American soccer players are as well-known as movie stars.
2. _____ Interest in soccer is slowly increasing in the United States.
3. _____ Most Americans watch soccer during the World Cup.

THINK ABOUT IT Discuss the questions with a partner or in a small group.

1. Is soccer popular in your country? When you were a child, did you dream of becoming a successful soccer player?
2. Discuss the dangers of playing soccer. Do you agree that soccer is safer than American football and ice hockey? Explain.

12.3 The Comparative Forms of Adjectives and Adverbs

	SIMPLE	COMPARATIVE
One-syllable adjectives and adverbs	high	higher
	large	larger
Two-syllable adjectives that end in *y*	easy	easier
	happy	happier
Other two-syllable adjectives	remote	more remote
	extreme	more extreme
Some two-syllable adjectives have two forms	simple	simpler
		more simple
	polite	politer
		more polite
Adjectives with three or more syllables	popular	more popular
	demanding	more demanding
-ly adverbs	quickly	more quickly
	directly	more directly
Irregular comparatives	good/well	better
	bad/badly	worse
	far	farther
Quantity words	little	less
	few	fewer
	a lot	more
	much	
	many	

Notes:

1. Other two-syllable adjectives that have two forms are:

    handsome, quiet, gentle, narrow, clever, friendly, angry, stupid

2. Adjectives that are past participles use *more*.

    tired—more tired

    fulfilled—more fulfilled

    worried—more worried

3. We use *than* before the second item of comparison.

    *Football is more popular **than** soccer in the U.S.*

EXERCISE 5 Listen to the following article. Fill in the blanks with the words you hear. 🎧 12.4

What are the differences between college sports and professional sports? Of course, professional athletes are __more experienced than__ college athletes, but college athletes are
1.
_____ and sometimes _____. The ticket prices are
2. 3.
_____ for professional sports _____ they are for college sports. In
4. 5.
professional sports, athletes make a lot of money, but college athletes don't. So college athletes are
_____ about the sport _____ they are about
6. 7.
financial gain.

In college baseball, players use aluminum bats; in professional baseball, players use wooden bats. Fans like the sound the wooden bat makes _____ the sound of the aluminum
8.
bat. The baseball stadium for professional baseball is _____ than the baseball stadium
9.
for college baseball.

Some fans think that college basketball is _____ professional basketball. The
10.
atmosphere of college basketball is _____ because college students cheer on their
11.
favorite team _____ after a score. The fans of professional basketball are
12.
_____ the fans of college basketball.
13.
College basketball is _____ either college baseball or football. The fans are
14.
_____ to the action. College football has a _____ crowd if the
15. 16.
home team is good that year.

In professional sports, fans are sometimes _____ in their favorite players
17.
_____ the whole team. In college sports, the team gets _____ than
18. 19.
the individual players.

Which do you think is _____?
20.

EXERCISE 6 Write the comparative form of each word.

1. fat   __fatter__   4. low   _____

2. important   __more important__   5. beautifully _____

3. exciting   _____   6. good   _____

318   Unit 12

7. remarkable _____
8. athletic _____
9. bad _____
10. rigorous _____
11. challenging _____

12. surprised _____
13. high _____
14. large _____
15. far _____
16. enthusiastically _____

12.4 Comparatives—Use

EXAMPLES	EXPLANATION
Basketball is **livelier than** baseball. Soccer is **more popular than** boxing.	We use the comparative form to show the difference between two people or things.
European children train **more rigorously** in soccer **than** American children.	We use *than* before the second item of comparison.
Soccer is **less popular than** football in the U.S.	We can use *less* to make a comparison.
College athletes have **less experience than** professional athletes. Soccer players have **fewer injuries than** football players.	We can put *more, less, fewer, better, worse,* and other comparative forms before a noun. We use *less* with noncount nouns; we use *fewer* with count nouns.
My sister **likes soccer more than** I do. You **play basketball better than** your brother does.	We can put *more, less, better, worse,* and other comparative forms after a verb (phrase).
Interest in soccer is **much lower** in the U.S. **than** it is in other countries. I like soccer **a little better than** I like baseball.	*Much, a lot,* or *a little* can come before a comparative form.
The more they practice, **the better** they play. **The older** you are, **the harder** it is to learn a new sport.	We can use two comparisons in one sentence to show cause and result.

Notes:

1. Omit *than* if the second item of comparison is not included.

    Basketball is popular in the U.S., but football is **more popular**.

2. When a pronoun follows *than*, the correct form is the subject pronoun (*he, she, I,* etc.). Usually an auxiliary verb follows (*is, do, did, can,* etc.). Informally, many Americans use the object pronoun (*him, her, me,* etc.) after *than* without an auxiliary verb.

    FORMAL: *You are taller than* **I am**.   FORMAL: *I can play soccer better than* **he can**.
    INFORMAL: *You are taller than* **me**.   INFORMAL: *I can play soccer better than* **him**.

EXERCISE 7 Circle the correct words to complete each statement.

1. Professional athletes make (**much more**/*more much*) money than college athletes.

2. A basketball player is (*more tall/taller*) than a gymnast.

3. A baseball game has (*little/less*) action than a soccer game.

continued

4. Football players use (*more padding/padding more*) than soccer players.

5. Football players are (*much/more*) heavier than soccer players.

6. A football team has (*much/more*) players than a baseball team.

7. Americans are (*enthusiastic less/less enthusiastic*) about soccer than Europeans.

8. Michael Phelps (*faster swims/swims faster*) than other swimmers.

9. Who plays (*better/more better*), college athletes or professional athletes?

10. College baseball has (*fewer/less*) fans than college basketball.

11. I think football is exciting, but soccer is (*more exciting/more exciting than*).

EXERCISE 8 Fill in the blank with the comparative of a word from the box. Include *than* when necessary.

| easily | tall | strong | slow | popular✓ | active | large | good |

1. In the United States, basketball is ____more popular than____ soccer.

2. Basketball players are usually _____ football players.

3. A golf game (18 holes) takes about three or four hours. It is much _____ most other sports.

4. A soccer ball is _____ a tennis ball.

5. Children learn sports _____ adults.

6. People who lift weights are _____ people who don't.

7. Soccer players are always moving. Soccer players are _____ baseball players.

8. Professional athletes are usually _____ college athletes.

EXERCISE 9 Use the information in the chart to write sentences that compare these two female Olympic swimmers. Answers may vary.

	MISSY FRANKLIN	NATALIE COUGHLIN
year born	1995	1982
height	6 feet 1 inches tall	5 feet 8 inches tall
weight	165 pounds	139 pounds
education	didn't finish college	graduated from college
age when she started to swim competitively	7	6
participation in Olympic Games	2012 and 2016	2004, 2008, and 2012
number of Olympic medals won	6	12

1. <u>Missy is younger than Natalie. OR Natalie is older than Missy.</u>
2. _____
3. _____
4. _____
5. _____
6. _____
7. _____

American gold medal swimmers Megan Romano, Shannon Vreeland, Natalie Coughlin, and Missy Franklin at the 2013 World Aquatics Championships in Barcelona, Spain.

ABOUT YOU Compare yourself to a family member or friend. Share your answers with a partner.

1. interested in baseball

   <u>My brother is more interested in baseball than I am.</u>

2. tall

   _____

3. strong

   _____

continued

4. athletic

   _____

5. competitive

   _____

6. enthusiastic about sports

   _____

7. a good swimmer

   _____

8. knowledgeable about soccer

   _____

EXERCISE 10 Fill in the blanks with the comparative or superlative form of the word given. Include *than* or *the* when necessary.

1. In the United States, baseball is __*more popular than*__ soccer.

popular

2. Baseball is one of __*the most popular*__ sports in the United States.

popular

3. A tennis ball is _____ a baseball.

soft

4. An athlete who wins the gold medal is _____ athlete in his or her sport.

good

5. Who is _____ basketball player in the world?

tall

6. I am _____ in baseball _____ in basketball.

interested

7. In my opinion, soccer is _____ sport in the world.

exciting

8. Weightlifters are _____ golfers.

muscular

9. Soccer is a _____ sport _____ baseball.

fast

10. A basketball team has _____ players _____ a baseball team.

few

11. My friend and I both jog. I run _____ my friend.

far

12. Who's a _____ soccer player—you or your brother?

good

13. In golf, the player who has _____ score wins.

low

14. European soccer players are _____ American soccer players.

well-known

322   Unit 12

An Amazing Athlete

Read the following article. Pay special attention to the words in bold. 🎧 12.5

Erik Weihenmayer is **as tough as** any mountain climber. In 2001, he made his way to the top of the highest mountain in the world—Mount Everest—at the age of 33. But Erik is different from other mountain climbers in one important way: he is completely blind. He is the only blind person to reach the top of the tallest mountain.

Erik was an athletic child who lost his vision in his early teens. At first, he refused to use a cane or learn braille[1], insisting he could do **as well as** any teenager. But he finally came to accept his disability. He couldn't play **the same** sports **as** he used to. He would never be able to play basketball or catch a football again. At 16, he became interested in rock climbing. Rock climbing led to mountain climbing, the greatest challenge of his life.

The members of his climbing team say that Erik isn't different from a sighted climber. He has **as much training as** the others. He is **as strong as** the rest. He is like any other climber: flexible, mentally tough, and able to tolerate physical pain.

Climbing Mount Everest was a challenge for every climber on Erik's team. The reaction to the mountain air for Erik was **the same as** it was for his teammates: lack of oxygen causes the heart to beat more slowly than usual, and the brain does not function **as clearly as** normal. To climb Mount Everest is an achievement for any athlete. Erik Weihenmayer showed that his disability wasn't **as important as** his ability.

---

[1] braille: a system of reading and writing for the blind that uses raised dots for letters, numbers, and symbols

Erik Weihenmayer on Mount Everest

COMPREHENSION Based on the reading, write T for *true* or F for *false*.

1. _____ When Erik became blind, he used a cane to get around.
2. _____ Erik doesn't have as much training as his teammates.
3. _____ At the highest altitudes, the brain functions as clearly as normal.

THINK ABOUT IT Discuss the questions with a partner or in a small group.

1. Reread the last line of the article. Can you give an example from your life or someone else's life where a disability wasn't as important as an ability?
2. Can you give an example of another amazing athlete? What did he or she do that was unusual?

12.5 As...As

EXAMPLES	EXPLANATION
Erik is **as strong as** his teammates. At high altitudes, the brain does**n't** function **as clearly as** normal.	We can show that two things are equal or unequal in some way by using: (*not*) *as* + adjective/adverb + *as*
Skiing is **not as difficult as** mountain climbing.	When we make a comparison of unequal items, we put the lesser item first.

Note:
Omit the second *as* if the second item of comparison is omitted.
   *Baseball is popular in the United States. Soccer is not **as popular**.*

EXERCISE 11 Fill in the blanks with a word from the box and *as . . . as*.

| strong | well | dangerous✓ | clearly | prepared |

1. Rock climbing is not _____as dangerous as_____ mountain climbing.
2. At high altitudes, you can't think _____ you can at lower altitudes.
3. Erik trained well, and he was _____ his teammates.
4. When Erik became blind, he wanted to do _____ any other teenager.
5. Erik is _____ other climbers.

EXERCISE 12 Change these comparative sentences to sentences using *not as . . . as*.

1. Europeans are more interested in soccer than Americans.

   Americans are not as interested in soccer as Europeans.

2. Soccer is more popular in Latin America than it is in the United States.

   _____

3. Football is more dangerous than soccer for children.

4. Missy Franklin is younger than Natalie Coughlin.

5. Missy Franklin is taller than Natalie Coughlin.

6. Professional European soccer players are more famous than professional American soccer players.

ABOUT YOU Compare yourself to another person. (Or compare two people you know.) Use the following words and *as . . . as*. You may add a comparative statement if there is inequality. Discuss your answers with a partner.

1. athletic

   I'm not as athletic as my uncle. He's much more athletic than I am.

2. interested in basketball

3. good at sports

4. walk fast

5. strong

6. excited about soccer

7. smart

8. good at languages

12.6 As Many/Much . . . As

EXAMPLES	EXPLANATION
Soccer players don't usually have **as many injuries as** football players. Erik had **as much training as** his teammates.	We can show that two things are equal or unequal in quantity by using: (*not*) *as many* + count noun + *as* (*not*) *as much* + noncount noun + *as*
I don't play soccer **as much as** I used to.	We can use *as much as* after a verb phrase.

EXERCISE 13 Fill in the blanks with *as much/many. . . as*.

1. Does Gregg Treinish get ____as much____ satisfaction from extreme sports ____as____ he used to?

2. Nancy Coughlin didn't win _____ medals in the 2012 Olympics _____ she did in the 2008 Olympics.

3. You don't hear about Michael Jordan _____ you used to.

4. Grandma Gatewood didn't carry _____ equipment on the Appalachian Trail _____ other hikers.

5. She didn't spend _____ money on equipment _____ other hikers.

6. Michael Phelps didn't win _____ gold medals in 2012 _____ he did in 2008.

7. American soccer teams don't win _____ games at the World Cup _____ European teams.

8. Americans don't show _____ interest in soccer _____ Latin Americans.

9. Americans don't know _____ about soccer _____ Europeans.

ABOUT YOU Fill in information about yourself. Then find a partner and compare your answers.

I don't spend as much time in nature as my partner does.

	NOT AT ALL	OCCASIONALLY	FREQUENTLY
1. I spend time in nature.	○	●	○
2. I exercise.	○	○	○
3. I read sports magazines.	○	○	○
4. I attend sporting events.	○	○	○
5. I watch basketball games.	○	○	○
6. I watch soccer on TV.	○	○	○

ABOUT YOU Compare yourself today to the way you were five years ago. Use *as . . . as, as much/many . . . as,* or a comparative form. Share your answers with a partner.

1. thin

    <u>I'm not as thin as I was five years ago. OR I'm heavier than I was five years ago.</u>

2. strong

    _____

3. physically fit

    _____

4. interested in sports

    _____

5. exercise

    _____

6. have time to relax

    _____

7. watch sports programs on TV

    _____

12.7 The Same . . . As

We can show that two things are equal or not with *the same . . . (as)*.

EXAMPLES	EXPLANATION
Pattern A: Erik had **the same ability as** his teammates.	**Pattern A:** Noun 1 + verb + *the same* noun *as* + noun 2.
Pattern B: Erik and his teammates had **the same ability**.	**Pattern B:** Noun 1 and noun 2 + verb + *the same* noun.

Note:
We can make statements of equality or inequality with many types of nouns, such as *size, shape, color, value, religion, age, height,* or *nationality*.

    He is **the same height as** his teammate. *(height = noun)*

    He is **as tall as** his teammate. *(tall = adjective)*

    Missy **isn't the same age as** Natalie. *(age = noun)*

    Missy **isn't as old as** Natalie. *(old = adjective)*

EXERCISE 14 Use the words to make statements with *(not) the same (... as)*.

1. a golf ball/a tennis ball (*size*)

   A golf ball isn't the same size as a tennis ball.

2. a basketball team/a soccer team (*number of players*)

   A basketball team and a soccer team don't have the same number of players.

3. a soccer ball/a football (*shape*)

   _____

4. a soccer player/a basketball player (*height*)

   _____

5. a college athlete/a professional athlete (*experience*)

   _____

6. a baseball/a softball (*size*)

   _____

7. football players/soccer players (*uniforms*)

   _____

8. a female athlete/a male athlete (*amount of money*)

   _____

EXERCISE 15 Use the information in the chart to compare two Olympic swimmers. Use two methods of comparison.

	MICHAEL PHELPS	NATHAN ADRIAN
year born	1985	1988
height	6 feet 4 inches tall	6 feet 6 inches tall
weight	185 pounds	225 pounds
education	received bachelor's degree	received bachelor's degree
age when he started swimming	7	2
participation in Olympic games	2000, 2004, 2008, 2012, and 2016	2008, 2012, and 2016
number of Olympic medals won	28	8

1. <u>Michael is older than Nathan.</u>

   <u>Nathan and Michael weren't born in the same year.</u>

2.

3.

4.

5.

6.

7.

Gold medalists Nathan Adrian and Michael Phelps thank the crowd at the 2016 Olympic Games in Rio de Janeiro, Brazil.

Superlatives, Comparatives 329

FOOTBALL and SOCCER

Tom Brady of the New England Patriots runs with the ball during a football game against the Buffalo Bills in Buffalo, New York, U.S.

Read the following article. Pay special attention to the words in bold. 12.6

It may seem strange that Americans give the name "football" to a game played mostly by throwing and carrying a ball with one's hands. Speakers of a language other than English usually refer to this sport as *American football*, but in the United States, it's simply *football*.

Many of the rules in soccer and football are the same. In both games, there are 11 players on each side, and a team scores its points by getting the ball past the goal of the other team. The playing fields for both sports **are** also very much **alike**.

When the action begins, the two games look very different. In addition to using their feet, soccer players are allowed to hit the ball with their heads. In football, the only person allowed to touch the ball with his feet is a special player known as the kicker. Also, in football, tackling[1] the player who has the ball is not only allowed but encouraged, whereas[2] tackling in soccer will get the tackler thrown out of the game.

Football players and soccer players **don't dress alike** or even **look alike** in many ways. Since blocking and tackling are a big part of American football, the players are often very large and muscular and wear heavy padding and helmets. Soccer players, on the other hand, are usually thinner and wear shorts and polo shirts. This gives them more freedom of movement so that they can show off the fancy footwork that makes soccer such a popular game around the world.

---

[1] tackling: knocking a player to the ground
[2] whereas: in contrast

COMPREHENSION Based on the reading, write T for *true* or F for *false*.

1. _____ A soccer team and a football team don't have the same number of players.
2. _____ It is common to see tackling in a football game.
3. _____ Football players need padding to protect their bodies.

THINK ABOUT IT Discuss the questions with a partner or in a small group.

1. Imagine that a soccer player wants to start playing football. Which rules or aspects of the game do you think could be most challenging to learn?
2. Which game do you prefer to watch? Why? Which would you prefer to play? Why?

12.8 Showing Similarity with *Like* and *Alike*

We can show that two things are similar (or not) with *like* and *alike*.

EXAMPLES	EXPLANATION
Pattern A: A soccer player **looks like** a rugby player. A soccer player **doesn't look like** a football player.	**Pattern A:** Noun 1 + verb + *like* + noun 2.
Pattern B: A soccer player and a rugby player **look alike**. A soccer player and a football player **don't look alike**.	**Pattern B:** Noun 1 and noun 2 + verb + *alike*.
Pattern A: He **is like** his brother in some ways. They both love soccer. He **is not like** his sister. They have different interests.	**Pattern A:** Noun 1 + *be like* + noun 2.
Pattern B: He and his brother **are alike** in some ways. He and his sister **are not alike**.	**Pattern B:** Noun 1 and noun 2 + *be alike*.

Notes:
1. We use the sense perception verbs (*look, sound, smell, taste, feel,* and *seem*) with *like* and *alike* to show an outward similarity or difference.
2. We can use other verbs with *like/alike*: act, sing, dress, think, etc.
    A soccer player doesn't **dress like** a football player.
    A soccer player and a football player **don't dress alike**.
3. We use *be like/be alike* to show an inward similarity or difference.
    Erik **is like** his teammates. He's a strong climber. (*be like* = an inward similarity)

GRAMMAR IN USE

Questions with *What + like* or *What + look like* don't ask for comparisons. They ask for a description:

What is he like? (asks about personality) *He's funny and really smart.*
What is it like? (asks for a description) *It's challenging.*
What does he look like? (asks for a physical description) *He's tall with brown hair.*

When *Who* is used instead of *What* in these questions, similarities are asked for:

Who is he like? He's like his brother. They are both athletic.
Who does he look like? He looks like his father. They are both tall and handsome.

Superlatives, Comparatives

EXERCISE 16 Fill in the blanks with an item from the box. You can use some items more than once.

| are alike | is like | don't look like | look like | aren't alike |
| dress alike | think alike | look alike | am not like | sound like |

1. **A:** You're so tall. You ___look like___ a basketball player.

   B: Everyone who sees me says the same thing.

2. **A:** _____ wrestling _____ boxing?

   B: In some ways, they _____ because they fight in a ring. But in many ways they're different.

3. **A:** My brother and I _____ in some ways.

   B: How?

   A: We're both very athletic.

4. **A:** Soccer players _____ football players at all.

   B: Football players are much bigger. And they wear completely different uniforms.

5. **A:** The swimming competition and the diving competition at the Olympics are very different.

   B: You're right. They _____ at all.

6. **A:** You _____ your brother.

   B: Everybody says that. We both talk about our favorite soccer team all the time.

7. **A:** My nieces are identical twins. They _____. Here's a picture of them.

   B: Oh, how cute. They're wearing the same outfit.

   A: Yes. They like to _____. But they _____ in all ways. One loves sports. The other doesn't.

8. **A:** I have a great idea. Let's take the day off and go to a baseball game.

   B: I had the exact same idea. You and I _____.

9. **A:** My sister is a great swimmer.

   B: What about you?

   A: When it comes to swimming, I _____ my sister at all. I'm afraid of the water.

   B: But you _____ in some ways. You're both interested in mountain climbing.

ABOUT YOU Compare yourself to someone in your family or compare two members of your family using the following words. Share your answers with a partner.

1. look like _I don't look like my mother. She's tall. I'm very short._ _____

2. be like _____

3. be alike _____

4. sing like _____

5. think alike _____

6. dress like _____

7. act like _____

EXERCISE 17 Fill in the blanks in the conversation. Use different methods of comparison from this unit. Use context clues to help you.

A: I heard that you have a twin brother. Do you and your brother look ____alike____ ?
                                                                            1.

B: No. He _____ look _____ me at all.
              2.   **3.**

A: But you're twins.

B: We're fraternal twins. That's different from identical twins. We're not even _____ height.
                                                                                      4.

He's not _____ I am. He's 5'8". I'm 6'2".
          5.

A: But you're _____ in some ways, aren't you?
                    6.

B: No. We're completely different. I'm athletic and I'm on the high school football team, but David hates sports. He's a much _____ student than I am. He gets all A's. He's more
                                      7.

_____ our mother, who loves to read and learn new things, and I _____ our
      8.   **9.**

father, who's athletic and loves to build things. Also, I'm outgoing, but he's very shy. And we don't dress

_____ at all. He likes to wear neat, conservative clothes, but I prefer torn jeans and
      10.

T-shirts. There's only one similarity: over the phone, people don't know if it's my brother or me. We

sound _____ .
        11.

Superlatives, Comparatives

SUMMARY OF UNIT 12

Simple, Comparative, and Superlative Forms

SHORT WORDS

Jacob is **tall**.
Mark is **taller than** Jacob.
Bart is **the tallest** member of the basketball team.

LONG WORDS

Basketball is **popular** in the United States.
Basketball is **more popular than** soccer in the United States.
Soccer is **the most popular** sport in the world.

Comparisons with *As . . . As* and *The Same . . . As*

Soccer players aren't **as tall as** basketball players.
Soccer players aren't **the same height as** basketball players.
Soccer players and basketball players aren't **the same height**.

I didn't swim **as many minutes as** you did.
I didn't spend **as much time** in the pool **as** you did.
I don't work out **as much as** you do.

Comparisons with *Like* and *Alike*

She**'s like** her mother. They're both interested in sports.
She and her mother **are alike**. They're both interested in sports.
She **looks like** her mother. They're both tall and strong.
She and her mother **look alike**. They're both tall and strong.

REVIEW

Fill in the blanks to complete the conversation. In some cases, answers may vary.

A: It's football season, and my husband doesn't pay as ____much____ attention to me
                                                                    1.

_____as_____ he does to his football games. Many women have _____ problem
    2.   3.

_____ I do. They call us "football widows" because we lose our husbands during football
    4.

season.

B: Your husband sounds _____ my husband. I feel _____ a widow, too. Most
                                5.   6.

men act _____ during football season. My husband isn't _____ interested in me as
            7.   8.

he is in watching TV. He looks _____ a robot in front of the TV. When I complain, he tells
                                    9.

me to sit down and join him. But I don't like football.

A: I think soccer is much _____ than football. My favorite team is the
                                    10.

Chicago Fire.

B: In my opinion, they're not _____ good _____ the Los Angeles Galaxy. I
                                        11.   12.

think the Galaxy is much _____. But _____ teams are from
                                13.   14.

Europe and Latin America.

A: Exactly! Soccer is _____ sport in the world. It's only in the U.S. that it
                            15.

isn't very popular. Even during the World Cup, Americans don't pay _____
                                                                        16.

attention to the games as Europeans and Latin Americans.

B: It's crazy! I think the action in soccer is _____ the action in football. And it's
                                                        17.

_____ fun to watch soccer players. Football players look _____ big
    18.   19.

monsters with their helmets and padding.

A: Did you watch the World Cup in 2016? The _____ game was between Germany and
                                                    20.

Argentina. I mentioned Lionel Messi to my husband, and he said, "Who's that?" I said,

"He's _____ player in the world."
            21.

B: I love Messi. He's a strong player. But Cristiano Ronaldo is even _____.
                                                                            22.

A: Well, let's do our favorite sport: shopping. We can spend _____ time shopping
                                                                        23.

_____ they do in front of the TV.
    24.

B: You and I think _____. We're football widows, so our husbands can be
                            25.

"shopping widowers."

Superlatives, Comparatives 335

FROM GRAMMAR TO WRITING

PART 1 Editing Advice

1. Don't use *more* and *-er* together.

    He plays baseball ~~more~~ better than his brother.

2. Use *than* before the second item of comparison.

    Soccer is more exciting ~~that~~ *than* baseball.

3. Use *the* before a superlative form.

    Mt. Everest is ^*the* tallest mountain in the world.

4. Use a plural noun in the phrase "one of the [superlative] [plural noun]."

    Lionel Messi is one of the best soccer player^*s* in the world.

5. Use the correct word order.

    I ~~more like sports~~ *like sports more* than you do.

    I have ~~interest more~~ *more interest* than you do in sports.

6. Use *be like* for inward similarity. Use *look like* for an outward similarity.

    He is ~~look~~ like his brother. They are both talented athletes.

    He ~~is~~ look^*s* like his brother. They are both tall and muscular.

7. Use the correct negative for *be like, look like, sound like, feel like,* etc.

    He ~~isn't~~ *doesn't* look like an athlete. He's not in good shape.

8. Use *the same* before nouns.

    A baseball isn't the same ~~big~~ *size* as a volleyball.

9. Use *as* before adjectives and adverbs.

    A baseball isn't ~~the same~~ *as* big as a volleyball.

10. With equality and inequality, use *as* with the second item.

    A football isn't the same shape ~~than~~ *as* a soccer ball.

11. Don't confuse *more* and *most*.

    Tierra del Fuego is the ~~more~~ *most* spectacular place he has ever seen.

PART 2 Editing Practice

Some of the shaded words and phrases have mistakes. Find the mistakes and correct them. If the shaded words are correct, write C.

    Soccer is the ~~more~~ *most* popular sport in the world. It is more popular *C* than football, baseball, and
                 1.   **2.**

basketball combined. I know Americans prefer football, but for me soccer is much more interesting **that**
                                                                       3.   **4.**

football. In fact, I think soccer is **the more exciting** sport in the world. There are some good American
                                        5.

teams, but they aren't **as good as** some of the European teams. I think Italy has one of the **best team.**
                6.   **7.** **8.**

    The name "football" is confusing. "Football" **is sounds like** a game where you use your feet, but
                                                                           9.

football players carry the ball. A football and a soccer ball don't **look alike** at all. A soccer ball is round, but
                                                                                          10.

a football isn't. The game of football isn't **look like** the game of soccer at all. These sports are completely
                                                                  11.

different. The players are different, too. Soccer players are not **the same** big as football players. There is
                                                                                  12.

just one similarity: a soccer team has **the same** number of players **as** a football team.
                                                  13.   **14.**

    I especially like Cristiano Ronaldo. In my opinion, he is **one of the best player** in the world. I love to
                                                                                          15.

watch soccer, but I like to play it even more. When I lived in my country, I played **more better** because I
                                                                                                       16.

more practiced. I played every weekend. But here I don't have **time as much** as before. I watch it on TV, but
17.   **18.**

it isn't **as much fun as** playing it.
       19.

WRITING TIP
When you write an essay, you need an introduction, a body, and a conclusion. The introduction includes your thesis statement, which expresses the central point of your essay. Each body paragraph introduces a main idea and supporting points. The conclusion is where you end your essay and restate your thesis. It is always good to create an outline to organize your ideas before you begin writing an essay.

PART 3 Write
Read the prompts. Choose one and write an essay about it.

1. Compare two athletes from the same sport. If you don't follow sports, compare two famous people from the same field (politics, movies, art, etc.). If you use information from an outside source, attach that source to your essay.
2. Write about a person who accomplished something amazing. You can write about a famous person or a person you know. If you use information from an outside source, attach that source to your essay.

PART 4 Edit
Reread the Summary of Unit 12 and the editing advice. Edit your writing from Part 3.

UNIT
13
Active and Passive Voice

THE LAW

Lady Justice's scale symbolizes fairness and balance, and her sword represents punishment. Her statue is often outside courthouses in the U.S.

Injustice anywhere is a threat to justice everywhere.

DR. MARTIN LUTHER KING, JR.

The Supreme Court

The U.S. Supreme Court Building, Washington, DC

Read the following article. Pay special attention to the words in bold. 13.1

You have probably heard of the Supreme Court of the United States. Why **was** this court **created**, how **are** the justices **selected**, and how is it different from other courts?

The Supreme Court **was created** by the U.S. Constitution to balance the power of the president and Congress. It has nine justices[1], one of whom is the Chief Justice. The president nominates a justice, but he doesn't have the final say. His choice has to **be confirmed**[2] by the Senate. Supreme Court justices **are** not **appointed** for a fixed number of years. According to the Constitution, they "shall hold their offices during good behavior." This usually means they serve for life or until they retire. Until 1981, all the justices were male. Then Sandra Day O'Connor, who **was nominated** by President Ronald Reagan, became the first female justice.

About 10,000 cases **are filed** every year, but the Supreme Court hears only about 75–80 cases. The Supreme Court hears cases that **are appealed**[3] from lower courts when these courts are not able to resolve a conflict. No new evidence[4] **is presented**, and no witnesses **are heard**. Attorneys[5] present their case in writing and orally. The judges listen to each side, review the evidence that **was presented** in the lower courts, and meet privately to decide the case. A simple majority of five justices is all that **is needed** to decide a case.

Once a case **is heard** on the Supreme Court, it **cannot be heard** in any other court. The justices' decision is final.

---

[1] justice: a judge in a court of law
[2] confirmed: formally accepted
[3] appealed: brought from a lower court to a higher court for review
[4] evidence: words or objects that support the truth of something
[5] attorney: a lawyer

COMPREHENSION Based on the reading, write T for *true* or F for *false*.

1. _____ The president has the final word in selecting a Supreme Court justice.
2. _____ To decide a case, all the justices must agree.
3. _____ A Supreme Court justice can serve for life.

THINK ABOUT IT Discuss the questions with a partner or in a small group.

1. Is there an institution similar to the Supreme Court in your country or other countries you know about?
2. What kinds of cases do you think go to the Supreme Court?

13.1 Active and Passive Voice—Overview

EXAMPLES	EXPLANATION
subject — Reagan / verb — **chose** / object — O'Connor.	Some sentences are in the **active voice**. The subject performs the action of the verb.
subject — O'Connor / verb (be + past participle) — **was chosen** / by + agent — by Reagan.	Some sentences are in the **passive voice**. The subject receives the action of the verb. To form the passive voice, we use *be* + the past participle of the verb. Some passive sentences have an agent, or performer of the action. The agent is in the *by* phrase.
O'Connor **was chosen** in 1981. About 10,000 cases **are filed** with the Supreme Court every year.	Many passive sentences don't mention an agent.

EXERCISE 1 Listen to the article about a famous case. Then write T for *true* or F for *false*. 🎧 13.2

1. _____ In Kansas in 1879, schools separated black and white children into different classrooms within schools.

2. _____ Oliver Brown was a teacher on the Topeka school board.

3. _____ In the case of *Brown v. The Board of Education*, the Supreme Court ruled in favor of segregation.

EXERCISE 2 Listen to the article again. Fill in the blanks with the words you hear. 🎧 13.2

One of the most famous cases heard in the Supreme Court ____is known____ as *Brown v.*
                                                              1.
The Board of Education. According to an 1879 Kansas law, elementary schools

_____ to segregate children—separate them according to race. Black and white
           2.

children _____ to different schools. School boards said that all children
                  3.

_____ "separate but equal" education.
           4.

In the early 1950s, when black parents tried to enroll their children in a neighborhood school in Topeka,

Kansas, they _____ . Oliver Brown was one of the parents. Brown's daughter
                        5.

_____ to walk six blocks to a school bus stop to ride a bus to her segregated school.
           6.

continued

The Topeka school board _____ in court. The District Court ruled in
7.
favor of segregated education. Then a group of black parents challenged this "separate but equal" law and took their case to the Supreme Court in 1953. The Supreme Court ruled that children
_____ by segregation. All nine justices agreed that segregation was
8.
unconstitutional.

All schools in the United States _____ by the Supreme Court's decision.
9.
All schools _____ to desegregate.
10.

13.2 The Passive Voice—Form

To form the passive voice, we use *be* + the past participle of the verb.

	ACTIVE	PASSIVE
Simple Present	The Constitution **protects** Americans.	Americans **are protected** by the Constitution.
Future	The judge **will make** a decision.	A decision **will be made** soon.
	The judge **is going to make** a decision.	A decision **is going to be made** soon.
Simple Past	Parents **challenged** the school board.	The school board **was challenged** in 1953.
Present Perfect	The court **has heard** the case.	The case **has been heard** by the court.
Infinitive	The court **has to make** a decision.	A decision **has to be made** by the court.
Modal	They **should change** the law.	The law **should be changed**.

Notes:
1. The tense of the sentence is shown by the verb *be*. The past participle of the main verb is used with every tense.
2. An adverb can be placed between the auxiliary verb and the main verb.
    *The attorneys **are** often **asked** questions.*
3. When the agent is included after a passive verb, we use *by* + noun or object pronoun.
    *I was helped **by the attorneys**.*   *My sister was helped **by them**, too.*
4. If two verbs in the passive voice are connected with *and*, we don't repeat the verb *be*.
    *All schools **were affected** and **required** to desegregate.*
5. Some active verbs have two objects: a direct object and an indirect object. When this is the case, the passive sentence can begin with either object. If the direct object becomes the subject of the passive sentence, *to* is used before the indirect object.
    Active: *They **gave** the child permission.*
    Passive: *The child **was given** permission.*   *Permission **was given to** the child.*

342   Unit 13

GRAMMAR IN USE

The passive voice is useful in reporting facts objectively. The passive puts emphasis on the receiver or object of the action (e.g., *Two people **were injured** in the accident.*). It also takes emphasis away from an unknown subject (e.g., *The painting **was stolen** from the museum.*).

The passive also allows a writer or speaker to adjust the focus. For example:

*Judge Brown **sentenced** Mel Simon to 10 years in prison.* (active)

*Mel Simon **was sentenced** to 10 years in prison.* (passive)

In the active voice, focus is placed on the judge. In the passive voice, Mel Simon is the focus.

EXERCISE 3 Change each sentence to passive voice. Use the same tense. Do not include the agent.

1. They **take** a vote. *A vote is taken.*

2. They **made** a decision. _____

3. They **will take** a vote. _____

4. They **are going to change** the law. _____

5. We **have paid** the attorneys. _____

6. We **must find** a good lawyer. _____

7. They **need to write** a report. _____

EXERCISE 4 Underline the verb. Then write *A* if the sentence is active or *P* if the sentence is passive.

1. The justices <u>discussed</u> the case in private. __*A*__

2. A decision <u>was made</u> to change the law. __*P*__

3. Sandra Day O'Connor became the first female justice on the Supreme Court. _____

4. About 75 cases are heard in the Supreme Court each year. _____

5. Some laws need to be changed. _____

6. The justices sometimes interrupt the attorneys. _____

7. Some justices will retire soon. _____

8. In many court cases, witnesses are brought in. _____

9. In criminal court, witnesses are questioned. _____

10. Schools in Kansas separated African-American children from other children. _____

11. The first African-American justice was appointed to the Supreme Court in 1967. _____

12. Things have changed a lot in the last 60 years. _____

JURY DUTY

Members of a jury listen to an attorney's argument.

Read the following article. Pay special attention to the words in bold. 13.3

All Americans **are protected** by the Constitution. No one person can decide if a person is guilty of a crime. Every citizen has the right to a trial by jury. When a person **is charged** with a crime, he or she **is considered** innocent until the jury decides he or she is guilty.

Most American citizens **are chosen** for jury duty at some time in their lives. How **are** jurors **chosen**? The court gets the names of citizens from lists of taxpayers, licensed drivers, and voters. Many people **are called** to the courthouse for the selection of a jury. From this large group, a limited number of people **is chosen**. Alternates[1] are also chosen. The lawyers and the judge ask each person questions to see if the person is going to be fair. If the person has made any judgment about the case before hearing the facts presented in the trial, he or she **is not selected**. If the person doesn't understand enough English, he or she **is not selected**. The court needs jurors who can understand the facts and be open-minded. When the final jury selection **is made**, the jurors must promise to be fair in deciding the case.

Sometimes a trial goes on for several days or more. Jurors **are not permitted** to talk with family members and friends about the case. In some cases, jurors **are not permitted** to go home until the case is over. They stay in a hotel and **are not permitted** to watch TV or read newspapers that give information about the case.

After the jurors hear the case, they have to reach a decision, or a verdict. They go to a separate room and talk about what they heard and saw in the courtroom. When they are finished discussing the case, they take a vote.

Jurors **are paid** for their work. They receive a small amount of money per day. Employers must give a worker permission **to take off work** to be on a jury. Jury duty **is considered** a very serious responsibility.

---
[1] alternate: a person who takes the place of a juror who cannot serve for some reason, such as illness

COMPREHENSION Based on the reading, write T for *true* or F for *false*.

1. _____ Only American citizens are selected for a jury in the United States.
2. _____ People with limited English are often not selected for jury duty.
3. _____ Jurors receive a small amount of money for serving.

THINK ABOUT IT Discuss the questions with a partner or in a small group.

1. Do you agree that a person is considered innocent until proven guilty of a crime? Why or why not? Is this true in your home country?
2. Have you ever had jury duty in the United States? If yes, describe the experience. If not, would you be eager to perform jury duty? Why or why not?

13.3 The Passive Voice—Use

EXAMPLES	EXPLANATION
Laws **should be obeyed**. The jurors **will be paid** at the end of the trial. A man **was charged** with a crime.	The passive voice is often used without an agent when: • the action is done by people in general. • the agent is unknown or unimportant. • the agent is obvious.
Active: The lawyers **presented** the case yesterday. **Passive**: The case **was presented** in two hours. **Active**: The judge and the lawyers **choose** 12 people. **Passive**: People who don't understand English **are not chosen**.	The passive voice is used to shift the emphasis from the agent to the receiver of the action.
A Supreme Court justice **is nominated** by the president.	The passive voice is sometimes used with an agent.
It **is considered** the responsibility of every citizen to serve on a jury.	Often the passive voice is used after *it* when talking about general beliefs, findings, and discoveries.

Notes:
1. The active voice is much more commonly used than the passive voice. Do not overuse the passive voice.
2. Informally, *they* is often used as the subject in an active sentence when the subject is not a specific person.
   They **give** you instructions in court. (Informal)
   You **are given** instructions in court. (Formal)

EXERCISE 5 Fill in the blanks with the passive voice of the verb given. Use the simple present.

1. Jurors ____are chosen____ from lists.
      (choose)
2. Only people over 18 years old _____ for jury duty.
                                        (select)
3. A questionnaire _____ out and _____.
                    (fill)   (return)
4. Many people _____ to the courthouse.
                  (call)
5. Not everyone _____.
                  (choose)
6. The jurors _____ a lot of questions.
                 (ask)
7. Jurors _____ time for lunch.
            (permit)
8. Jurors _____ a paycheck at the end of the trial if they are not employed.
            (give)

Active and Passive Voice 345

EXERCISE 6 Fill in the blanks with the passive voice of the verb given. Use the simple past.

1. I ___was sent___ a letter.
   _{send}
2. I _____ to go to the courthouse on Fifth Street.
   _{tell}
3. My name _____.
   _{call}
4. I _____ a form to fill out.
   _{give}
5. A video about jury duty _____ on a large TV.
   _{show}
6. The jurors _____ to the third floor of the building.
   _{take}
7. I _____ a lot of questions by the lawyers.
   _{ask}
8. I _____ for the jury.
   _{choose}

EXERCISE 7 Fill in the blanks with the passive voice of the verb given. Use the present perfect.

1. The jurors ___have been given___ a lot of information.
   _{give}
2. Many books _____ about the courts.
   _{write}
3. Many movies _____ about criminal trials.
   _{make}
4. Many people _____ for jury duty.
   _{choose}
5. Your name _____ for jury duty.
   _{select}
6. The check _____ with the clerk.
   _{leave}
7. The check _____ in an envelope.
   _{put}
8. A notice about jury duty _____ to your house.
   _{send}

EXERCISE 8 Fill in the blanks with the passive voice of the verb given. Use the future with *will*.

1. You ___will be taken___ to a courtroom.
   _{take}
2. You _____ to stand up when the judge enters the room.
   _{tell}
3. Each of you _____ a lot of questions.
   _{ask}
4. The lawyers _____.
   _{introduce}
5. Information about the case _____ to you.
   _{present}
6. Twelve of you _____.
   _{select}
7. Besides the 12 jurors, two alternates _____.
   _{choose}
8. All of you _____.
   _{pay}

Unit 13

EXERCISE 9 Fill in the blanks with the passive voice for each of the underlined verbs.

1. The jury took a vote. The vote _____was taken_____ after three hours.

2. The lawyers asked a lot of questions. The questions _____ in order to find facts.

3. The court will pay us. We _____ $20 a day.

4. They told us to wait. We _____ to wait on the second floor.

5. They gave us instructions. We _____ instructions about the law.

6. People pay for the services of a lawyer. Lawyers _____ a lot of money for their services.

7. You should use a pen to fill out the form. A pen _____ for all legal documents.

8. They showed us a film about the court system. We _____ the film before we went into the courtroom.

9. Someone needs to tell us what to do. We _____ how the jury system works.

10. Many people consider *Brown v. The Board of Education* a very important case. It _____ an important step toward the end of inequalities.

13.4 Negatives and Questions with the Passive Voice

Compare statements, *yes/no* questions, short answers, *wh-* questions, and subject questions.

AFFIRMATIVE STATEMENT:	They **are permitted** to talk to other jurors.
NEGATIVE STATEMENT:	They **aren't permitted** to talk to family members.
YES/NO QUESTION:	**Are** they **permitted** to eat in the courtroom?
SHORT ANSWER:	No, they **aren't**. /No, they**'re not**.
WH- QUESTION:	What **are** they **permitted** to do in the courtroom?
NEGATIVE WH- QUESTION:	Why **aren't** they **permitted** to talk to family members?
SUBJECT QUESTION:	Who **is permitted** in the courtroom?

EXERCISE 10 Write *A* if the sentence is active. Write *P* if the sentence is passive.

1. Did you go to court last week? _____A_____

2. Which courtroom were you sent to? _____

3. The jurors didn't agree with each other. _____

4. Jurors aren't paid a lot of money. _____

5. I haven't been selected for a jury. _____

continued

6. Some jurors won't be needed. _____

7. How many questions did the lawyers ask you? _____

8. Did you receive a letter for jury duty? _____

9. How are justices selected for the Supreme Court? _____

10. Which justice will resign next? _____

EXERCISE 11 Fill in the blanks with the negative form of the underlined verbs.

1. I <u>was selected</u> for jury duty last year. I _____wasn't selected_____ this year.

2. The jurors <u>are paid</u>. They _____ a lot of money.

3. Twelve people <u>were chosen</u>. People who don't understand English well _____.

4. We <u>are allowed</u> to eat in the waiting room. We _____ to eat in the courtroom.

5. We <u>were told</u> to keep an open mind. We _____ how to vote.

EXERCISE 12 Change the statements to questions using the words given.

1. The jurors are paid. (*how much*)

   How much are the jurors paid?

2. The jurors are given a lunch break. (*when*)

   _____

3. I wasn't chosen for the jury. (*why*)

   _____

4. You were given information about the case. (*what kind of information*)

   _____

5. Several jurors have been sent home. (*which jurors*)

   _____

FUN WITH GRAMMAR

Be a news reporter. Work with a partner to prepare a short TV news report. The goal is to use the passive voice correctly and effectively. The news can be true or made up. You can talk about any news topic: the weather, famous people, crime, politics, personal interest stories, etc. The class will listen and write down uses of the passive. Then the class will vote on the most engaging news report.

Who Owns the Photo?

Read the following article. Pay special attention to the bold and underlined verbs. 13.4

In 2011, wildlife photographer David Slater <u>traveled</u> to Indonesia to photograph an endangered type of monkey, the crested black macaque. For days, Slater followed a group of these animals through a forest. One afternoon, when the group stopped to rest, Slater put his camera on a stand and moved away. A few minutes later, several monkeys approached the camera and started to play with it. Some pressed buttons and began taking photos of themselves. By the end, Slater had hundreds of monkey selfies[1]. One **was taken** by a female macaque. In the photo, she <u>seems</u> to be smiling. The image **was published** by different news media and <u>became</u> famous worldwide.

In the summer of 2011, Slater's famous photo <u>appeared</u> on Wikipedia, a popular U.S. website. Slater contacted the company and <u>complained</u>. He asked the website to remove the photo, or to pay him for using it. His request **was rejected**. Why? Slater didn't hold the copyright[2], Wikipedia said. It **was owned** by the monkey—because she took the picture. But since a copyright **cannot be held** by an animal, Wikipedia argued, the photo **could be used** by anyone for free.

Today, the famous monkey selfie <u>remains</u> on Wikipedia—where it **can be downloaded** by anyone—and Slater's fight with the company continues. A photographer does more than just press a button on a camera, Slater has said. When this case **is heard** in court, he hopes a judge will agree.

Some good <u>has come</u> from this situation, though. The legal case has attracted a lot of international attention, and people have begun protecting the crested black macaque. Slater has also agreed to help. He is donating 10 percent of the money that **is made** from the sale of the monkey photos to a conservation group. "I only wanted to help these animals—and I still do," says Slater. Now he hopes the legal system will help him.

The monkey in the photo took this picture of herself.

Crested black macaques **are hunted** for their meat. Their environment **is** also **threatened** by human development. Because of this, there are only about 100,000 of them today.

---
[1] selfie: a photo that someone takes of himself or herself
[2] copyright: the legal ownership of a photo, book, song, etc., which gives a person the exclusive right to publish or sell the material and make money from it

Active and Passive Voice

COMPREHENSION Based on the reading, write T for *true* or F for *false*.

1. _____ The photo of the smiling monkey was taken by David Slater.
2. _____ In Wikipedia's opinion, the monkey photo isn't owned by David Slater.
3. _____ Because of David Slater's legal case, people have begun protecting the crested black macaque.

THINK ABOUT IT

1. Imagine that you are Wikipedia's lawyer. Why, in your opinion, can the monkey photo be used for free? Then imagine that you are David Slater's lawyer. Why, in your opinion, does your client own the photo?
2. Which side do you agree with and why?

13.5 Transitive and Intransitive Verbs

Transitive verbs have an object. Intransitive verbs have no object.

EXAMPLES	EXPLANATION
(A) Wikipedia **published** the photo of the monkey. (P) The photo of the monkey **was published** by Wikipedia.	Transitive verbs have an active (A) and a passive (P) form.
(A) A monkey **took** the photo. (P) The photo **was taken** by a monkey.	The active voice is more common than the passive voice when there is a specific agent.
In the photo, the monkey **seems** to be smiling. The photo **became** famous worldwide. The photo **appeared** on Wikipedia. Slater **complained** about this. The famous photo **remains** on Wikipedia.	Intransitive verbs don't have a passive form. Some intransitive verbs are: *arrive, be, become, come, complain, depend, die, fall, go, grow* (in a natural way), *happen, laugh, leave* (a place), *occur, rain, recover* (from an illness), *remain, run, sleep, stay,* and *work*. The sense perception verbs are also usually intransitive: *appear, feel, look, seem, smell, sound,* and *taste*.

Notes:

1. Even though *have* and *want* are followed by an object, these verbs are not usually used in the passive voice.

    *Slater **has** a famous photo.* (NOT: *A famous photo is had by Slater.*)

    *He **wants** a new camera.* (NOT: *A new camera is wanted by him.*)

2. Some verbs can be used both as transitive verbs and intransitive verbs.

    *The monkeys **stopped** to rest.* (intransitive)

    *The reporter **stopped** Slater and asked a question. Slater **was stopped** by the reporter.* (transitive)

EXERCISE 13 Circle the correct word(s) to complete each sentence.

1. David Slater (**takes**/*is taken*) photos of endangered animals.
2. The photo of a smiling monkey (*took*/*was taken*) in Indonesia.
3. Wikipedia (*used*/*was used*) the photo without Slater's permission.
4. Slater contacted Wikipedia. He said the photo (*should remove*/*should be removed*) from the website.
5. Slater said, "An artist's work (*cannot use*/*cannot be used*) for free."
6. Wikipedia (*rejected*/*was rejected*) Slater's request.
7. Now the case (*will go*/*will be gone*) to court.
8. Some good things (*have happened*/*have been happened*) because of this case.
9. For years, crested black macaques (*have hunted*/*have been hunted*) for their meat or (*have kept*/*have been kept*) as pets.
10. As a result, many of these animals (*have died*/*have been died*).
11. But now, the monkeys (*protected*/*are protected*) in some places.
12. Conservationists hope that more of the monkeys (*can save*/*can be saved*).

EXERCISE 14 Look at each underlined verb in the conversation. If it is correct, put a check (✓). If it is incorrect, write the correct active or passive form.

A: Why weren't you in school yesterday?

B: I ___was had___ [had] jury duty. It ___was___ [✓] interesting.
    1.   2.

A: What ___was happened___ ?
          3.

B: A woman ___was sued___ her employer.
              4.

A: Why?

B: The woman ___was injured___ on the job. She ___complained___, but the company ___wasn't helped___
                 5.   6.   7.
   her. The case ___went___ to court, and the woman ___won___ a lot of money.
                    8.   9.

A: How much ___was___ she ___paid___?
               10.   11.

B: She ___gave___ three million dollars by the court.
         12.

A: Wow! Was the woman happy?

B: Yes. She ___was appeared___ to be very happy.
               13.

A: Now that jury duty is over, you don't have to do it again. Right?

B: No, that's not true. A person ___can chosen___ for jury duty more than once.
                                    14.

EXERCISE 15 Find and underline the verb in each sentence. Then identify which sentences can be changed to the passive voice and change those sentences. If no change is possible, write *NC* (*no change*).

1. In the photo, the monkey <u>appears</u> to be smiling.

   NC

2. Wikipedia <u>used</u> the photo without Slater's permission.

   The photo was used (by Wikipedia) without Slater's permission.

3. Slater became angry about this.

   _____

4. Wikipedia didn't pay Slater for his work.

   _____

5. Anyone can download the photo of the smiling monkey.

   _____

6. In the future, a judge will decide Slater's case.

   _____

7. Laws protect us.

   _____

8. Some court cases seem silly.

   _____

9. The Supreme Court has decided important cases.

   _____

10. Jurors should arrive on time to court.

    _____

ABOUT YOU Read the sentences in the chart. Write the correct active or passive form of the verb in parentheses. Think about a country's legal system you know about. For each sentence, check *yes* or *no*. Then work with a partner. Use the sentences in the chart to ask and answer questions.

Country: _____

	YES	NO
1. Citizens (select) _____are selected_____ to be on a jury.		
2. People (represent) _____ by lawyers in court.		
3. Jurors (pay) _____ for their service in court.		
4. The laws (be) _____ fair.		
5. Famous trials (show) _____ on TV.		
6. The death penalty (use) _____ in some cases.		
7. The country (have) _____ a Supreme Court.		
8. Lawyers (respect) _____, and they make good money, so many people (become) _____ attorneys.		

A: I know about the legal system in Spain.
B: In Spain, are citizens selected to be on a jury?
A: Yes. In some cases, people are selected to be on a jury.

Among major law schools in the U.S., Yale University had the lowest acceptance rate for the fall of 2018.

SUMMARY OF UNIT 13

Active and Passive Voice—Forms

ACTIVE	PASSIVE
Sam **drove** the car.	The car **was driven** (by Sam).
Sam **didn't drive** the car.	The car **wasn't driven** (by Sam).
Sam **will drive** the car.	The car **will be driven** (by Sam).
Sam **has driven** the car.	The car **has been driven** (by Sam).
Sam often **drives** the car.	The car **is** often **driven** (by Sam).
Sam **should drive** the car.	The car **should be driven** (by Sam).
Sam **needs to drive** the car.	The car **needs to be driven** (by Sam).
Did Sam **drive** the car?	**Was** the car **driven** (by Sam)?
When **did** Sam **drive** the car?	When **was** the car **driven** (by Sam)?
Why **didn't** Sam **drive** the car?	Why **wasn't** the car **driven** (by Sam)?

The Active Voice—Use

EXAMPLES	EXPLANATION
I **hired** an attorney. The attorney **prepared** the evidence. She **will present** the evidence in court.	In most cases, when either the active or passive can be used, we use the active voice.
The accident **happened** last month. She **went** to court.	When the verb is intransitive (it has no object), the active voice must be used. There is no choice.

The Passive Voice—Use

EXAMPLES	EXPLANATION
I **was chosen** for jury duty.	The agent is not known or is not important.
The criminal **was taken** to jail.	The agent is obvious.
Jury duty **is considered** a responsibility of every citizen.	The agent is everybody or people in general.
The court paid me. I **was paid** at the end of the day.	The emphasis is shifted from the agent to the receiver of the action.
It **was discovered** that many accidents are the result of driver distraction.	When talking about general beliefs and findings, we begin with *It*.
Accidents **are caused** by distracted drivers.	The emphasis is on the receiver of the action more than on the agent. (In this case, the agent is included in a *by* phrase.)

REVIEW

Fill in the blanks with the active or passive voice of the verb given.

In many countries, laws __have been passed__ (1. present perfect: *pass*) that prohibit drivers from using cell phones while driving. In a few countries, such as Japan, both hand-held and hands-free cell phone use _____ (2. present perfect: *ban*). In the United States, the law _____ (3. simple present: *depend*) on the place where you _____ (4. simple present: *live*). States _____ (5. present perfect: *start*) to become tougher on drivers who use cell phones. In New York, for example, the use of hand-held cell phones while driving _____ (6. simple present: *prohibit*), but the use of hands-free devices _____ (7. simple present: *permit*). A driver who _____ (8. simple present: *not/obey*) this law can be fined $50 for a first offense, $50–$200 for a second offense, and $50–$400 after that. In addition, a driver _____ (9. *can/lose*) his or her license for two to six months. In Alaska, the fine for using a hand-held device while driving is $10,000. A driver _____ (10. *can/even/send*) to jail for up to one year. Texting while driving _____ (11. present perfect: *become*) an even greater problem. Drivers _____ (12. simple present: *need*) to look away from the road in order to text. The risk of causing an accident while texting is 23 times higher than it is while driving without this distraction. Each year, nearly 390,000 people _____ (13. simple present: *injure*) in cell phone-related crashes.

But the problem of driver distraction is not only a result of cell phones and texting. According to one study, it _____ (14. simple past: *find*) that 80 percent of accidents _____ (15. simple present: *cause*) by drivers who are not paying attention. This study _____ (16. simple past: *determine*) that drivers _____ (17. simple present: *distract*) by many things: eating, putting on makeup, reading, reaching for things, and changing stations on the radio.

Over 3,000 people _____ (18. simple past: *kill*) in 2018 as a result of driver distraction. It is clear that all drivers _____ (19. simple present: *need*) to give driving their full attention.

Active and Passive Voice   355

FROM GRAMMAR TO WRITING

PART 1 Editing Advice

1. Never use *do, does,* or *did* to form the passive voice.

   The criminal ~~didn't find~~ wasn't found.

   Where ~~did~~ were the jurors taken?

2. Don't use the passive voice with *happen, die, become, sleep, work, live, fall, seem,* or other intransitive verbs.

   The accident ~~was~~ happened three weeks ago.

3. Don't confuse the *-ing* form with the past participle.

   The criminal was ~~taking~~ taken to jail.

4. Don't forget the *-ed* ending for a regular past participle.

   My cousin was select**ed** to be on a jury.

5. Don't forget to use *be* with a passive sentence.

   The evidence **was** presented in court.

6. Use the correct word order with adverbs.

   I was ~~selected never~~ never selected to be on a jury.

PART 2 Editing Practice

Some of the shaded words and phrases have mistakes. Find the mistakes and correct them. If the shaded words are correct, write C.

I ~~wasn't~~ didn't come to class last week. My classmates **wanted** (C) to know if I was sick. I explained that I **had**
1.   2.   3.
jury duty. Only citizens of the United States **can serve** on a jury, so my friends were surprised. But I
                                                                 4.
was become a citizen six months ago. Last month, I **was received** a letter in the mail telling me I had to
5.   6.
report for duty. I'm still an ESL student, and my English is far from perfect, but I **was selected**. I **was ask**
                                                                                                                              7.   8.
a lot of questions, and I **answered** them without a problem. Many people **were rejected**, and I don't know
                                       9.   10.
why, but I **chosen**.
                  11.

The case was about a traffic accident. Here's what **was happened**: A man **hit** a woman's car and
                                                                                   12.   13.
was left the scene of the accident. Her car **was badly damage**. Luckily, the woman **didn't injured**. The
14.   15.   16.
woman **saw** the driver's license plate and **wrote** down the number. She also **was taken** a picture of the car
             17.   18.   19.
with her cell phone as the driver was leaving. She called the police. The police **caught** him. He **was driven**
                                                                                                                                           20.   21.
without a license. They also determined that the man **was texting** while driving. My friends asked me,
                                                                                    22.

356 Unit 13

"How was that determined? The police checked the phone records and was found that at the exact time
              23.   24.
of the accident, he was texting. The case lasted for two days. All the jurors were agreed that the man was
                                          25.   26.
guilty. The man was given a $500 fine. His driver's license was suspended for one year.
              27.   28.

I think a lot of accidents are cause by people talking on the phone or texting while driving. According
                               29.
to the law, we're not permit to text and drive. But in some places, you can talk on the phone and drive. I
           30.
hope that the law will be changed and talking on a cell phone will be against the law, too.
                    31.   32.

WRITING TIP
When writing, think carefully about whether the active or passive voice is more appropriate. For example, if you choose prompt 1 below, you might use constructions such as:

I was told/asked/instructed to . . .

For prompt 2, you might use constructions such as:

The man was sentenced/convicted/released.

After you complete a writing assignment, read it through and check for uses of the passive. Confirm that each passive construction is suitable. If you aren't sure, try putting the sentence into active voice and see if this makes the sentence stronger. Sometimes you may need additional information in order to use the active voice.

The man was sentenced to five years in prison. (passive) → *Judge Andrews sentenced the man to five years in prison.* (active)

PART 3 Write
Read the prompts. Choose one and write a paragraph about it.

1. Write about an experience you have had with the court system in the United States or your native country.
2. Write about a famous court case that you know of. Do you agree with the decision of the jury?
   (If you research your topic, attach a copy of your sources.)

PART 4 Edit
Reread the Summary of Unit 13 and the editing advice. Edit your writing from Part 3.

UNIT

14

Articles
Other/Another
Indefinite Pronouns

MONEY

Workers compare blown-up sections of counterfeit, or fake, $100 bills with a real bill enlarged 400 times.

> Making money isn't hard in itself. What's hard is to earn it doing something worth devoting your life to.
> CARLOS RUIZ ZAFÓN

Millennials AND Money

Read the following article. Pay special attention to the words in bold. 14.1

You've probably been hearing a lot about millennials these days. What, exactly, is **a millennial**? **A millennial** is **a person** born between 1981 and 1996. This is **the** largest **group** of Americans, 78 million. Within the next two years, **millennials** will make up 50 percent of **the workforce**[1]. By 2030, they will be **the majority** of **the workforce** at 75 percent and **the largest group** of consumers, so **marketers** are especially interested in this group and their spending habits.

Millennials' attitudes towards **money** and spending are different from those of their parents, **the "Baby Boomers"** (born between 1946 and 1964), or **"Generation Xers,"** (born between 1965 and 1980). First, they often shop online, where they can compare **prices**, **products**, and **vendors**. They are more influenced by **the opinions** of other consumers than by **the recommendations** of family and friends. Second, they prefer to rent **things** rather than own them; they prefer movie and music **subscriptions** rather than **ownership** of DVDs or CDs. They get their music and movies on their smartphones, tablets, or computers. A significant number of them don't even own **a television**. Third, they like to spend their money on life experiences, such as **entertainment**, **restaurants**, and **travel** rather than on **goods**. They often have **the attitude** of "YOLO": You Only Live Once. They want to experience all **life** has to offer. Generally, they are optimistic[2] about **the future**.

What influences these attitudes? At **the end** of 2007, the United States went into a deep economic recession[3]. **The** average **salary** for a person just out of college in 2013 was $34,500. This was **the** lowest starting **salary** for a college graduate since 1998. And recent college graduates have been entering **the** job **market** with huge college **debt**[4]. As a result, millennials have learned to be careful with **money**. They are getting married later than previous **generations**, and many don't believe in spending a lot of **money** on an expensive **wedding**. They often use **public transportation** and **bicycles** for short **trips** or use car-sharing **services**. They prefer to rent **an apartment** rather than buy **a house** because they don't want large financial **commitments**.

American **millennials** spend $600 billion **dollars** a year. **Marketers** need to understand **the mentality** and **habits** of millennnials if they wish to attract their dollars.

---

[1] workforce: all workers employed in a specific area
[2] optimistic: believing that good things will happen
[3] recession: a time when economic activity is not strong
[4] debt: an amount of money owed

Percent of Annual Spending on Major Categories
by Millennials, Gen Xers, & Baby Boomers

Category	Millennials	Gen Xers	Baby Boomers
Food at home	7.2	7.1	7.2
Food away from home	6.3	5.8	5.1
Housing	35.7	32.7	31.5
Clothing	3.7	3.2	2.7
Transportation	16.8	16.1	15.9
Healthcare	5.6	6.5	9.4
Entertainment	4.9	5.8	5.4

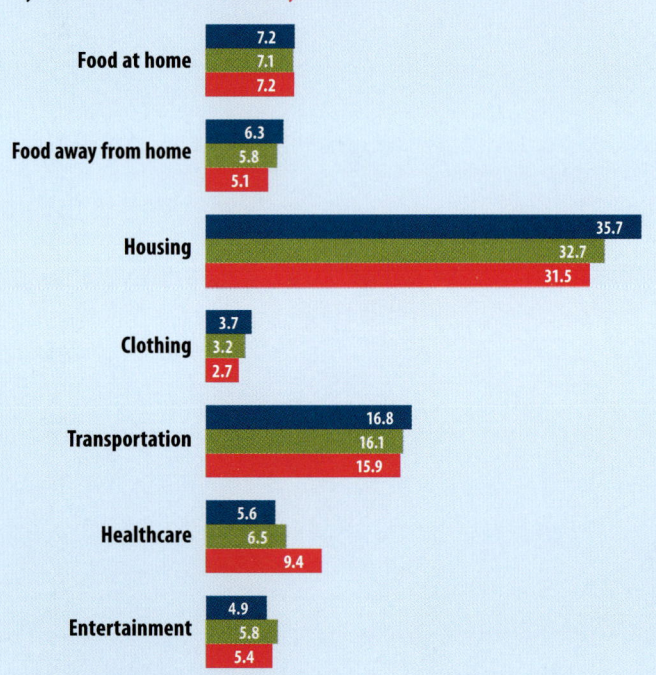

Data source: Bureau of Labor Statistics

Marketers need to do more research on millennial spending habits. Despite differences in values, these three generations have some similar spending habits.

COMPREHENSION Based on the reading, write T for *true* or F for *false*.

1. _____ Millennials make their buying decisions mostly on recommendations from friends.
2. _____ Millenials buy a lot of CDs and DVDs.
3. _____ Millennials make up the largest portion of Americans today.

THINK ABOUT IT Discuss the questions with a partner or in a small group.

1. Which generation do you belong to—Millennial? Gen X? Baby Boomer? Do you think the article describes these generations correctly?
2. What does "You only live once" (YOLO) mean to you? Do you share the YOLO attitude?

14.1 Articles—An Overview

EXAMPLES	EXPLANATION
Do you want **an** expensive wedding? **A** college graduate wants to find **a** good job.	The indefinite articles *a* and *an* are used before a noun to refer to non-specific things and people (singular only).
Many people use **the** Internet to shop online. **The** boomers were born between 1946 and 1964.	The definite article *the* is used before a noun to refer to specific things and people (singular or plural).
Marketers are interested in **millennials**. **Ownership** of DVDs does not interest **millennials**.	A noun can be used without an article to refer to non-specific things and people.

EXERCISE 1 Listen to the paragraphs. Then write T for *true* or F for *false*. 14.2

1. _____ Historically, each generation in America has had a better standard of living than their parents.
2. _____ Millennials aren't different from their parents in spending.
3. _____ Getting married isn't a top priority for millennials.

EXERCISE 2 Listen to the paragraphs again. Fill in the blanks with the article you hear. If you don't hear an article, fill in the blank with Ø. 14.2

___Ø___ Millennials are ___the___ first generation in American history to have
1.   2.

_____ lower standard of living than their parents. Millennials looking for _____ job
3.   4.

in 2010 faced _____ unemployment rate of almost 10 percent. _____ average debt for
                        5.   6.

_____ millennial college graduate in 2013 was approximately $30,000. In _____
7.   8.

recent book called _____ *Next America*, _____ author, Paul Taylor, describes
                                    9.   10.

_____ economic changes we will see as boomers retire.
11.

continued

Millennials are not only different from their parents' generation in spending. They are _____ 12. first generation to grow up with _____ 13. technology. _____ 14. amount of time it takes _____ 15. product to reach a 50 percent adoption by _____ 16. consumers has become much shorter. It took 31 years for radio to reach 50 percent of consumers; television, 28 years; home computers, 18 years; smartphones, three and a half years. Consumers have adopted _____ 17. smartphones 10 times faster than they adopted _____ 18. computers.

Millennials also have _____ 19. different values from their parents. In 2018, 27 percent of millennials between 18 and 32 were married. In 1980, 48 percent of _____ 20. boomers in this age group were married. Millennials value _____ 21. fun and _____ 22. discovery. Boomers value _____ 23. family and _____ 24. practicality.

14.2 Making Generalizations

EXAMPLES	EXPLANATION

Smartphones are more popular than **flip phones**.
A smartphones is more popular than **a flip phone**.
	We can make a generalization about a count subject in two ways:
	    no article + plural noun
	    OR
	    a or *an* + singular noun

Fun is important for young people. **Ownership** is not important for millennials.	We don't use an article to make a generalization about a noncount subject.
Millennials like **movies**. Millennials value **discovery**.	To make a generalization about an object, count or noncount, we don't use an article. We use the plural form for count nouns. Noncount nouns are always singular.

EXERCISE 3 Match the subject on the left with the verb phrase on the right.

1. A shopper
2. TVs
3. Kids
4. Parents
5. Advertising
6. Parents often tell kids that
7. Grandparents
8. A child
9. Life

are expensive.
is short. You only live once (YOLO).
is often directed at millennials.
wants to get a good price.
often buy toys for their children.
like to give gifts to their grandchildren.
money doesn't grow on trees.
needs to learn about money.
want to have toys.

362 Unit 14

EXERCISE 4 Complete the sentences to make generalizations about the subjects given. You may work with a partner.

1. Millennials _____ have different values from their parents. _____
2. A college graduate _____
3. Consumers _____
4. Life for older Americans _____
5. Good jobs _____
6. A wedding _____
7. Technology _____
8. Marketers _____
9. Boomers _____
10. DVDs _____
11. Money _____

ABOUT YOU Put a check (✓) next to the statements that are generally true in your country. Discuss your answers with a partner.

___ 1. A bank is a safe place to keep your money.
___ 2. Doctors make a lot of money.
___ 3. Teenagers have part-time jobs.
___ 4. Children work.
___ 5. Teachers earn a good salary.
___ 6. A government official makes a lot of money.
___ 7. Businesses are closed on Sundays.
___ 8. A college degree is needed to earn a good salary.

14.3 Classifying or Defining the Subject

EXAMPLES	EXPLANATION
A millennial is **a** person born between 1981 and 1996. "Recession" is **an** economic term.	We classify or define a singular count noun like this: Singular noun + *is* + *a(n)* + (adjective) + noun.
Boomers are **Americans** born between 1946 and 1964. CDs are compact **discs**.	We classify or define a plural count noun like this: Plural noun + *are* + (adjective) + noun.
What's a millennial? **What** are boomers?	We can ask for a definition with *what*.

Note:
We can also use *the* in a definition if the noun is specific.
   The Next America *is **the** name of a book.*
   *A salary is **the** amount of money you get from working at your job.*

EXERCISE 5 In the left column, fill in the blank with the verb and an article if needed. Then match the subject on the left with the definition or classification on the right.

1. YOLO _____is an_____ person born between 1946 and 1964.

2. A boomer _____ owed money.

3. A recession _____ book about the future of the United States.

4. Debt _____ abbreviation.

5. A vendor _____ kids between the ages of 13 and 19.

6. *The Next America* _____ person or company that sells something.

7. Paul Taylor _____ time when the economy isn't strong.

8. Teenagers _____ man who wrote *The Next America*.

EXERCISE 6 Define or classify the subject given. You may work with a partner.

1. A CD __is a disk that contains digital music.__

2. A quarter _____

3. A dime _____

4. A credit card _____

5. A debit card _____

6. A diamond _____

7. Silver and gold _____

8. Marketers _____

9. Consumers _____

10. A bank _____

11. A wallet _____

12. Expenses _____

> **GRAMMAR IN USE**
>
> When defining or classifying a subject, it is important to be aware of the verbs. Use the simple present for things, concrete or abstract, that exist in the current day, and for people who are alive.
>
> *Identity theft **is** the illegal use of another person's private identifying information.*
> *Bill Gates **is** an entrepreneur and businessman who founded Microsoft.*
>
> However, to describe something from the past, you would use the simple past.
>
> *Vikings **were** Scandinavian pirates who **attacked** the coasts of Europe from the 8th to 10th centuries.*

Many children have to do chores around the house.

KIDS and MONEY

Read the following article. Pay special attention to the words in bold. 14.3

Kids like to spend money. With part-time jobs, **an** allowance[1] from their parents, gifts from grandparents and others, and no bills to pay, kids have **the** most disposable income[2] of **any** part of American society. According to **a** 2019 statistic, teens between 15 and 17 have $4,900 **a** year to spend. While **some** teens think about saving their money, about 21 percent say they don't save **any** money at all.

The average American child gets **an** allowance of about $800 **a** year. In 90 percent of American homes, kids are expected to do **some** chores[3] in exchange for their allowance. In many cases, this is no more than one hour **a** week. What does **an** allowance teach **a** child about money? Many experts believe **the** answer is nothing!

Parents need to talk to kids about money early. When is **the** best time? **The** earlier **the** better, according to experts. Even preschool children can learn about money. For example, they can learn that you need money to buy things and that you earn money by working. They can learn that there is **a** difference between **the** things you want and **the** things you need. Between six and 10, children can learn to make choices and to compare prices. Between 11 and 13, they can learn that they should save 10 cents of every dollar they receive. Between 14 and 18, they should start to compare **the** cost of different colleges.

Warren Buffet is one of **the** most famous billionaires in **the** world. He says that **the** age at which parents teach their kids good financial habits will determine how successful **the** child will be later in life. Buffet taught his children **the** value of learning from experience. He allowed them to succeed and fail on their own. He did not help them financially if they got in **any** trouble. Interestingly, he is not planning on leaving his grown children **a** large inheritance[4]. He said, "I want to give my kids just enough so that they would feel that they could do anything, but not so much that they would feel like doing nothing."

---

[1] allowance: money children get from their parents for everyday expenses
[2] disposable income: money a person can spend after expenses
[3] chore: a household job, such as washing the dishes
[4] inheritance: money a person receives from someone who died

Articles, Other/Another, Indefinite Pronouns

COMPREHENSION Based on the reading, write T for *true* or F for *false*.

1. _____ Many experts believe that giving children an allowance teaches them the value of money.
2. _____ Most kids who get an allowance are expected to do several hours a week of chores.
3. _____ Warren Buffet plans to leave his children the majority of his wealth.

THINK ABOUT IT Discuss the questions with a partner or in a small group.

1. What is your opinion about giving a child an allowance? Is this common in your culture?
2. Reread the quote by Warren Buffet at the end of the article. Why might a person who has a lot of money feel like doing nothing? Do you think Warren Buffet is right to have this concern for his kids?

14.4 Non-Specific Nouns

EXAMPLES	EXPLANATION
She has **a** job. She gets **an** allowance.	We use *a* or *an* to introduce a singular non-specific count noun.
He has to do (**some**) chores. He doesn't have (**any**) chores on weekdays. Does he have (**any**) chores on Sunday?	We use *some* or *any* to introduce a plural non-specific count noun. *Some* and *any* can be omitted.
He needs (**some**) money. He doesn't have (**any**) cash. Is there (**any**) money in your checking account?	We use *some* and *any* to introduce a non-specific noncount noun.

Notes:
1. Both *some* and *any* can be used in questions with plural nouns and noncount nouns.
    *Do you have **some** money? Do you have **any** quarters?*
2. *Some* and *any* can be omitted.
    Do you have money? Do you have quarters?

EXERCISE 7 Fill in the blanks with *a, an, some, any,* or Ø (for no article) to complete the conversation between a son (A) and his mother (B). In some cases, more than one answer is possible.

A: Mom, I want to get ____*a*____ job.
   1.

B: But you're only 16 years old.

A: I'm old enough to work. I need to make _____ money.
                                              2.

B: Grandma and Grandpa always give you _____ money for your birthday. And we give you
                                         3.

_____ 15 dollars a week. Isn't that enough money for you?
   4.

A: It's not even enough to take _____ girl to _____ movie.
                                   5.   6.

B: What are you going to do about school? You won't have _____ time to study.
                                                           7.

A: You know I'm _____8._____ good student. I'm sure I won't have _____9._____ problems

working part-time. We don't have _____10._____ homework on weekends.

B: I'm worried about your grades falling. Maybe we should raise your allowance. Then you won't have to work.

A: I want to have my own money. I want to buy _____11._____ new clothes. And I'm going to save

_____12._____ money each week. Then I can buy _____13._____ car someday.

B: Why do you want a car? You have _____14._____ bike.

A: Bikes are great for exercise, but if my job is far away, I'll need a car for transportation.

B: So, you need _____15._____ job to buy _____16._____ car, and you need _____17._____

car to get to work.

A: Yes. My friends work, and they're good students. I'm not _____18._____ baby anymore. I really want

to work.

14.5 Specific Nouns

EXAMPLES	EXPLANATION
The reading on page 365 is about kids and money. **The photos** in this unit are related to money. What did you do with **the money** I gave you?	We use *the* with a specific noun. A noun is specific if it is defined in the phrase or clause after the noun.
The first reading in this unit is about millennials and money. When is **the right** time to talk to kids about money?	We use *the* when there is only one of something. We usually use *the* with the following words: *first, second, next, last, only, same, back, front,* and *right*.
Where's **the teacher**? I have a question about **the reading** on kids and money.	We use *the* when there is a shared experience. Students in the same class talk about *the* teacher, *the* textbook, *the* homework, *the* board.
Teenagers should put some of their savings in **the** bank. They want money to go to **the** movies with their friends.	We use *the* with certain familiar places and people: the bank the beach the bus the zoo the post office the train the park the doctor the movies the store the hospital
Warren Buffet is one of **the richest** people in the world. What's **the best** way to teach kids about money?	We use *the* before a superlative form.
Millennials often use **the Internet** to shop.	We use *the* before a unique noun.
You have **an allowance**. You can use **the allowance** to go out with your friends. There is **some money** on the table. You can use **the money** to go to the movies.	After a non-specific noun is introduced with *a/an/some/any*, we use the definite article to refer to a specific example of this noun.

continued

Notes:

1. We don't use *the* to make a generalization. Compare:

    Life today is very different from **life** 40 years ago. (Life *is general.*)

    The life of my grandparents is different from my life. (The life *is specific.*)

2. When we introduce a noun with *there + be*, we use the indefinite article. We can refer to the noun again with *the*.

    There was **a recession** in 2007. **The recession** affected a lot of people.

EXERCISE 8 Fill in the blanks with *a* or *the*.

A: I need to buy _____a_____ new laptop.

B: What's wrong with _____ laptop you have now?

A: It's too old.

B: There's _____ good website that compares computer prices.

A: Can you show me _____ website?

B: Sure. Let's look at my tablet.

A: That's _____ cool tablet you have.

B: Thanks. I don't even use _____ computer anymore.

A: Was _____ tablet expensive?

B: I got _____ good deal online.

EXERCISE 9 Fill in the blanks with *the, a, some,* or *any*.

A: Where are you going after class?

B: I'm going to ___the___ cafeteria. I want to buy _____ cup of coffee.

A: You don't have to go to _____ cafeteria. There's _____ coffee machine on this floor.

B: I only have _____ $10 bill. Do you have _____ change?

A: I have _____ change, but I need it for the parking meters. There's _____ dollar-bill changer next to _____ coffee machine.

B: Uh-oh. _____ coffee machine is out of order. I guess I'll have to go to _____ cafeteria after all. Do you want to go with me?

A: Sorry. I don't have _____ time.

368   Unit 14

EXERCISE 10 Fill in the blanks with *the, a, an, any, some* or Ø for no article. In some cases, more than one answer is possible.

1. **A:** Mom, I need to buy _____some_____ new jeans.
      a.

   B: There are _____ jeans on this rack. Which ones do you like?
              b.

   A: I love these. Don't you?

   B: But they're torn.

   A: That's _____ style these days.
                   c.

   B: I'll never understand _____ kids. In my day, _____ torn clothes meant you
                                        d.   e.

   were poor.

   A: That's silly.

   B: I think _____ life was better back then.
                    f.

   A: You always compare your childhood with today's kids, but _____ times have changed. So,
                                                                              g.

   what did you decide about _____ jeans? Can I buy them? I have enough money from
                                      h.

   _____ job I had last summer.
         i.

   B: I suppose so. Go try them on. _____ dressing room is over there.
                                                j.

2. **A:** Where are you going?

   B: To _____ store. I want to deposit _____ check, and I need to get
              a.   b.

   _____ cash. There's _____ ATM at _____ supermarket on
         c.   d.   e.

   _____ corner.
         f.

   A: I'll go with you.

   (At the ATM)

   B: Oh, no. Look. _____ ATM is out of order.
                              g.

   A: Don't worry. There's _____ ATM on _____ next corner.
                                        h.   i.

   B: That ATM doesn't belong to my bank. If I use it, I'll have to pay _____ fee.
                                                                                    j.

   A: How much is _____ fee?
                              k.

   B: It's usually $3.00 or $3.50. That's a lot of money to me. _____ more I save,
                                                                              l.

   _____ more I have to spend on _____ things I want.
         m.   n.

continued

3. **A:** I'm going to _____ post office. I need to buy _____ stamps.
   　　　　　　　　　　　　a.　　　　　　　　　　　　　　　　　　b.

   B: I'll go with you. I want to mail _____ package to my parents.
   　　　　　　　　　　　　　　　　　　　　c.

   A: What's in _____ package?
   　　　　　　　　　　d.

   B: _____ coat for my sister and _____ money for my mother.
   　　　e.　　　　　　　　　　　　　　　　　　　f.

   A: You should never send _____ money by mail. You should buy _____ money
   　　　　　　　　　　　　　　　　g.　　　　　　　　　　　　　　　　　　　　　　　　　h.

   order at _____ bank.
   　　　　　　i.

   B: How much does it cost?

   A: Well, if you have _____ account in _____ bank, it's usually free. If not, you'll
   　　　　　　　　　　　　　j.　　　　　　　　　　　k.

   probably have to pay _____ fee.
   　　　　　　　　　　　　l.

14.6 Specific or Non-Specific Nouns with Quantity Words

EXAMPLES	EXPLANATION
All children like toys. **Most** American homes have a television. **Few** people are billionaires.	We use *all, most, many, some, (a)/(very) few,* and *(a)/(very) little* before non-specific nouns.
All of the readings in this unit are about money. **Very few of the** people in my country are rich. **None of the** readings gives information about how to make money.	We use *all of the, most of the, many of the, some of the, (a)/(very) few of the, (a)/(very) little of the,* and *none of the* before specific nouns.

Notes:

1. After *all*, *of* is often omitted.

   All the readings in this unit are about money.

2. After *none of the* + plural noun, a singular verb is correct. However, a plural verb is often used in less formal speech or writing.

   None of the readings is long. (correct)

   None of the readings are long. (common)

3. Delete *the* when there is a possessive form.

   *He spent **all of his money** on a new car.*

4. Remember, *few* and *little* without *a* mean "not enough." We often put *very* before these words to emphasize that the quantity is not enough.

ABOUT YOU Fill in the blanks with *all, most, some,* or *(a)/(very) few* to make a general statement about your country or another country you know about. Discuss your answers with a partner.

1. _____Some_____ people have a car.
2. _____ schools have computers.
3. _____ teachers have a good salary.
4. _____ people use credit cards.
5. _____ kids get an allowance.
6. _____ parents buy a lot of toys for their children.
7. _____ college graduates can find a good job.
8. _____ people have a checking account.
9. _____ grandparents give their grandchildren a lot of gifts.

ABOUT YOU Fill in the blanks with a quantity word to make a statement about specific nouns.

1. ___A few of the___ students in this class are boomers.
2. _____ people I know are millennials.
3. _____ my friends shop online.
4. _____ students in this class have a job.
5. _____ people I know have a smartphone.
6. _____ older people in my family use technology.
7. _____ kids in my family use technology.
8. _____ computers at this school are new.

> **FUN WITH GRAMMAR**
>
> Role-play a conversation. Work with a partner. The teacher will write six quantity words on the board. Continue the conversation below for several exchanges, incorporating two of the quantity words correctly. Then role-play your conversation for the class as students listen for the quantity words and correct use of specific or non-specific nouns.
>
> A: I think **all Americans** are friendly.
> B: Well, . . .

Billionaires Jeff Bezos and Mark Zuckerberg

Billionaires

Read the following article. Pay special attention to the words in bold. 14.4

It's hard to imagine having over a billion dollars. Only about 2,100 people in the world are billionaires. The United States leads the world with the largest number. In 2018, the United States had over 500 billionaires. At the top of the list is Jeff Bezos, the founder of Amazon, with over $130 billion. **Another** area of the world that produces a large number of billionaires is China, with close to 400.

As hard as it is to imagine having over a billion dollars, try to imagine accumulating[1] this wealth before the age of 40! In 2018, Kylie Jenner became the youngest self-made billionaire ever at the age of 21. In 2014, a financial website, Bankrate.com, listed the 10 youngest billionaires in the world at the time. The richest, Mark Zuckerberg, the founder of Facebook, now has a net worth of over $62 billion. But he's not the only one to get rich from Facebook. **Another** person who became a billionaire from Facebook is Dustin Moskovitz. While **other** billionaires prefer to live a life of luxury, Moskovitz rides his bike to work and flies commercial airlines. Both Zuckerberg and Moskovitz have signed the Giving Pledge, which Warren Buffet and **another** famous billionaire, Bill Gates, started. The Giving Pledge has gotten the commitment[2] of Zuckerberg, Moskovitz, and **others** to give the majority of their wealth to philanthropy[3] while they're still alive.

The second richest person on Bankrate's list in 2014 was Yang Huiyan, from China. She made her money in real estate. She also inherited money from her father. She was the only woman on the list of young billionaires in 2014. All **the others** were men. With over $22 billion in 2018, she is on the list of global billionaires along with 241 **other** women.

Some of the billionaires on the list became rich mainly by inheriting family money. One of these is Fahd Hariri of Lebanon. He and his five siblings inherited their father's wealth when their father, the prime minister of Lebanon, was assassinated[4] in 2005. Hariri now owns a furniture company, which supplies furniture to **other** wealthy people, mostly in Saudi Arabia.

If we think about inheriting this large amount of money, we might think of what a nice life we can have. On **the other** hand, we might think, "Would easy money kill our motivation?"

---
[1] to accumulate: to gather together
[2] commitment: a promise
[3] philanthropy: the practice of giving money to people in need
[4] to assassinate: to kill

COMPREHENSION Based on the reading, write T for *true* or F for *false*.

1. _____ The wealthiest person in the world is from the United States.
2. _____ The richest person on Bankrate's list is a woman.
3. _____ All of the people on the list inherited money from their family.

THINK ABOUT IT Discuss the questions with a partner or in a small group.

1. If you had a billion dollars, would you commit to the Giving Pledge and give the majority of your wealth to philanthropy? Why or why not? If yes, which causes in particular would you contribute to?
2. Do you think easy money could kill your motivation? Do you think motivation is important for a happy life?

14.7 *Other* and *Another*

The use of *other* and *another* depends on whether a noun is singular or plural, specific or non-specific.

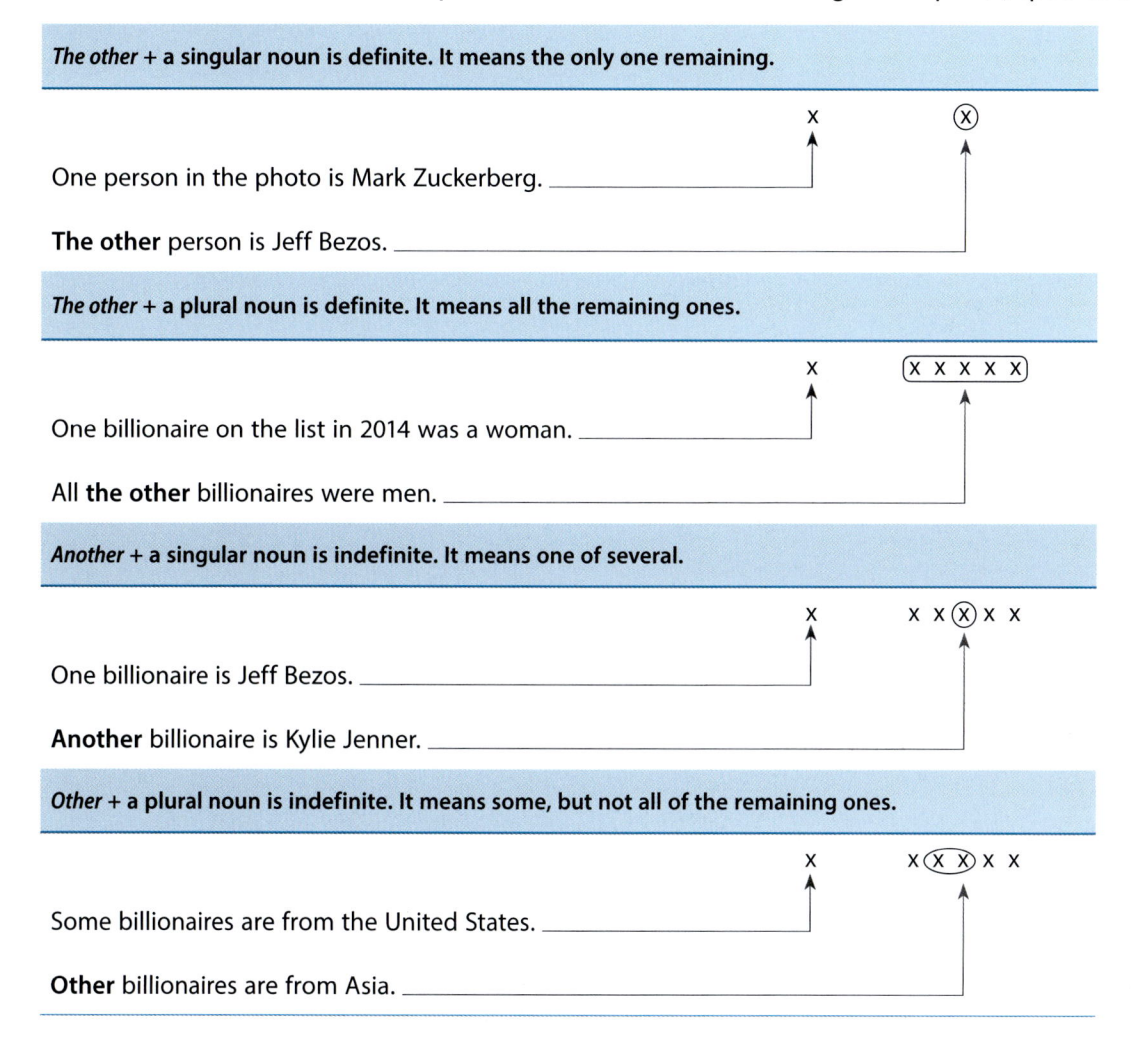

The other + a singular noun is definite. It means the only one remaining.

One person in the photo is Mark Zuckerberg.

The other person is Jeff Bezos.

The other + a plural noun is definite. It means all the remaining ones.

One billionaire on the list in 2014 was a woman.

All **the other** billionaires were men.

Another + a singular noun is indefinite. It means one of several.

One billionaire is Jeff Bezos.

Another billionaire is Kylie Jenner.

Other + a plural noun is indefinite. It means some, but not all of the remaining ones.

Some billionaires are from the United States.

Other billionaires are from Asia.

EXERCISE 11 Circle the correct words to complete this conversation.

A: Last month, I went to the doctor, and she sent me to get an X-ray. I got a bill and paid it, but then I got (**another**/*the other*) bill. Can you help me figure this out?

B: Let's see. Well, one bill is from the doctor. (*The other*/*Another*) bill is from the X-ray lab.

A: This is crazy.

B: I know, right? Wait for your insurance to pay. After your insurance pays, they'll send you (*another*/*other*) bill that shows the amount you have to pay.

A: There are two phone numbers. Which one should I call for information?

B: The first number is for telephone service. (*The other*/*Another*) number is a fax number.

A: How do I pay?

B: There are two methods of payment: One method is by check. (*Other*/*The other*) method is by credit card.

A: I hate paying bills. Every month, I get a gas bill, a cell phone bill, an electricity bill, a cable bill, and (*other*/*another*) bills. This is so confusing.

B: Some people send a check, but (*other*/*another*) people set up direct payment. Call the electric company and all (*other*/*the other*) companies to see if you can set up an automatic payment from your checking account. That way, you don't have to think about bills every month.

14.8 More about *Other* and *Another*

EXAMPLES	EXPLANATION
One young billionaire is Mark Zuckerberg. **Another billionaire** is Dustin Muskovitz. **Another one** is Dustin Muskovitz. **Another** is Dustin Muskovitz.	After *another* or *the other*, we can substitute a singular noun with *one*. We can also omit *one*.
One billionaire is a woman. **The other billionaires** are men. **The other ones** are men. **The others** are men.	After *other* or *the other*, we can substitute a plural noun with *ones*. We can also omit *ones*. If we omit it, we use *others*, not *other*.
This $10 bill is torn. Please give me **another** one.	*Another* is sometimes used to mean a different one, or one more.

Note:
We omit *the* when we use a possessive form.

   I have two bank accounts. One account is a checking account. **My other** *account is a savings account.* (NOT: *My the other*)

EXERCISE 12 Fill in the blanks with *the other, another, the others,* or *other* to complete the conversation between a grandson (A) and his grandfather (B).

A: I want to buy __another__ pair of sneakers.
        1.

B: You already have about six pairs of sneakers. I bought you a new pair for your last birthday.

A: The new pair is fine, but all _____ are too small for me. You know I'm growing very
                                            2.
fast, so I threw them away.

B: Why did you throw them away? _____ boys in your neighborhood could use them.
                                            3.

A: They wouldn't like them. They're out of style.

B: You kids are so wasteful today. What's wrong with the sneakers I bought you last month? If they fit you, why

do you need _____ pair?
                    4.

A: Everybody in my class at school has red sneakers with the laces tied backward.

B: Do you always have to have what all _____ kids in school have? Can't you think for
                                                    5.
yourself?

A: Didn't you ask your parents for stuff when you were in middle school?

B: My parents were poor, and my two brothers and I worked to help them. When we outgrew our clothes, we

gave them to _____ families nearby. And our neighbors gave us the things that their
                    6.
children outgrew. One neighbor had two sons. One son was a year older than me.

_____ one was two years younger. So we were constantly passing clothes back and
        7.
forth. We never threw things out. We didn't waste our parents' money. My oldest brother worked in a factory

and gave all his salary to our parents. My _____ brother and I helped our father in
                                                    8.
his business. My dad didn't give us a salary. It was our duty to help him.

A: You don't understand how important it is to look like all _____ kids.
                                                                        9.

B: I guess I don't. I'm old-fashioned. Every generation has _____ way of looking at
                                                                        10.
things.

Articles, *Other/Another*, Indefinite Pronouns **375**

14.9 Definite and Indefinite Pronouns

EXAMPLES	EXPLANATION
A: Did you read **the article** about **the billionaires**? **B:** Yes, I read **it** yesterday. Five of **them** are Americans.	We use definite pronouns *him, her, them,* and *it* to refer to specific count nouns.
I'm going to buy a laptop. I need **one** to take notes in class.	We use the indefinite pronoun *one* to refer to a non-specific singular count noun.
NONCOUNT: My son asked me for money. I didn't give him **any**. Do you think I should give him **some**? **COUNT:** I told him not to buy video games, but he bought **some**. I wanted him to buy books, but he didn't buy **any**.	With noncount nouns and plural count nouns, we refer to a non-specific noun as follows: • *some* for affirmative statements. • *any* for negative statements. • *some* or *any* for questions.

Notes:

1. We often use *any* and *some* before *more*.

    Son: *I don't have enough money. I need **some more**.*

    Dad: *I'm not going to give you **any more**.*

2. We can start with a non-specific noun, but when referring to it specifically, we use a definite pronoun.

    *I have **some questions** about one of the billionaires. Can you answer **them** for me?*

EXERCISE 13 Fill in the blanks with *one* or *it* to complete the conversation between a mother (A) and her teenage daughter (B).

A: I have a brochure from the state university. Do you want to look at ___it___ with me?
                                                                              1.

B: I don't know, Mom. I don't know if I want to go to college when I graduate.

A: Why not? We've been planning for _____ since the day you were born.
                                          2.

B: College isn't for everyone. I want to be an artist.

A: Artists don't make any money! You can be _____ and still go to college. Please choose a more
                                                  3.

practical career, like teaching.

B: I'm not really interested in a college degree.

A: But it's good to have _____ anyway.
                              4.

B: I don't know why. In college, I'll have to study general courses, too, like math and biology. You know I

hate math. I'm not good at _____.
                            5.

A: Maybe we should look at art schools. There's one downtown. Do you want to visit _____?
                                                                                          6.

B: We can probably find information about _____ online.
                                              7.

A: (*Looking at the art school website*) This school sounds great. Let's call and ask for an application.

B: I'm sure you can get _____ online.
8.

A: Oh, yes. Here it is. Let's print a copy of _____.
9.

B: You can fill _____ out online and submit _____ electronically.
10.   11.

EXERCISE 14 Fill in the blanks with *one, some, any, it, a, an, the,* or Ø (for no article) to complete the conversation between a teenager (A) and her mother (B). In some cases, more than one answer is possible.

A: Can I have 15 dollars? I want to buy _____a_____ poster of my favorite singer.
1.

B: I gave you _____ money last week. What did you do with _____?
2.   3.

A: I spent _____ on a movie.
4.

B: No, you can't have _____ more money until next week. Besides, why do you want a poster? You
5.

already have _____ of your favorite singer in your room.
6.

A: I took _____ down. I don't even like her anymore.
7.

B: What happened to all _____ money Grandpa gave you for your birthday?
8.

A: I don't have _____ money anymore. I spent _____.
9.   10.

B: You have to learn that _____ money doesn't grow on trees. If you want me to give you
11.

_____, you'll have to work for it. You can start by cleaning your room.
12.

A: But I cleaned _____ two weeks ago.
13.

B: That was two weeks ago. It's dirty again.

A: I don't have _____ time. I have to meet my friends.
14.

B: You can't go out. You need to do your homework.

A: I don't have _____. Please let me have 15 dollars.
15.

B: When I was your age, I had _____ job.
16.

A: I wanted to get a job last summer, but I couldn't find _____.
17.

B: You didn't try hard enough. When I worked, I gave my parents half of _____ money I earned. You
18.

kids today have _____ easy life.
19.

A: Why do _____ parents always say that to _____ kids?
20.   21.

B: Because it's true. It's time you learn that _____ life is hard.
22.

Articles, *Other/Another*, Indefinite Pronouns   **377**

SUMMARY OF UNIT 14

Indefinite Articles

	COUNT—SINGULAR	COUNT—PLURAL	NONCOUNT
General	*A/AN* **A child** likes toys.	*Ø ARTICLE* **Children** like toys. I love **children**.	*Ø ARTICLE* **Money** can't buy happiness. Everyone needs **money**.
Non-Specific	*A/AN* I bought **a toy**.	*SOME/ANY* I bought **some toys**. I didn't buy **any games**. Did you buy **any games**?	*SOME/ANY* I spent **some money**. I didn't buy **any candy**. Do you have **any time**?
Classification/Definition	*A/AN* "Recession" is **an economic term**.	*Ø ARTICLE* Teenagers are **young adults**.	

Definite Articles

	COUNT—SINGULAR	COUNT—PLURAL	NONCOUNT
Specific	**The reading** on page 365 is about kids and money.	**The photos** in this unit are about money.	**The information** about millennials is interesting.
Unique	**The Internet** is a great tool.	**The Hawaiian Islands** are beautiful.	

Other/Another

	SPECIFIC	NON-SPECIFIC
Singular	the other book the other one the other my other book	another book another one another
Plural	the other books the other ones the others my other books	other books other ones others

Indefinite Pronouns

We use *one/some/any* to substitute for non-specific nouns.

Singular Count	I need a quarter. Do you have **one**?
Plural Count	I need some pennies. You have **some**.
Noncount	I don't have any change. Do you have **any**?

REVIEW

Circle the correct words to complete the conversation. (Ø means no article is needed.)

A: I bought my daughter (*a*/*the*/*some*) new doll for her birthday. Now she's asking me to buy her
    1.

(*the other*/*another*/*other*) one. There's nothing wrong with (*a*/*the*/*Ø*) doll I bought her last month. She just got
    2.   3.

bored with it.

B: That's how (*Ø*/*the*/*a*) kids are. They don't understand (*a*/*the*/*Ø*) value of money.
            4.   5.

A: You're right. They think that (*a*/*the*/*Ø*) money grows on trees.
                                     6.

B: I suppose it's our fault. We have to set (*Ø*/*a*/*the*) good example. On the one hand, we tell them to be careful
                                                 7.

about money. On (*the other*/*other*/*another*) hand, we buy a lot of things we don't really need. We use (*a*/*the*/*Ø*)
                   8.   9.

credit cards instead of (*a*/*the*/*Ø*) cash and worry about paying (*a*/*the*/*Ø*) bill later.
                          10.   11.

A: I suppose you're right. Last month, we bought (*the*/*a*/*Ø*) new TV.
                                                       12.

B: I thought you bought (*it*/*one*) last year.
                             13.

A: We did. But we were at the appliance store last month looking for (*the*/*a*/*Ø*) new dishwasher when we saw a
                                                                           14.

much bigger, better TV. We decided to get (*it*/*one*).
                                            15.

B: What did you do with (*the other*/*another*/*other*) TV?
                              16.

A: We put (*it*/*one*) in (*the*/*a*/*Ø*) basement. I suppose we didn't really need (*other*/*any other*/*another*) one.
                17.   18.   19.

B: Last weekend, my husband bought (*a*/*some*/*the*) new phone. He said (*a*/*the*/*Ø*) new one has better apps than
                                         20.   21.

(*another*/*other*/*the other*) one. And it has better games. He got tired of (*another*/*the others*/*the other*) games.
    22.   23.

A: Our kids are imitating us. We need to make (*some*/*any*/*the*) changes in our own behavior. I'm going to start
                                                    24.

(*a*/*the*/*Ø*) budget tonight. I'm going to start saving (*a*/*any*/*some*) money each month.
    25.   26.

B: Do you need (*a*/*any*/*the*) help with it? There's (*a*/*the*/*Ø*) course at the community college on how to manage
                     27.   28.

your money. Do you want to take it with me?

A: That's (*a*/*Ø*/*the*) good idea. How much does it cost?
                29.

B: I'm not sure. Some courses are $50 a course. (*Others*/*Other*/*Another*) courses are $100 a credit hour. We should
                                                       30.

take it no matter what it costs.

FROM GRAMMAR TO WRITING

PART 1 Editing Advice

1. Choose the correct article or Ø for no article.

   Warren Buffet is famous billionaire. *(a)*

   What is first job you had? *(the)*

   You should save ~~a~~ money for college.

2. Use *the* after a quantity word when the noun is specific.

   I spent most of money my grandparents gave me. *(the)*

3. Use a plural count noun after a quantity expression.

   A few of my friend have a part-time job. *(friends)*

4. *Another* is always singular.

   Some teenagers save their money. ~~Another~~ *Other* teenagers spend it without thinking about their future.

5. *A* and *an* are always singular.

   Mark Zuckerberg and Warren Buffet are ~~a~~ billionaires.

6. Use *a* or *an* for a definition or a classification of a singular count noun.

   A millennial is person born between 1981 and 1996. *(a)*

7. Don't use the definite article with a possessive form.

   I use two cards for my purchases. One is my credit card. My ~~the~~ other card is a debit card.

8. Don't use *the* to make a general statement about a noun.

   ~~The~~ Money doesn't buy happiness.

   ~~The~~ Children like toys.

9. Use an indefinite pronoun to substitute for a non-specific noun.

   I have a checking account. Do you have ~~it~~? *(one)*

10. Before a plural noun or pronoun, use *other*, not *others*.

    Some billionaires are from the United States. Other~~s~~ billionaires are from Asia.

PART 2 Editing Practice

Some of the shaded words and phrases have mistakes. Find the mistakes and correct them. If the shaded words are correct, write C.

I'm **a** teenager and I know this: ~~the~~ teenagers think a lot about **the** money. We want **money** to
    1. *C*   2.   3.   4.
buy **a new jeans** or sneakers. Or we want money to go out with our friends. We sometimes want
    5.
to go to **the** restaurant or to **a** movie. Most of **the my** friends try to get a job in the summer to
         6.   7.   8.
make **some** money. At the beginning of every summer, my friends always say, "I need **a** job. Do
     9.   10.
you know where I can find **it**?"
                           11.
    One of my **friend** found a summer job at Bender's. Bender's is **small bookstore**. **Another**
              12.   13.   14.
friend found a job at a summer camp. But I have **the other** way to make money. I prefer to
                                                 15.
work in my neighborhood. **Most of people** in my neighborhood are working or elderly. I ask
                          16.
my neighbors for work. Some neighbors pay me to take care of **the** lawn in front of their house.
                                                              17.
Another neighbors pay me to clean their garage. In the winter, I shovel **a sidewalks** in front of
   18.   19.
their houses. I like these jobs. I love **a music**, and I listen to my favorite music while I work.
                                         20.
    What do I do with **the** money I get from my jobs? I buy songs on **Internet**. I used to buy
                      21.   22.
CDs, but I only liked a few songs. **Some of songs** on the CDs were great, but I never listened to
                                    23.
anothers. Now I can download **the** songs I like and not pay for all **the others** songs on a CD. This
  24.   25.   26.
helps me save money. With the money I save, I can buy **the other** things I want.
                                                       27.

WRITING TIP
When writing an introduction, grab the readers' attention with an interesting piece of information. If you choose prompt 1, you can start with some statistics. For example, *Did you know that kids in the U.S. earn an average of $67.80 per month?* For prompt 2, one possible way to pull in the reader is with a series of questions directed at a teen. For example, *Do you need money to upgrade your phone or to get a new pair of sneakers?* Engaging openers captivate readers and make them want to read more.

PART 3 Write
Read the prompts. Choose one and write about it.

1. Do you think children should get an allowance from their parents? How much? Does it depend on the child's age? Should the child have to do chores for the money? Write a few paragraphs explaining your point of view.
2. Write a short essay giving advice to teenagers on how to earn and save money.

PART 4 Edit
Reread the Summary of Unit 14 and the editing advice. Edit your writing from Part 3.

APPENDIX A

SUMMARY OF VERB TENSES

VERB TENSE	FORM	MEANING AND USE
SIMPLE PRESENT	I **have** class Mondays. He **doesn't have** class today. **Do** you **have** class today? **What do** you **do** every day?	• facts, general truths, habits, and customs • used with frequency adverbs, e.g., *always, usually, sometimes, never* • regular activities and repeated actions
PRESENT CONTINUOUS	I **am studying** biology this semester. He **isn't studying** now. **Are** you **studying** this weekend? **What is** she **studying** at college?	• actions that are currently in progress • future actions if a future time expression is used or understood
PRESENT PERFECT	I **have seen** the movie *Titanic*. He **has seen** *Titanic* five times. **Have** you **seen** *Titanic*? **Why have** you never **seen** *Titanic*?	• action that started in the past and continues to the present • action that repeats during a period of time from the past to the present • action that occurred at an indefinite time in the past
PRESENT PERFECT CONTINUOUS	She **has been working** there for years. I **haven't been working** regularly in a while. **Have** you **been working** here long? **Where have** you **been working** lately?	• an action that started in the past and continues to the present
SIMPLE PAST	The students **liked** the class discussion. They **didn't like** the homework. **Did** you **like** the discussion? **What did** you **like** about the discussion?	• a single, short past action • a longer past action • a repeated past action
PAST CONTINUOUS	She **was watching** TV when I called. I **wasn't watching** TV when you called. **Were** you **watching** TV around 10? **What were** you **watching**?	• an action in progress at a specific past time • often with the simple past in another clause to show the relationship of a longer past action to a shorter past action
PAST PERFECT	I **had** just **left** when she arrived. We **hadn't left** yet when she arrived. **Had** you already **left** the party when she arrived? **How long had** you **known** each other before you got married?	• used to indicate the first of two past events
PAST PERFECT CONTINUOUS	The movie **had been playing** for 10 minutes when they arrived. The movie **hadn't been playing** for too long when they arrived. **How long had** the movie **been playing**?	• a continuous past action that was completed before another past action • used with action verbs, e.g., *arrive, ask, eat, enter*
FUTURE WITH *WILL*	I **will go** to the store. He **won't go** to the store. **Will** you **go** to the store? **When will** you **go** to the store?	• future plans/decisions made in the moment • strong predictions • promises and offers to help

FUTURE WITH *BE GOING TO*	He's **going to study** all weekend. He **isn't going to study** Saturday. **Are** you **going to study** Saturday? **What are** you **going to study** Saturday?	• future plans that are already made • predictions
FUTURE CONTINUOUS	I **will be sleeping** at midnight. They'**re going to be attending** a concert at that time.	• actions that will occur in the future and continue for an expected period of time
FUTURE PERFECT	She **will have finished** by 10 o'clock.	• actions that will be completed before another point in the future
FUTURE PERFECT CONTINUOUS	I **will have been standing** here for an hour when the train finally arrives.	• actions that will continue up until a point in the future

APPENDIX B

NONACTION VERBS

DESCRIPTION	FEELINGS	DESIRES	MEASUREMENTS	MENTAL STATES	SENSES
appear* be* consist of look* look like resemble seem	appreciate care dislike forgive hate like love mind miss	hope need prefer want wish	cost measure* weigh*	agree believe concern disagree doubt forget guess know imagine mean recognize remember* suppose surprise think* understand	belong contain feel* have* hear* hurt notice own possess see* smell* sound*

*Words that also have an active meaning

APPENDIX C

IRREGULAR VERB FORMS

BASE FORM	PAST FORM	PAST PARTICIPLE	BASE FORM	PAST FORM	PAST PARTICIPLE
be	was/were	been	fight	fought	fought
bear	bore	born/borne	find	found	found
beat	beat	beaten	fit	fit	fit
become	became	become	flee	fled	fled
begin	began	begun	fly	flew	flown
bend	bent	bent	forbid	forbade	forbidden
bet	bet	bet	forget	forgot	forgotten
bid	bid	bid	forgive	forgave	forgiven
bind	bound	bound	freeze	froze	frozen
bite	bit	bitten	get	got	gotten
bleed	bled	bled	give	gave	given
blow	blew	blown	go	went	gone
break	broke	broken	grind	ground	ground
breed	bred	bred	grow	grew	grown
bring	brought	brought	hang	hung	hung
broadcast	broadcast	broadcast	have	had	had
build	built	built	hear	heard	heard
burst	burst	burst	hide	hid	hidden
buy	bought	bought	hit	hit	hit
cast	cast	cast	hold	held	held
catch	caught	caught	hurt	hurt	hurt
choose	chose	chosen	keep	kept	kept
cling	clung	clung	know	knew	known
come	came	come	lay	laid	laid
cost	cost	cost	lead	led	led
creep	crept	crept	leave	left	left
cut	cut	cut	lend	lent	lent
deal	dealt	dealt	let	let	let
dig	dug	dug	lie	lay	lain
dive	dove/dived	dove/dived	light	lit/lighted	lit/lighted
do	did	done	lose	lost	lost
draw	drew	drawn	make	made	made
drink	drank	drunk	mean	meant	meant
drive	drove	driven	meet	met	met
eat	ate	eaten	mistake	mistook	mistaken
fall	fell	fallen	overcome	overcame	overcome
feed	fed	fed	overdo	overdid	overdone
feel	felt	felt	overtake	overtook	overtaken

BASE FORM	PAST FORM	PAST PARTICIPLE	BASE FORM	PAST FORM	PAST PARTICIPLE
overthrow	overthrew	overthrown	stick	stuck	stuck
pay	paid	paid	sting	stung	stung
plead	pled/pleaded	pled/pleaded	stink	stank	stunk
prove	proved	proven/proved	strike	struck	struck/stricken
put	put	put	strive	strove	striven
quit	quit	quit	swear	swore	sworn
read	read	read	sweep	swept	swept
ride	rode	ridden	swell	swelled	swelled/swollen
ring	rang	rung	swim	swam	swum
rise	rose	risen	swing	swung	swung
run	ran	run	take	took	taken
say	said	said	teach	taught	taught
see	saw	seen	tear	tore	torn
seek	sought	sought	tell	told	told
sell	sold	sold	think	thought	thought
send	sent	sent	throw	threw	thrown
set	set	set	understand	understood	understood
sew	sewed	sewn/sewed	uphold	upheld	upheld
shake	shook	shaken	upset	upset	upset
shed	shed	shed	wake	woke	woken
shine	shone/shined	shone/shined	wear	wore	worn
shoot	shot	shot	weave	wove	woven
show	showed	shown/showed	wed	wedded/wed	wedded/wed
shrink	shrank/shrunk	shrunk/shrunken	weep	wept	wept
shut	shut	shut	win	won	won
sing	sang	sung	wind	wound	wound
sink	sank	sunk	withdraw	withdrew	withdrawn
sit	sat	sat	withhold	withheld	withheld
sleep	slept	slept	withstand	withstood	withstood
slide	slid	slid	wring	wrung	wrung
slit	slit	slit	write	wrote	written
speak	spoke	spoken			
speed	sped	sped			
spend	spent	spent			
spin	spun	spun			
spit	spit/spat	spit/spat			
split	split	split			
spread	spread	spread			
spring	sprang	sprung			
stand	stood	stood			
steal	stole	stolen			

Note:

The past and past participle of some verbs can end in *-ed* or *-t.*

burn	burned or burnt
dream	dreamed or dreamt
kneel	kneeled or knelt
learn	learned or learnt
leap	leaped or leapt
spill	spilled or spilt
spoil	spoiled or spoilt

APPENDIX D

GERUNDS AND INFINITIVES

Verbs Followed by Gerunds

admit	detest	miss	resent
advise	discuss	permit	resist
anticipate	dislike	postpone	risk
appreciate	enjoy	practice	stop
avoid	finish	put off	suggest
can't help	forbid	quit	tolerate
complete	imagine	recall	understand
consider	keep	recommend	
delay	mention	regret	
deny	mind	remember	

Verbs Followed by Infinitives

agree	claim	know how	seem
appear	consent	learn	swear
ask	decide	manage	tend
attempt	demand	need	threaten
arrange	deserve	offer	try
be able	expect	plan	volunteer
beg	fail	prepare	want
can afford	forget	pretend	wish
care	hope	promise	would like
choose	intend	refuse	

Verbs Followed by Either Gerunds or Infinitives

begin	love	start
continue	prefer	stop*
hate	remember*	try (in past form *tried*)*
like	can (not) stand	

*Difference in meaning between use of gerund and infinitive

Adjectives Followed by Infinitives

afraid	easy	lucky	sad
ashamed	embarrassed	necessary	shocked
careful	excited	pleased	sorry
certain	glad	prepared	stupid
challenging	good	proud	surprised
delighted	happy	ready	upset
determined	hard	relieved	useful
difficult	important	reluctant	willing
disappointed	impossible	rewarding	wrong
eager	likely	right	

APPENDIX E

VERBS AND ADJECTIVES FOLLOWED BY A PREPOSITION

MANY VERBS AND ADJECTIVES ARE FOLLOWED BY A PREPOSITION.

accuse someone of	(be) familiar with	(be) prepared for/to
(be) accustomed to	(be) famous for	prevent (someone/something) from
adjust to	(be) fond of	prohibit (someone/something) from
(be) afraid of	forget about	protect (someone/something) from
agree with	forgive (someone) for	(be) proud of
(be) amazed at/by	(be) glad about	recover from
(be) angry about	(be) good at	(be) related to
(be) angry at/with	(be) grateful (to someone) for	rely on/upon
apologize for	(be) guilty of	(be) responsible for
approve of	(be) happy about	(be) sad about
argue about	hear about	(be) satisfied with
argue with	hear of	(be) scared of
(be) ashamed of	hope for	(be) sick of
(be) aware of	(be) incapable of	(be) sorry about
believe in	insist on/upon	(be) sorry for
blame someone for	(be) interested in	speak about
(be) bored with/by	(be) involved in	speak to/with
(be) capable of	(be) jealous of	succeed in
care about	(be) known for	(be) sure of/about
care for	(be) lazy about	(be) surprised at
compare to/with	listen to	take care of
complain about	look at	talk about
concentrate on	look for	talk to/with
(be) concerned about	look forward to	thank (someone) for
consist of	(be) mad about	(be) thankful (to someone) for
count on	(be) mad at	think about
deal with	(be) made from/of	think of
decide on	(be) married to	(be) tired of
depend on/upon	object to	(be) upset about
(be) different from	(be) opposed to	(be) upset with
disapprove of	participate in	(be) used to
(be) divorced from	plan on	wait for
dream about/of	pray to	warn (someone) about
(be) engaged to	pray for	(be) worried about
(be) excited about		worry about

APPENDIX F

NONCOUNT NOUNS

GROUP A	**Nouns that have no distinct, separate parts**			
	milk	juice	paper	cholesterol
	oil	yogurt	rain	blood
	water	poultry	air	electricity
	coffee	bread	soup	lightning
	tea	meat	butter	thunder

GROUP B	**Nouns with parts too small or insignificant to count**		
	rice	hair	sand
	sugar	popcorn	corn
	salt	snow	grass

GROUP C	**Nouns that are classes or categories**	
	money or cash (nickels, dimes, dollars)	mail (letters, packages, postcards, flyers)
	furniture (chairs, tables, beds)	homework (compositions, exercises, readings)
	clothing (sweaters, pants, dresses)	jewelry (necklaces, bracelets, rings)

GROUP D	**Abstract nouns**					
	love	happiness	nutrition	patience	work	nature
	truth	education	intelligence	poverty	health	help
	beauty	advice	unemployment	music	fun	energy
	luck/fortune	knowledge	pollution	art	information	friendship

GROUP E	**Subjects of study**		
	history	grammar	biology
	chemistry	geometry	math (mathematics*)

*Note: Even though *mathematics* ends with *s*, it is not plural.

Quantity Words with Count and Noncount Nouns

SINGULAR COUNT	PLURAL COUNT	NONCOUNT
a tomato	tomatoes	coffee
one tomato	**two** tomatoes	**two cups of** coffee
	some tomatoes	**some** coffee
no tomato	**no** tomatoes	**no** coffee
	any tomatoes (with questions and negatives)	**any** coffee (with questions and negatives)
	a lot of tomatoes	**a lot of** coffee
	many tomatoes	**much** coffee (with questions and negatives)
	a few tomatoes	**a little** coffee
	several tomatoes	**several cups of** coffee
	How many tomatoes?	**How much** coffee?

Count or Noncount Nouns with Changes in Meaning

COUNT	NONCOUNT
Avocados and nuts are **foods** with healthy fats.	We have a lot of **food** at home.
He wrote a **paper** about hypnosis.	I need some **paper** to write my composition.
He committed three **crimes** last year.	There is a lot of **crime** in a big city.
I have 200 **chickens** on my farm.	We ate some **chicken** for dinner.
I don't want to bore you with my **troubles**.	I have some **trouble** with my car.
She went to Puerto Rico three **times**.	She spent a lot of **time** on her project.
She drank three **glasses** of water.	The window is made of bulletproof **glass**.
I had a bad **experience** on my trip to Paris.	She has **experience** with computers.
I've learned about the **lives** of my grandparents.	**Life** is sometimes happy, sometimes sad.
I heard a **noise** outside my window.	Those children are making a lot of **noise**.
Some **fruits** have a lot of sugar.	I bought some **fruit** at the fruit store.

APPENDIX G

USES OF ARTICLES

The Indefinite Article

A. To classify a subject

EXAMPLES	EXPLANATION
Chicago is **a** city. Illinois is **a** state. Abraham Lincoln was **an** American president.	• We use *a* before a consonant sound. • We use *an* before a vowel sound. • We can put an adjective before the noun.
Chicago and Los Angeles are cities. Lincoln and Washington were American presidents.	We do not use an article before a plural noun.

B. To make a generalization about a noun

EXAMPLES	EXPLANATION
A dog has sharp teeth. **Dogs** have sharp teeth. **An elephant** has big ears. **Elephants** have big ears.	We use an indefinite article *(a/an)* + a singular count noun or no article with a plural noun. Both the singular and plural forms have the same meaning.
Coffee contains caffeine. **Love** makes people happy.	We do not use an article to make a generalization about a noncount noun.

C. To introduce a new noun into the conversation

EXAMPLES	EXPLANATION
I have **a cell phone**. I have **an umbrella**.	We use the indefinite article *a/an* with singular count nouns.
I have **(some) dishes**. Do you have **(any) cups**? I don't have **(any) forks**. I have **(some) money** with me. Do you have **(any) cash** with you? I don't have **(any) time**.	We use *some* or *any* with plural nouns and noncount nouns. We use *any* in questions and negatives. *Some* and *any* can be omitted.
There's **an elevator** in the building. There isn't **any money** in my wallet.	*There* + a form of *be* can introduce an indefinite noun into a conversation.

The Definite Article

A. To refer to a previously mentioned noun

EXAMPLES	EXPLANATION
There's **a dog** in the next apartment. **The dog** barks all the time.	We start by saying *a dog*. We continue by saying *the dog*.
We bought **some grapes**. We ate **the grapes** this morning.	We start by saying *some grapes*. We continue by saying *the grapes*.
I need **some sugar**. I'm going to use **the sugar** to bake a cake.	We start by saying *some sugar*. We continue by saying *the sugar*.
Did you buy **any coffee**? Yes. **The coffee** is in the cabinet.	We start by saying *any coffee*. We continue by saying *the coffee*.

B. When the speaker and the listener have the same reference

EXAMPLES	EXPLANATION
The number on this page is 391.	The object is present, so the speaker and listener have the same object in mind.
The president is talking about **the** economy.	People who live in the same country have things in common.
Please turn off **the lights** and shut **the door** before you leave **the house**.	People who live in the same house have things in common.
The house on the corner is beautiful. I spent **the money you gave me**.	The listener knows exactly which one because the speaker defines or specifies which one.

C. When there is only one in our experience

EXAMPLES	EXPLANATION
The sun is bigger than **the moon**. There are many problems in **the world**.	The *sun*, the *moon*, and the *world* are unique objects.
Write your name on **the top** of the page.	The page has only one top.
Alaska is **the biggest** state in the U.S.	A superlative indicates that there is only one.

D. With familiar places

EXAMPLES	EXPLANATION
I'm going to **the store** after work. Do you need anything? **The bank** is closed now. I'll go tomorrow.	We use *the* with certain familiar places and people—*the bank, the zoo, the park, the store, the movies, the beach, the post office, the bus, the train, the doctor, the dentist*—when we refer to the one that we habitually visit or use.

Notes:

1. Omit *the* after a preposition with the words *church, school, work,* and *bed*.
   - He's **in church**.   They're **at work**.
   - I'm going **to school**.   I'm going **to bed**.
2. Omit *to* and *the* with *home* and *downtown*.
   - I'm going **home**.   Are you going **downtown** after class?

continued

E. To make a formal generalization

EXAMPLES	EXPLANATION
The shark is the oldest and most primitive fish.	To say that something is true of all members of a group, use *the* with singular count nouns.
The computer has changed the way people deal with information.	To talk about a class of inventions, use *the*.
The ear has three parts: outer, middle, and inner.	To talk about an organ of the body in a general sense, use *the*.

Note:

For informal generalizations, use *a* + a singular noun or no article with a plural noun.
    The computer has changed the way we deal with information. (Formal)
    A computer is expensive. (Informal)
    Computers are expensive. (Informal)

Special Uses of Articles

NO ARTICLE	ARTICLE

Personal names:
  John Kennedy
	The whole family:
	  the Kennedys

Title and name:
  Queen Elizabeth
	Title without name:
	  the Queen

Cities, states, countries, continents:
  Cleveland
  Ohio
  Mexico
  South America
	Places that are considered a union:
	  the United States
	Place names: the _____ of _____
	  the District of Columbia

Mountains:
  Mount Everest
	Mountain ranges:
	  the Rocky Mountains

Islands:
  Staten Island
	Collectives of islands:
	  the Hawaiian Islands

Lakes:
  Lake Superior
	Collectives of lakes:
	  the Great Lakes

Beaches:
  Palm Beach
  Pebble Beach
	Rivers, oceans, seas:
	  the Mississippi River
	  the Atlantic Ocean
	  the Dead Sea

Streets and avenues:
  Madison Avenue
  Wall Street
	Well-known buildings:
	  the Willis Tower
	  the Empire State Building

Parks:
  Central Park
	Zoos:
	  the San Diego Zoo

NO ARTICLE	ARTICLE

Seasons:
    summer   fall   spring   winter
    Summer is my favorite season.
Note: After a preposition, *the* may be used.
    In (the) winter, my car runs badly.
	Deserts:
	    the Mojave Desert
	    the Sahara Desert

Directions:
    north   south   east   west
	Sections of a piece of land:
	    the West Side (of New York)

School subjects:
    history   math
	Unique geographical points:
	    the North Pole the Vatican

Name + *College* or *University*:
    Northwestern University
	The University/College of _____
	    the University of Michigan

Magazines:
    Time   *Sports Illustrated*
	Newspapers:
	    the *Tribune* the *Los Angeles Times*

Months and days:
    September   Monday
	Ships:
	    the *Titanic* the *Queen Elizabeth II*

Holidays and dates:
    Mother's Day
    July 4 (month + day)
	The day of month:
	    the fifth of May
	    the Fourth of July

Diseases:
    cancer   AIDS
    polio   malaria
	Ailments:
	    a cold a toothache
	    a headache the flu

Games and sports:
    poker
    soccer
	Musical instruments, after *play*:
	    the drums the piano
	Note: Sometimes *the* is omitted.
	    She plays (the) drums.

Languages:
    English
	The _____ language:
	    the English language

Last month, year, week, etc. = the one before this one:
    I forgot to pay my rent last month.
    The teacher gave us a test last week.
	The last month, the last year, the last week, etc. = the last in a series:
	    December is the last month of the year.
	    Vacation begins the last week in May.

In office = in an elected position:
    The president is in office for four years.
	In the office = in a specific room:
	    The teacher is in the office.

APPENDIX H

CONNECTORS

Sentences Types

There are three basic sentences types: simple, compound, and complex.
Simple sentences usually have one subject and one verb.

    S   V
Students love textbooks.

Simple sentences can have more than one subject and/or verb.

   S   S   V
Children and adults like pizza.

Compound sentences are usually made up of two simple sentences (independent clauses) with a **connector** (a coordination conjunction such as *and, but, or, yet, so,* and *for*):

                       coord
S   V   conj S   V
They worked hard all semester, **but** they did not finish the project.

Complex sentences have one independent clause and at least one dependent clause. The dependent clause is often an adverb clause, which begins with a **connector** (a subordinating conjunction such as *while, although, because,* and *if*):

sub
conj dependent clause   independent clause
Although the test was very difficult, all the students received a passing grade.

Coordinating Conjunctions

Coordinating conjunctions join two independent clauses to form a compound sentence. Use a comma before a coordinating conjunction in a compound sentence.

                      coord
independent clause   conj   independent clause
The test was very difficult, **but** all the students received a passing grade.

Subordinating Conjunctions

Subordinating conjunctions introduce a dependent clause in a complex sentence. When a dependent clause begins a sentence, use a comma to separate it from the independent clause.

      dependent clause   independent clause
Although the test was very difficult, all the students received a passing grade.

When a dependent clause comes after an independent clause, no comma is used.

     independent clause   dependent clause
All the students received a passing grade **although** the test was very difficult.

Transition Words

Transition words **show the relationship between ideas in sentences**. A transition followed by a comma can begin a sentence.

    independent clause   transition   independent clause

The test was very difficult. **However**, all the students received a passing grade.

Connector Summary Chart

PURPOSE	COORDINATING CONJUNCTIONS	SUBORDINATING CONJUNCTIONS	TRANSITION WORDS
To give an example			For example, To illustrate, Specifically, In particular,
To add information	and		In addition, Moreover, Furthermore,
To signal a comparison			Similarly, Likewise, In the same way,
To signal a contrast	but, yet	while, although	In contrast, However, On the other hand, Conversely, Instead,
To signal a concession	yet	although, though, even though	Nevertheless, Even so, Admittedly, Despite this,
To emphasize			In fact, Actually,
To clarify			In other words, In simpler words, More simply,
To give a reason/cause	for	because, since	
To show a result	so	so	As a result, As a consequence, Consequently, Therefore, Thus,
To show time relationships		after, as soon as, before, when, while, until, since, whenever, as	Afterward, First, Second, Next, Then, Finally, Subsequently, Meanwhile, In the meantime,
To signal a condition		if, even if, unless, provided that, when	
To signal a purpose		so that, in order that	
To signal a choice	or		
To signal a conclusion			In conclusion, To summarize, As we have seen, In brief, In closing, To sum up, Finally,

APPENDIX I

CAPITALIZATION AND PUNCTUATION

Capitalization Rules

RULE	EXAMPLES
The first word in a sentence	**M**y friends are helpful.
The word *I*	My sister and **I** took a trip together.
Names of people	**A**braham **L**incoln; **G**eorge **W**ashington
Titles preceding names of people	**D**octor (**D**r.) **S**mith; **P**resident **L**incoln; **Q**ueen **E**lizabeth; **M**r. **R**ogers; **M**rs. **C**arter
Geographic names	the **U**nited **S**tates; **L**ake **S**uperior; **C**alifornia; the **R**ocky **M**ountains; the **M**ississippi **R**iver **Note:** The word *the* in a geographic name is not capitalized.
Street names	**P**ennsylvania **A**venue (**A**ve.); **W**all **S**treet (**S**t.); **A**bbey **R**oad (**R**d.)
Names of organizations, companies, colleges, buildings, stores, hotels	the **R**epublican **P**arty; **C**engage **L**earning; **D**artmouth **C**ollege; the **U**niversity of **W**isconsin; the **W**hite **H**ouse; **B**loomingdale's; the **H**ilton **H**otel
Nationalities and ethnic groups	**M**exicans; **C**anadians; **S**paniards; **A**mericans; **J**ews; **K**urds; **I**nuit
Languages	**E**nglish; **S**panish; **P**olish; **V**ietnamese; **R**ussian
Months	**J**anuary; **F**ebruary
Days	**S**unday; **M**onday
Holidays	**I**ndependence **D**ay; **T**hanksgiving
Important words in a title	*Grammar in Context; The Old Man and the Sea; Romeo and Juliet; The Sound of Music* **Note:** Capitalize *the* as the first word of a title.

Punctuation Rules

PUNCTUATION	EXAMPLES
A period (.) is used at the end of a declarative sentence.	This is a complete sentence.
A question mark (?) is used at the end of a question.	When does the movie start?
An exclamation mark (!) is used at the end of an exclamation. It expresses a strong emotion. It can also be called an exclamation point.	This book is so interesting!
A comma (,) is used:	
• before the connectors *and*, *but*, *so*, and *or* in a compound sentence.	• She gave Tomas a pen, but he wanted a pencil.
• between three or more items in a list.	• He needs a notebook, a pen, and a calculator.
• after a dependent clause at the beginning of a complex sentence. Dependent clauses include time clauses, *if* clauses, and reason clauses.	• If it's cold outside, you should wear a coat.
• between the day and the date and between the date and the year.	• The test will be on Friday, May 20. The school opened on September 3, 2010.
• between and after (if in the middle of a sentence) city, state, and country names that appear together.	• She lived and taught in Shanghai, China, for five years.
• after time words and phrases, prepositional phrases of time, and sequence words (except *then*) at the start of a sentence.	• Finally, the test was over, and the student could leave. After the movie, they decided to go out for coffee.
An apostrophe (') is used to indicate either a contraction or a possession:	
• Use an apostrophe in a contraction in place of the letter or letters that have been deleted.	• I'm happy to see you. You've read a lot of books this year.
• Add an apostrophe and the letter *-s* after the word. If a plural word already ends in *-s*, just add an apostrophe.	• That is Yusef's book. The teachers' books include the answers.
Quotation marks (") are used to indicate:	
• the exact words that were spoken by someone. Notice that the punctuation at the end of a quote is inside the quotation marks.	• Albert Einstein said, "I have no special talent. I am only passionately curious."
• language that a writer has borrowed from another source.	• The dictionary defines punctuation as "the use of specific marks to make ideas within writing clear."
• when a word or phrase is being used in a special way.	• The paper was written by a "professional" writer.

GLOSSARY

- **Adjective** An adjective gives a description of a noun.

    It's a *tall* tree.   He's an *old* man.   My neighbors are *nice*.

- **Adverb** An adverb describes the action of a sentence or an adjective or another adverb.

    She speaks English *fluently*.   I drive *carefully*.

    She speaks English *extremely* well.   She is *very* intelligent.

- **Adverb of Frequency** An adverb of frequency tells how often an action happens.

    I *never* drink coffee.   They *usually* take the bus.

- **Affirmative** Affirmative means "yes."

    They *live* in Miami.

- **Apostrophe '** We use the apostrophe for possession and contractions.

    My *sister's* friend is beautiful. (possession)

    Today *isn't* Sunday. (contraction)

- **Article** An article comes before a noun. It tells if the noun is definite or indefinite. The indefinite articles are *a* and *an*. The definite article is *the*.

    I have *a* cat.   I ate *an* apple.   *The* teacher came late.

- **Auxiliary Verb** An auxiliary verb is used in forming tense, mood, or aspect of the verb that follows it. Some verbs have two parts: an auxiliary verb and a main verb.

    You *didn't* eat lunch.   He *can't* study.   We *will* return.

- **Base Form** The base form of the verb has no tense. It has no ending (*-s*, *-ed*, or *-ing*): be, go, eat, take, write.

    I didn't *go*.   We don't *know* you.   He can't *drive*.

- **Capital Letter** A B C D E F G . . .

- **Clause** A clause is a group of words that has a subject and a verb. Some sentences have only one clause.

    She speaks Spanish.

    Some sentences have a **main clause** and a **dependent clause**.

MAIN CLAUSE	DEPENDENT CLAUSE (reason clause)
She found a good job	because she has computer skills.
MAIN CLAUSE	DEPENDENT CLAUSE (time clause)
She'll turn off the light	before she goes to bed.
MAIN CLAUSE	DEPENDENT CLAUSE (*if* clause)
I'll take you to the doctor	if you don't have your car on Saturday.

- **Colon :**

- **Comma ,**

- **Comparative** The comparative form of an adjective or adverb is used to compare two things.

    My house is *bigger* than your house.

    Her husband drives *faster* than she does.

    My children speak English *more fluently* than I do.

- **Consonant** The following letters are consonants: *b, c, d, f, g, h, j, k, l, m, n, p, q, r, s, t, v, w, x, y, z*.

  NOTE: *Y* is sometimes considered a vowel, as in the world *syllable*.

- **Contraction** A contraction is two words joined with an apostrophe.

  He's my brother. *You're* late. They *won't* talk to me.

  (*He's* = He is) (*You're* = You are) (*won't* = will not)

- **Count Noun** Count nouns are nouns that we can count. They have a singular and a plural form.

  1 *pen*–3 *pens* 1 *table*–4 *tables*

- **Dependent Clause** See **Clause**.

- **Exclamation Mark** !

- **Frequency Word** Frequency words (*always, usually, generally, often, sometimes, rarely, seldom, hardly ever, never*) tell how often an action happens.

  I *never* drink coffee. We *always* do our homework.

- **Hyphen** -

- **Imperative** An imperative sentence gives a command or instruction. An imperative sentence omits the subject pronoun *you*.

  Come here. *Don't be* late. Please *help* me.

- **Infinitive** An infinitive is *to* + the base form.

  I want *to leave*. You need *to be* here on time.

- **Linking Verb** A linking verb is a verb that links the subject to the noun, adjective, or adverb after it. Linking verbs include *be, seem, feel, smell, sound, look, appear,* and *taste*.

  She *is* a doctor. She *looks* tired. You *are* late.

- **Main Clause** See **Clause**.

- **Modal** The modal verbs are *can, could, shall, should, will, would, may, might,* and *must*.

  They *should* leave. I *must* go.

- **Negative** *Negative* means "no."

  She *doesn't speak* Spanish.

- **Nonaction Verb** A nonaction verb has no action. We do not use a continuous tense (*be* + verb *-ing*) with a nonaction verb. Nonaction verbs include: *believe, cost, care, have, hear, know, like, love, matter, mean, need, own, prefer, remember, see, seem, think, understand, want,* and sense-perception verbs.

  She *has* a laptop. We *love* our mother. You *look* great.

- **Noncount Noun** A noncount noun is a noun that we don't count. It has no plural form.

  She drank some *water*. He prepared some *rice*.

  Do you need any *money*? We had a lot of *homework*.

- **Noun** A noun is a person, a place, or a thing. Nouns can be either count or noncount.

  My *brother* lives in California. My *sisters* live in New York.

  I get *advice* from them. I drink *coffee* every day.

- **Noun Modifier** A noun modifier makes a noun more specific.

  fire department *Independence* Day *can* opener

- **Noun Phrase** A noun phrase is a group of words that form the subject or object of a sentence.

     A very nice woman helped me.   I bought *a big box of cereal*.

- **Object** The object of a sentence follows the verb. It receives the action of the verb.

     He bought *a car*.   I saw *a movie*.   I met *your brother*.

- **Object Pronoun** We use object pronouns (*me, you, him, her, it, us, them*) after a verb or preposition.

     He likes *her*.   I saw the movie. Let's talk about *it*.

- **Paragraph** A paragraph is a group of sentences about one topic.
- **Parentheses** ( )
- **Period** .
- **Phrasal Modal** Phrasal modals, such as *have to* and *be able to,* are made up of two or more words.

     You *have got to* see the movie.   We *have to* take a test.

- **Phrase** A group of words that go together.

     Last month my sister came to visit.   There is a strange car *in front of my house*.

- **Plural** *Plural* means "more than one." A plural noun usually ends with *-s*.

     She has beautiful *eyes*.   My *feet* are big.

- **Possessive Form** Possessive forms show ownership or relationship.

     Mary's coat is in the closet.   *My* brother lives in Miami.

- **Preposition** A preposition is a short connecting word. Some common prepositions are: *about, above, across, after, around, as, at, away, back, before, behind, below, by, down, for, from, in, into, like, of, off, on, out, over, to, under, up,* and *with*.

     The book is *on* the table.   She studies *with* her friends.

- **Present Participle** The present participle of a verb is the base form + *-ing*.

     She is *sleeping*.   They were *laughing*.

- **Pronoun** A pronoun takes the place of a noun.

     John likes Mary, but *she* doesn't like *him*.

- **Punctuation** The use of specific marks, such as commas and periods, to make ideas within writing clear.
- **Question Mark** ?
- **Quotation Marks** " "
- **Regular Verb** A regular verb forms the simple past with *-ed*.

     He *worked* yesterday.   I *laughed* at the joke.

- **-s Form** A simple present verb that ends in *-s* or *-es*.

    He *lives* in New York.   She *watches* TV a lot.

- **Sense-Perception Verb** A sense-perception verb has no action. It describes a sense. Some common sense-perception verbs are: *look, feel, taste, sound,* and *smell*.

    She *feels* fine.   The coffee *smells* fresh.   The milk *tastes* sour.

- **Sentence** A sentence is a group of words that contains a subject and a verb and gives a complete thought.

    SENTENCE: She came home.

    NOT A SENTENCE: When she came home

- **Singular** *Singular* means "one."

    She ate a *sandwich*.   I have one *television*.

- **Subject** The subject of the sentence tells who or what the sentence is about.

    My sister got married last April. *The wedding* was beautiful.

- **Subject Pronoun** We use a subject pronoun (*I, you, he, she, it, we, you, they*) before a verb.

    They speak Japanese.   *We* speak Spanish.

- **Superlative** The superlative form of an adjective or adverb shows the number one item in a group of three or more.

    January is the *coldest* month of the year.

    My brother speaks English the *best* in my family.

- **Syllable** A syllable is a part of a word. Each syllable has only one vowel sound. (Some words have only one syllable.)

    change (one syllable)   after (af·ter = two syllables)

    look (one syllable)   responsible (re·spon·si·ble = four syllables)

- **Tag Question** A tag question is a short question at the end of a sentence. It is used in conversation.

    You speak Spanish, *don't you?*   He's not happy, *is he?*

- **Tense** Tense shows when the action of the sentence happened. Verbs have different tenses.

    SIMPLE PRESENT: She usually *works* hard.

    PRESENT CONTINUOUS: She *is working* now.

    SIMPLE PAST: She *worked* yesterday.

    FUTURE: She *will work* tomorrow.

- **Verb** A verb is the action of the sentence.

    He *runs* fast.   I *speak* English.

    Some verbs have no action. They are linking verbs. They connect the subject to the rest of the sentence.

    He *is* tall.   She *looks* beautiful.   You *seem* tired.

- **Vowel** The following letters are vowels: *a, e, i, o, u*.

    NOTE: *Y* is sometimes considered a vowel, as in the world *syllable*.

INDEX

A
A few, several, a little, 143–144, 146
Ability/permission, modals, 202–203
Action verbs, present continuous, 53–54
Active voice, 341–342, 354
   summary, 354
Adjectives, 168
   adverbs versus, 162–163
   clauses, 284–307
   comparatives, 317–319
   gerunds, with, 267
   infinitives after, 273–274
   modifiers, 154–156
   possessive, 98–99
   superlatives, 311–313
   too, too much, too many, enough, 165–166, 168
   too, very, 166–168
Adjective clauses, 284–307
   relative pronouns, objects, 291–294, 304
   relative pronouns, objects of prepositions, 295–297, 304
   relative pronouns, place, 301–304
   relative pronouns, possessive, 298–299, 304
   relative pronouns, subjects, 288–290, 304
   relative pronouns, time, 301–304
   summary, 304
   where and *when*, 301–304
   who/that, 290
   whose + noun, 298–299, 304
Adverbs, modifiers, 153–154, 160–162, 168
   adjectives versus, 162–163
   comparatives, 317–319
   nouns, modifying, 153–154
   present perfect, 233
   summary, 168
   superlatives, 311–313
Advice, modals, 205–207
Affirmative statements
   simple present, 16–17
Another and *other*, 373–375, 378
Articles, 361–381
   another and *other*, 373–375, 378
   definite pronouns, 376–378
   generalizations, 362–363
   indefinite pronouns, 376–378
   nonspecific nouns, 366–367, 370–371
   quantity words, 370–371
   specific nouns, 367–371
   subjects, classifying, 363–364
   subjects, defining, 363–364
   summary, 378
As . . . as, comparatives, 324–325, 334
As many/much . . . as, comparatives, 326–327

B
Be
   contractions, 5, 10–11
   forms, simple present, 5–10, 36
   going to, 60–64
   negative statements, 8
   present continuous, 43–44
   simple past, 76–77, 88
   there + be, 138–140
   uses, 7
   wh- questions, 12–14
Be + not, 8
Be going to, 60–64
Be supposed to, 201–202

C
Can, could, modals, 202–203
Clauses, adjectives, 284–307
Comparatives, 316–337
   adjectives, 317–319
   adverbs, 317–319
   as . . . as, 324–325, 334
   as many/much . . . as, 326–327
   like and *alike*, 331–334
   long words, 334
   same . . . as, 327–329, 334
   short words, 334
   similarity, 331–333
   summary, 334
   use, 319–322
Comparison nouns, 141
Complements, questions about, 114–116, 118
Comprehension exercises
   a few, several, a little, 142–143
   adjective clauses, 286–287, 300–301
   adverbs, modifiers, 152–153
   articles, 360–361, 365–366, 372–373
   as . . . as, 323–324
   be forms, 4–5
   comparatives, 316–317
   count and noncount nouns, 130–131
   frequency words, 28–29
   future, 57–58

gerunds, 260–261
habitual past, 85–86
infinitives, 270–271
like and *alike*, 330–331
modals, 196–197, 204–205, 211–212, 216–217
nouns, plural, 124–125
object pronouns, 102–103
past continuous, 179–180, 185–186
possessive forms, 94–95
present continuous, 42–43
present perfect, 226–227, 234–235, 240–241
present perfect continuous, 248–249
relative pronouns, objects of prepositions, 295–296
simple past, 72–73, 75–76
simple past negatives, 81–82
simple present affirmative, 15–16
simple present questions, 20–21
simple present vs. present continuous, 50–51
superlatives, 310–311
time words, 174–175
transitive and intransitive verbs, 349–350
voice, 340–341
Conclusions, deductions, modals, 212–213
Contractions
  be, 5, 10–11
Count and noncount, 131–136, 141, 146

D

Definite pronouns, 376–378
Direct and indirect objects, 109–111, 118
  complements, questions about, 114–116, 118
  questions, 112–117
  say and *tell*, 110–111
  subjects, questions about, 113–116, 118
  wh- questions, 117
Discussion questions
  a few, several, a little, 143
  adjective clauses, 287, 301
  adverbs, modifiers, 153
  articles, 361, 366, 373
  as . . . as, 323–324
  be forms, 5
  comparatives, 317
  count and noncount nouns, 131
  frequency words, 29
  future, 58
  gerunds, 261
  habitual past, 86
  infinitives, 271
  like and *alike,* 331
  modals, 197, 205, 212, 217

nouns, plural, 125
object pronouns, 103
objects, direct and indirect, 108
past continuous, 180, 186
possessive forms, 95
present continuous, 43
present perfect, 227, 235, 241
present perfect continuous, 249
relative pronouns, objects of prepositions, 296
simple past, 73, 76
simple past negatives, 82
simple present affirmative, 16
simple present questions, 21
simple present vs. present continuous, 51
subject, 113
superlatives, 311
time words, 175
transitive and intransitive verbs, 350
voice, 341

E

Ever, simple present questions with, 32–33
Expectation, modals, 201–202

F

Frequency words/expressions, 29–31, 36
Future, 57–66
  be going to, 60–64
  if clause, 64–65
  present continuous, 62–64
  summary, 66
  time +, 64–65
  will, with, 58–60, 62–64

G

Generalizations, 128, 362–363
Gerunds, 258–269, 278–280
  adjective +, 267
  after verb, 278–279
  form, 262
  go + gerund, 265
  infinitives versus, 280
  objects, 265–266
  phrase, 261, 265
  preposition +, 267–269
  subjects, 262–264
  summary, 280
Go + gerund, 265

H

Habitual past, 85–88
How often, simple present questions with, 33–35

I

If clause, future, 64–65
Indefinite pronouns, 376–378
Indefinite time, present perfect, 243–245
Infinitives, 271–280
    after adjectives, 273–274
    after *it*, 272–273
    after verbs, 274–276, 278–279
    gerunds versus, 280
    objects before, 276
    phrase, 274–275
    show purpose, 277
    summary, 280
    to +, 277–278
Intransitive verbs, 350–353
Irregular verbs, simple past, 78–80, 88
It, infinitives after, 272–273

L

Like and *alike*, comparatives, 331–334
Long words, comparatives, 334

M

May, modals, 200–201
May/might, modals, 214–215
Modals, 194–223
    ability/permission, 202–203
    advice, 205–207
    be supposed to, 201–202
    can, could, and, 202–203
    conclusions, deductions, 212–213
    expectation, 201–202
    may and, 200–201
    may/might, 214–215
    must and, 199–200, 212–213
    negatives, 207–210
    obligation/necessity, 199–200
    permission/prohibition, 200–201
    phrasal, 197–200, 220
    politeness, 217–219
    possibility, 214–215
    should, ought to, had better, 205–207
    summary, 220
Modifiers; *see also* Adjectives, Adverbs, Nouns
    adjectives as, 154–156
    adverbs as, 153–154, 160–162, 168
    nouns, 153–154, 157–158, 168
Must, modals, 199–200, 212–213

N

Negative statements
    be, 8
    modals, 207–210
    passive voice, 347–348, 354
    simple past, 82–84
    simple present, 18–19, 36
Nonaction verbs, present continuous, 53–54
Non-specific nouns, 366–367, 370–371
Nouns
    a few, several, a little, 143–144, 146
    comparison, 141
    count and noncount, 131–136, 141, 146
    generalizations, 128
    modifiers, 153–154, 157–158, 168
    non-specific, 366–367, 370–371
    plural, 125–129
    possessive, 96–97, 118
    quantity, 135–136
    singular, 129
    specific, 367–371
    summary, 146
    there + be, 138–140, 146
    too much/too many, a lot of, 145–146

O

Object pronouns, 103–105, 118
Objects
    gerunds, 265–266
    infinitives after, 276
    relative pronouns, 291–294, 304
Objects of prepositions, relative pronouns, 295–297, 304
Obligation/necessity, modals, 199–200
Other and *another*, 373–375, 378

P

Passive voice, 341–348, 354
    form, 342–343
    negatives, 347–348
    questions, 347–348
    summary, 354
    use, 345–347
Past continuous, 180–184, 190
    present participle, 180
    simple past versus, 188
    specific time, 182–183
    summary, 190
    verb + *ing*, 189
    wh- questions, 180
    when clause, 184, 188
    while clause, 186–187
    yes/no questions, 180
Past participle, present perfect, 228–232
Past to present continuation, present perfect, 236–237
Past to present repetition, present perfect, 241–243
Permission/ability, modals, 202–203
Permission/prohibition, modals, 200–201

Phrasal modals, 197–200, 220
Phrases
    gerunds, 261, 265
    infinitives, 274–275
Place, relative pronouns, 301–304
Plural nouns, 125–129
Politeness, modals, 217–219
Possessive forms, 95–101, 118
    adjectives, 98–99
    nouns, 96–97, 118
    pronouns, 95–96, 99–100, 118
    summary, 118
    whose, questions with, 101
Possessive nouns, 96–97, 118
Possessive relative pronouns, 298–299, 304
Possibility, modals, 214–215
Preposition + gerund, 267–269
Present continuous, 41–56, 62–64, 66
    action verbs, 53–54
    be verb form, 43–44
    future with, 62–64
    nonaction verbs, 53–54
    use, 45–46
    questions, 46–48
    summary, 66
    versus simple present, 51–53, 55–56
    wh- questions, 46
    yes/no questions, 47
Present participle, past continuous, 180
Present perfect, 227–247
    adverb with, 233
    forms, 227–228
    indefinite time, past, 243–245
    past participle, 228–232
    past to present continuation, 236–237
    past to present repetition, 241–243
    simple past, 238–239, 246–247, 254
    simple present, 238–239
    summary, 254
    uses, 235
Present perfect continuous, 249–254
    forms, 249–251
    summary, 254
    use, 251–253
    wh- questions, 249
    yes/no questions, 249
Pronouns, 95–96, 99–107, 118
    object pronouns, 103–105, 118
    possessive forms, 95–96, 99–100, 118
    reflexive, 106–107
Purpose, show, 277

Q
Quantity nouns, 135–136, 146
Quantity words, articles, 370–371
Questions
    complement, 114–118
    passive voice, 347–348

R
Reflexive pronouns, 106–107, 118
Regular verbs, simple past, 77–78, 88
Relative pronouns
    objects, 291–294, 304
    objects of prepositions, 295–297, 304
    place, 301–304
    possessive, 298–299, 304
    subjects, 288–290, 304
    time, 301–304

S
Same . . . as, comparatives, 327–329, 334
Say and *tell*, 110–111
Short words, comparatives, 334
Should, ought to, had better, modals, 205–207
Similarity, comparatives, 331–333
Simple past, 72–84
    be, 76–77, 88
    habitual past, *used to*, 86–88
    irregular verbs, 78–80, 88
    negatives, 82–84
    past continuous versus, 188
    present perfect, 238–239, 246–247, 254
    regular verbs, 77–78, 88
    summary, 88, 254
    use, 74
    wh- questions, 82–84
    yes/no questions, 82–84
Simple present, 3–39, 66
    affirmative statements, 16–17, 36
    be, 5–10, 36
    ever, questions with, 32–33
    frequency words/expressions, 29–31, 36
    how often, questions with, 33–35
    negative statements, 18–19, 36
    present perfect, 238–239
    questions, 21–27
    summary, 36
    use, 17–18
    versus present continuous, 51–53, 55–56
    wh- questions, 21, 25–27, 36
    yes/no questions, 21, 32, 36
Singular nouns, 129
Specific nouns, 367–371

Specific time, past continuous, 182–183
Subjects
    classifying, articles, 363–364
    defining, articles, 363–364
    gerunds, 262–264
    questions about, 113–116, 118
    relative pronouns, 288–290, 304
Superlatives, 308–315
    adjectives, 311–313
    adverbs, 311–313
    summary, 334
    use, 313–315

T

There + be, 138–140, 146
Time + future, 64–65
Time words, 175–178, 189–190
    relative pronouns, 301–304
    summary, 190
To + infinitives, 277–278
Too, too much, too many, enough, 165–166, 168
Too, very, 166–168
Too much/too many, a lot of, 145–146
Transitive verbs, 350–353

U

Units of measure, 133–134
Used to, habitual past, 86–88

V

Verb + *ing*, past continuous, 189
Verbs
    gerunds after, 278–279
    infinitives after, 274–276, 278–279
    intransitive verbs, 350–353
    transitive verbs, 350–353

Voice
    active voice, 341–342, 354
    negatives, 347–348
    passive voice, 341–348, 354
    questions, 347–348
    summary, 354

W

Wh- questions
    be, 12–14
    direct and indirect objects, 117
    past continuous, 180
    present continuous, 46
    present perfect continuous, 249
    simple past, 82–84
    simple present, 21, 25–27, 36
When, whenever, 178
When clause, past continuous, 184, 188
Where and *when*, 301–304
While clause, past continuous, 186–187
Who/that, 290
Whose, questions with, 101
Whose + noun, 298–299, 304
Will, future with, 58–60, 62–64

Y

Yes/no questions
    past continuous, 180
    present continuous, 47
    present perfect continuous, 249
    simple past, 82–84
    simple present, 21, 32, 36

NOTES

NOTES